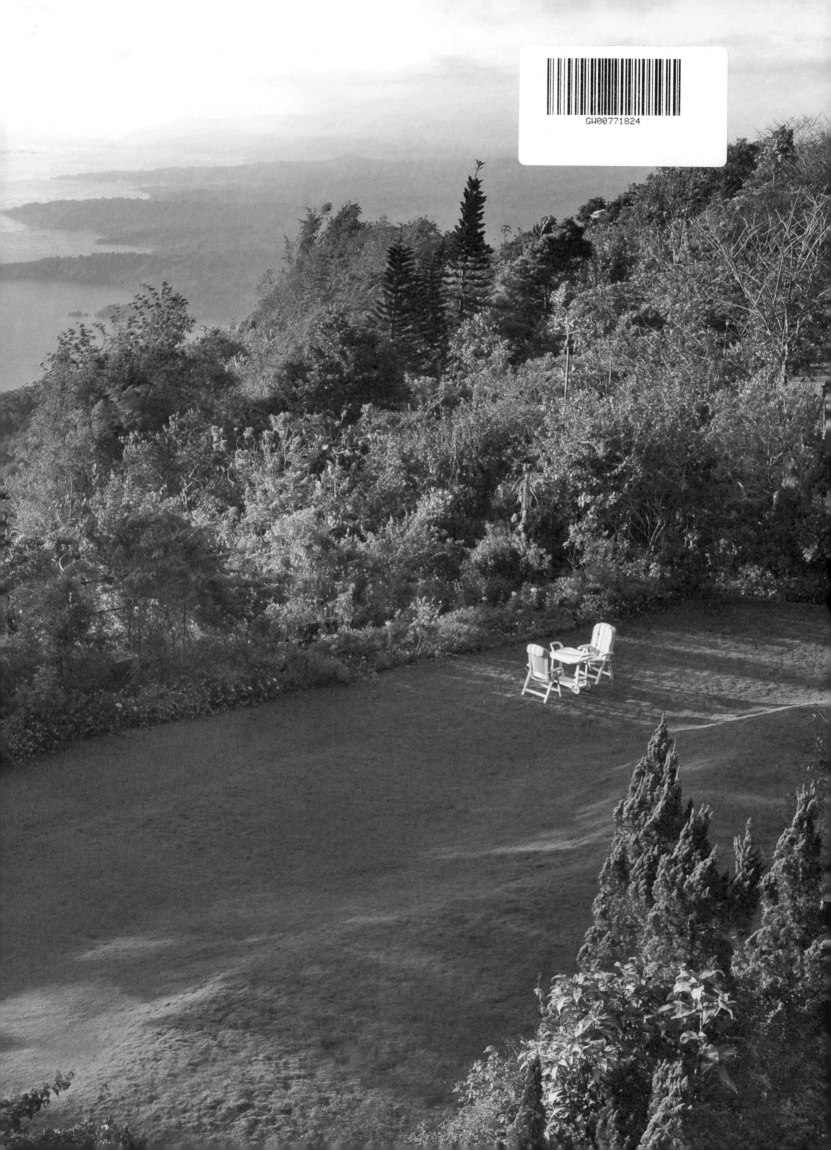

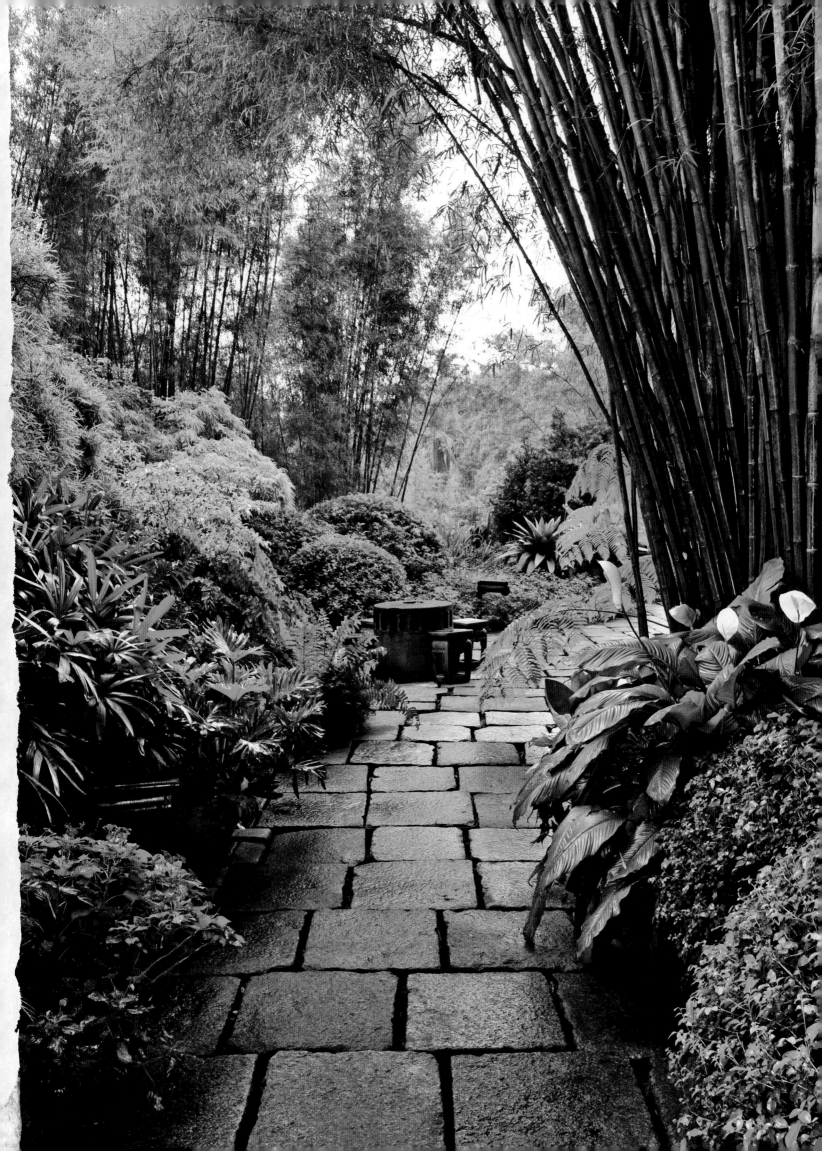

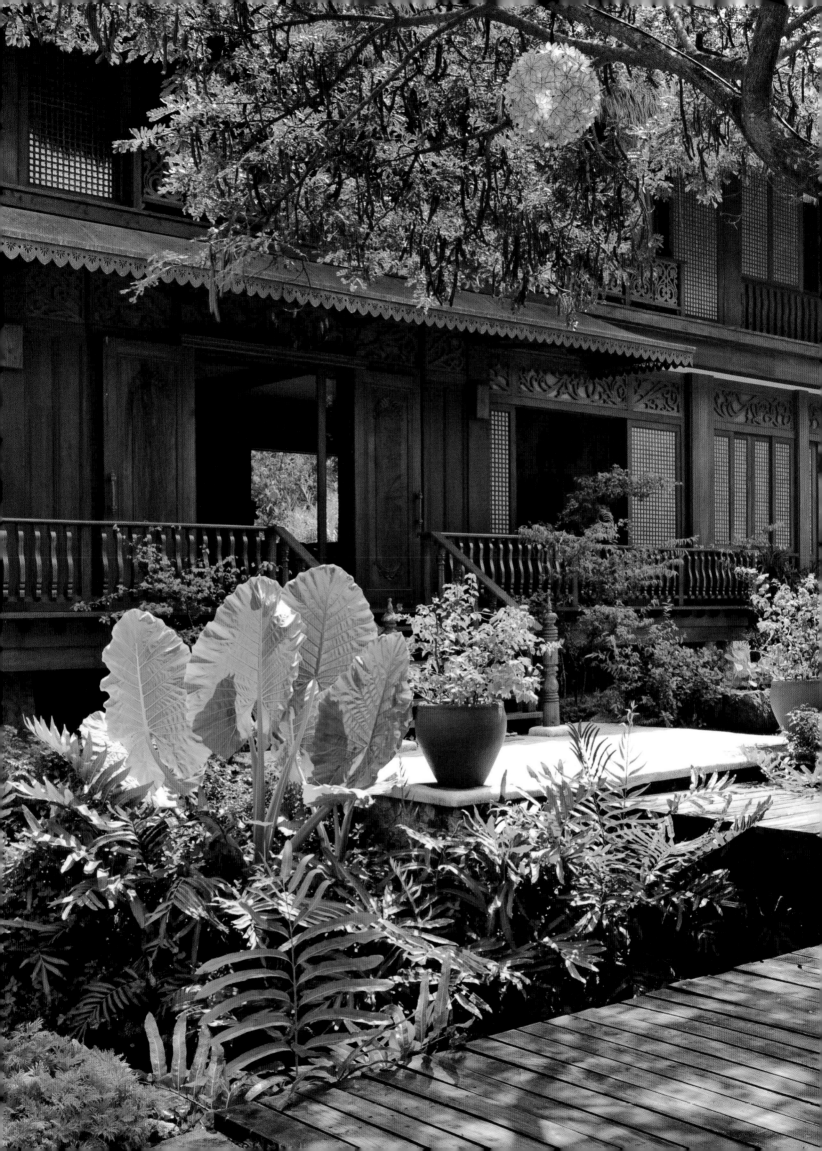

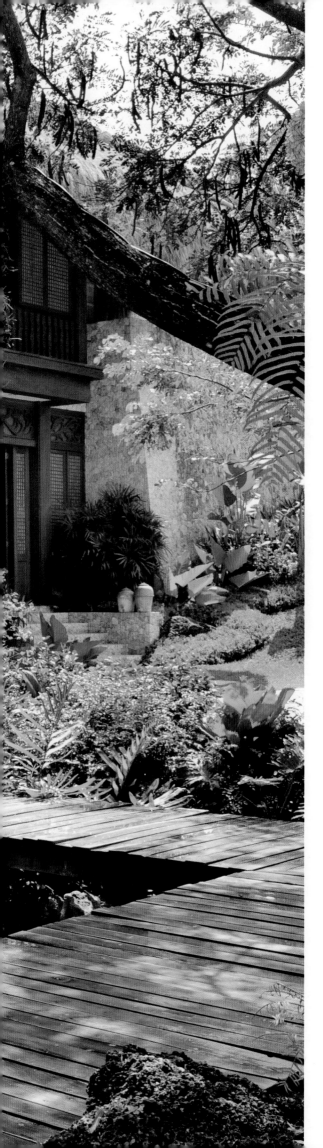

TROPICAL GARDENS
of the Philippines

By Lily Gamboa O'Boyle and Elizabeth V Reyes

photography by Luca Invernizzi Tettoni

TUTTLE Publishing

Tokyo | Rutland, Vermont | Singapore

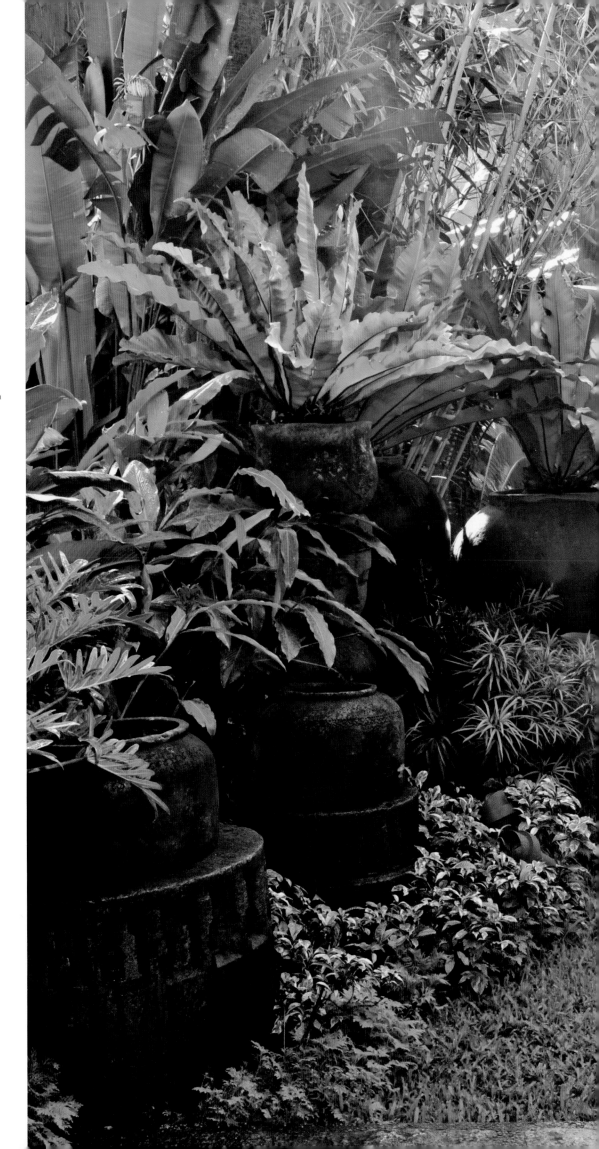

Published by Tuttle Publishing, an imprint
of Periplus Editions (HK) Ltd

www.tuttlepublishing.com

Text © 2010 Lily Gamboa O'Boyle and
Elizabeth V Reyes
Photos © 2010 Luca Invernizzi Tettoni

ISBN 978-0-8048-4154-3

Distributed by

**North America, Latin America &
Europe**
Tuttle Publishing
364 Innovation Drive
North Clarendon, VT 05759-9436 USA
Tel: 1 (802) 773-8930
Fax: 1 (802) 773-6993
info@tuttlepublishing.com
www.tuttlepublishing.com

Japan
Tuttle Publishing
Yaekari Building, 3rd Floor
5-4-12 Osaki
Shinagawa-ku
Tokyo 141 0032
Tel: 81 (3) 5437 0171
Fax: 81 (3) 5437 0755
sales@tuttle.co.jp
www.tuttle.co.jp

Asia Pacific
Berkeley Books Pte Ltd
61 Tai Seng Avenue, #02-12
Singapore 534167
Tel: (65) 6280 1330
Fax: (65) 6280 6290
inquiries@periplus.com.sg
www.periplus.com

15 14 13 12 11   8 7 6 5 4 3 2 1

Printed in Singapore

TUTTLE PUBLISHING® is a registered
trademark of Tuttle Publishing, a division
of Periplus Editions (HK) Ltd

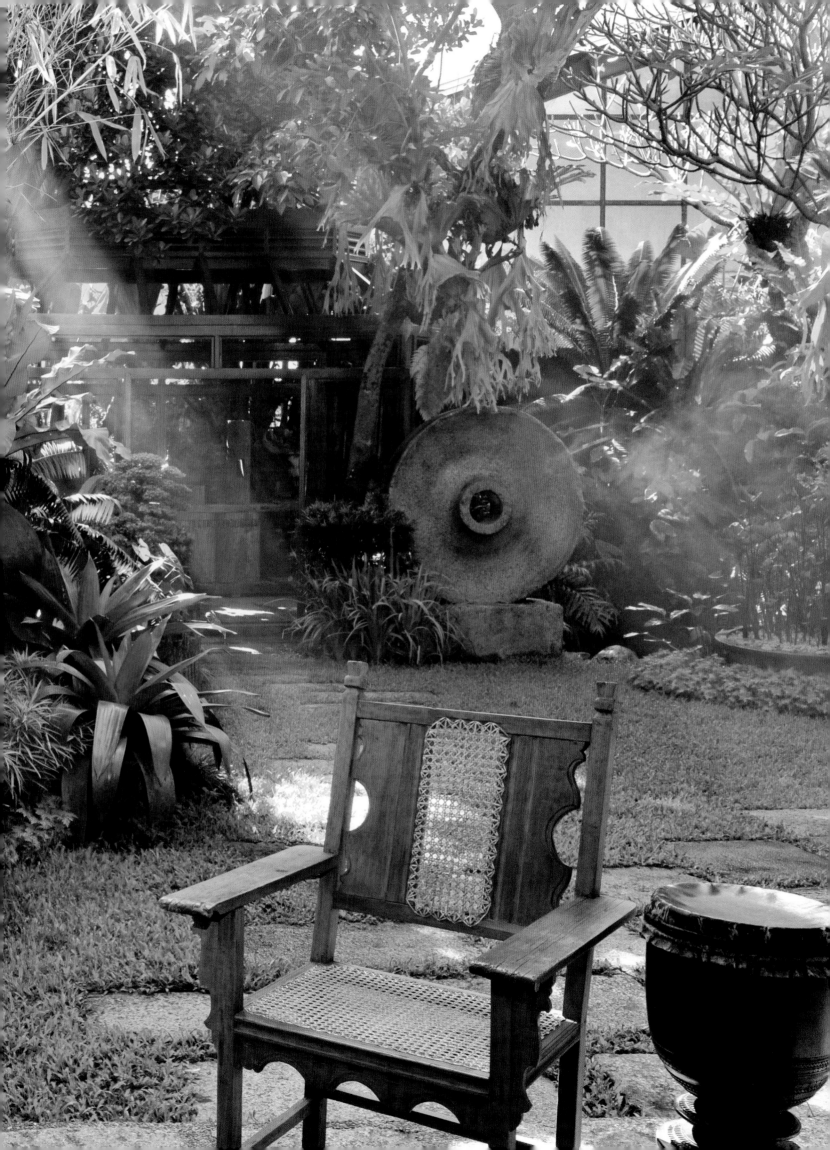

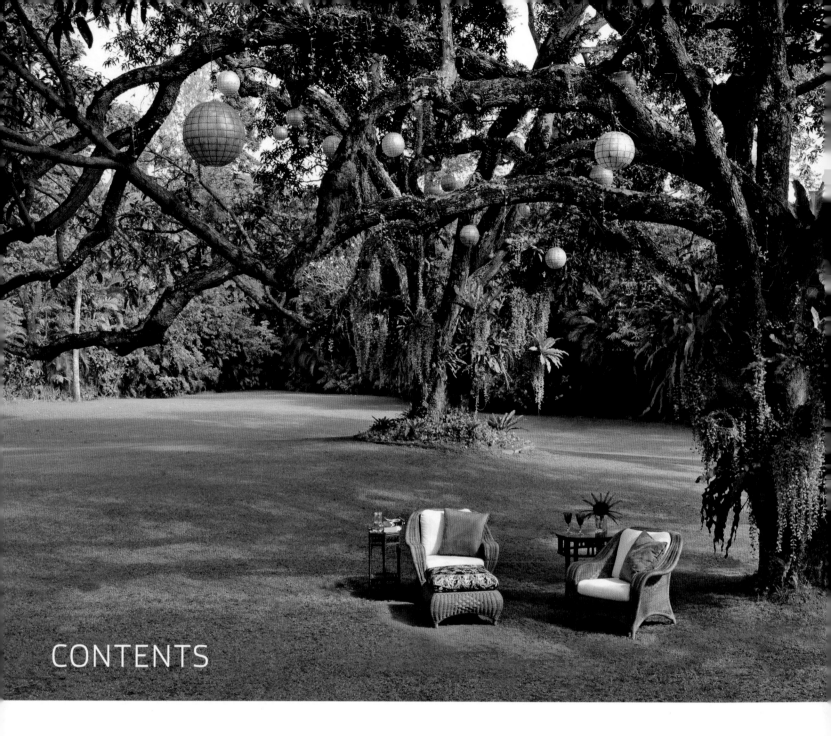

CONTENTS

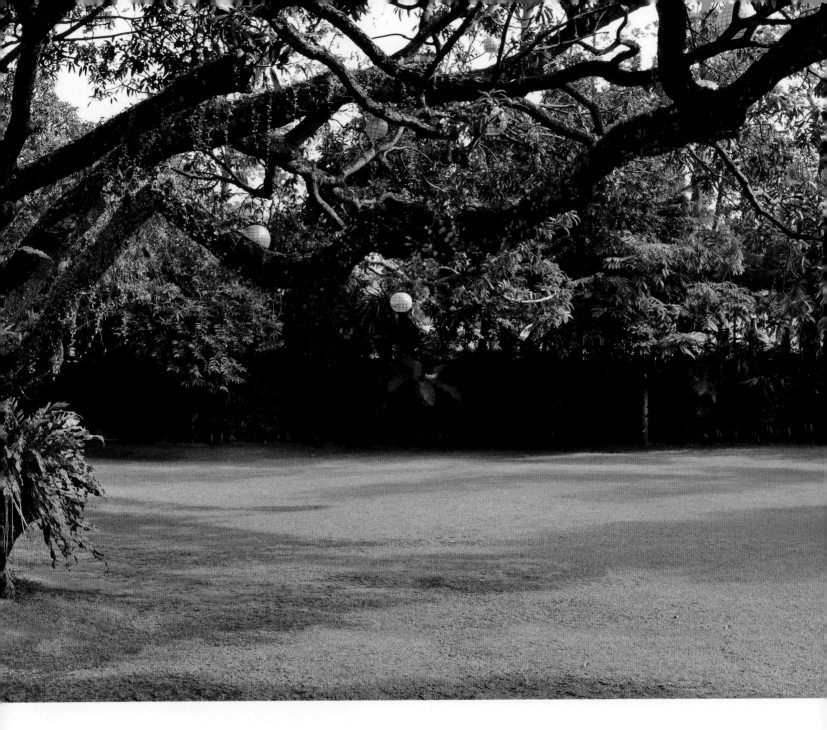

THE PHILIPPINE TROPICAL GARDEN

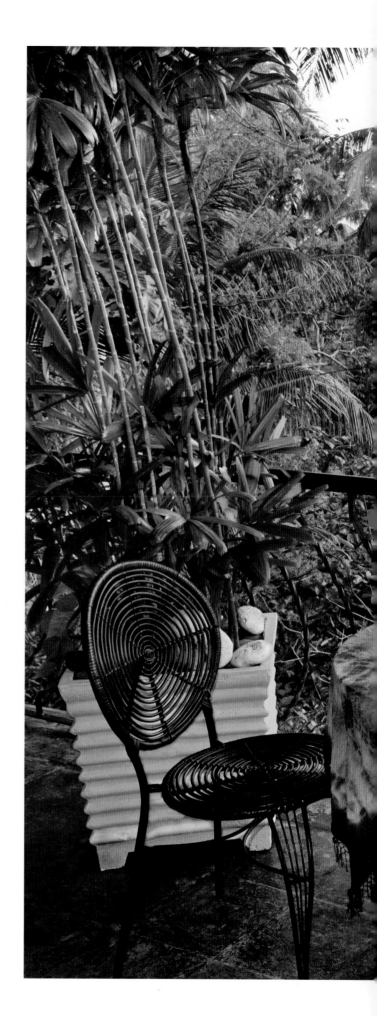

The Philippines—from rice terraces that climb to the heavens to little cottage plots found along the outskirts of towns combining orchard, vegetables and flowers—is one big garden. A varied topography, diverse tropical climate, cultural assimilation from outsiders, and an inate love of nature all contribute to the huge variety of gardens we find in the Philippines today.

The Philippines did not have royal palaces and water temples that in places like Bali and Thailand helped define a garden model. The early Filipinos believed that spirits called *anitos* animated the forests. They worshipped the spirits along with nature in forested groves. Plants were grown mainly for food and medicinal purposes.

Prior to Spanish colonization, there was no tradition of ornamental horticulture in the Philippines. A 17th century depiction of a Philippine garden from the book *Our Islands And Their People* cites palm, *nipa*, banana and fruit trees of the village as surrounding the house. "The rice fields are nearby, as are the streams and rivers where men can fish or sail and trade with the Chinese junks at sea." It was only after the arrival of the Spanish in the 16th century that gardens planted for viewing pleasure came into being. Along with a newfound affection for water, the Filipinos developed a fascination for the plants introduced by foreigners from Mexico and Spain. *Flora de Filipinas*, published in 1837 by priest and scientist Fray Manuel Blanco, documented the rich plant life of the Philippines and was lauded by botanists all over the world. By the 19th century, townhouses with gardens and courtyards featuring fountains and flat open terraces called *azoteas* where old-fashioned favorites were grown in pots became the norm.

The concepts and implementation of landscape design came much later with the arrival of the Americans who also brought with them a love of lawns and open spaces. The Japanese subsequently introduced their disciplined traditions of pruning and plantsmanship. Stories abound of Japanese spies working as gardeners in the Philippines before the outbreak of World War II.

So, what are the influences that have made their mark on today's Philippine garden? Certainly, the formality of the Chinese and Japanese garden which the Filipinos somehow minimize and modernize at every turn with unexpected plant combinations; the Latin flamboyance of the Mediterranean garden which they fine-tune with a more selective plant palette; and the fertile and skilled tradition of Philippine plantsmanship that plays like a melodic refrain through their gardens. Today, a spirit of innovation and creativity is sweeping the gardening world.

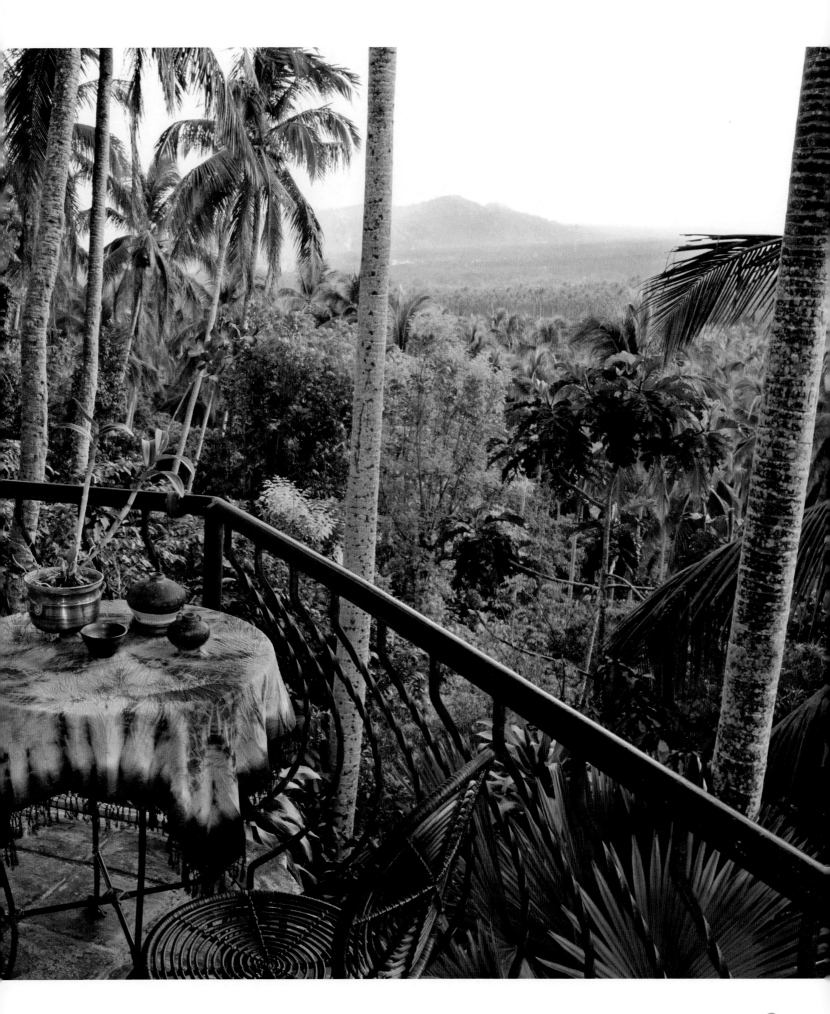

Previous pages The Philippine house and garden draw their vitality from the country's rugged geography and diverse tropical climate. The balcony of the home of Ely Bautista and Bill Lewis overlooks the lush tropical vegetation of Meros and the surrounding Laguna countryside.

Opposite right top The Philippines benefits from an extraordinary array of exotic and native plants available in the country. The *sanggumay*, *Dendrobium anosmum*, is one of 60 recorded orchid species in the Philippines.

Opposite right 2nd from top *Kapa kapa*, *Medinilla magnifica*, is one of the most beautiful tropical epiphytic shrubs. Endemic to the Philippines, it is grown for its lush foliage and brightly colored flowers.

Opposite right 3rd from top *Mussaenda 'Dona Luz'*, an old-fashioned favorite named after one of the Philippine first ladies. This shrub is native to the Philippines.

Opposite right bottom The jade vine (*Strongylodon macrobotrys*), a native of the tropical forests of the Philippines, is marked by a deep blue-green color and has the texture of jade, hence its name.

Right A contemporary country house with a huge garden designed by Noel Saratan was inspired by Philippine traditional architecture. A mural by Emmanuel Cordova depicts some of the country's diverse plant life that can be found on the property.

Below and bottom Orchids are among the favorites of tropical gardeners not only for their wide variety but also for their long lived blooms. Below is one of many Dendrobium hybrids and at bottom is a yellow-orange *Staurochilus loheriana sp.* This small to medium sized monopodial species is endemic to the Philippines on the island of Luzon.

Pages 12/13 Creating a cool, sheltered area, which serves as an extension of the landscape is an integral part of the design of the tropical house. The home of Doris Ho is a union of indoor and outdoor living.

Pages 14/15 Traditional stone features are being updated in sophisticated ways for the modern garden. White granite pavers cut horizontally and seamed with grass add a modern touch to this Thunbergia arbor designed by Jun Obrero for a Tagaytay client.

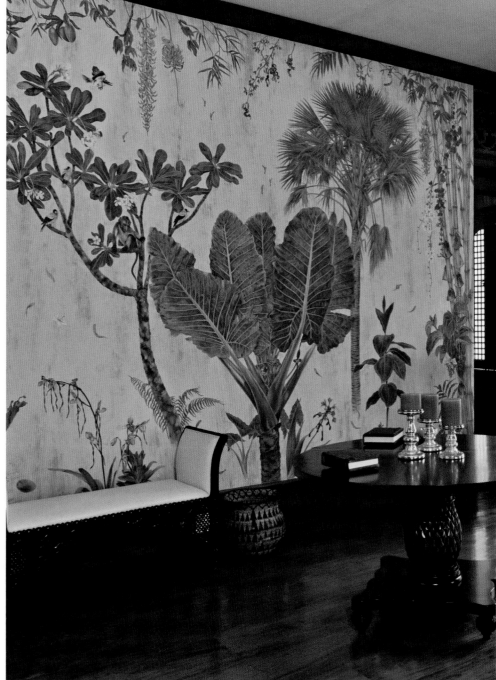

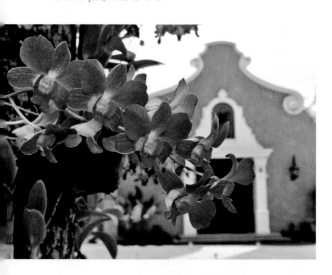

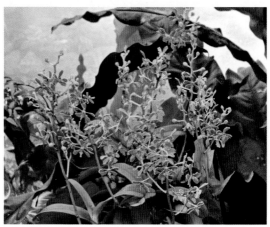

A renewed interest in modern architecture has seen a similar interest in the garden. The garden is becoming a laboratory where new materials, plants and local artifacts can connect with the Philippine design heritage to create fun and livable contemporary spaces that exude a type of tropical modern vibe. There is the "high style" of the contemporary Philippine country house and garden, the "new style" look of the modern, chic suburban garden in and around Manila, as well as the "exotic style" of the romantic garden where the Filipino is at his best. Along with this comes a new breed of landscape designer and gardener, all trying to define a Philippine gardening style that is truly unique.

Jerry Araos, perhaps best described as a "philosopher gardener," has long been an exponent of the "enhanced nature" or nature-inspired movement that is steadily gaining ground in the USA and Europe to the advantage of wildlife and biodiversity. Like Piet Oudolf and other German proponents of the New Wave Movement, he

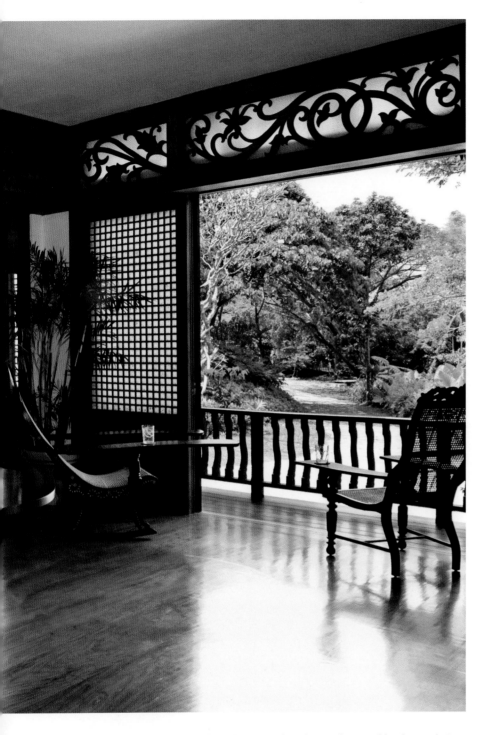

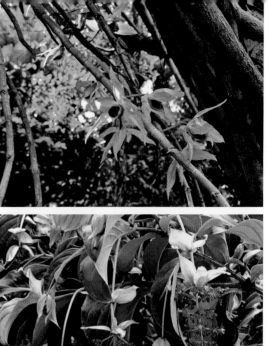

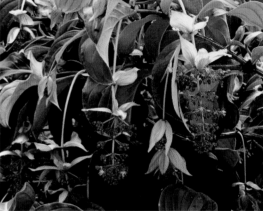

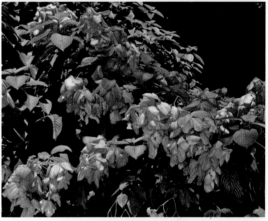

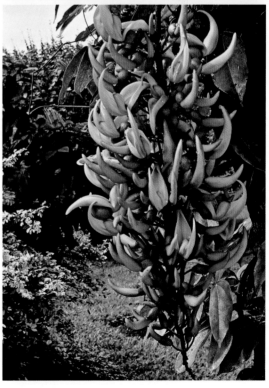

has crafted his own earth-friendly approach to horticulture and landscape design. For more than 20 years he has been designing wild, naturalistic gardens that call for dynamic, ecological plantings that are wildlife-friendly and at the same time self-sustaining without pesticides, complicated water systems and a large labor force. He is credited for redesigning the Manila Hotel gardens in time for the APEC Conference of 1997. A decade earlier, he had created a garden for himself and his family in a swampy piece of land in Antipolo. Today it is a tropical paradise where his poetic and sensitive interpretation of the garden form offers an inspiring and timely model for Philippine gardeners. Araos' approach brings natural elements—earth, stone, water and plants—into a harmonious whole to convey personal philosophies about humanity and man's relationship to nature.

Yuyung LaO', a master landscape artist, is another name on the contemporary scene who has mentored many of the country's young landscape designers.

His innovative use of plants gives an international appeal to his landscape design, and also offers fresh ideas for how these plants can be used in a modern tropical landscape. The garden designer, Ponce Veridiano, is outstanding in creating tropical gardens. His career now extends into Sarawak, Hongkong and Brunei, but his breakthrough project was the Pearl Farm Resort in Samal Island, Davao. Here, he showcased his skill in combining the exuberant growth of native and introduced plants with an exacting attention to detail, texture, color and decorative accents. Recent work at his own home shows how his work continues to evolve.

The gardens of Jun Obrero, Toni Parsons and Bobby Gopiao, along with those of Rading Decepida and Jojo Lazaro, abound with a new naturalism. Proponents of the "nature managed" concept of gardening, their works exhibit an ecological sensitivity to the nuances of water, stone and vegetation. Outstanding tropical border designs tend to be composed of key plants, which are repeated through the garden to create rhythm and evoke the idea of plantings in the wild. To highlight the contrast between areas of strong light and deep shade, light-catching plants such as ferns and bamboo are used for their delicately textured leaves. Though naturalistic in feel, they become contemporary when combined with modern paving, and carefully maintained lawns. Sculpture and decorative objects are used around the garden to enhance and add interest while water is given special attention in the landscape.

The gardens of Ramon Antonio, Noel Saratan and Frank Borja all reflect an architect's eye for space and a gardener's passion for plants. A sculpted, spatial quality resonates throughout their work. Their modern tropical gardens are usually based on strong, clear structural lines, with winding, elegant curves in the ground plan and hardscapes, and a preference for bamboo and clipped boxed shrubs. Borja worked abroad for many years with the prestigious landscaping firm Belt Collins and has supervised many of the firm's landscaping projects in the Philippines. His work, like Antonio's, is designed not just to showcase plants but also to cater to clients' leisure needs. This design trend, born out of functionalist and Modernist ideas of the 1920s, has been reinforced by gardening design shows and western makeover programs promoting the pleasures of water features such as pools and Jacuzzis, patios, barbecues and showy architectural plants in ornamental pots.

In Asia, where gardeners have traditionally been male, a number of women are now playing creative roles in the landscaping arena. Shirley Sanders, a self-taught landscape artist well known for her skillful and meticulous plantsmanship, is famous for designing huge resort-type gardens but she is equally adept with small spaces. Her modest-sized garden and nursery in the bucolic countryside of Los Banos, known for its mineral hot springs, is of particular note. Michelle Magsaysay, who designed the Alejandrino and Olbes gardens, has also established herself as a sought-after designer in the urban scene; she specializes in small-scale designs that combine an Asian formality with a contemporary slant.

Thanks to the now-famous vertical tropical landscapes of French botanist and artist Patrick Blanc, ornamental tropicals are the new darlings of the horticultural establishment. Many a visitor has stopped dead in his tracks at the sight of the hundreds of plants cascading down the walls of the Musée du Quai Branly and the Fondation Cartier in Paris. Taking their cue from this phenomenon, home-grown designers are also experimenting with tropical plants of varying leaf colors, sizes and patterns to transform contemporary architecture into living works of art. The extraordinary array of exotic and native plants available in the country today, as well as the advances in water filtration and irrigation, have benefitted the garden designer. New and hardier varieties of Anthuriums and Alocasias and more sun tolerant species of Philodendrons and *Excoecaria cochinchinensis* are enhancing many of the newer gardens, while excellent substitutes for yew and boxwood, much used in the west for hedges and topiary rounds, are found in Fukien tea, *kamuning* (*Muraya paniculata*) and Eugenia shrubs.

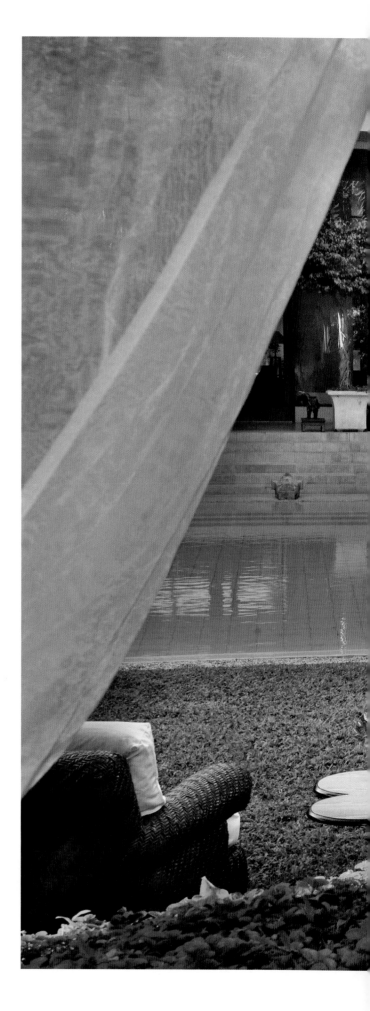

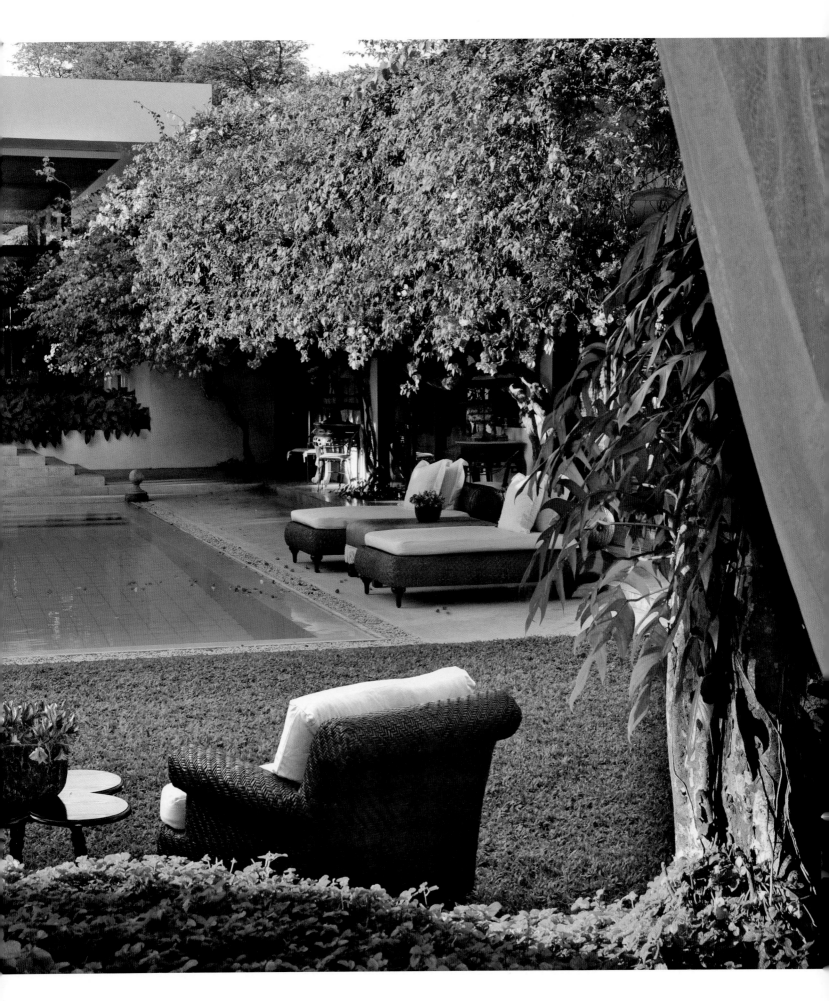

In general, gardens exhibit a wide variety of plant material mostly imported from neighboring Bangkok, Indonesia and Malaysia. The garden of Malyn and Ochie Santos in Lipa, Batangas is an outstanding example of a garden with a wide variety of introduced plants. Their amazing collection of unusual Philodendrons, Anthuriums and variegated palms showcased artfully by species is a horticulturist's dream. While a notable few, such as Patis Tesoro and Cecilia Locsin, have made their mark with the combination of indigenous and imported species, others delight in combining the formal and informal gardening traditions of their Asian neighbors. Western models inspire others like Vicky Hererra: Her garden in the windy ethereal landscape of Tagaytay is particularly impressive with seemingly wild borders of perennials and annuals woven in delicate shifting tones.

Last but not least, there are those who showcase their artistry in stone in the great tradition of the Ifugaos, the Philippine mountain people who built the famous Banaue rice terraces. This engineering marvel, crafted of stone and water 2,000 years ago, covers an area of nearly 400 square kilometers (155 square miles) and reaches 1,500 meters (5,000 feet) in height in some places. Known for their skills as wall builders and stone craftsmen, many Ifugaos have been forced from their mountain homes to seek jobs elsewhere due to hard economic times. Their migration, unfortunate as it may be, has inadvertently made their skills available elsewhere to the benefit of the garden world. As a result, some of the most unique contemporary Philippine gardens excel in stone artistry.

Extensive and imaginative stone features, planted beds with sinuous edges and retaining walls, intricately constructed "rip-rap" walls, and more, are all commonly found in many of today's gardens à la mode. Although stonework has been used in garden design since time immemorial, a high profile comeback has occurred recently in its practical and artistic uses. Though the essentials of construction remain the same, the sculptural qualities of the stone itself and the fluidity of design to which the techniques apply themselves are making dry-stone walling more relevant to contemporary as well as traditional gardens. The popularity of both garden walls and paving in modern gardens confirms the recent rise in demand for dry-stone work. Imaginative and influential designers such as Jerry Araos and Yuyung LaO' and landscape artists such as Augusto Bigyan and Rading Decepida have recognized the potential of this ancient craft and have answered the call with highly pleasing sculptural, yet functional, creations.

The Cordillera wall of Jerry Araos in his Antipolo garden exhibits both mastery of and sensitivity to stone. He prefers to work with natural stone from Bulacan and Antipolo and creates many of his own designs relying on the old trusted techniques. Augusto Bigyan, on the other hand, specializes in exquisite stone and terracotta mosaics and uses a variety of stone materials in his walls and hardscapes. The stones in Bigyan's projects vary widely depending upon the geographic location, but most are sourced from the provinces of Bulacan, Rizal and Mindoro. *Escombro*, a porous stone from Bulacan, is a favorite of many designers because of its ability to weather beautifully. The Andres' garden waterfall, designed by Rading Decepida, is another example of how traditional garden features are being updated in sophisticated ways for the modern garden.

Clearly, there exists a myriad of different styles. During the three months we traveled around the country viewing and photographing gardens, we tried to showcase this variety, along with the wild enthusiasm of the country's gardeners and designers. We wanted to get a sense of how the real Philippines connects with the garden and celebrate some of the best contemporary Philippine gardens. We hope that the gardens featured here will be an inspiration for gardeners, landscapers and garden designers in other parts of the world—those looking for something new, something borrowed, something true.

Lily Gamboa O'Boyle

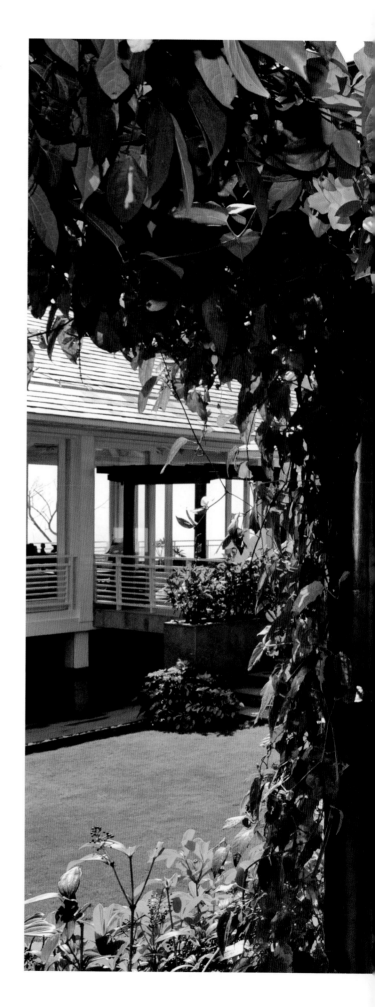

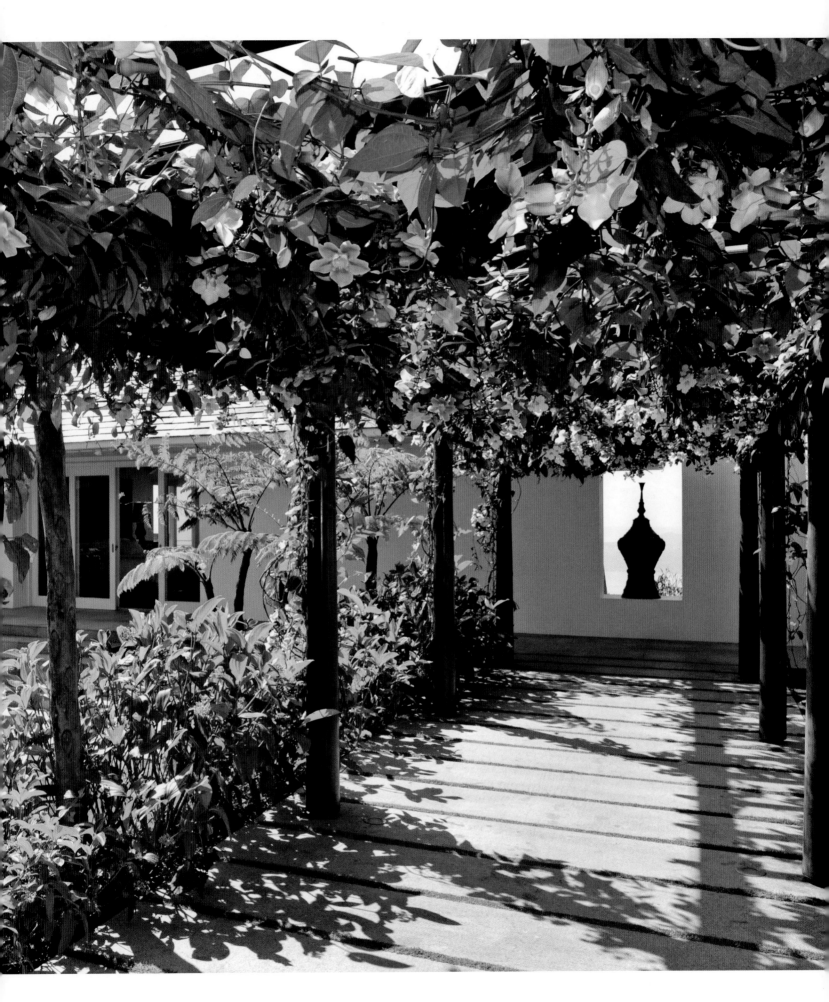

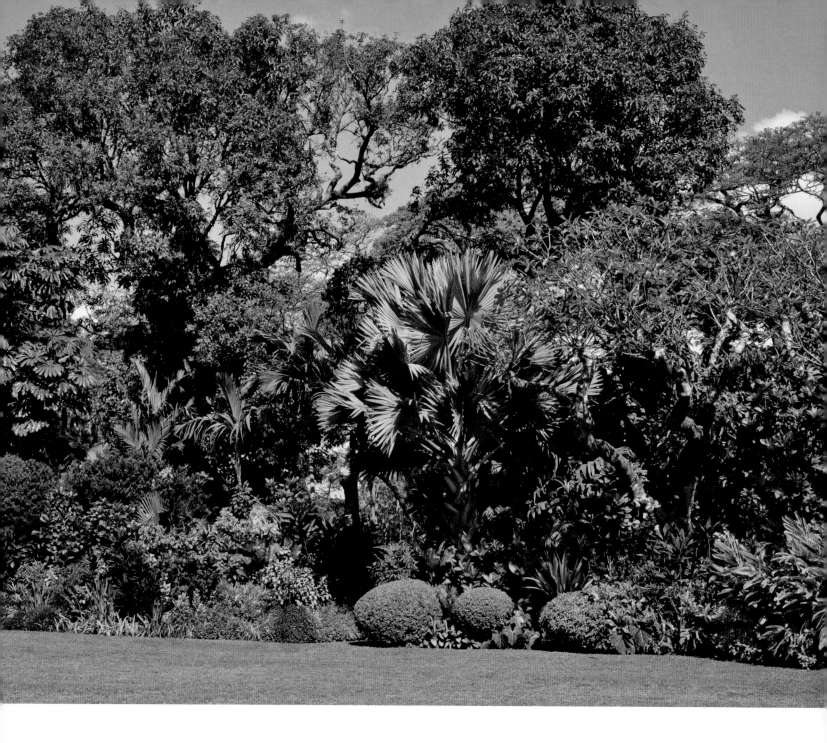

CASA DE NIPA

Canlubang, Laguna

Designed by Cecilia Yulo Locsin

You get to Casa de Nipa down one of those narrow, dusty country roads (meant to be a shortcut!) that pass through a subdivision under construction, via an industrial zone, uphill and down until you get deeper and deeper into the Canlubang countryside. Just when you conclude you are on the road to nowhere, you reach a wooden gate with a guard who assures you that you have arrived at your intended destination.

The gate opens onto a heavily wooded entrance drive. Ahead is a large house, perched on a platform of lawn surrounded by lavishly planted borders of the most exquisite tropical plants you have ever seen. Originally built in 1915 and renovated in 1999, the dwelling was designed along the lines of a modern *bahay kubo*, sometimes referred to as a *nipa* hut, after the leaves that are used for the roofs of this kind of abode. The house was the result of a collaboration between Andy Locsin of LV Locsin Partners and Noel Saratan. The garden, except for a new water garden added recently, was the creation of Cecilia Yulo Locsin.

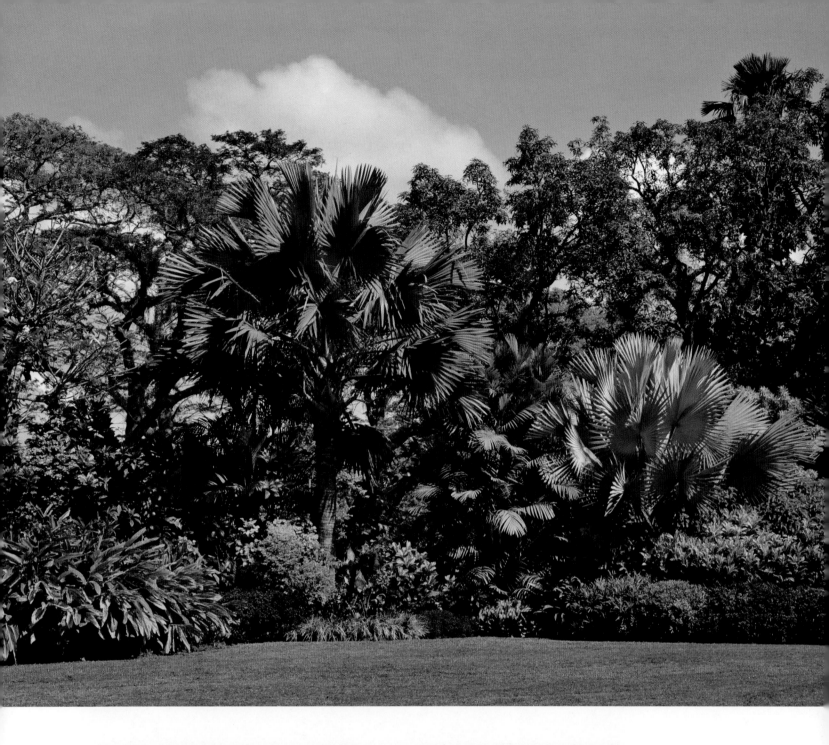

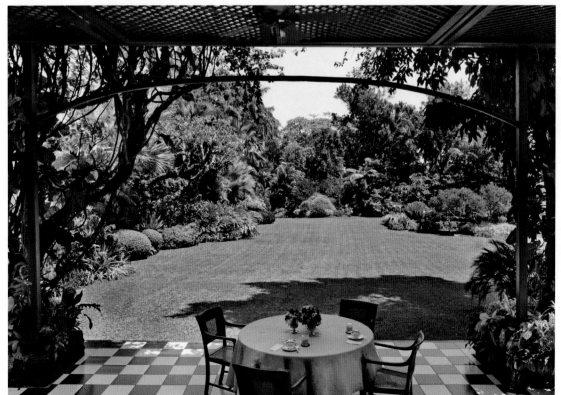

Above *Narra*, frangipani
and Bismark fan palms cast
dappled shade over groupings of
Acalyphas, Crotons, Cordylines,
Heliconias, Rhapis palms, Fukien
tea and *Osmoxylon geelvinkianum*
in the exquisite and richly planted
borders of Casa de Nipa.

Left The shaded front entrance
with a checkerboard floor also
serves as a dining area and
viewing spot from where one
can admire the garden.

The garden is divided stylistically into three parts: The first part, around the house, is all gentle curves following the perimeter of the property. There is an abundant profusion of copper Acalyphas, thick, leathery Crotons and green and variously-tinged Cordylines backed by stands of *Heliconia caribaea 'Pupurea'* and Rhapis palms. Beneath an impressive *kamuning* tree (*Muraya paniculata*) by a natural pond is a giant clump of *Osmoxylon geelvinkianum* underplanted with purple elephant ears, *Chrysothemis pulchella* and maroon-colored *Aerva sanguinolenta*.

Away from the house, the middle part comprises a swimming pool and a patio laid out in *piedra China* pavers. Structured plantings of Ficus, palms and Dracaena work well with sculptural stone seats; both indicate the presence of the owner's controlling hand. Garden and water meet and merge here in a new manmade pond designed by Ponce Veridiano. Complementing the design, the shapes become more organic and the planting more natural. Different varieties of bamboo are juxtaposed against boxed forms of Eugenia, Miagos, grasses and aquatic plants; all provide a contrasting play of light and shadows in this delightful area.

The third part of the garden is a large stone patio with a vine-laden stone and wooden arbor and a pond alive with koi. This space, designed by Noel Saratan, was intended as a dining pavilion as well as a reception area.

The abundance of well-established trees—*Ficus balete*, Saraca, *narra* (timber trees in the genus Pterocarpus), sea hibiscus, frangipani or Plumeria, as well as mango and *santol* fruit trees and a wide variety of palms (Bismark, *Corypha elata*, Areca sp), gives this garden an integral unity and lasting bond with the landscape.

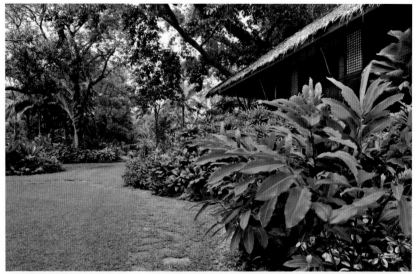

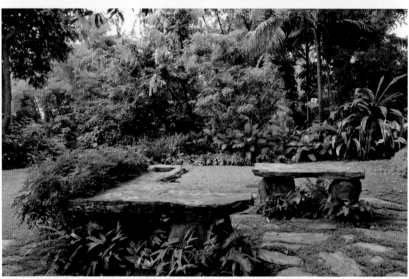

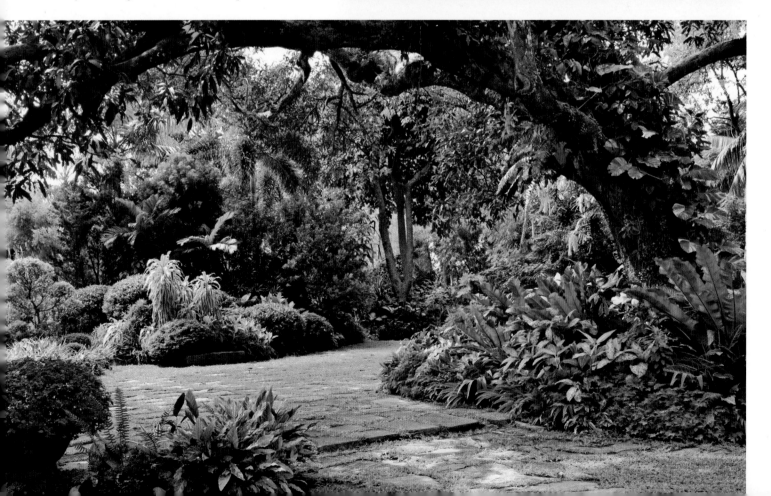

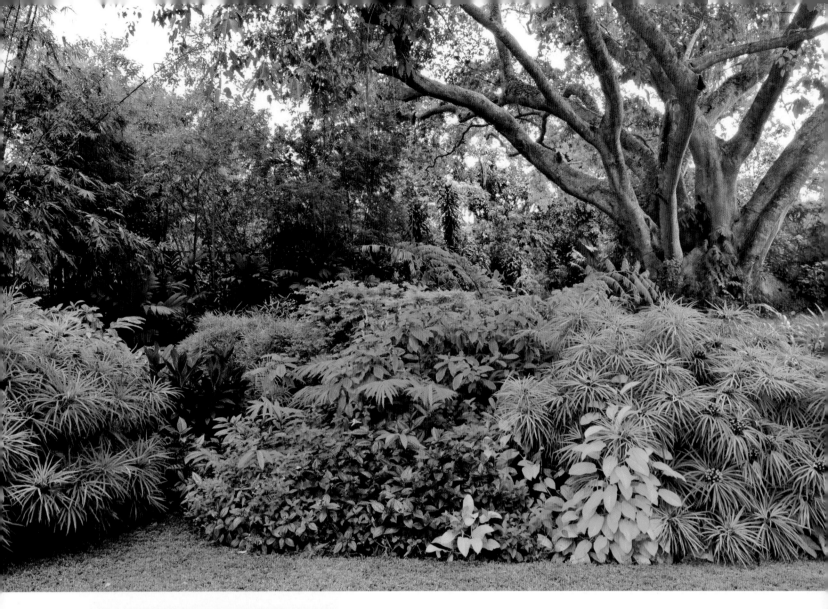

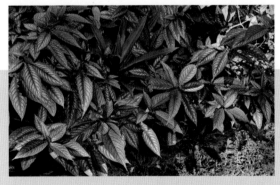

Opposite top Wide, capiz framed windows look out onto a border teeming with pink ginger or *Alpinia purpurata*.

Opposite middle A pair of stone benches invites visitors to pause and take a break.

Opposite bottom Luscious tropicals are skillfully arranged in beds beneath an old tree.

Top Thick plantings of green Miagos, *Osmoxylon geelvinkianum*, contrast with the yellow-green foliage of Philodendrons, maroon *ti* plants and Acalyphas.

Above The silver-purple tints of a patch of *Strobilanthes dyerianus* add subtle color in a bed.

Right A *narra* tree, *Pterocarpus indicus*, commands the landscape. *Narra* hardwood is purplish and rose-scented; as it is termite resistant, it is a popular wood for furniture and flooring.

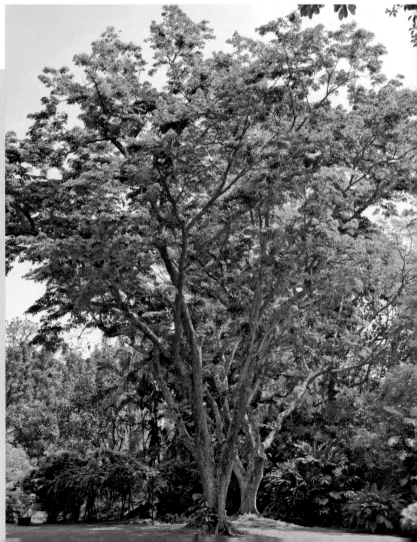

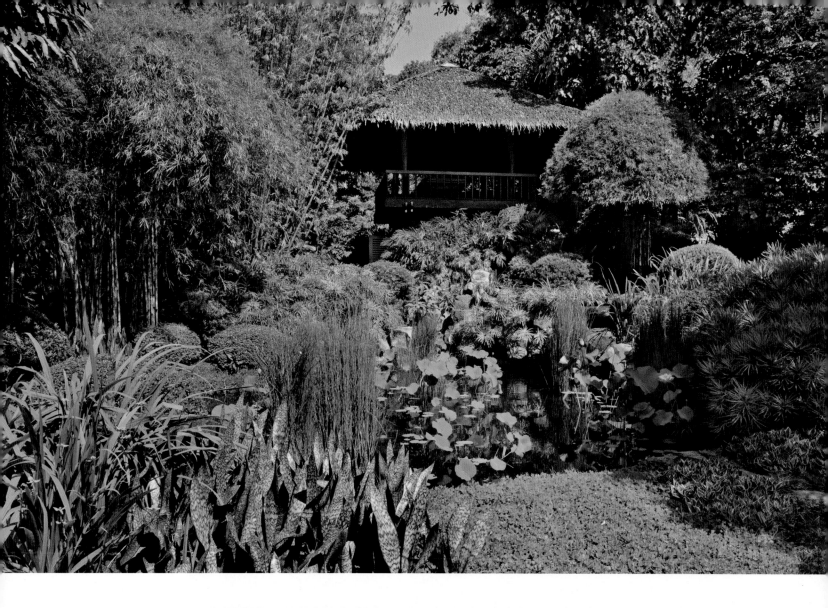

Above and right A thatched gazebo overlooks a new man-made pond (seen on right from above). Designed by landscaper Ponce Veridiano, it is planted with several varieties of bamboo, clipped Eugenia shrubs, grasses, *Osmoxylon geelvinkianum*, *Sanseviera trifasciata*, irises and lotus.

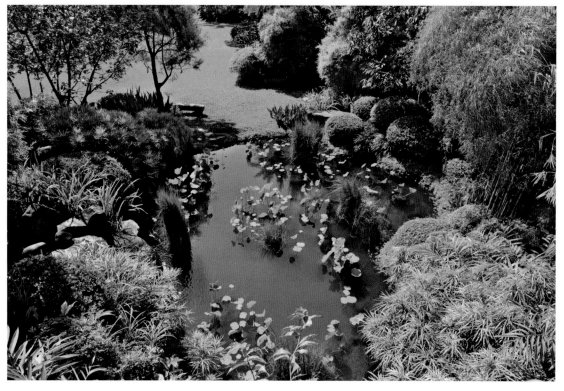

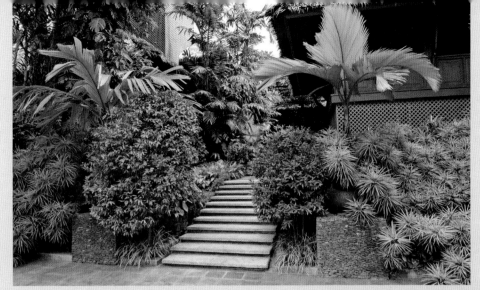

Above A stairway leading to the house is given special treatment with selected ornamental plantings.

Below A swimming pool with a Jacuzzi is nestled against a backdrop of luxuriant tropical vegetation.

Right The large stone pavilion with a vine-laden arbor and adjacent koi pond.

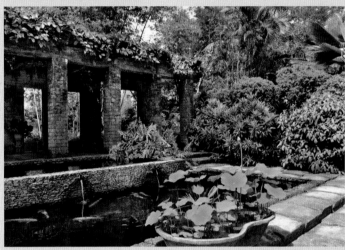

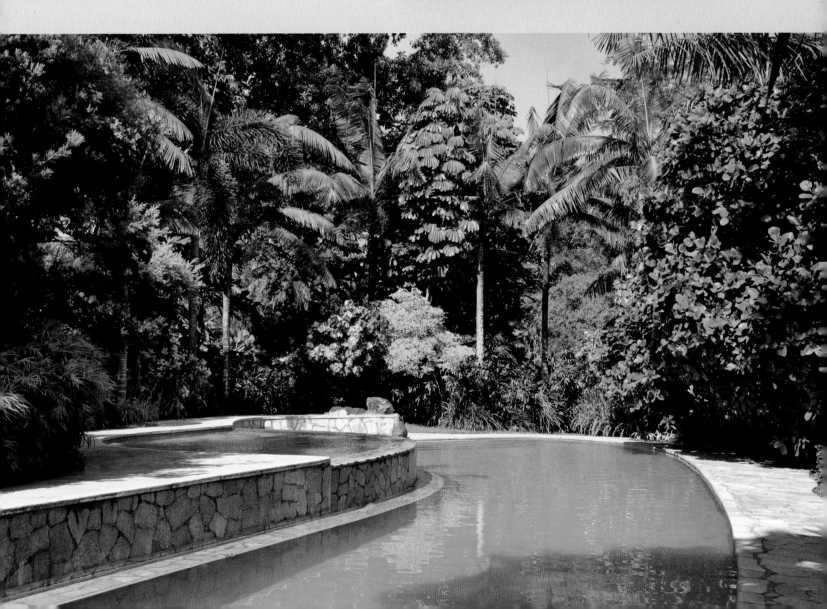

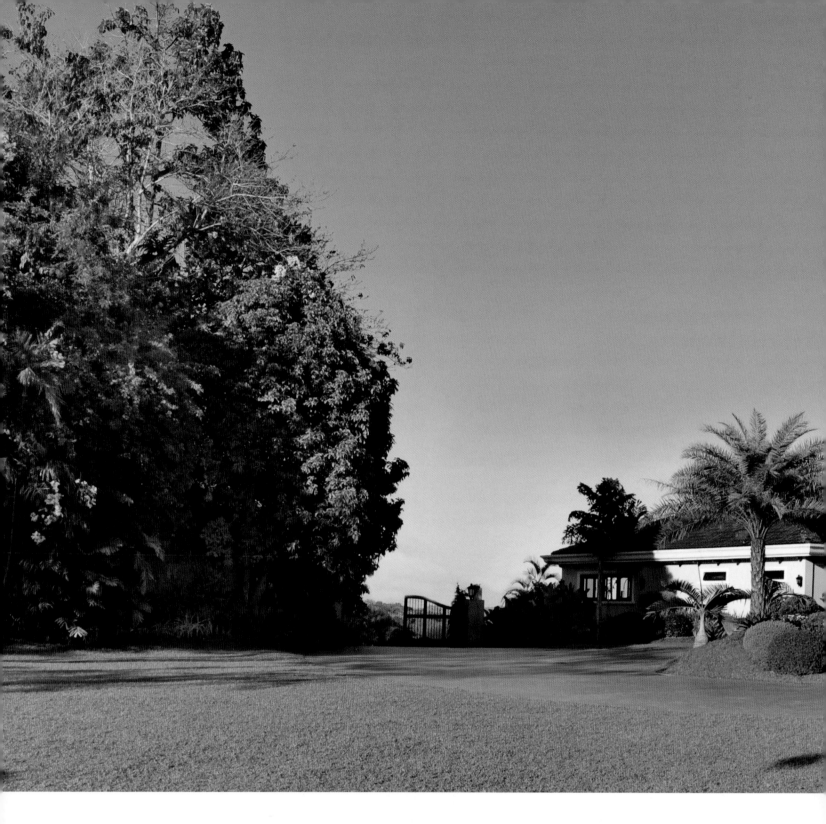

LA VISTA HILLTOP GARDEN

Maria Luisa Subdivision, Cebu

Designed by Jaime Chua and Celine Borja

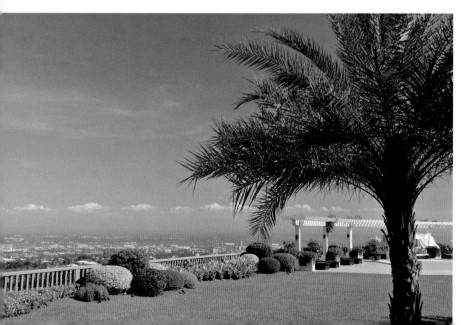

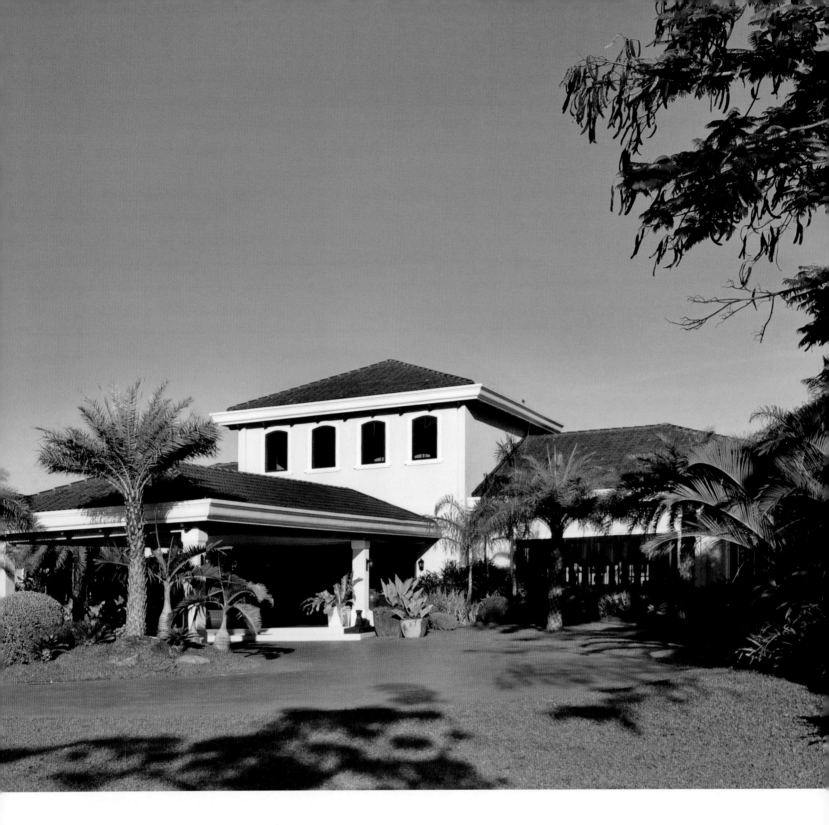

What strikes you most about this garden is the view. Once within its grounds, no other gardens are visible—just sky, mountains, and Cebu City down below. The principal façade of the house gazes outwards to embrace the natural horizon of surrounding hills and mountains. The vertical lines of the trees, the profile of the hills and the huge Mediterranean-style house harmonize with the horizontal lines of the multi-level garden.

The marvelous rear garden with an entertainment area and giant pool spreads like a great viewing gallery, looking out onto the vast scenic panorama of Cebu. The owners have enlarged their vision and made the country-side part of the garden, playing with the background and distant views and incorporating them into the garden by means of a succession of planes. Understanding that a strict formality would not work here, they have followed a more sinuous, flowing approach. But rather than abandon formal design altogether, they absorbed formal touches such as the level ground, gravel areas, boxed shrubs, and paving into a larger more natural design of curvy lawns, voids and lines of trees and shrubs. They focused on round and circular rather than square and rectangular shapes.

As you walk towards the house, a door on your right opens onto a private garden with round, clipped shrubs.

Above The large yet inviting house looks out onto a vast scenic panorama of city and mountain views.

Opposite A stone balustrade overlooking the city of Cebu reins in the border of clipped ornamental shrubs.

This is the Oriental Garden, designed by Cebu-based landscaper Jaime Chua. A collection of boxed Fukien tea, silver dust (*Atriplex halimus*), Duranta and Acalypha contrasts with Bromeliads in vats. Chinese statues, including the goddess Kuan Yin, punctuate the border and reinforce the Oriental theme. Access from here to the house's master suite is marked by tall stands of bamboo. Colorful box forms continue along the border of the garden, contrasting in color as well as shape with the less rigid forms of Schefflera, Euphorbia, Bougainvillea and Crinum lilies.

Away from the house—just adjacent to the driveway, is a secret garden with several water features. You climb down a long flight of marble steps under a canopy of green-colored and variegated-leafed plants until you reach the bottom of the steps, whereupon a small pond and two waterfalls are dramatically revealed. Framed with orchids, tree ferns, ornamental gingers and Bromeliads, these water features enhance the serenity of the place and endow it with magic.

Right A pristine, rectangular pool complements the house's architecture.

Below A white pergola newly planted with vines provides shade and structure to the pool area.

Bottom Bright pink Bougainvillea and golden Crinum lilies frame the magnificent view.

Opposite bottom Circular boxed shrubs echo the curvy silhouette of the hills beyond.

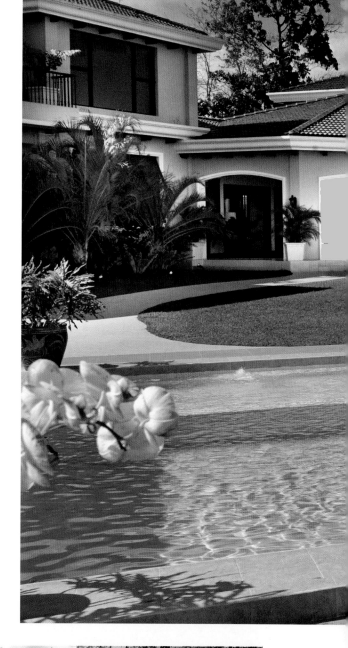

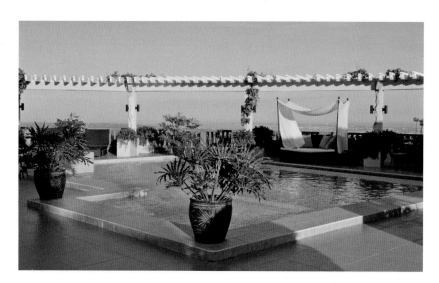

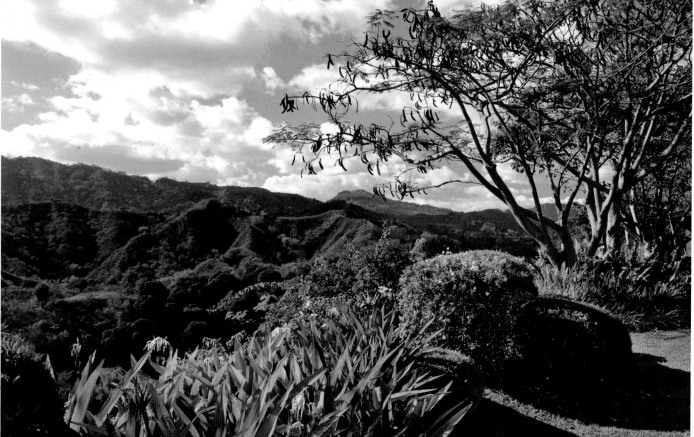

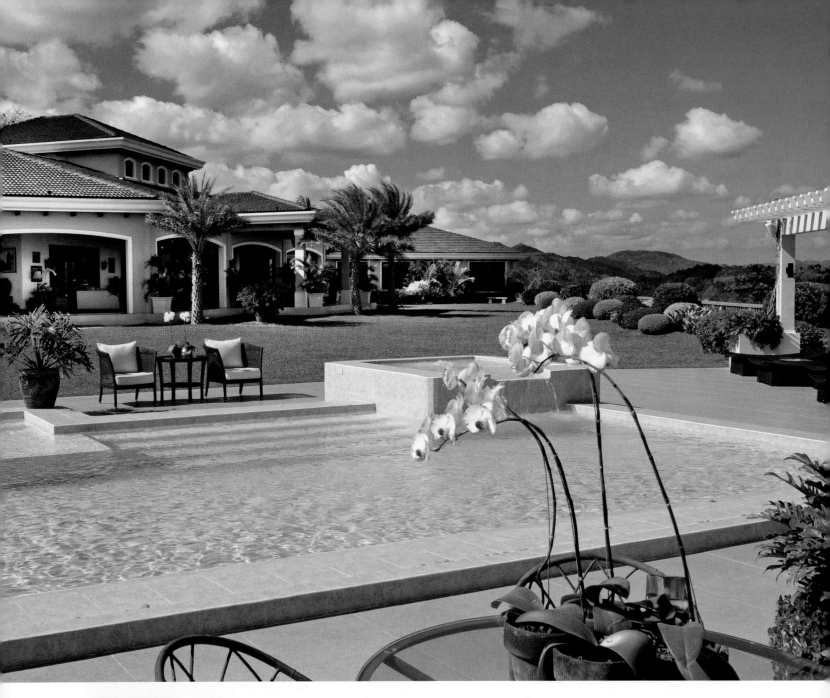

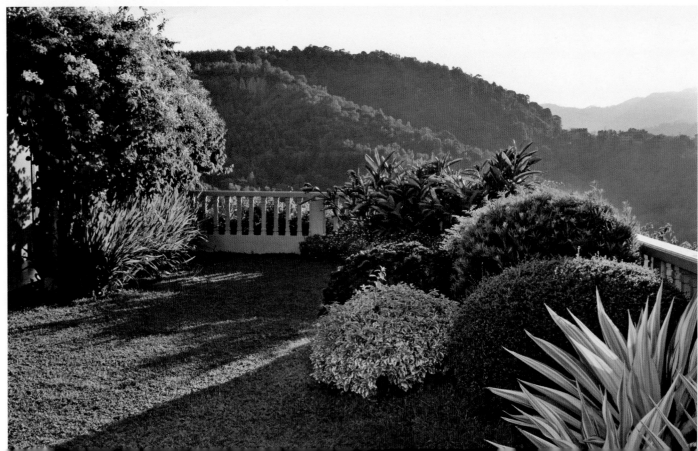

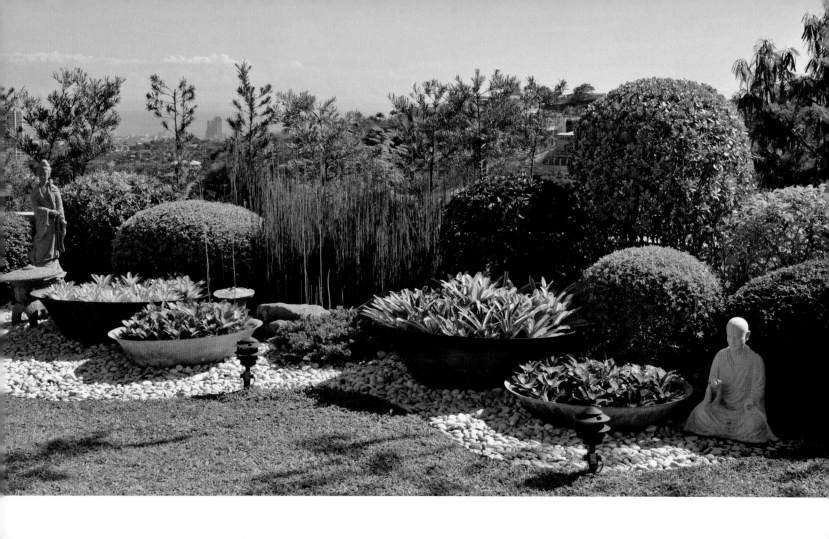

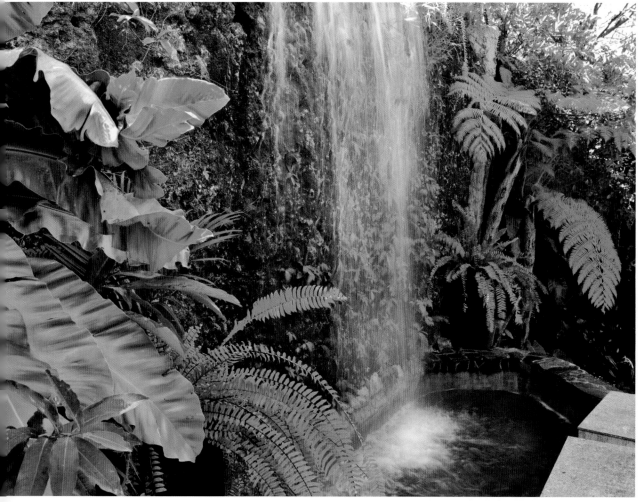

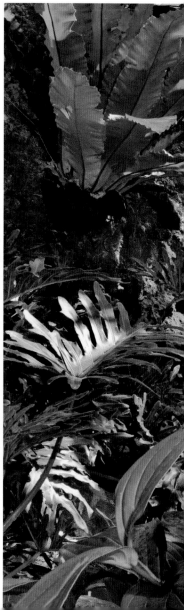

Left Statues of Chinese deities on a bed of white pebbles grace the Oriental-themed garden that is designed with round, clipped boxes of Fukien tea, silver dust (*Atriplex halimus*), Duranta and Acalypha along with iron vats filled with Vrieseas.

Right and bottom A special garden project along the approach road features a small pond and two manmade waterfalls. Intensely tropical, this "Secret Garden" at the bottom of a marble stairway provides a spot for quiet reflection for the owners and their family.

Opposite bottom Close-up of one of the waterfalls fringed with a variety of epiphytic and terrestrial ferns. The plantings of ferns were started by the plant-lover and home owner Michel Lhuillier while the garden hardscape was designed by his architect Celine Borja.

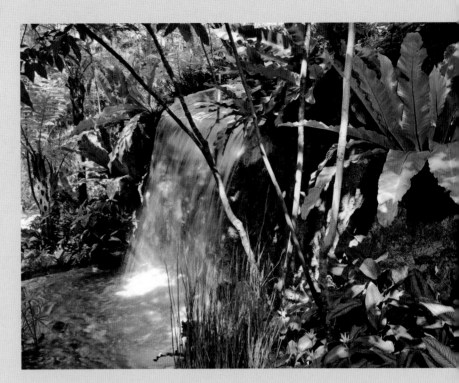

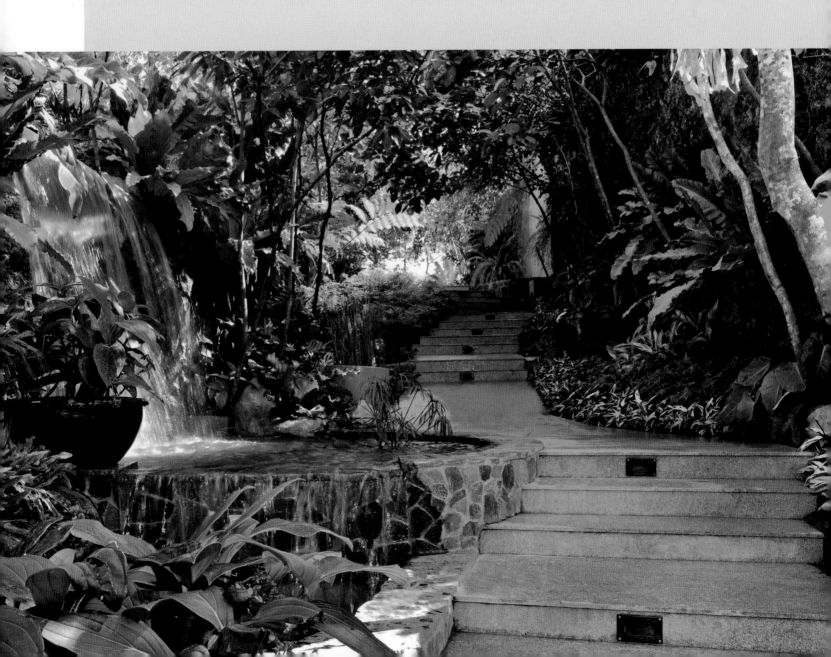

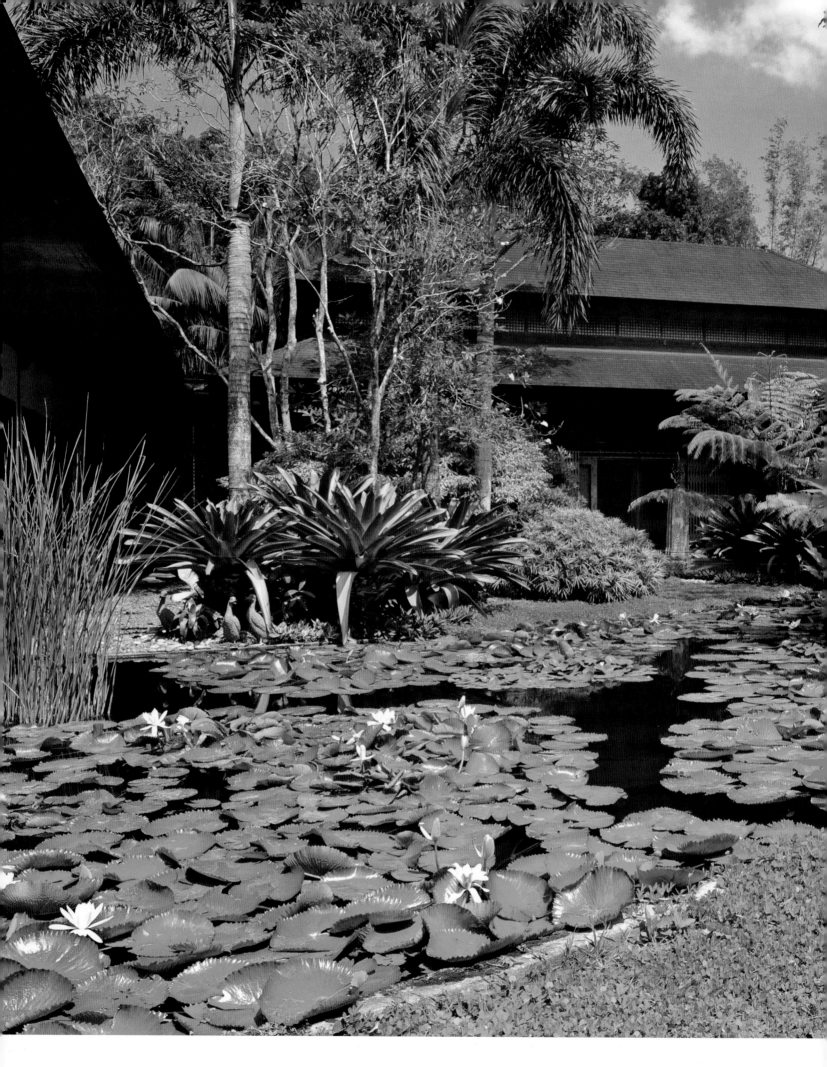

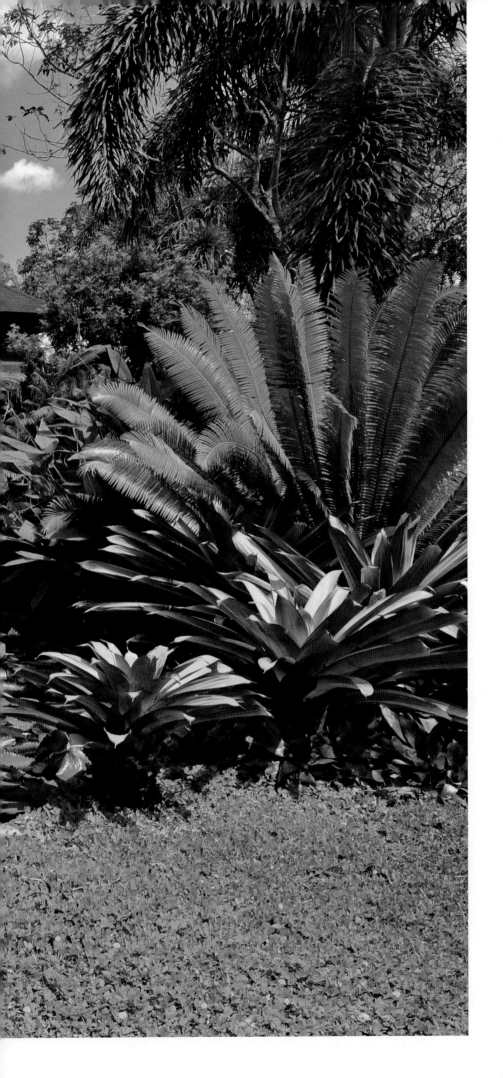

THE SUNBURST FARM GARDEN

Lipa Batangas

Designed by Yuyung LaO' and
Ponce Veridiano

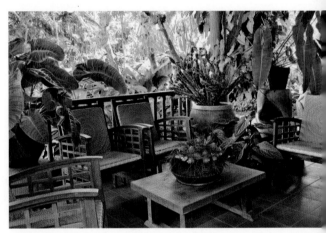

Sunburst Farm is the country home of Ochie Santos,
a gentleman farmer who raises horses and koi fish and
his wife, Malyn, a keen gardener and plant enthusiast.
Together, they garden five of the 23 hectares (57 acres) that
comprise the property along with a number of dedicated
gardeners. A pond, resplendent with white tropical water
lilies, by the front patio provides the link between the
house and the landscape originally designed by noted
Philippine designer, Yuyung LaO'. A friend and mentor
to the owners, LaO', laid out the structural planting of
the garden. When he retired, Ponce Veridiano took over.

Box forms of Fukien tea and Eugenia anchor the garden,
giving it a more intimate scale, as well as providing
bold foreground shapes to contrast with the adjoining
woodland. One of the design principles evident here and
evocative of the styles of both designers is the planting in
big sweeps to achieve an effect. In a setting such as this
where a major part of the garden is revealed at once but
also has to connect to the countryside beyond, a proper,
graceful scale of planting is necessary to avoid chaos.

Just below the house are long banks of Heliconias,
Miagos and Bromeliads along with wild ginger, so-called

zigzag plants, *Pedilanthus tithymaloides 'Variegatus'* and Cordylines. These banks also support a stand of mahogany trees whose fallen leaves have lent an air of unlikely autumn color on the ground. On a slope near the top of the garden are Sansevierias, Cycads and Bromeliads animated by a smiling Buddha statue.

The owners have overseen the planting of a comprehensive botanical collection of not only native trees and plants but of new and rare species from abroad. It is a plant enthusiast's garden, with a huge range of ornamental species from Bangkok, Singapore and Australia. As such, it is a challenge to combine all the different elements into harmoniously pleasing plant schemes and integrate them seamlessly with the surrounding landscape. Having some stabilizing, repetitive element in the borders—whether at tree or ground level—helps to quiet down an otherwise busy garden. Here, harmony is reinforced by sizeable green swathes of *Tabernaemontana variegata* known locally as *pandakaki*, Dieffenbachias, Philodendrons, bird's nest ferns, Alocasias and Aglaonemas which tie together some of the colorful, more exotic specimens.

The owners have ensured endless variety by combining their spectacular collection with everything from coarse terrestrial ferns, golden Crinum lilies, red-berried *ti* plants to drifts of towering bamboo and variegated fishtail palms. It makes for a new vista at every turn.

Previous pages main photo A pond resplendent with white tropical water lilies by the front patio provides the link between the house and the landscape.

Previous pages small photo The front patio provides a cool, sheltered spot from which to view the garden.

Right A small pond with a gazebo ringed by plantings of Bromeliads, Euphorbias, golden Crinum lilies and *Osmoxylon geelvinkianum*.

Below Clipped shrubs of Fukien tea, tall Heliconias and Bromeliads play off formal and informal contrasts in the front entrance walkway.

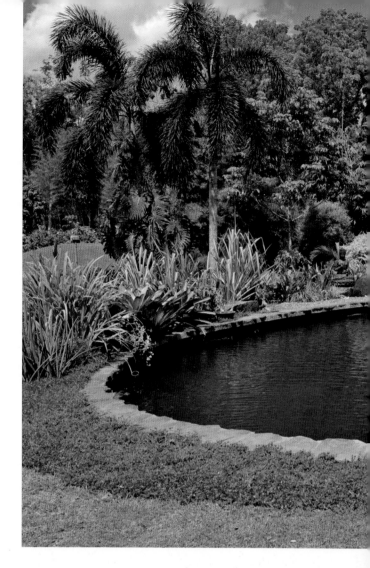

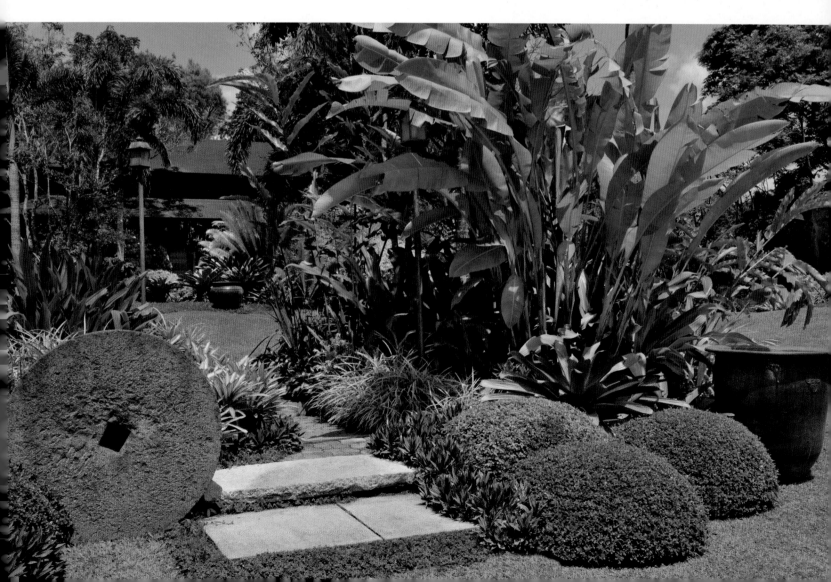

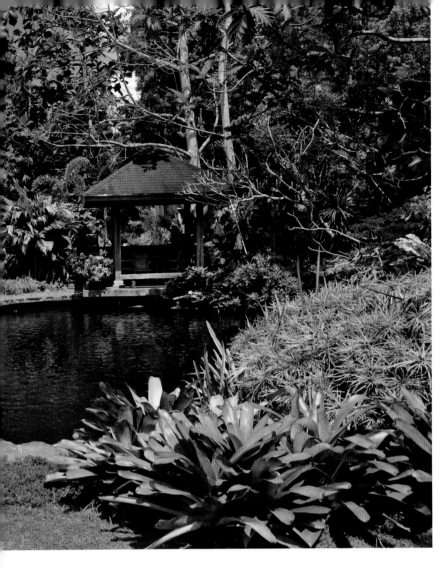

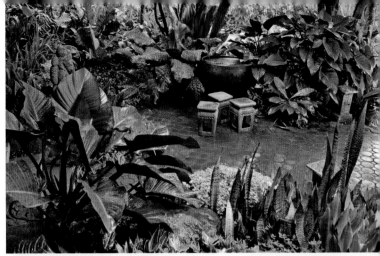

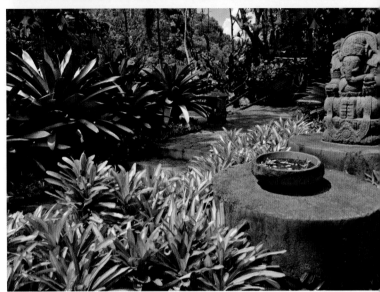

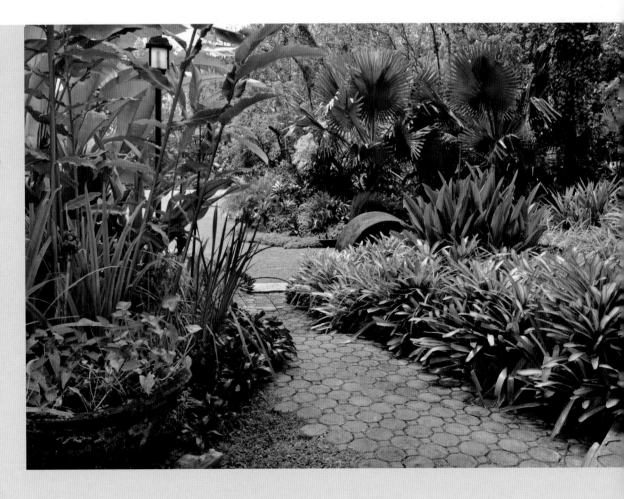

Top right Some of the owners' outstanding Anthurium collection is conveniently potted for display and easily moved to mix with other ornamentals such as ferns, Sansevierias and Philodendron.

Middle right Along this path, a dramatic assemblage of *Alcantarea imperialis rubra* in the background and Vrieseas in the foreground are mixed with stone sculpture and an old cart.

Right The masterful layering of plants and use of color adds tremendous visual appeal to this garden.

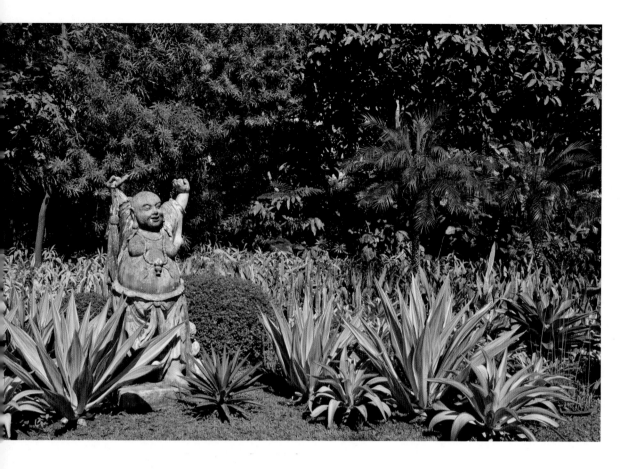

Left A smiling Buddha statue draws focus to a border of Bromeliads, Sansevierias, golden Crinum lilies and Cycads.

Below A spectacular grouping of *Philodendron erubescens* 'Golden' and *Alcantarea imperialis rubra* highlights a lily pond adjacent to the master bedroom.

Opposite top Giant sweeps of carefully chosen plant specimens create a special effect.

Opposite middle left Red Anthuriums provide some welcome color in this otherwise green corridor.

Opposite middle right Silvery green Dieffenbachia grace the ends of the curtain plant vine, *Vernonia elaeagnifolia*.

Opposite bottom left One of many seating areas in the garden.

Opposite bottom right A calming palette of greens and greys provides a serene backdrop to this walkway.

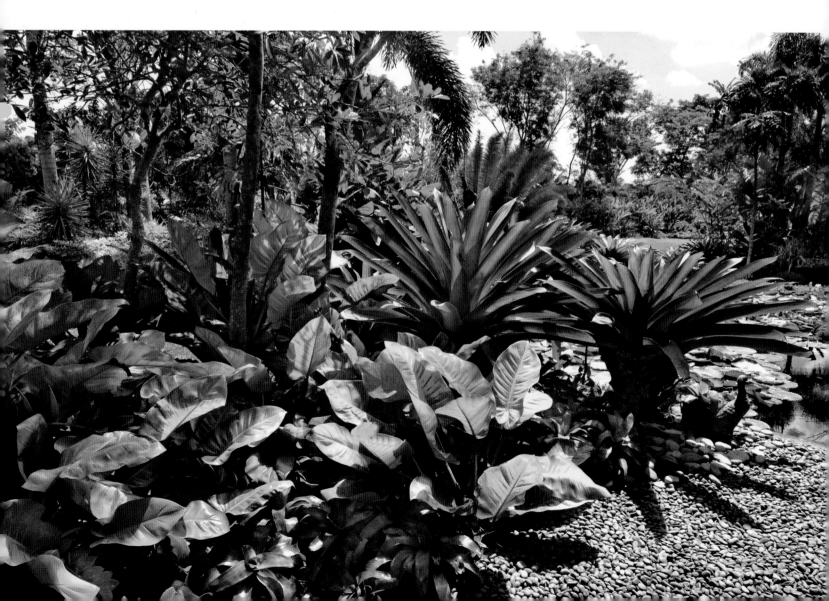

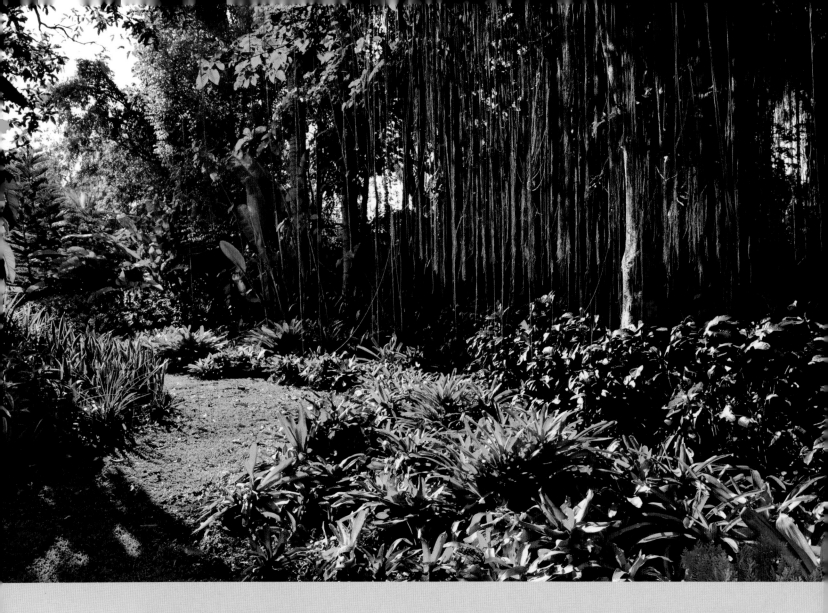

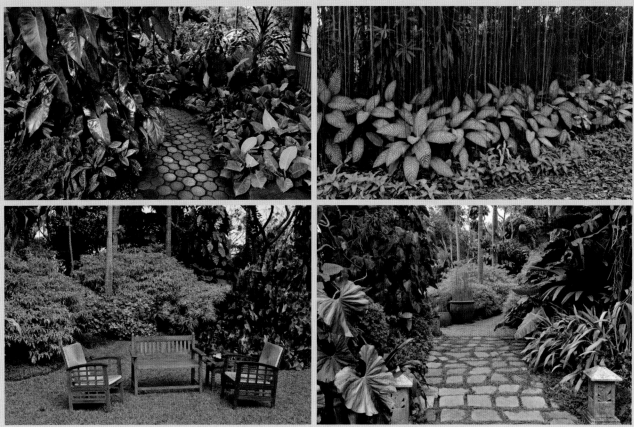

LU YM GARDEN

Maria Luisa Subdivision, Cebu

Designed by Annabelle Lu Ym and Jaime Chua

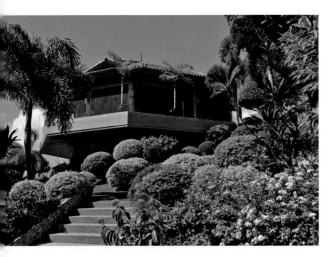

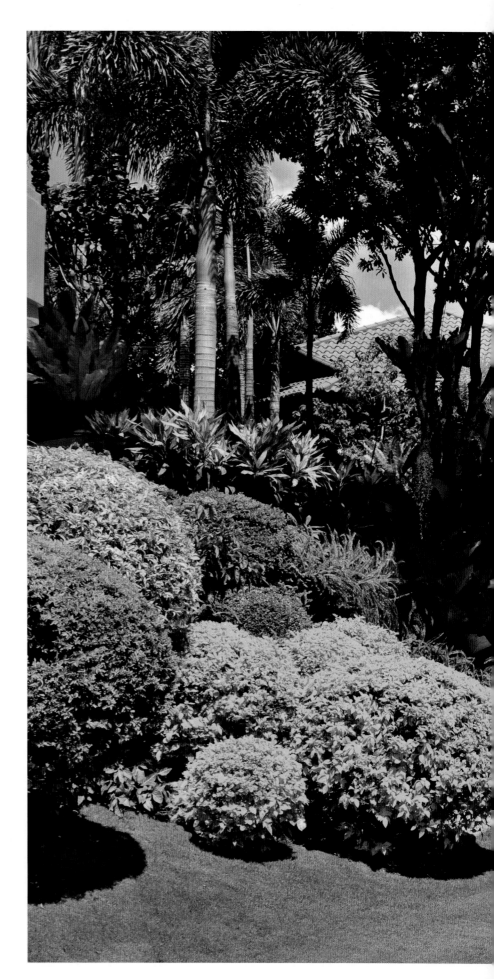

A sweep of stately palms ushers you into the driveway of the Lu Ym property and up to the sprawling house set on a hill designed by Bobby Manosa. The hillside setting is spectacular with wide, well-tended lawns, lush ornamental borders and airy views.

From the house one gets a glimpse of the luxurious and flowing design of the garden. Wide stone steps softened by greenery lead to the different terraced levels that have been incorporated into the garden through the skillful use of elevation. Palms are a major component with royal palms (*Roystonea elata*) currently dominating the scene. The owners have planted them in a naturalistic style distilling a feeling for the landscape into the structure of the garden.

The silhouettes of these palms enhance the many different vistas fully appreciated from above. From the top, the eye is led down the central vista to focus on the more free-flowing spaces that are to be found in the lower part of the garden such as the small natural pond and the lavish beds and borders along the perimeter wall. Farther away from the house, the formal elements are translated

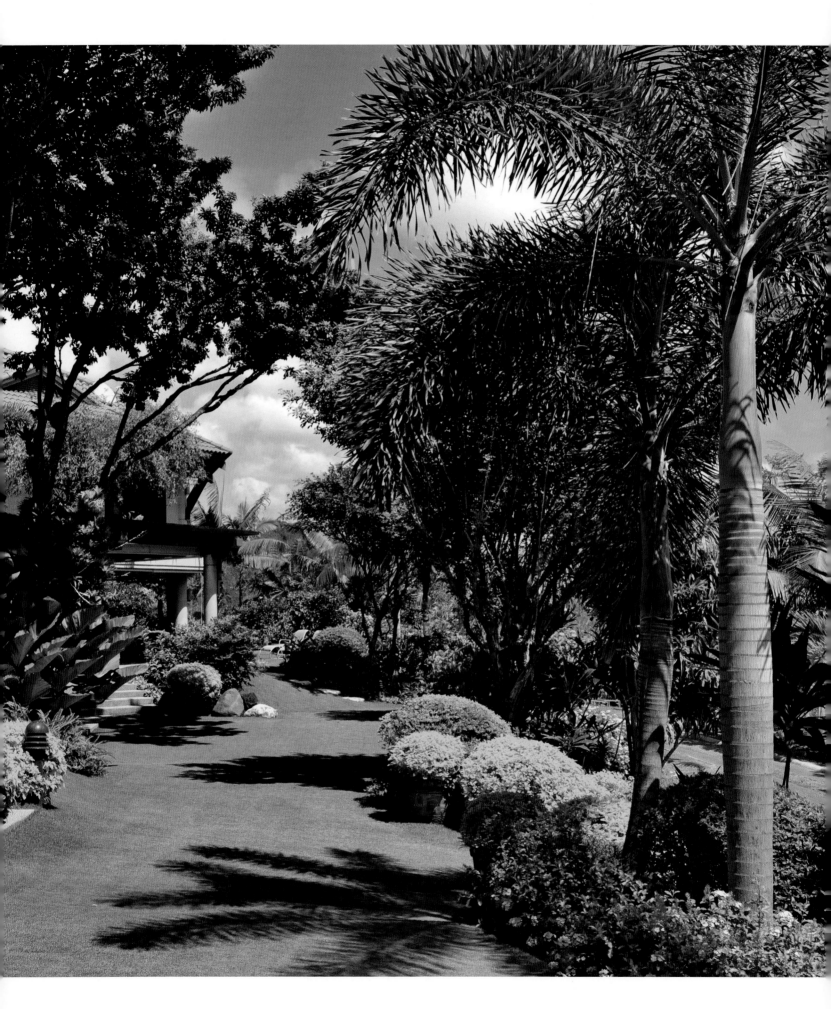

into softer, more rounded forms of clipped shrubs and meticulously sheared ground covers.

The sound of flowing water comes from a contemporary fountain, which features a cascade of water trickling over a series of vats. Traveler's palms (*Ravenala madagascariensis*) and date palms dominate the top end of this water feature, while Bromeliads and bright red ornamental gingers contribute colorful accents. The repeated groupings of Heliconias and Philodendrons create a harmonious look.

A small gravel-paved courtyard in the house displays a collection of exotic ornamentals such as Bromeliads, Anthuriums and Philodendrons, along with some ferns. Annabelle Lu Ym, the lady of the house, known around here as the "constant gardener" loves to have potted plants that can be moved easily around the garden to maintain interest and variety.

The garden's structure with its steep central planted vistas going up the hillside, and its pattern of paths that rise, pause, join and intersect until they reach the house from where one can look out at magnificent views of the surrounding countryside is a distinct expression of the combination of *yin* and *yang*: Areas of dense shade are worked with areas of light and energy together creating a harmonious whole.

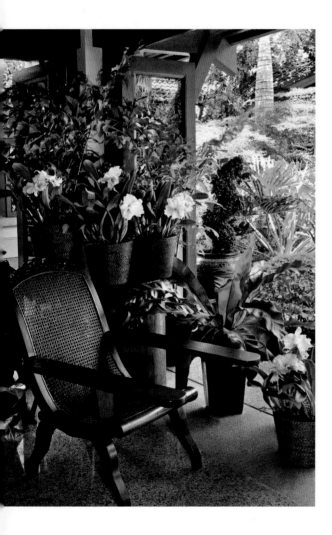

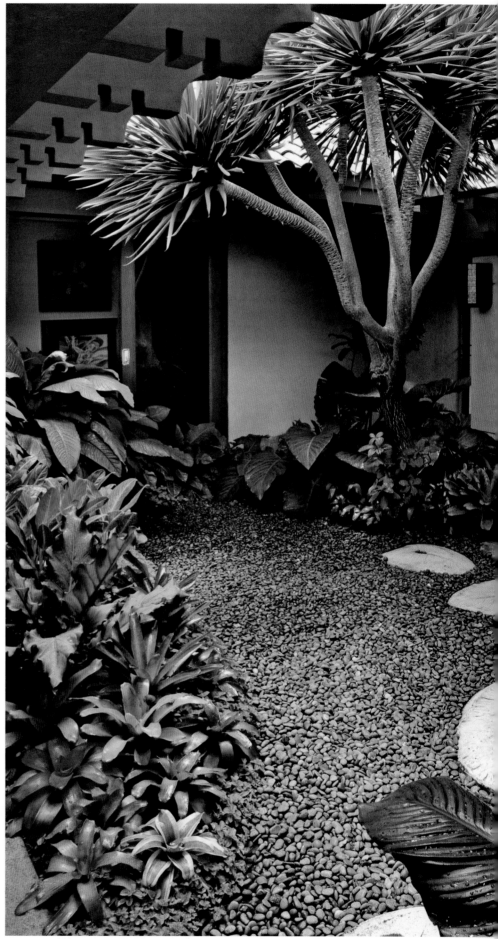

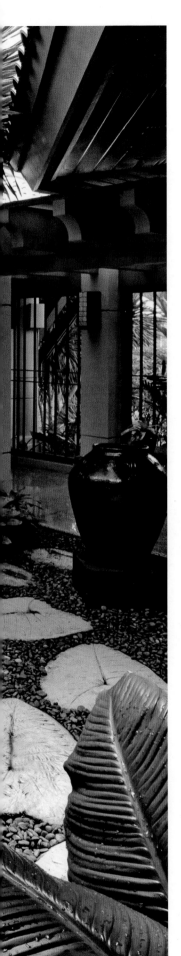

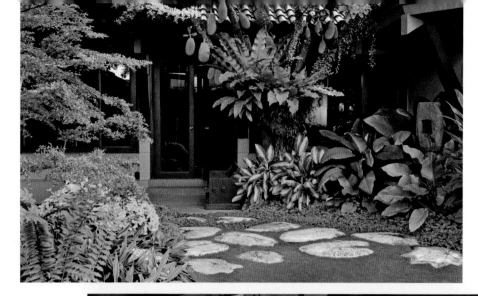

Previous pages main photo The spectacular hillside setting features wide well tended lawns, lush ornamental borders and airy views.

Previous pages small photo The house looks out onto magnificent views of the garden and the surrounding countryside.

Opposite bottom White Cattleyas decorate one side of the spacious *lanai*.

Left A striking *Dracaena arborea* dominates a corner of the indoor court garden that is tightly planted with Bromeliads, Anthuriums and Philodendrons.

Right top Giant pavers in leaf patterns provide a whimsical touch adjacent the house.

Right middle Potted ornamental plants such as ferns, palms and Bromeliads are used skillfully to make movable displays for the indoor plantings.

Right bottom An ornamental pond adjoining the house mirrors the sky and surrounding greenery.

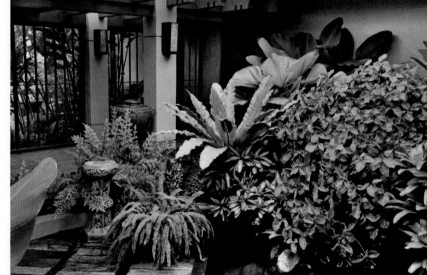

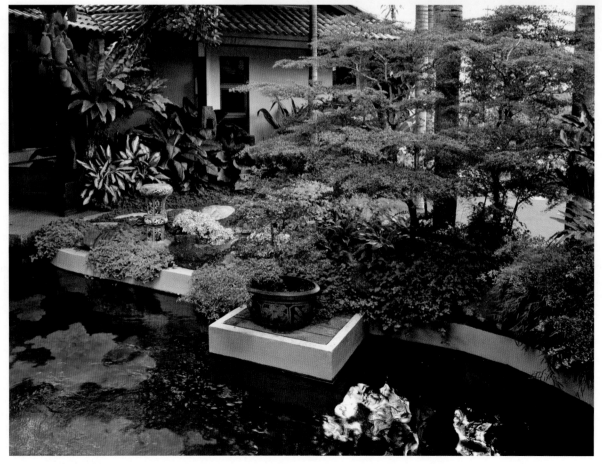

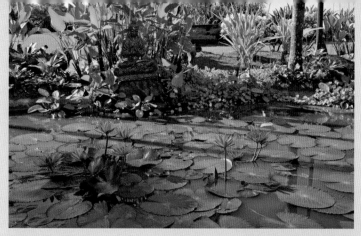

Above A statue of Buddha casts a meditative spell over a pond of tropical water lilies.

Right Wide steps softened by tightly clipped shrubs and ground covers lead to different terraced levels in this garden.

Bottom A cascade of water trickles down a series of vats that has been designed as a fountain.

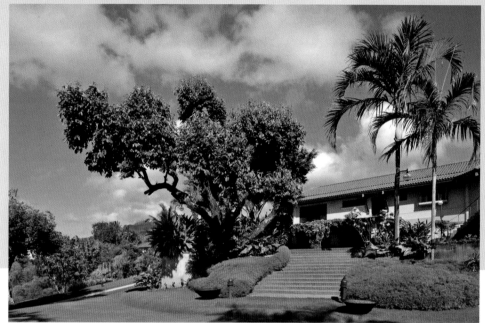

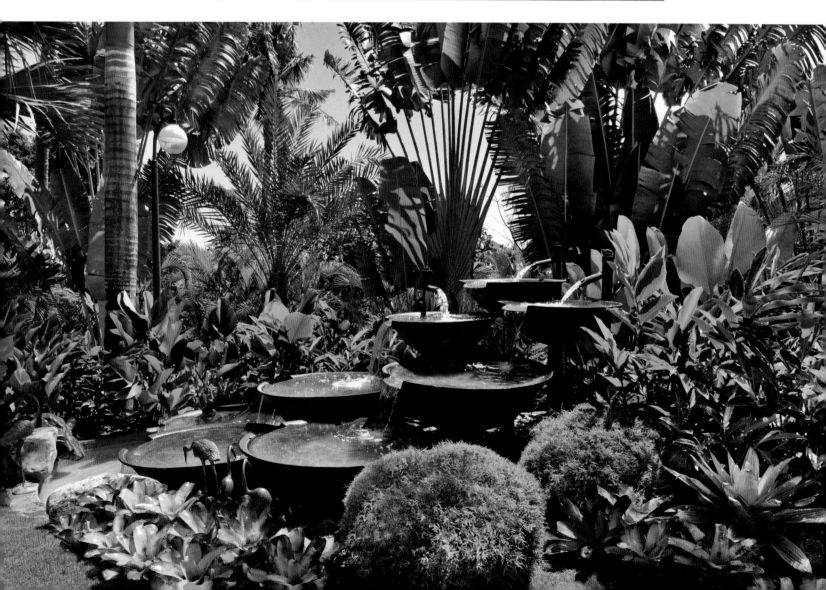

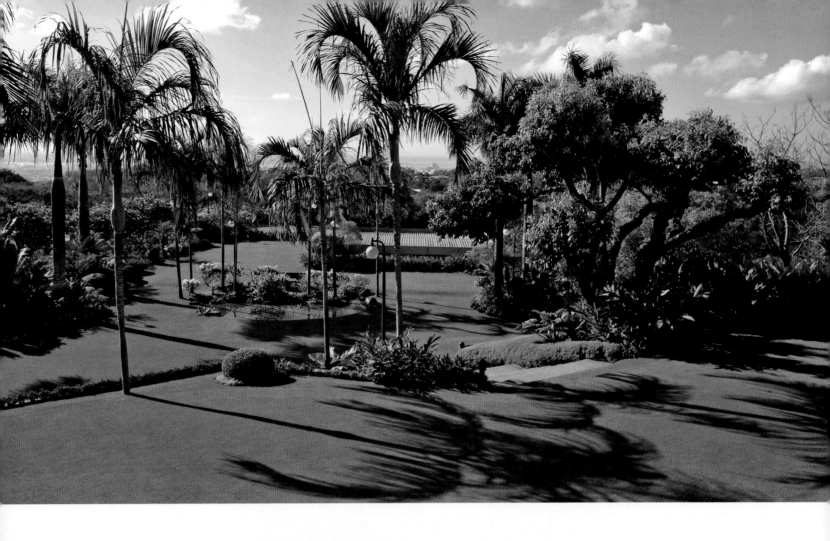

Above The silhouettes of palms enhance the many different vistas fully appreciated from the top of the property.

Right *Plumbago auriculata* weaves through the borders in great sweeps. Known as Cape or Blue Plumbago, the species is native to South Africa.

Bottom Royal palms, *Roystonea elata*, underplanted with boxed Duranta and plumbago line the driveway. Native to the Caribbean islands, and the adjacent coasts of Florida, Central and South America, they are commonly found in Asia nowadays.

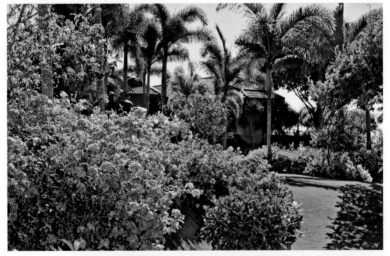

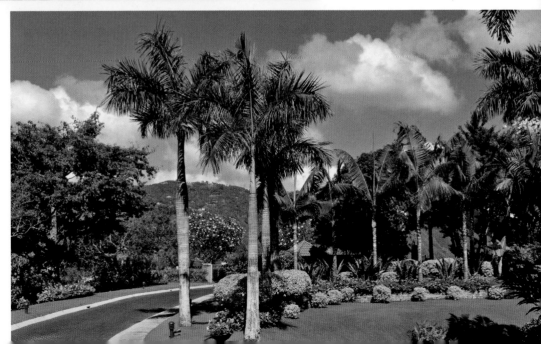

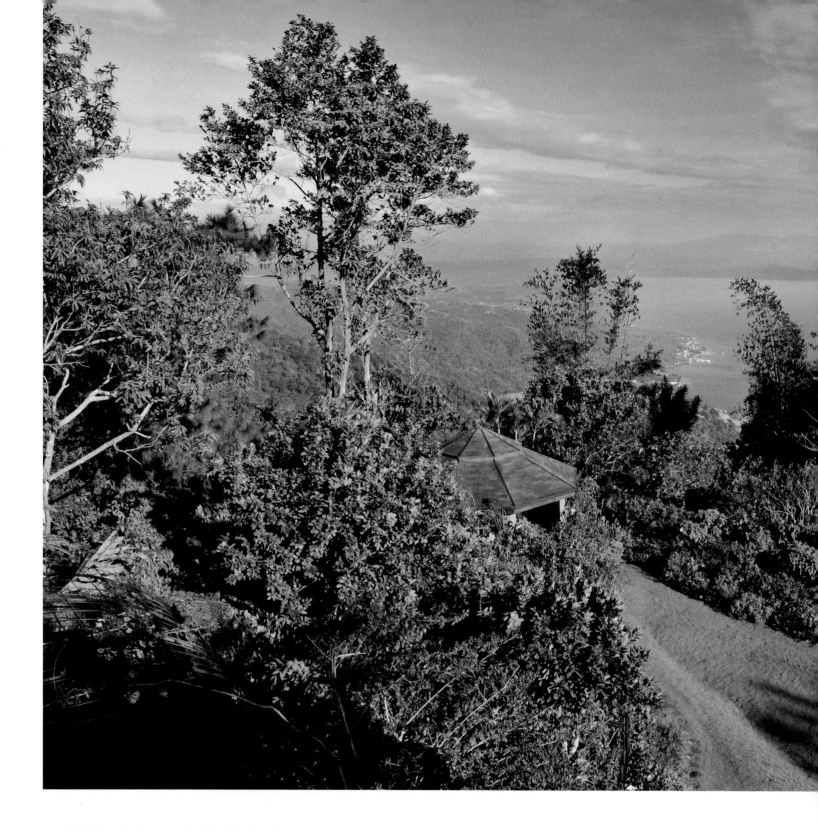

VICKY HERRERA'S GARDEN

Tagaytay City, Cavite

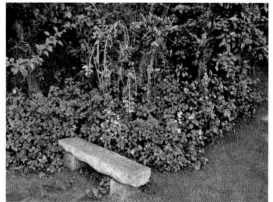

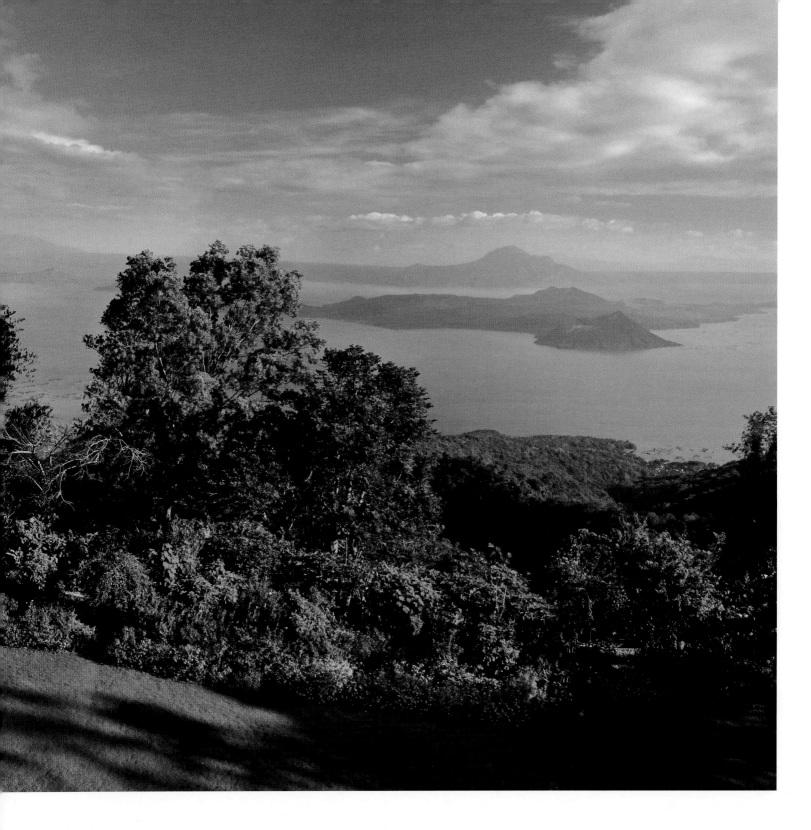

Perched on the side of a hill in scenic Tagaytay, the garden of Vicky Herrera looks out onto one of the most magical views in the Philippines, that of Taal volcano and its lake. One would think this would pose a serious challenge to anyone intent on creating a garden here: it's not just the views the owner had to contend with but also the ferocious winds that sweep off Taal Lake and Laguna de Bay. Herrera met the challenge by designing a garden of mostly colorful and sweet-scented perennials that thrive in rich volcanic soil and hardy annuals that tolerate the wind. She believes that the soft and airy growth habits of annual species make for natural plantings when combined with perennials.

Today, the garden's bold and wild color palette frames and enhances the mostly quiet and tranquil panorama. After more than 20 years, the once bare hillside is now home to many colorful and healthy plants. Evergreen shrubs and pine trees form the backbone of the design, and these are reinforced by the contour of the lawns and exuberantly planted borders. In July, orange and red Impatiens is planted in groups of ten or 20 in the borders. Fast growing, they soon compete with the equally vigorous *Lantana camara* in yellow and pink. Petunias, Cosmos and Hibiscus, along with brightly flowering Salvias, contribute to the explosion of color.

Above A panoramic view of the garden overlooking the majestic Taal volcano and lake.

Opposite A stone bench nestles against plantings of colorful Impatiens and wildly fragrant, native *sanggumay* orchids, *Dendrobium anosmum*. Somewhat surprisingly, the orchid's scientific name translates as "without scent," which is a bit of a misnomer as this plant has a strong perfume.

Everywhere, flowering plants drift and flow, fall and climb over each other in an unorchestrated ballet with the wind. A daring colorist, Herrera is fearless about combining brilliant hues and prefers reds and oranges to soft pastels. She encourages the unlikely combinations of red Salvia, orange Impatiens, dark pink Azalea and yellow daisies, which she contrasts with blue ginger and feathery Cleomes (spider flowers). The strong, dark colors are used to strengthen the borders. Since this is, in large part, a naturalistic garden, plants are allowed to reseed themselves and choose their own places in the planting scheme.

Around the back, the garden is divided into two levels. Encircled by loose waves of *Salvia splendens*, the first level slopes to a mossy embankment profuse with a dazzling display of yellow, pink and white Lantana to reveal a secret nook with stone paved benches and a pergola cloaked with the owner's prized Jade vine now in flower. This hidden enclosure provides another spot from which to admire the view. On the second level there is a wooden gazebo that provides shelter from the elements. Except for a magnificent grouping of Medinilla and a tree fern here and there, Herrera has resisted the temptation to plant the more exotic and ornamental plants that have become fashionable in many tropical gardens. She is content to grow the modest and common cultivars and concentrate instead on planting more of the scented flowers such as Gardenias, Honeysuckle, Champaca and the wildly fragrant *sanggumay* or *Dendrobium anosmum*, all of which provide her house with a welcome scent.

Vicky Herrera has made her mark on this dramatic landscape. While respecting its splendid location, she has also made it her own.

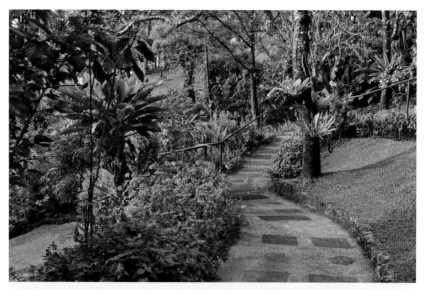

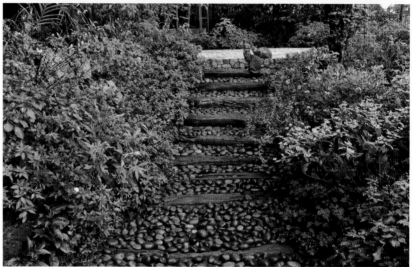

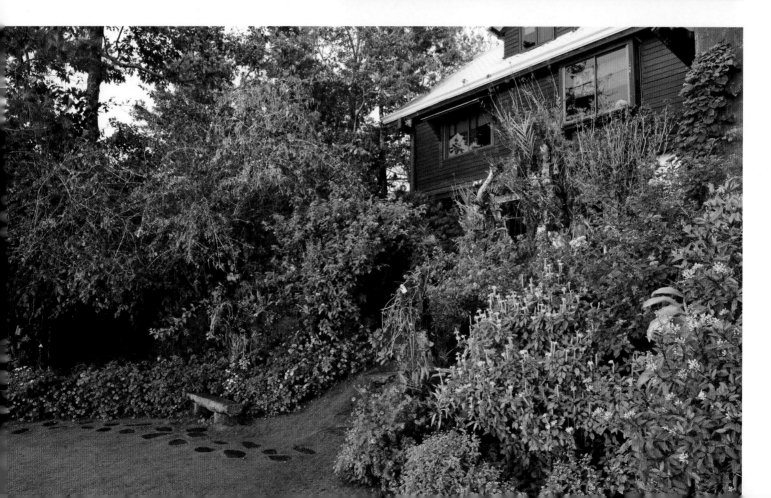

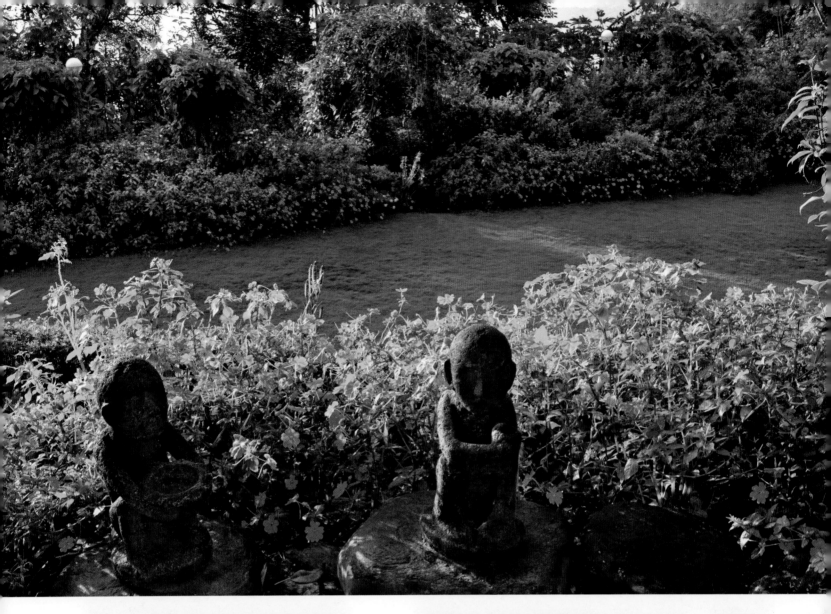

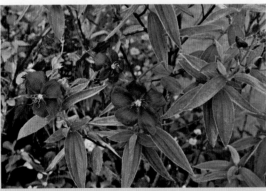

Opposite top Lush plantings of red Salvia and orange Impatiens provide color along the winding garden paths.

Opposite center Brightly colored annuals highlight steps fashioned out of river stones and railroad sleepers.

Opposite bottom A glimpse of the house through the dense floral display of modest and common cultivars mixed in with variously scented flowers.

Top Stone sculptures of *anitos* (spirit gods) provide a dramatic note in this wild and naturalistic garden.

Above The purple flowered *Tibouchina urvilleana* contrasts with red *Salvia splendens*.

Right A cool, green respite from all the color. A jade vine can be seen hanging above the bird's nest fern on the post.

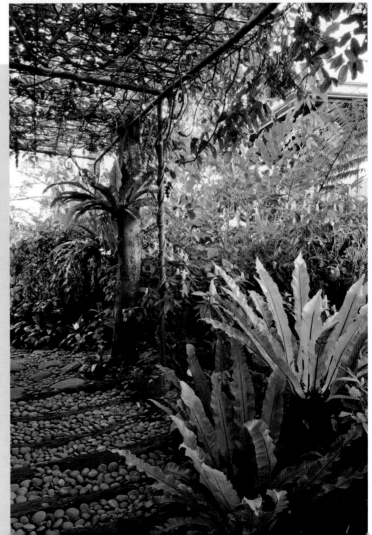

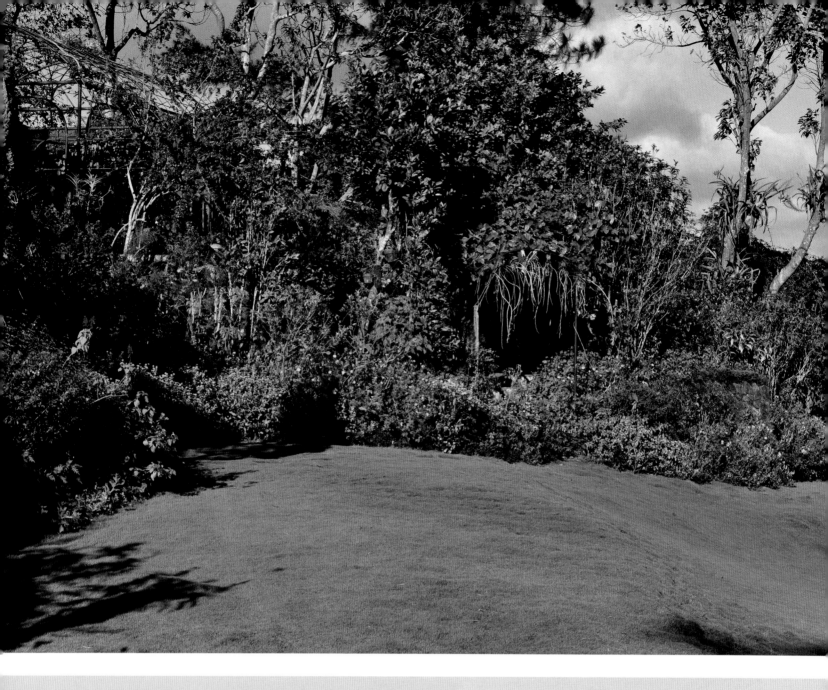

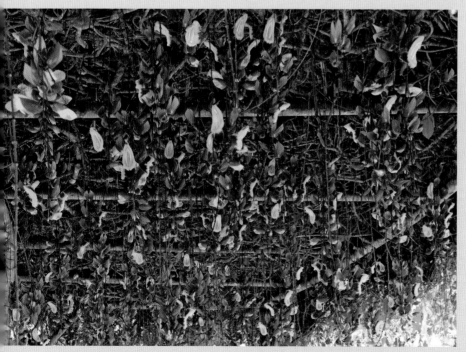

Above A sweet wooden gazebo provides shelter from the elements as well as views over the lake and volcano below.

Left *Thunbergia mysorensis* makes a dazzling display on a pergola. This woody-stemmed, evergreen flowering vine is native to India. The name, *mysorensis*, is derived from the city of Mysore in South India.

Right A wonderful example of the amazing Philippine jade vine, *Strongylodon macrobotrys*.

Far right The spiky pink *Celosia argentea*, an annual herb sometimes considered a weed looks perfectly at home in this garden.

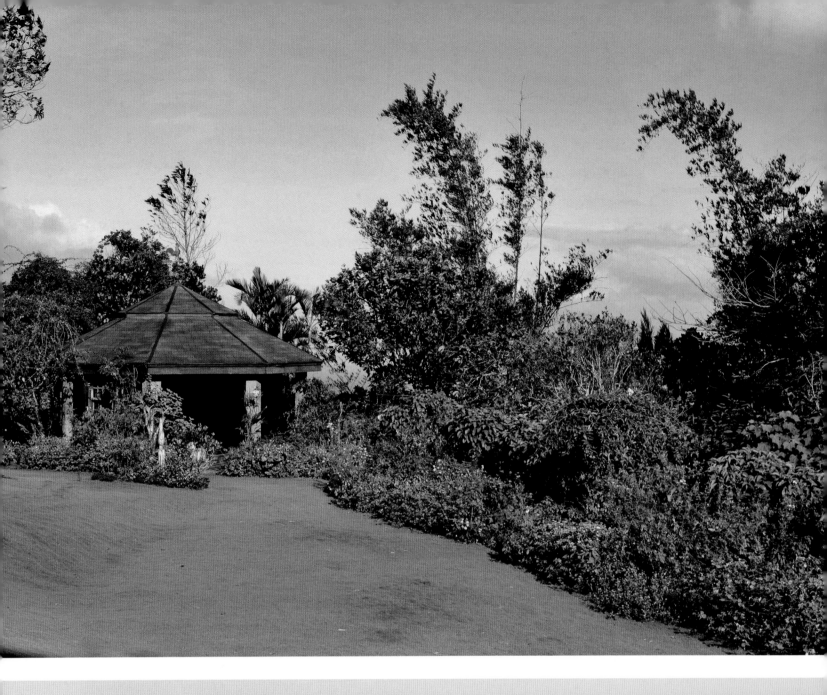

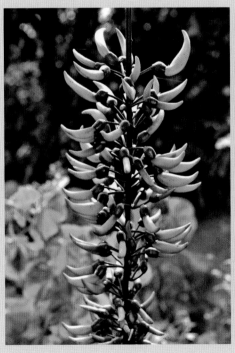

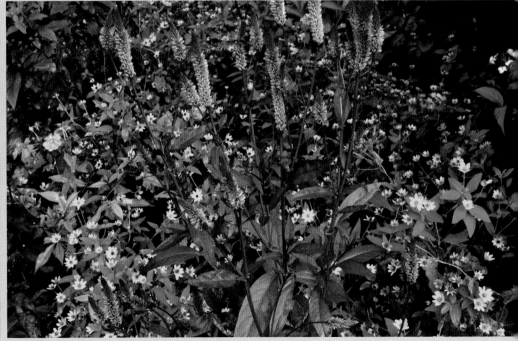

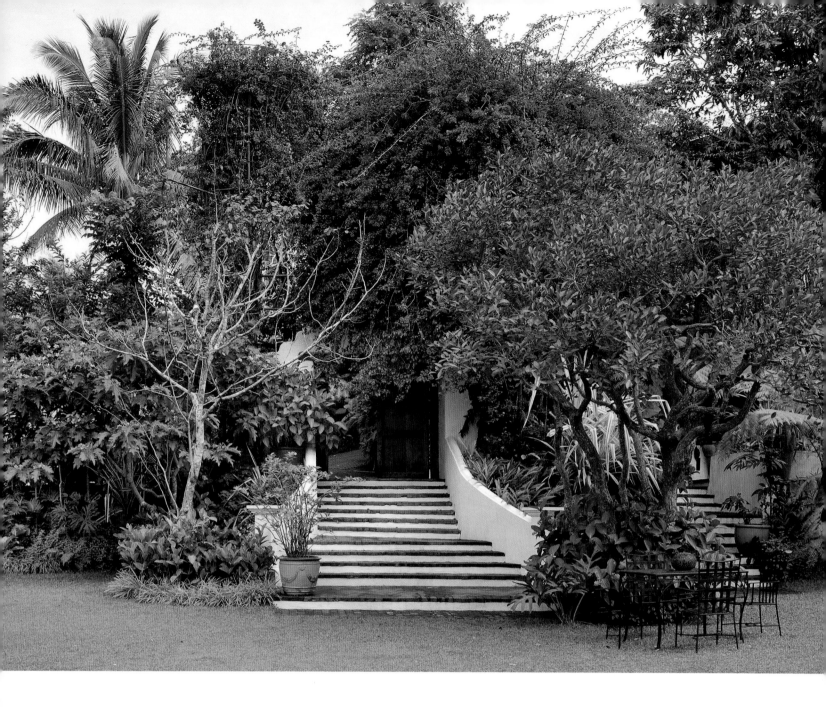

ANTONIO'S FINE DINING GARDEN

Tagaytay City, Cavite
Designed by Jun Obrero

The secret of the elegant garden at Antonio's Fine
Dining lies in the cool climate of Tagaytay. Located 2,500
feet (760 m) above sea level, with an average temperature
of 22 degrees Celsius, low humidity and abundant rain-
fall, Tagaytay is the Philippines' second summer capital. Its
cool temperate climate makes it conducive for growing
a wide range of plants.

Antonio's garden is tucked away down a hillside, a
mile or so (2 km) off the main road, accessed by a long
narrow road that ends at an imposing garden gate with
a white wood door. The highly rated country restaurant,
designed by chef owner Antonio Escalante, is reminiscent
of a grand Philippine colonial home decorated with hanging glass lamps, decorative floor tiles and antique wooden
furniture. Surrounded by a lush forest garden, the work
of landscape designer Jun Obrero, it features tall glass
windows that look out over abundant greenery. Tree ferns
preside over a wealthy assortment of plants that include
Medinillas, Heliconias, ornamental ginger and ferns.

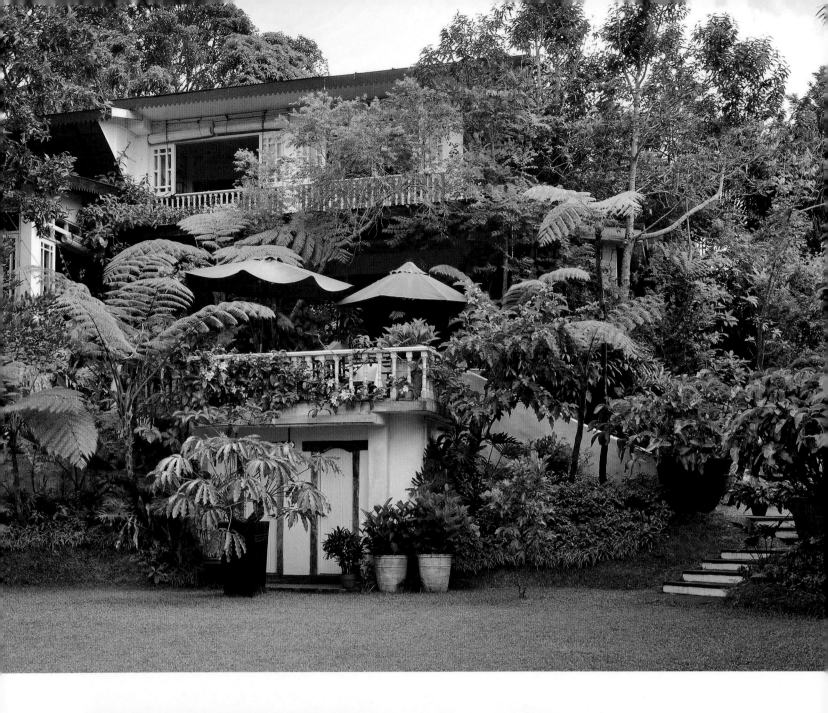

Above The restaurant, reminiscent of a grand Philippine colonial house, is surrounded by a lush garden of shade trees and a rich assortment of ornamental plants. Dazzling maroon Bougainvillea works well with the delicate light green shades of the tree ferns.

Left Tall glass windows look out at parasols of tree ferns, Cyathea.

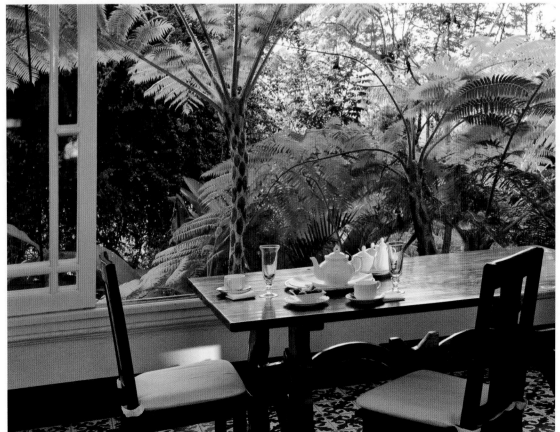

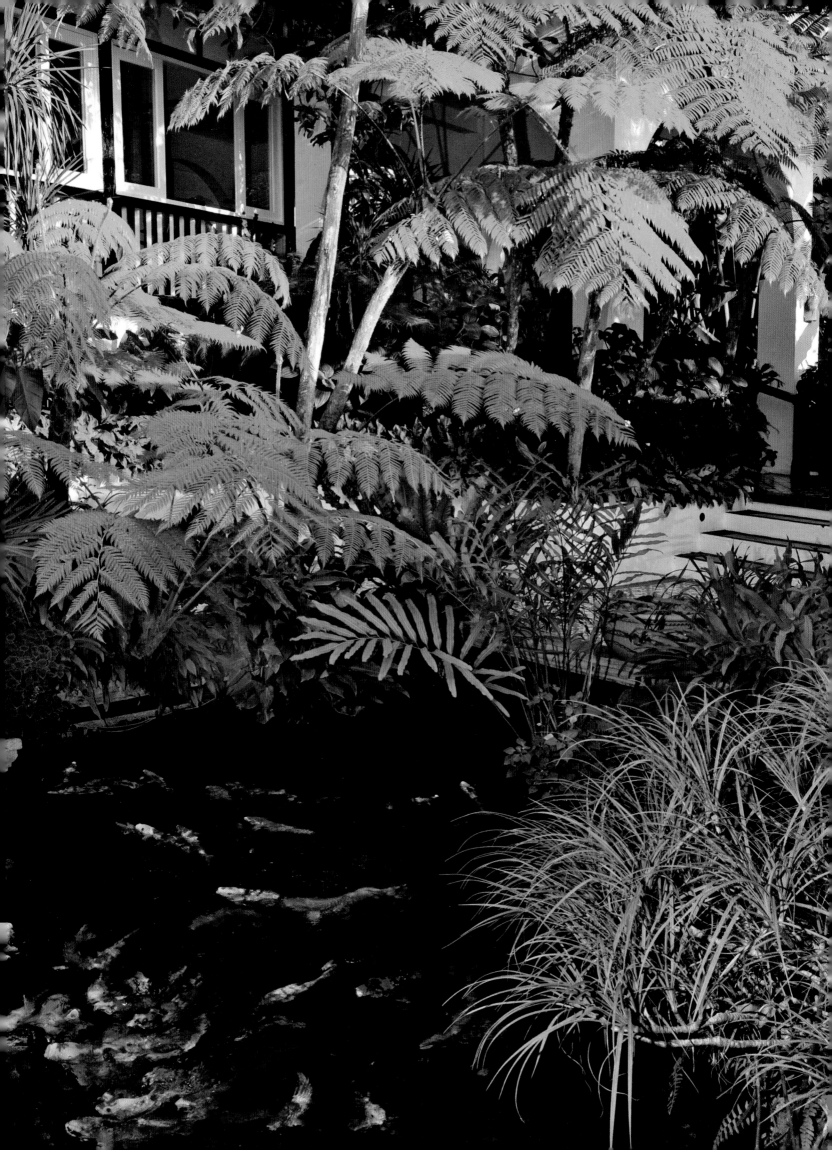

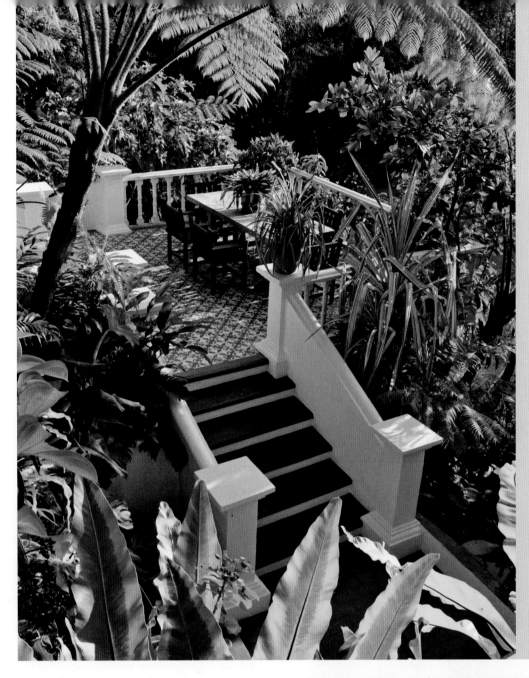

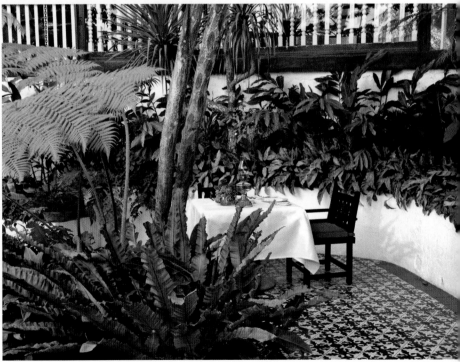

Opposite A pond teeming with colorful koi surrounds the first terrace of the restaurant.

Left Tree ferns preside over a wealthy assortment of plants that includes bird's nest ferns, *Pandanus odoratissimus* 'Veitchii' and red ginger, *Alpinia purpurata*.

Below A terrace ringed with Aglaonemas, red ginger and bird's nest ferns reminds one of the *azotea* of the 19th century, a flat open terrace suitable for growing old-fashioned potted plant varieties and cottage garden favorites.

A wide wooden staircase leads to the outdoor terrace. Here, tables are set under majestic parasols of tree ferns underplanted with bird's nest ferns and Aglaonemas. A square pond teeming with colorful koi centers the space. Down another flight of stairs is a second balustraded terrace that overlooks a garden planted with more tree ferns, Philodendrons and variegated Pandanus. Here, Escalante and his designer have taken cues from the *azoteas* of the 19th century Filipinos. The *azotea* was a raised, flat open terrace with a balustrade running along its edge. Supported by stone arches and decorated with Spanish tiles, these areas were suitable for growing old-fashioned, cottage garden favorites. Here one could focus on the beauty and specific function of individual plants. Surrounded by shade trees and perfumed with scented flowers, they often looked out onto distant views.

Escalante's contemporary take on a traditional house and garden bodes well with patrons from Manila who keep returning not just for the food, but for the romantic ambiance of the forested surroundings that they find both relaxing and invigorating.

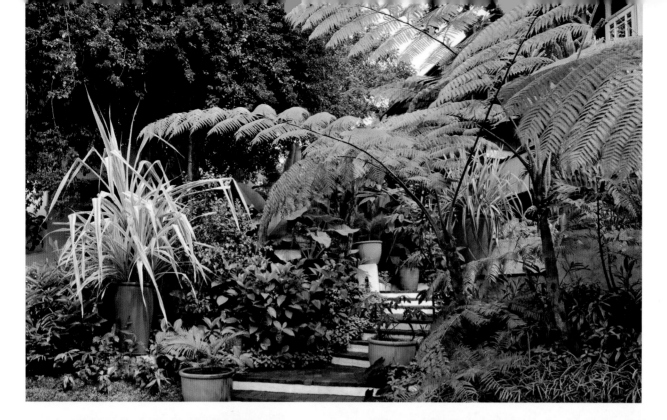

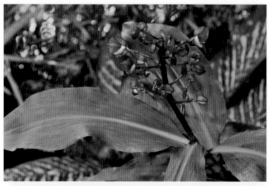

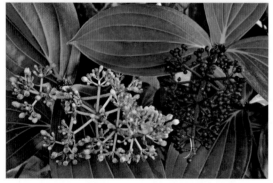

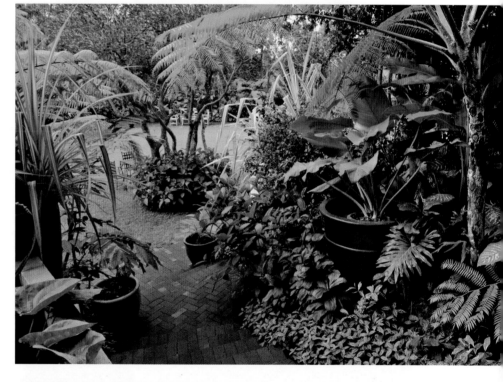

Top Umbrellas of giant tree ferns and shrubs of Medinilla provide contrasting leaf textures together with a potted variegated Pandan along a stairway.

Above and opposite bottom left There are over 100 species of Medinilla in the Philippines. They have short hanging panicles that add color to any garden.

Above middle The perrenial herb *Dichorisandra thyrsiflora* with small blue-violet flowers is sometimes called the blue ginger. It favors wet, loamy soil.

Above right A brick path weaves through a forest of tree ferns punctuated with potted ornamentals.

Right Purple-white flowers from the potato tree, *Solanum macranthum*. A bushy tree, native to Brazil, it can grow to a height of 5 meters (15 feet).

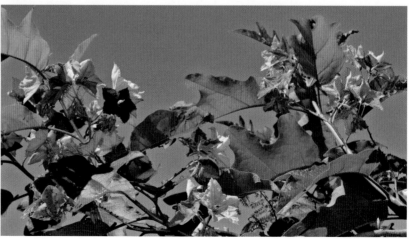

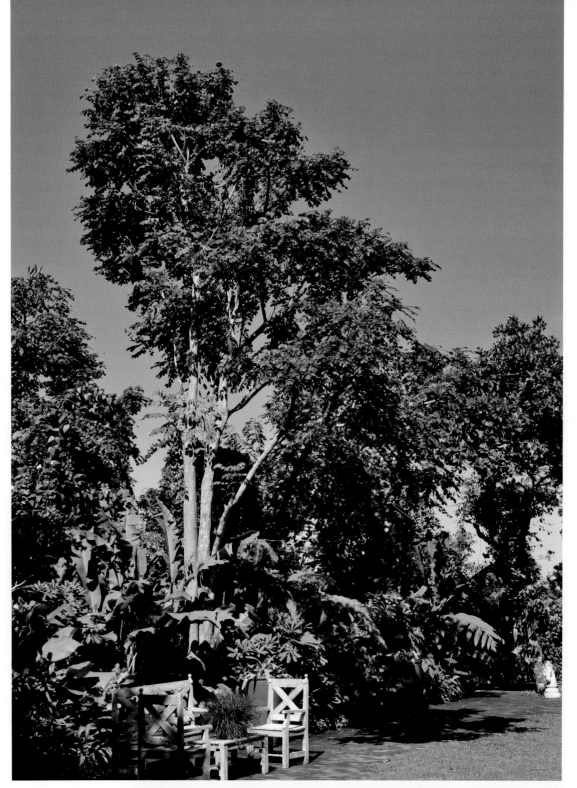

Left A towering African tulip tree, *Spathodea campanulata*, dwarfs a seating arrangement in the garden. A close up of its large orange, bell-shaped flowers can be seen on bottom right photo.

Below The fragrant blooms of *Saraca thaipingensis*, the yellow Saraca tree, which is native to Southeast Asia.

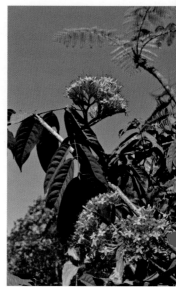

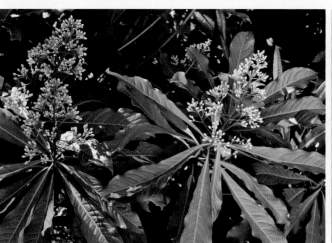

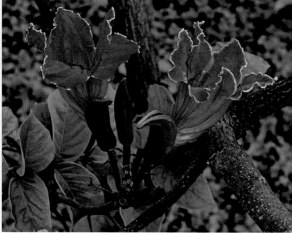

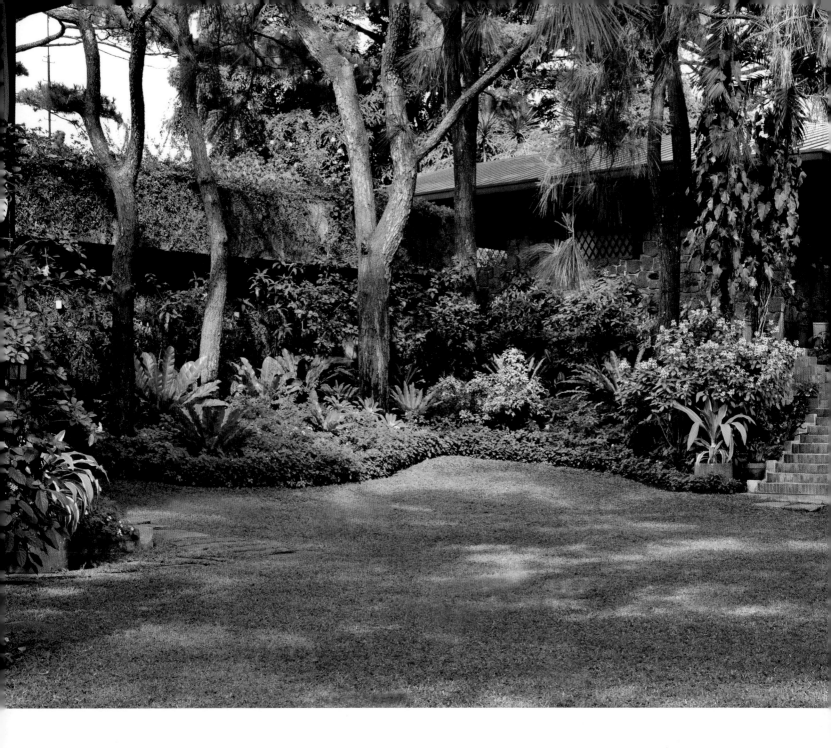

A PINE FOREST GARDEN

Tagaytay City, Cavite

Designed by Ging S de los Reyes and Popo San Pascual

A magical hillside setting in the Tagaytay countryside is home to a lovely and elegant woman who is devoted to flowers. Ging S de los Reyes manages a thriving business engaged in the cultivation and sale of ornamental flowers such as Heliconias, gingers, chrysanthemums and Gerberas. Her house and garden are part of a woodland aerie that looks out onto spectacular views of Taal lake and volcano far below.

An architectural framework of stone walls, terraces and paths defines this garden's structure and sense of place. The charming house made from dramatic roughly hewn stone overlooks a manicured lawn with beds of ornamental shrubs and simple, cottage variety plants that make a colorful display all year round. The borders near the house spill over with red Hibiscus and orange and red Impatiens. Marble-leaved *picara*, *Excoecaria cochinchinensis* does a star turn, tall shrubs of blue Plumbago tone

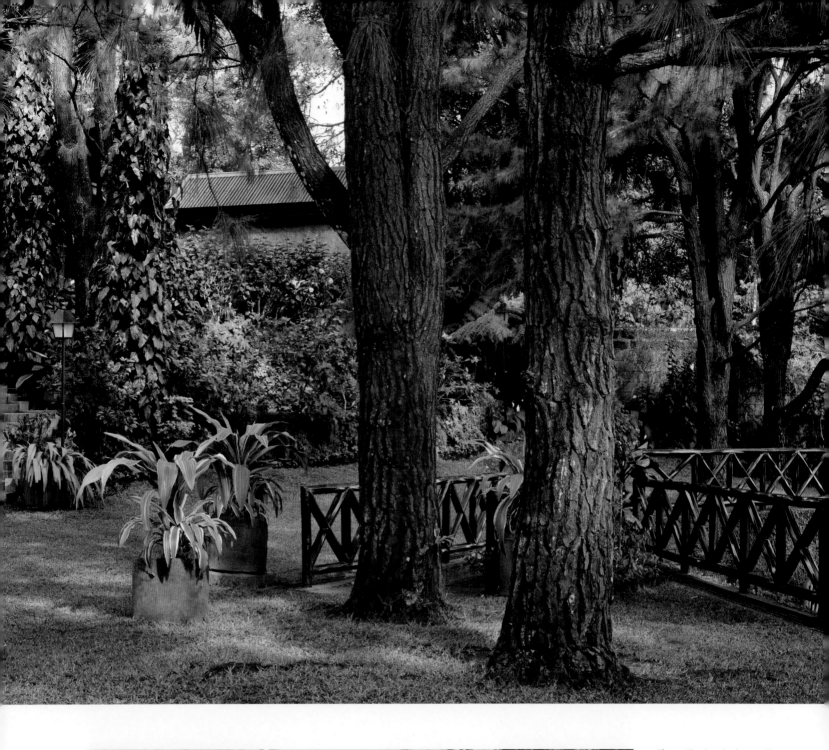

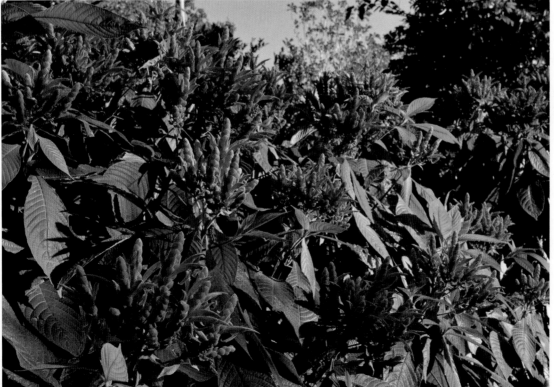

Above The charming house with dramatic stone walls overlooks a manicured lawn with beds of ornamental shrubs and simple, cottage variety plants that make a colorful display all year round.

Left Showy red-orange bracts of the bright and wooly *Aphelandra sinclairiana* make a dramatic statement. Native to central America, the plant is also known as the Panama queen and the orange shrimp plant.

down the borders while repeating rosettes of bird's nest ferns provide a unifying effect. By using plants with varying textures, the owner, along with her consultant Popo San Pascual, have created greater interest as the difference in flower size, habit, color and leaf form provides interesting contrasts in the borders. An added attraction is the collection of pine trees alongside the house that play host to dark green climbing Philodendrons.

The fresh, sweet scent of pine accompanies you everywhere, up and down the gently undulating terrain thickly planted with towering pines, Datura and tree ferns. Ivy and fern clad walls form backdrops to lively groups of colorful annuals and bright and wooly clusters of *Aphelandra sinclairiana*. It is the use of color that adds a new dimension to this garden.

A sparkling pool on a paved terrace provides a water element and ample room for entertaining and dining. The owner loves to sit out here with her friends and admire the way her exquisite pine tree garden crowns the landscape of Tagaytay with its exclusive view of Taal volcano on the lake.

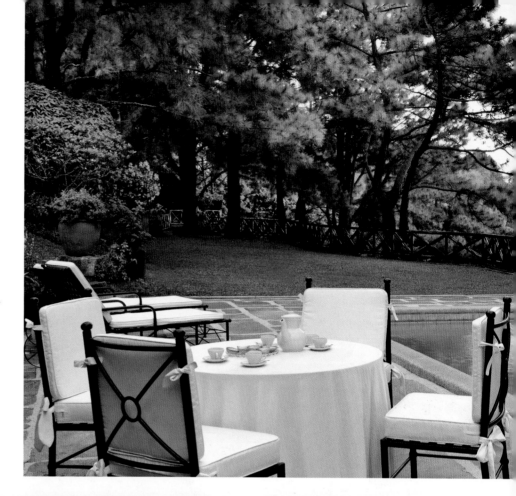

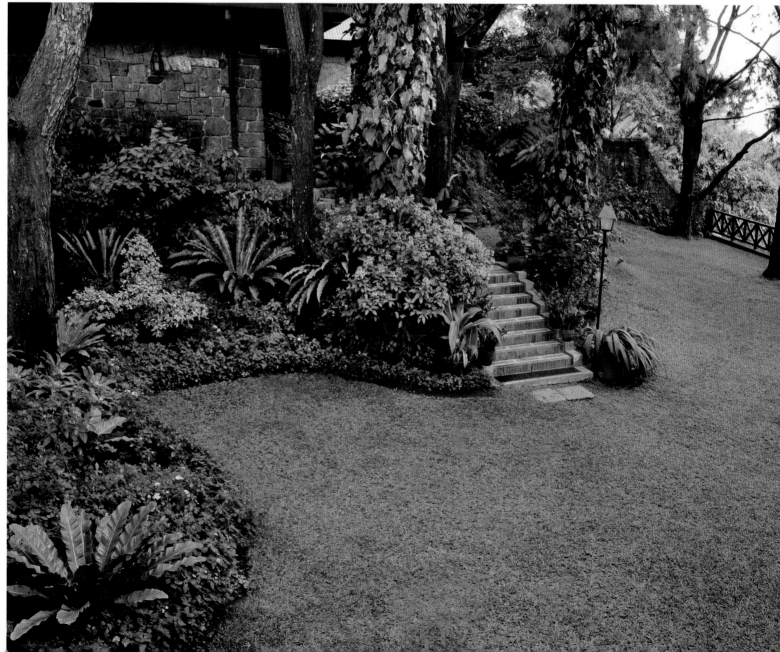

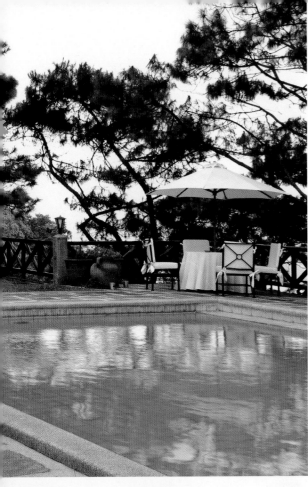

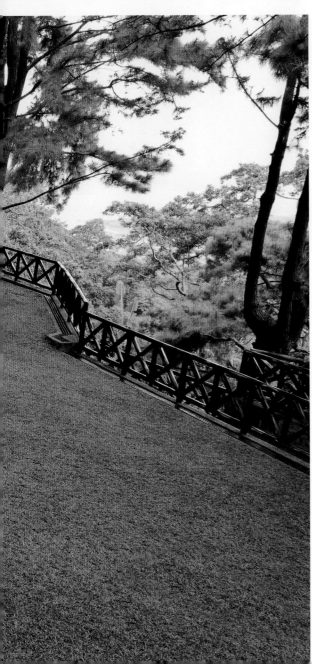

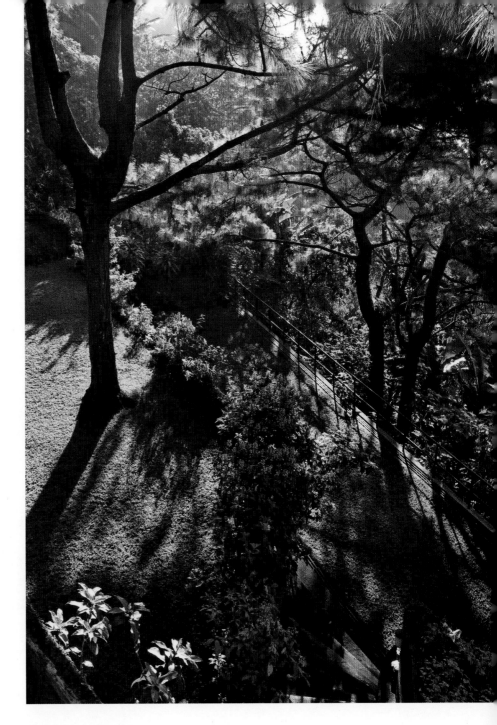

Above left A sparkling pool on a paved terrace provides a distinct water element and ample room for entertaining and dining.

Left The borders near the house are neatly planted with red Hibiscus, orange and red Impatiens, *Excoecaria cochinchinensis*, tall shrubs of blue Plumbago and repeating rosettes of bird's nest ferns. Their undulating shape match the contours of the balustrade at the end of the lawn.

Above The garden basking in a golden glow reaches out from its seclusion to embrace the wooded landscape of Tagaytay.

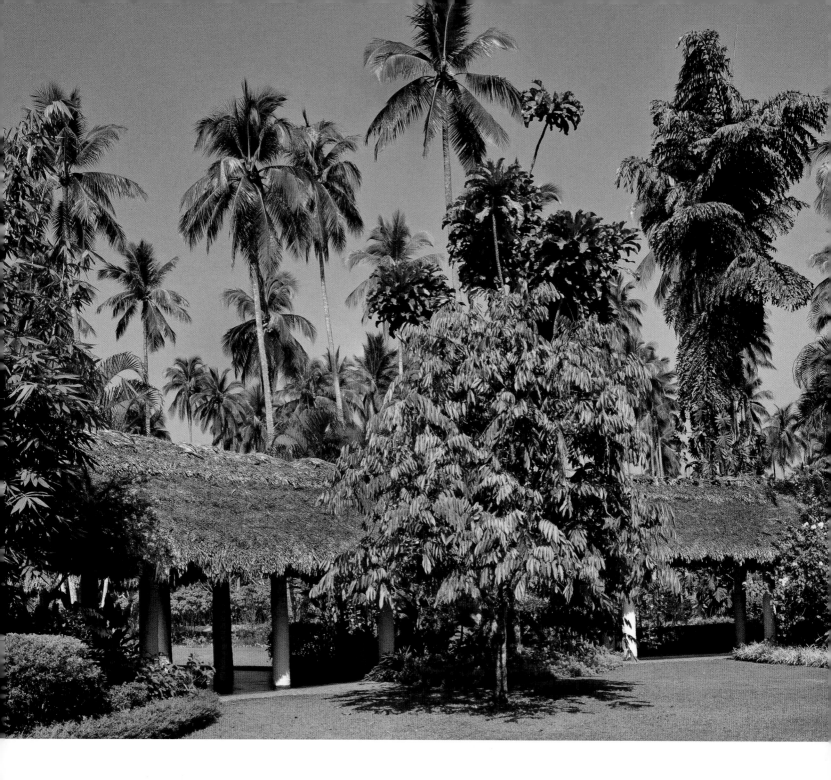

ESCUDERO GARDENS

San Pablo, Laguna

Designed by Dr. Salvador Bautista

Villa Escudero has belonged to the Escudero family
for generations. Although it has become more popularly
known as a resort in the last two decades and, more
recently, as an exclusive gated community, the Escuderos
have maintained a sizable portion of the vast estate as
the seat of their family home.

There are a number of houses for different members
of the family with the main pink stucco house (see over-
leaf), built in 1933, serving as the focal point of the complex. It boasts an extensive formal front garden, European
in design and feeling with clipped beds of Ixora and
three central fountains. Neoclassical urns on pedestals
stand in perfect symmetry under towering royal palm
trees. Behind the house, entered through a red Japanese
gate, is a pond thriving with exotic water lilies.

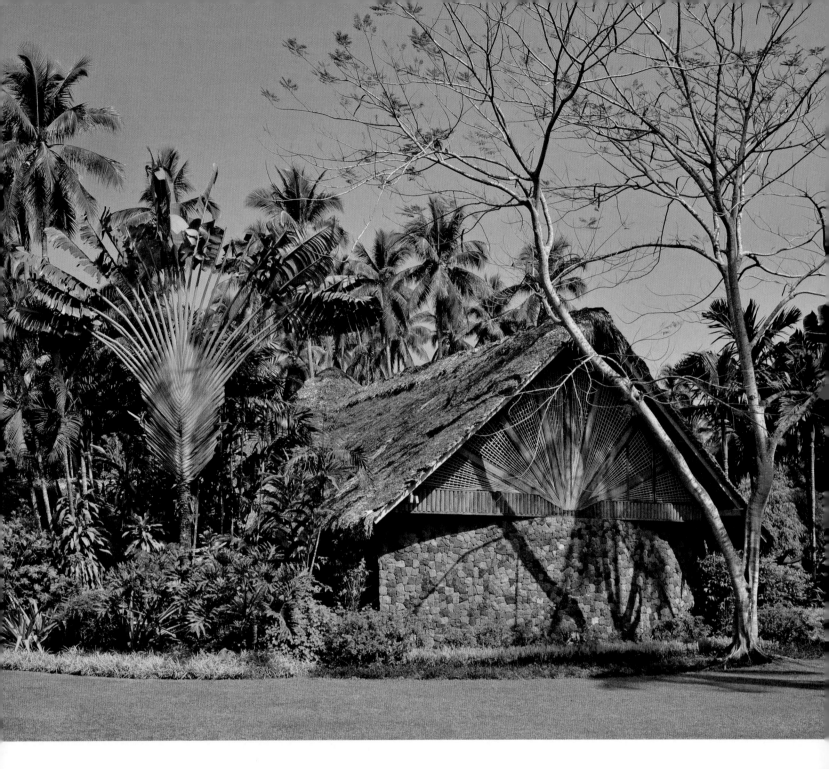

Above A thatched roofed walkway leads to the main guest pavilion lushly planted with Philodendrons, Bromeliads, Ophiopogon grass, palms and a traveler's palm.

Right A gently sloping border of ornamental plantings in front of the guest cottages. On left is a white frangipani or Plumeria with fragrant blooms.

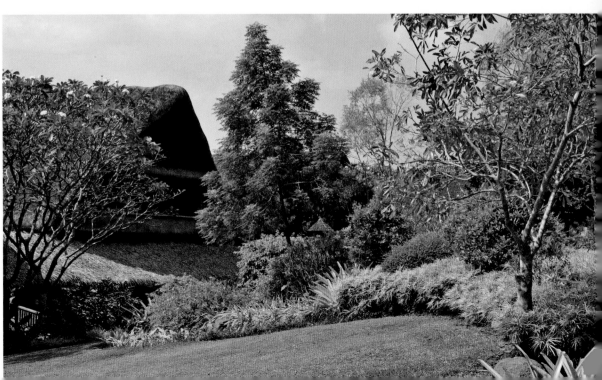

In direct contrast to the formality of the gardens of the main house are the newer, free form plantings of the guest cottages and pavilions. Tropical in mood and design, the gardens are at once natural and contrived with a thatch-roofed walkway connecting several pavilions. In one corner, along a stone walled pavilion is a long bed of Philodendrons, Bromeliads and an old-favorite, *Mussaenda 'Dona Aurora'*, under planted with golden Ophiopogon grass. In another border, a Mickey Mouse tree, *Ochna serrulata*, native to Africa, and introduced to the Philippines after World War II, is a specimen of interest in the way its yellow-green flowers become enlarged, reflexed and bright red in fruit. Also with bright yellow flowers is the *Dillenia suffruticosa,* indigenous to the Philippines.

For outstanding foliage there are Medinillas with showy, pink hanging panicles, variegated bamboo and pink ornamental gingers. And for contrast, groupings of Song of India have been staged beside Rhapis palms. The beds also support a variety of native trees, *ti* plants, Schefflera and variegated Pandan along with a vast selection of flowering plants such as Bougainvillea, Plumbago, Begonias and *Pachystachys lutea,* just to name a few. Although many of the plantings are new, cultivation standards are impressive throughout the garden.

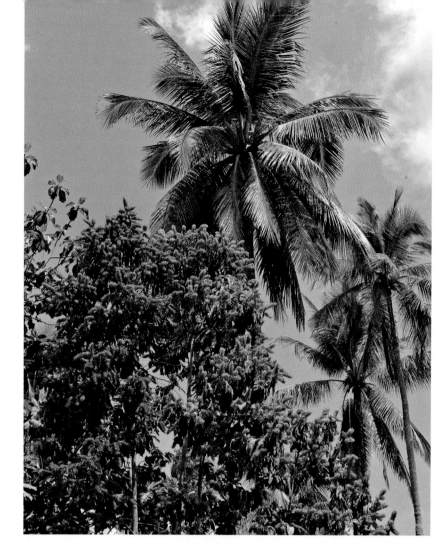

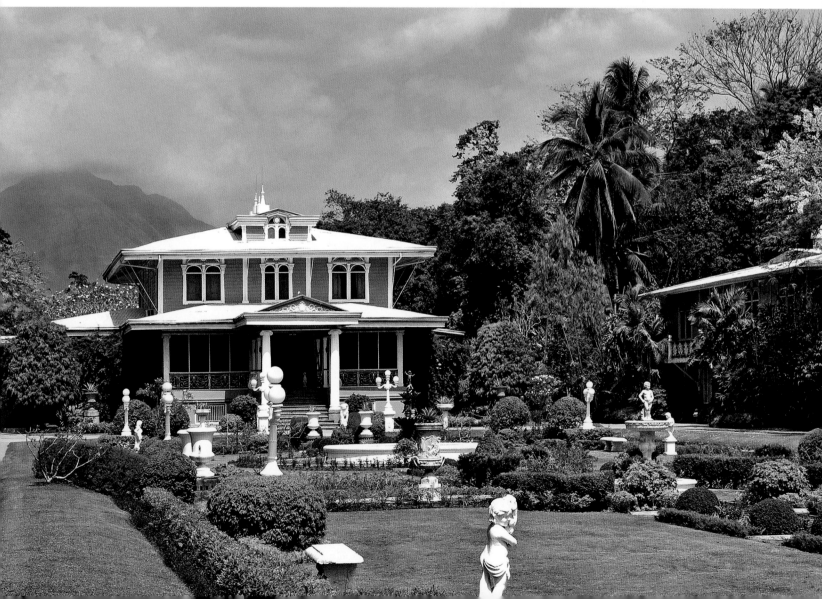

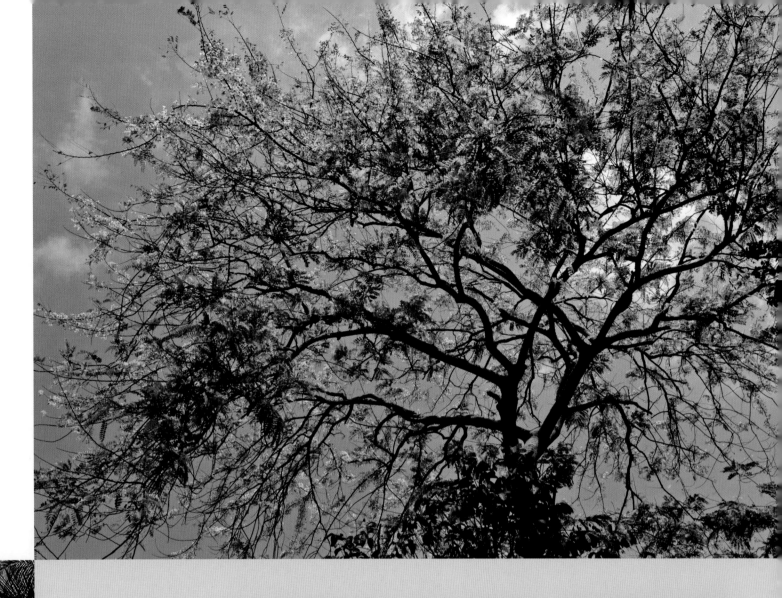

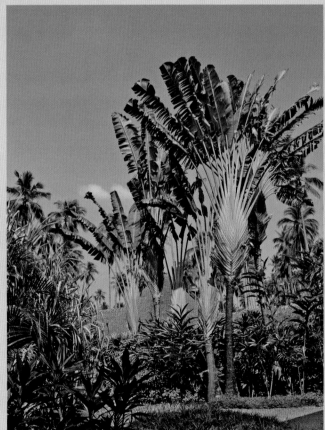

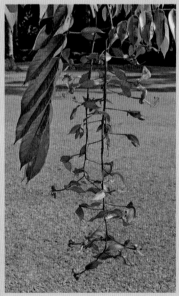

Opposite top *Palo santo* or *Triplaris cumingiana* is a valuable shade as well as ornamental tree.

Oposite bottom The pink stucco house fronts a formal garden with clipped beds of Ixora and three central fountains.

Above A pink and white shower tree, *Cassia nodosa*.

Right Towering specimens of traveler's palm, *Ravenala madagascariensis*, dwarf the colorful maroon colored stands of *Cordyline fruticosa* below.

Far right The delicate orange flower of *Amherstia nobilis* hangs above the lawn. This striking tree is native to Burma (Myanmar), hence its common name is Pride of Burma.

PONCE VERIDIANO'S GARDEN

Nagcarlan, Laguna
Designed by Ponce Veridiano

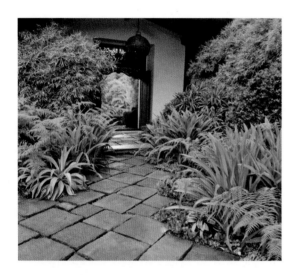

It could be said that creating a big impact is one of
the hallmarks of the tropical look. In Ponce Veridiano's
garden in Nagcarlan, Laguna this is achieved with the
careful selection of tropical plants, the use of bold foliage
and forms, and striking infusions of color. A master of the
"instant effect," Veridiano relies on a framework of densely
planted borders to give architectural coherence and flow
to his design. Flowering specimens such as Impatiens and
Spathiphyllum are concentrated in blocks against finely
textured bamboos and ferns to provide a strong contrast.
Alocasias, Philodendrons and palms with large, architectural
leaves are used as bold statements, while thick stands of a
wide variety of bamboo along with prickly and thick-leaved
Bromeliads create focal points. These are complemented by a
carefully selected assortment of Philippine artifacts.

In the warm, humid climate of Laguna this tropical
garden has grown amazingly well, metamorphosing into
a lush oasis in the span of 14 years, thanks to the hard
work and daring imagination of its landscaper/owner.
Veridiano delights in testing the limits of contrast by combining unlikely flowers and foliages to heighten the sense of

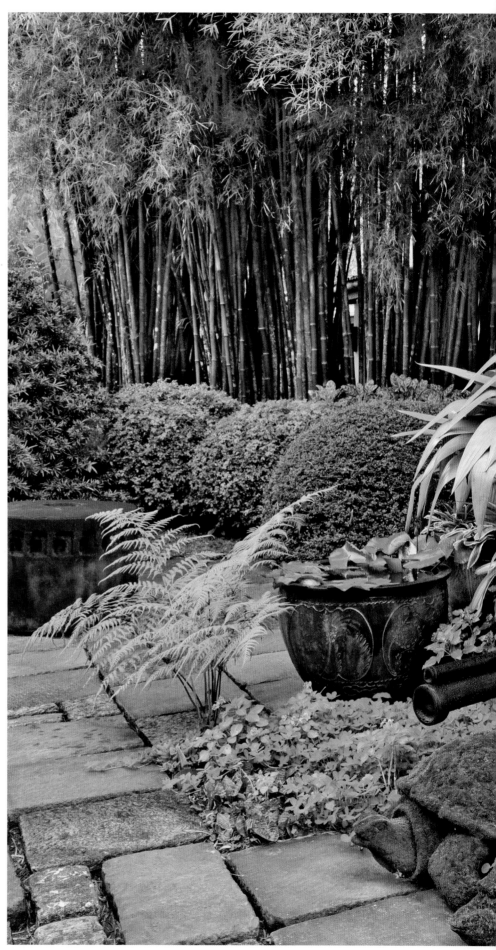

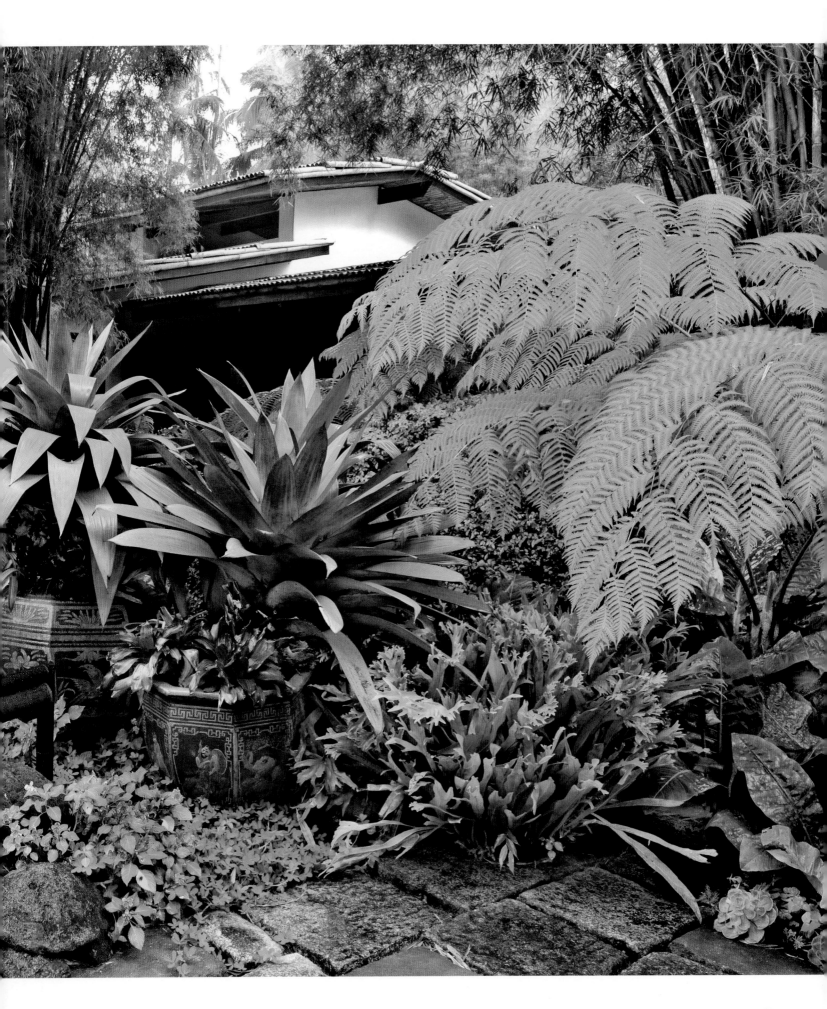

drama. He employs a system of "monosweeps" and box combinations to great effect by using blocks of same type plants as well as same color plants. For him, every project demands an interplay between structure and plant selection. Dense planting schemes that may require a lot of upkeep somehow maintain a naturalistic feel, and, wherever possible, the designer incorporates views of the surrounding landscapes to blend naturally into his rich horticultural tapestry.

A sparkling, circular pool on one side of the guest pavilion is edged with Philodendrons, Rhapis palms, majestic tree ferns, and Schefflera. A concealed path runs around the back of the pool to reveal more surprises— a jar filled with lotus or a dramatic piece of sculpture. Groundcovers such as Selaginella and yellow peanut, *Arachis pintol*, soften the transitions between thresholds and create pattern and rhythm on the garden's floor.

Even in the farther reaches of the garden, Veridiano, ever the consummate plantsman, continues to blend structure into nature with the use of lush, jungle-like plantings, set off by lawns or paved courtyards. In all his projects, there is a happy partnership between the cultivated and the wild, man and nature, architecture and the surrounding countryside; his own home, with its very contemporary style, is no different.

Previous pages main photo
Ponce Veridiano has made the Big Impact his hallmark in tropical contemporary garden design. Here, the tough leathery leaves of *Alcantarea imperialis rubra* planted in jars make a bold statement.

Previous pages small photo
Slightly irregular pavers form a walkway edged by lush plantings.

Right A colonnaded front entry accesses this open-air living room with garden views. The white columns and giant black jars stand directly upon the pond surrounding the entire house, embraced in turn by the garden-scape.

Below A sparkling, circular pool by the guest pavilion is rimmed with Philodendrons, Heliconias, tree ferns and lacy bamboo.

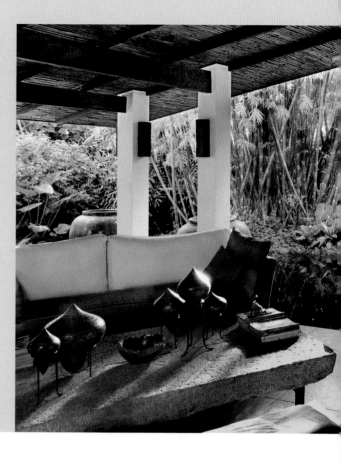

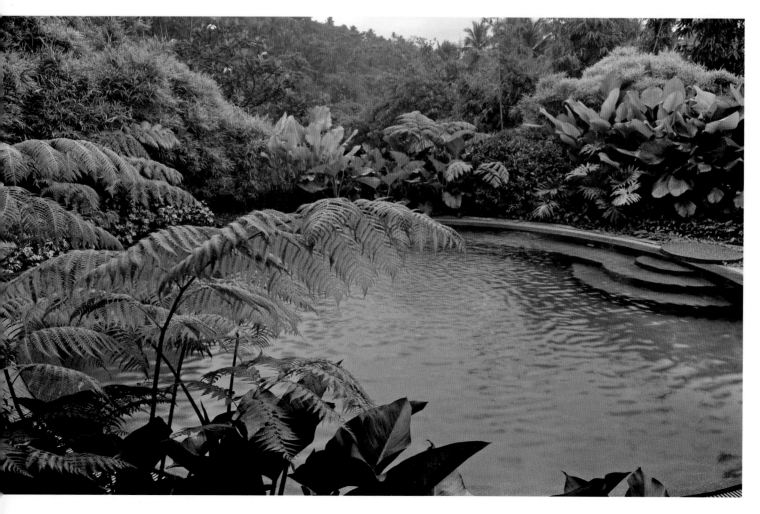

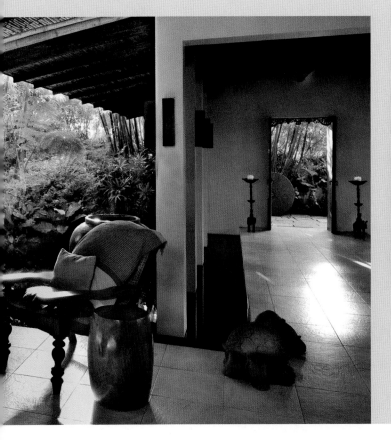

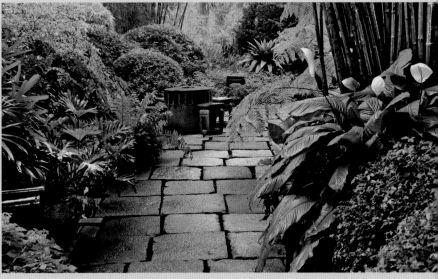

Above A scenic walled garden, comprising roughly hewn stones, giant ferns and pocket-sized water features, is wrapped around every bedroom's picture window.

Below Plantings of bamboo and tree ferns are used in waves to create sweeping gestures. They blend in with the landscape behind.

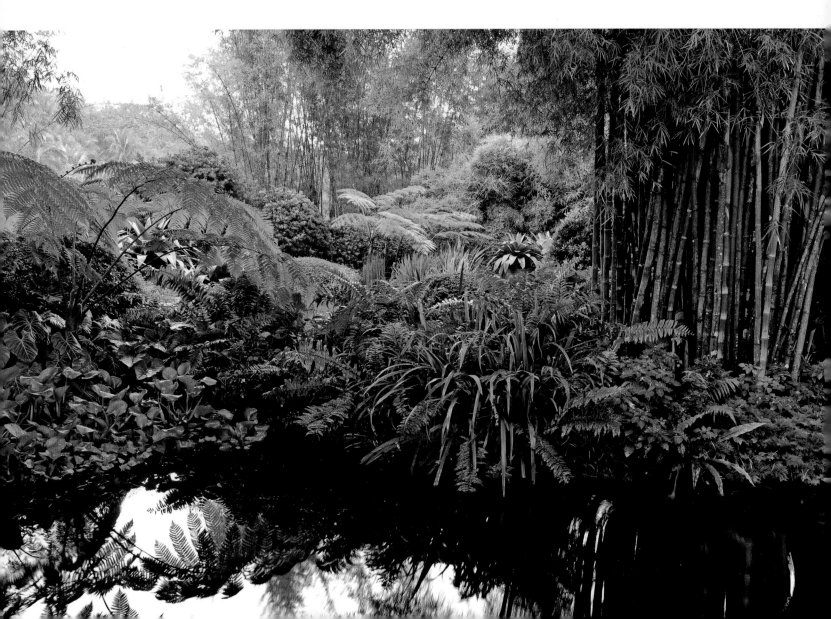

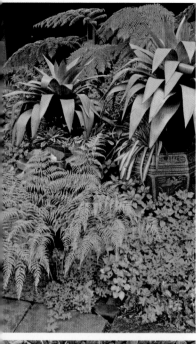

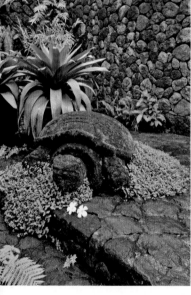

Top, above and right The
combinations of unlikely flowers
and foliages, architectural forms,
and textures heighten the sense of
drama in this garden.

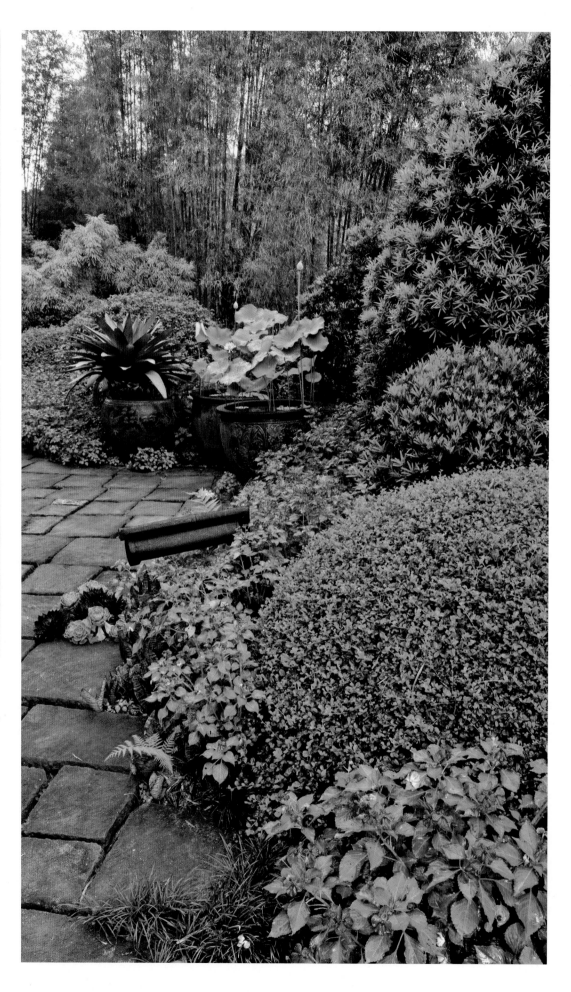

Right Hand-hewn stone walls mellowed with greenery divide and screen the property. Built by Ingorot workers from the Cordillera, they have become moss encrusted over time.

Below A pocket garden viewed from the guest bedroom. Grey pebbles, larger boulders and the stone wall mix with tree ferns and other foliage in artful-natural style.

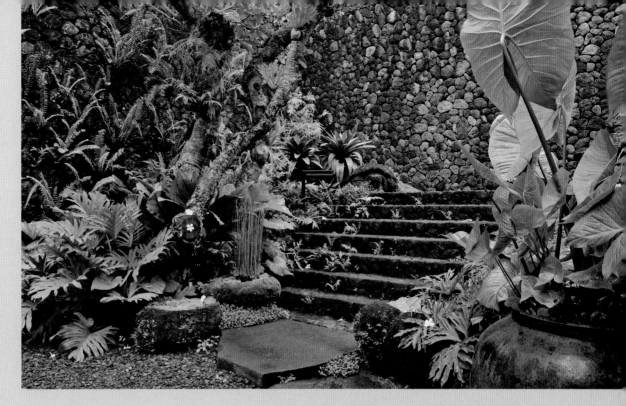

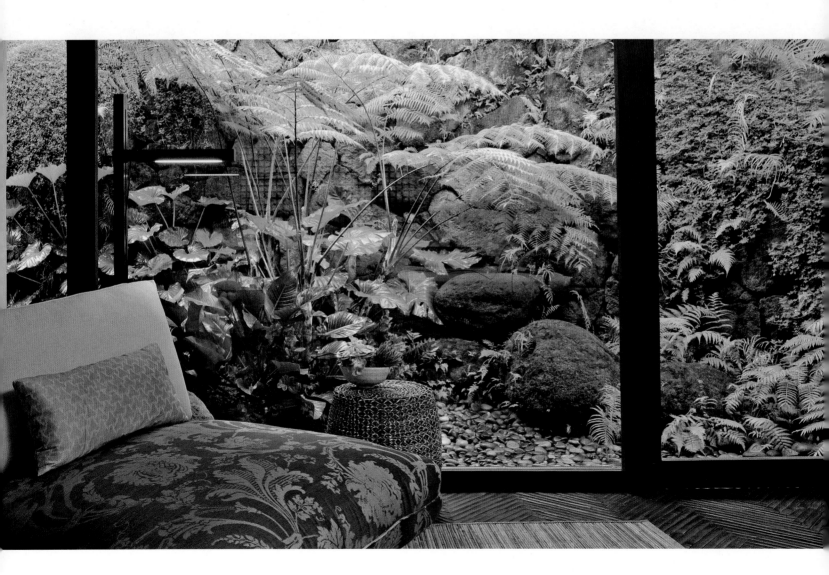

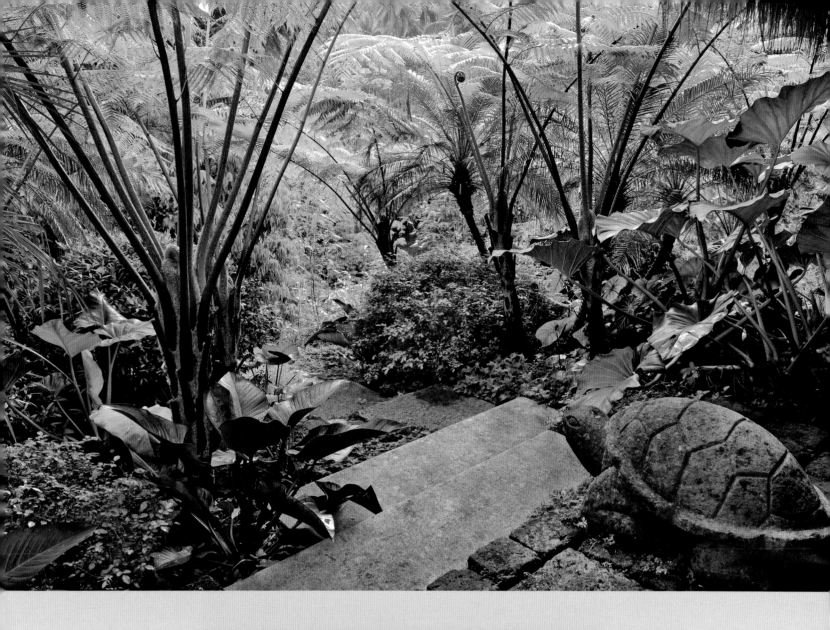

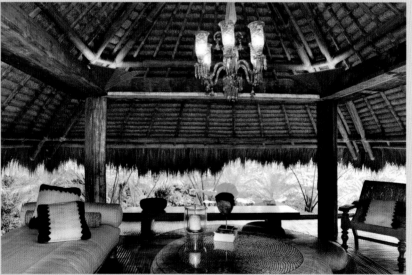

Top A stone turtle contemplates a pathway flanked by tree ferns, Philodendron and Alocasias.

Left The owner's rustic teahouse with long overhanging eaves is situated within a giant fern garden. The stylish pavilion features the finest *cogon*-thatch sheltering over tropical eclectic furnishings.

Bottom Surprises lurk in the greenery in the form of a stone turtle lost among plantings of Fukien tea, Bromeliads and tree ferns.

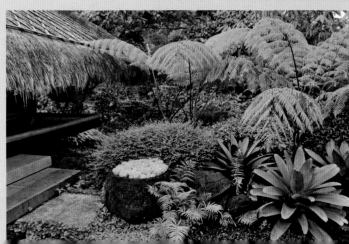

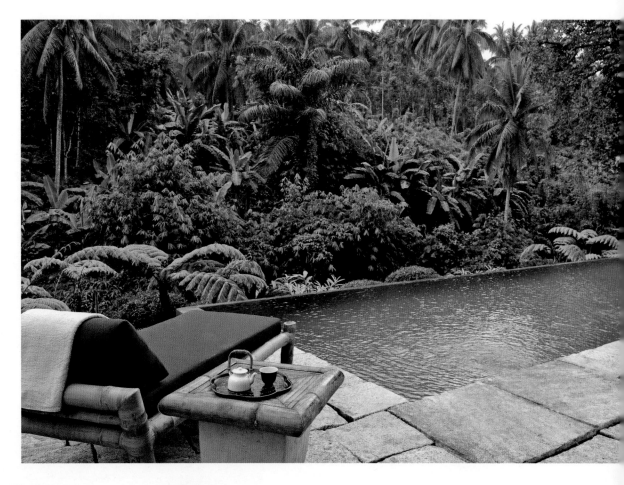

Right An infinity edge pool looks out onto a dreamy landscape skillfully incorporated into the natural landscape behind.

Below Blocks of same type plants like the ferns and the Bromeliads shown here are used repeatedly in waves to create sweeping gestures.

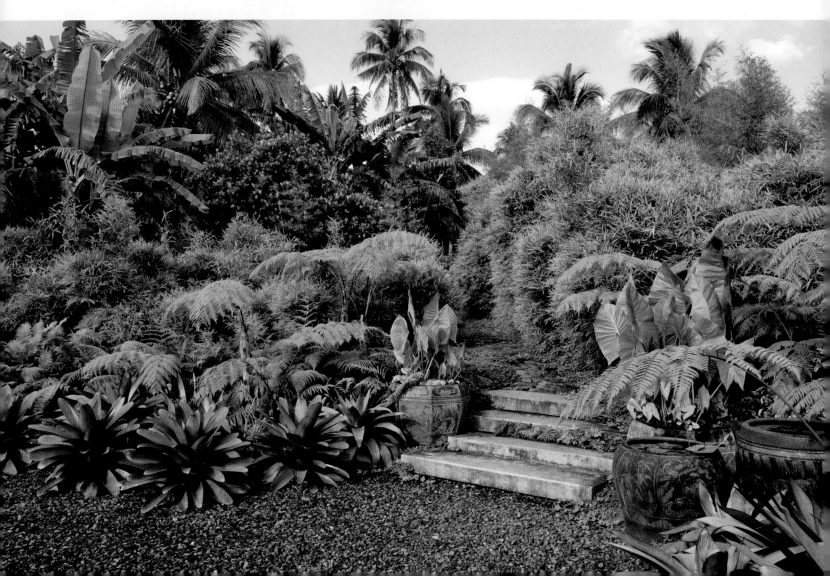

OF EARTH AND STONE

Forbes Park, Makati

Designed by Yuyung LaO' and Rod Cornejo

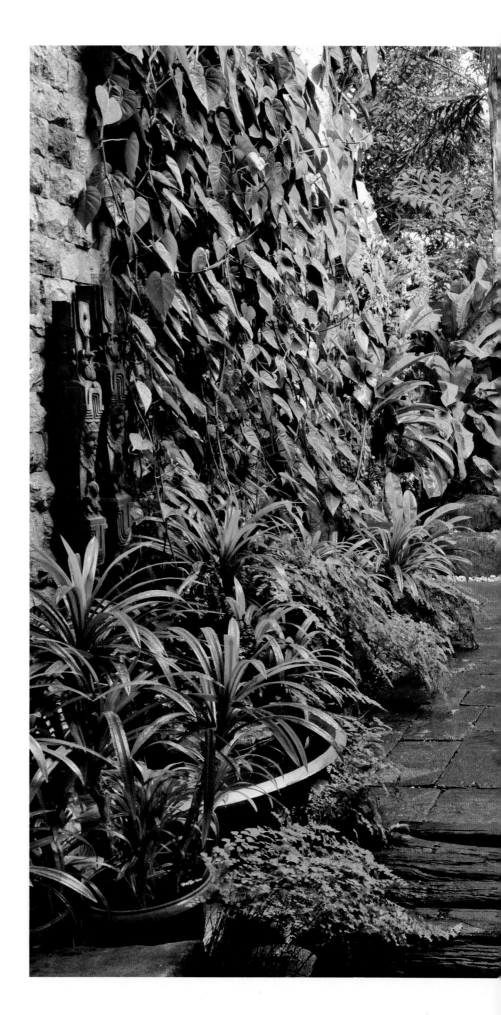

Yuyung LaO' has designed many gardens in the Philippines condensing in each site the unique tropical planting traditions of the Philippines. To this end, he combines artistry with exceptional plantsmanship honed over many years of working on both private and public landscapes. Today, the name Yuyung LaO' still conjures up images of exuberance and luxurious planting—be it at this garden in Forbes Park, the Santos garden in Dasmarinas Village, or at any other garden for that matter.

This densely planted garden at the home of Belen King, punctuated here and there with rocks and boulders, invites close inspection of LaO''s plantings. Lacy Selaginella segues into thicker, textured ferns and the texture is repeated further along a border with low plantings of feathery Miagos. Another border planted with two-toned Bromeliads and miniature Sansevieria highlights the contrast between the two different specimens.

A highly imaginative composition at the front of the property facing the street is another example of LaO''s mastery of plant material. Here, cool serene patches of green and silver ground covers weave and hug a stone wall and decorative boulders; they make you pause, before inviting you in. Another area along one side of the house features a tapestry of many different shades of green, while elsewhere borders and beds combine plants of varying dimensions and shapes with a daring, bold eye.

One of the highlights is the swimming pool area. Here, a lively combination of ferns and Euphorbias interact with natural boulders at the rim of the pool. LaO' relies on a framework of thickly planted spaces focused around a specific focal point. As such, his work reaffirms his position as one of the country's foremost landscape designers working in the modern tropical idiom.

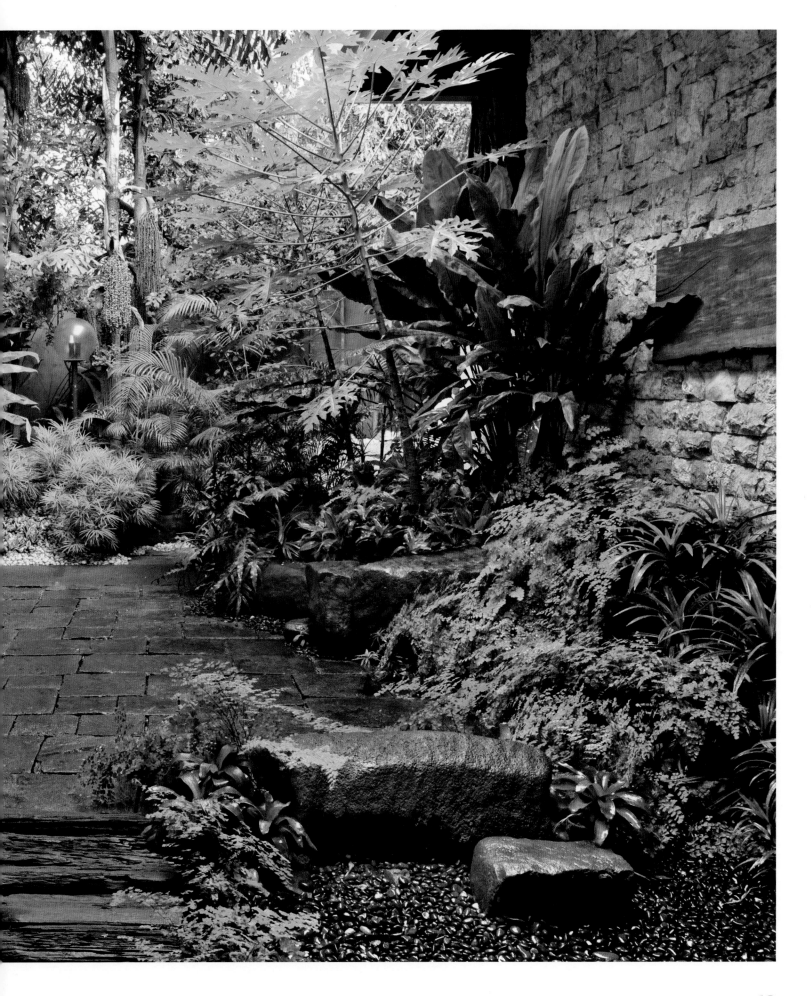

Previous pages This side garden is a detailed tapestry of texture, foliage and color.

Right A bed of Neoregelia and miniature Sansevieria highlights the contrast between the two specimens.

Opposite top A variety of green and silver ground covers weaves and hugs the stone wall and boulders in the sidewalk garden.

Opposite bottom A closeup of Euphorbia planting by the pool.

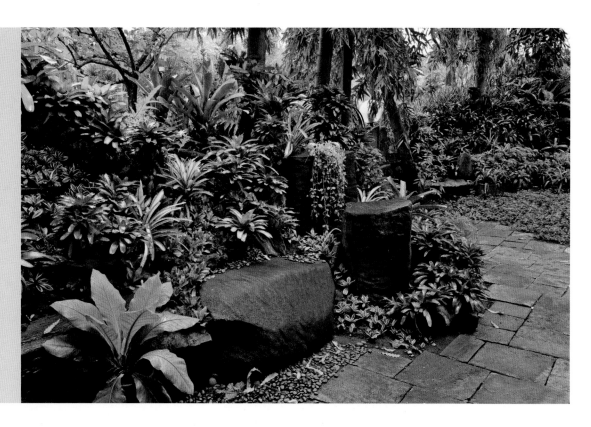

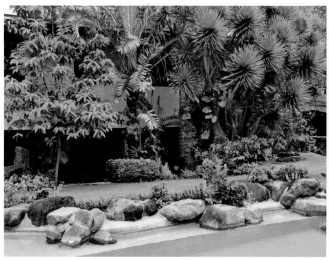

Above Groupings of river stones placed around the rim of the pool draw the focus around a specific focal point—the large naturalistic swimming pool. Euphorbias play co-starring roles with boulders at the pool's rim.

Right A sculptural Dracaena frames the pool's stunning waterfall, created by the late Rodney Cornejo, one of the Philippines' earliest landscape designers.

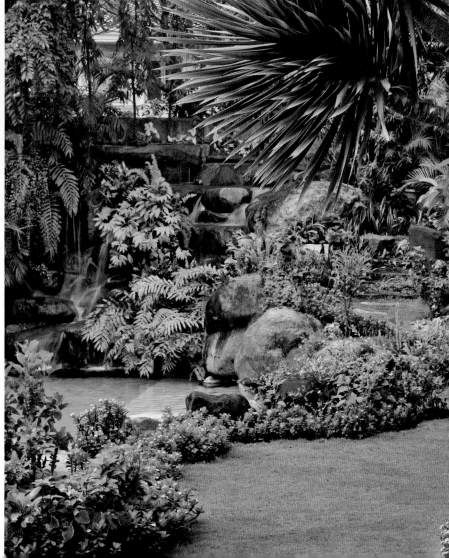

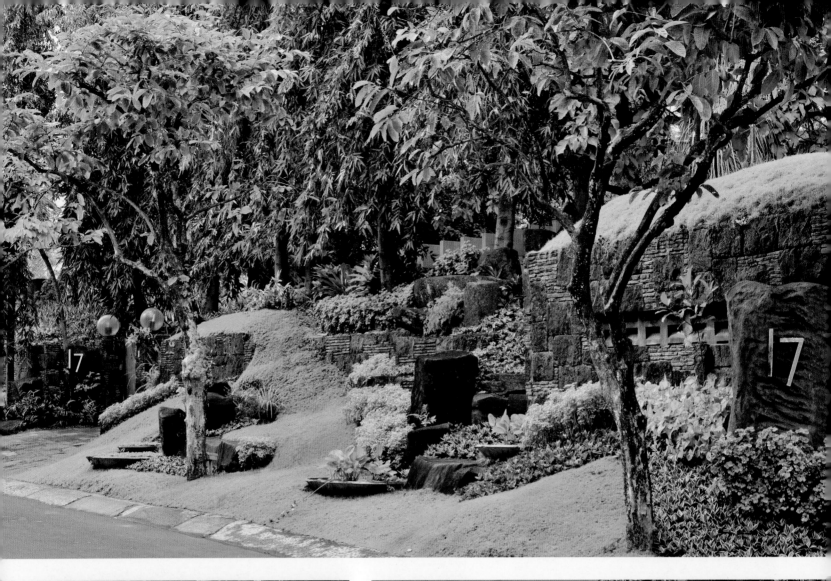

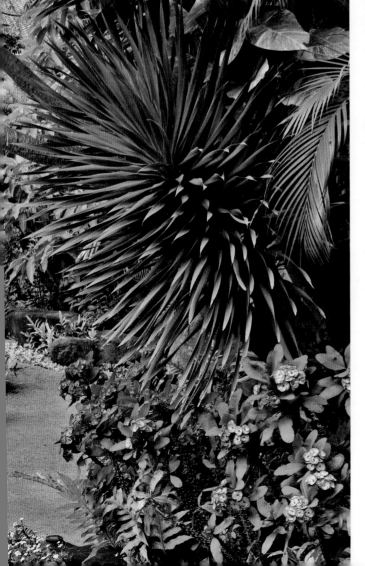

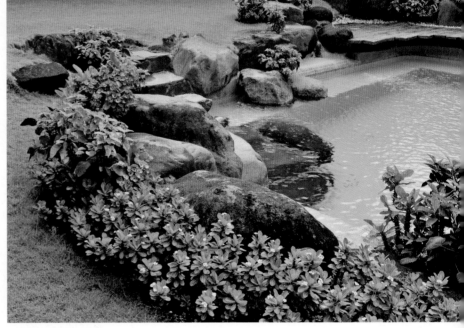

SANTOS KOI POND GARDEN

Dasmarinas Village, Makati
Designed by Yuyung LaO'

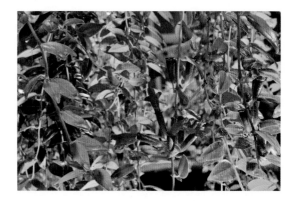

One can happily spend hours discussing the hundreds
of species and cultivars creatively planted in this garden
by master designer Yuyung LaO'. This designer clearly
has a flair for combining plants in unusual yet winning
combinations. He has always been interested in exotics
and tropical species: giant bird's nest and staghorn ferns,
Philodendrons, Alocasias and Bromeliads, to name a few.

In this exquisite garden belonging to Ochie and Malyn
Santos, LaO' uses an infinite variety of tropical plants, shrubs,
palms and ground covers to provide a rich horticultural
scenario. Many of the plants were chosen for foliage—
such as the grayish green banded *Sansevieria trifasciata*
Hahnii; *Zebrina pendula* with finely divided dark green
and purple foliage; an irregularly patchy leaved Aglaonema;
Philodendron x Burgundy with arrow-shaped leaves
sporting a red cast; and *Rhapis humilis* with stiff, arching
fan-like leaves.

In the back garden surrounded by a layered tapestry of
green one gets a self-satisfied, relaxed feeling that results
when plants grow together and form their own micro-
climates. Beneath towering palms and lacy bamboo, tiny
ferns have sprouted from spores along the path's edges

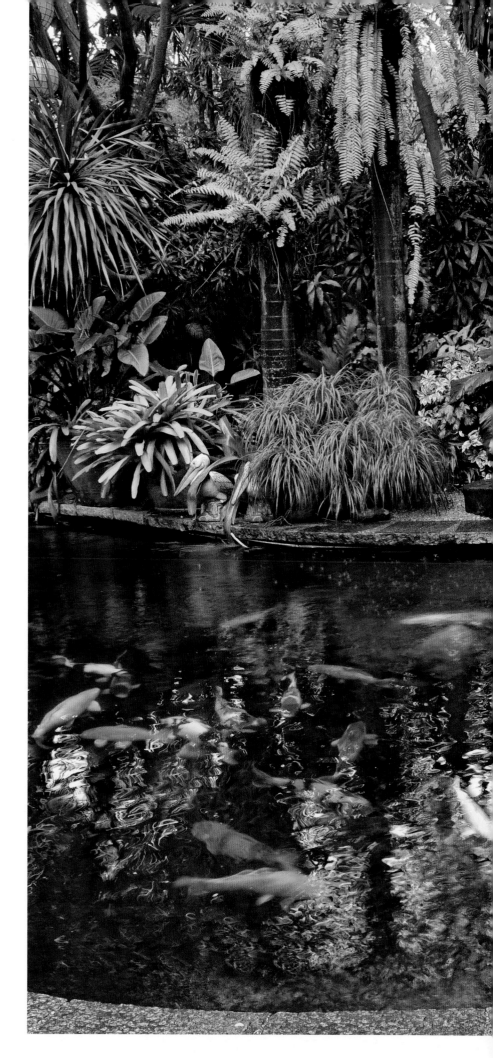

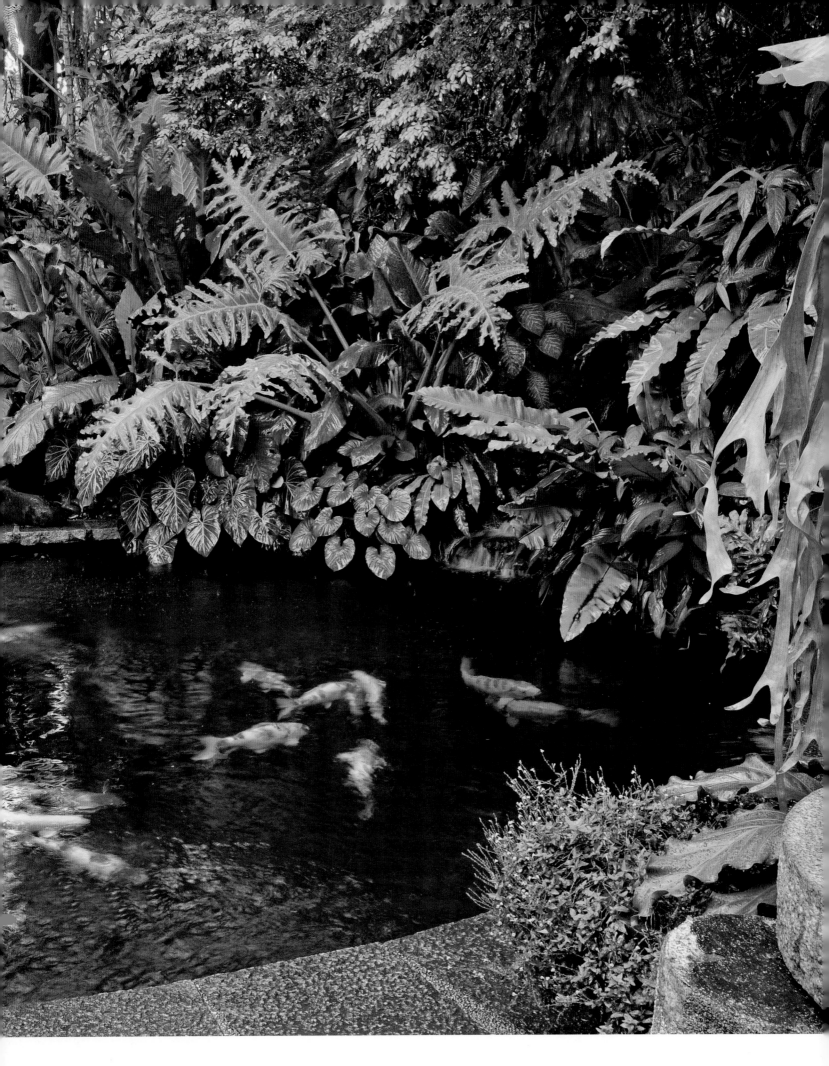

together with self-sown seedlings of other plants. There are several water features in the garden: a circular stone-edged pond bordered by Fukien tea, Sansevierias, Bromeliads and Alocasias and a raised one with tropical water lilies plus a few more in pots tucked in among the foliage.

The Santos garden is a good example of how to maximize space with the imaginative use of plantings linked by winding paths. Copious use of statuary, Thai ceramic jars and different textured hardscapes also complement the plethora of plantings. Water plays an important role too.

Gardens such as these are a source of inspiration for many aspiring gardeners who would like to transform a basic suburban plot into a tropical paradise. As the master knows, it is not as easy at it looks!

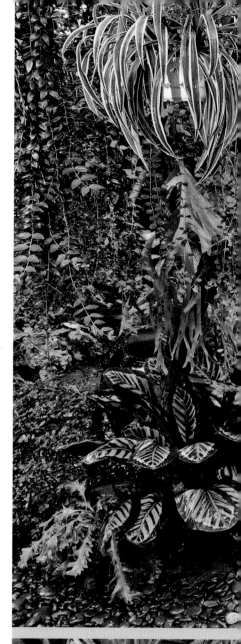

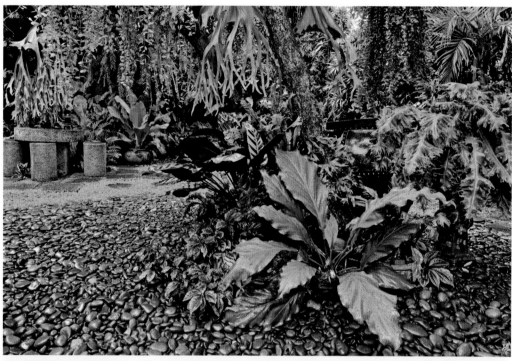

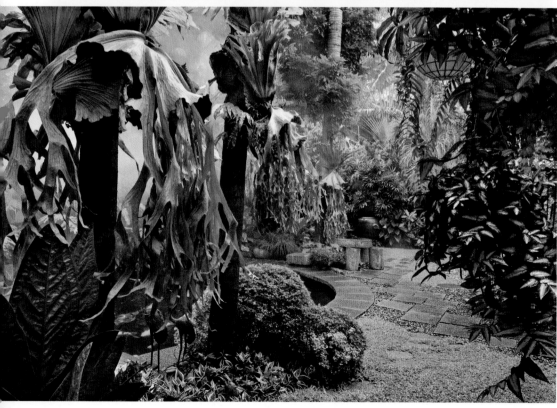

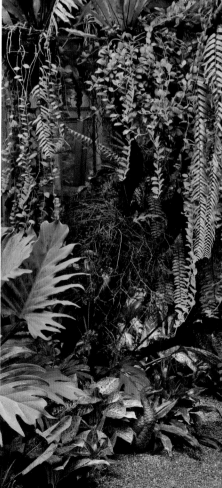

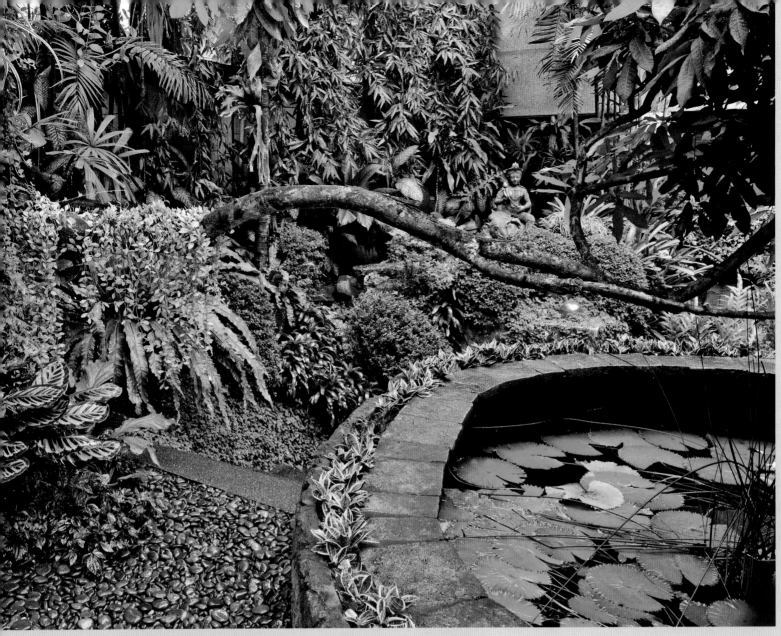

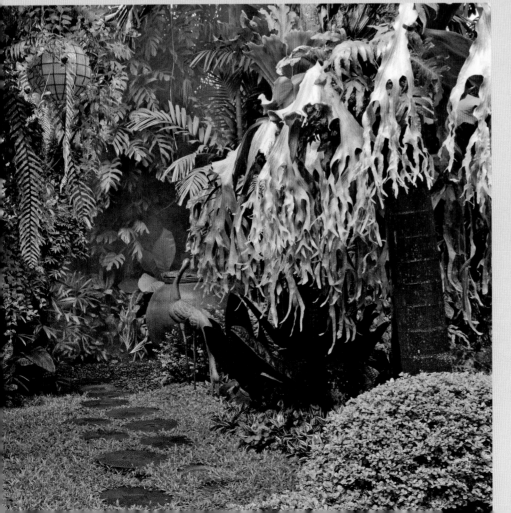

Previous pages main photo The main water feature in the garden is a circular, stone-edged pond animated with colorful koi.

Previous pages small photo Close-up of blooms of *Aeschynanthus javanica*, a vine called the red lipstick plant as it looks like a lipstick emerging from its case.

Opposite top Dark pebbles and irregular pavers in paths act as a foil to the verdant greenery.

Opposite bottom Dripping from trees, the common staghorn fern, *Platycerium bifurcatum*, adds drama and a sense of mystery.

Above A circular, stone-edged-pond, woven around the edges with miniature Sansevieria, is one of several water features in the garden.

Left Epiphytic ferns such as *Goniophlebium persicifolium* and *Platecerium bifurcatum* lend a tropical forest feeling to the surroundings. The fern's pendant, simply pinnate fronds hang almost straight down and can reach close to 2 meters (6 feet) in length.

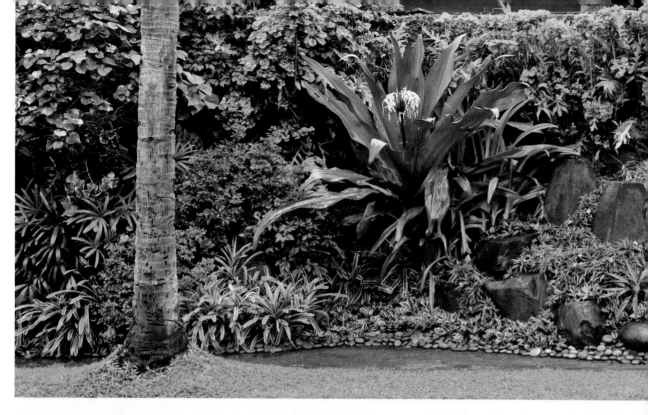
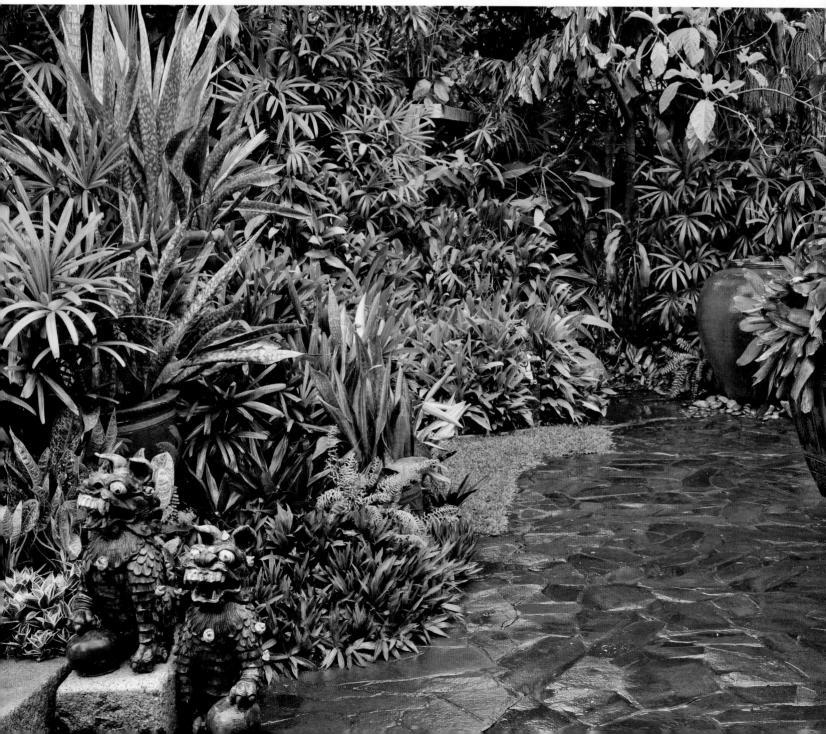

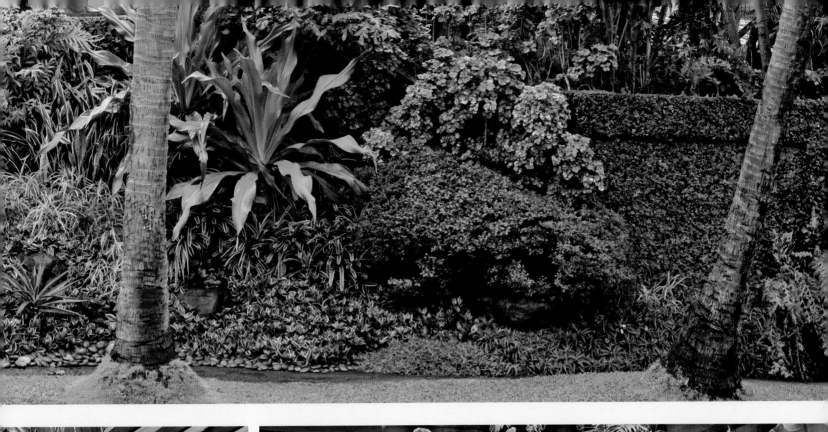

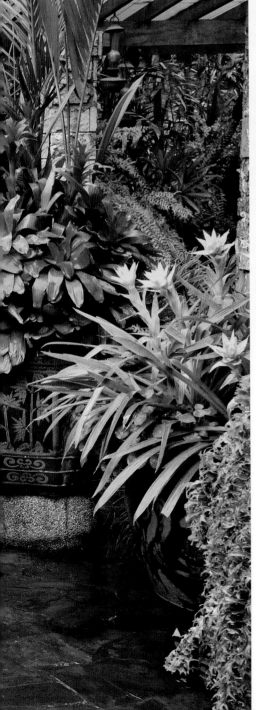

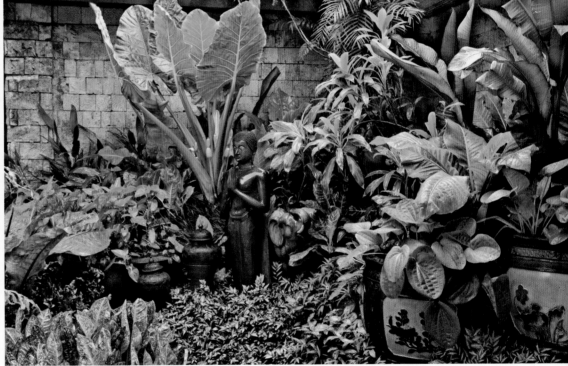

Top A *Crinum augustum* with a pale pink flower stands out in the rich tapestry of ornamental greens in this suburban sidewalk garden.

Above An indoor garden with potted Alocasias, Aglaonemas, Heliconias and Anthuriums.

Left Colorful Bromeliads and *Sansevieria trifasciata* in large ornamental jars add oomph to a courtyard arrangement.

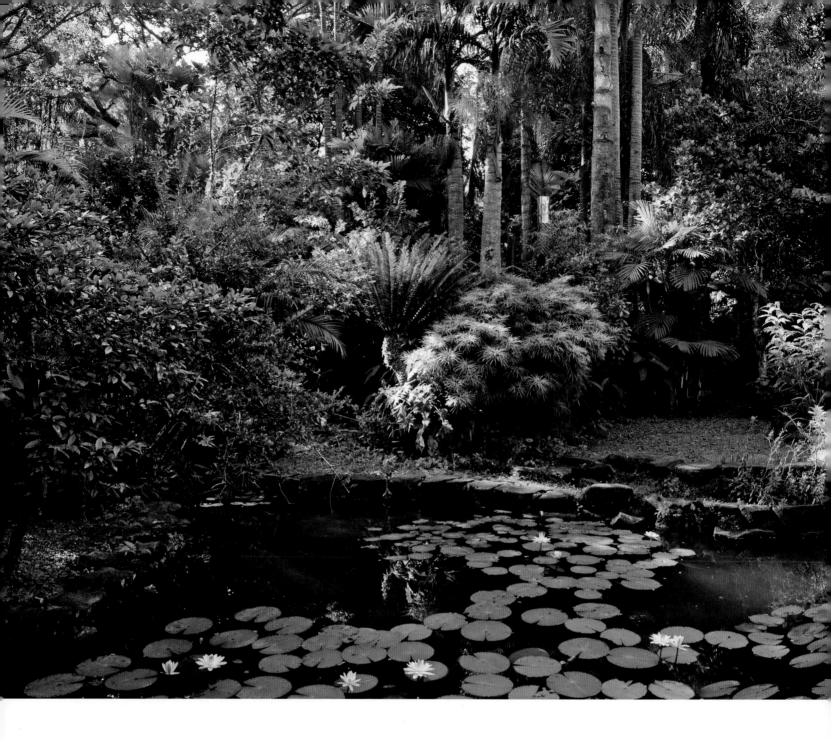

JERRY ARAOS GARDEN

Antipolo City, Rizal
Designed by Jerusalino Araos

Jerusalino Araos, better known as "Jerry" to his friends and the tight knit garden circle, is a legend among gardeners and plant lovers. His colorful past as a NPA guerilla and Camp Crame prisoner along with his multiple talents as a sculptor and furniture designer have made his transformation to horticulturist and garden philosopher even more intriguing. His garden located in Antipolo, a town named after the local *tipolo* tree that grows wild in the area and whose sap was used for traps and caulking boats, was once grassland with a natural spring. Today it is a magical leafy oasis of tall trees and bamboo groves teeming with wildlife and botanical interest.

Upon entering the gate, the visitor has the choice of two winding paths that lead through the garden. The path to the left takes you around a bend dominated by a spectacular *Freycinetia multiflora*, a climbing Pandanus

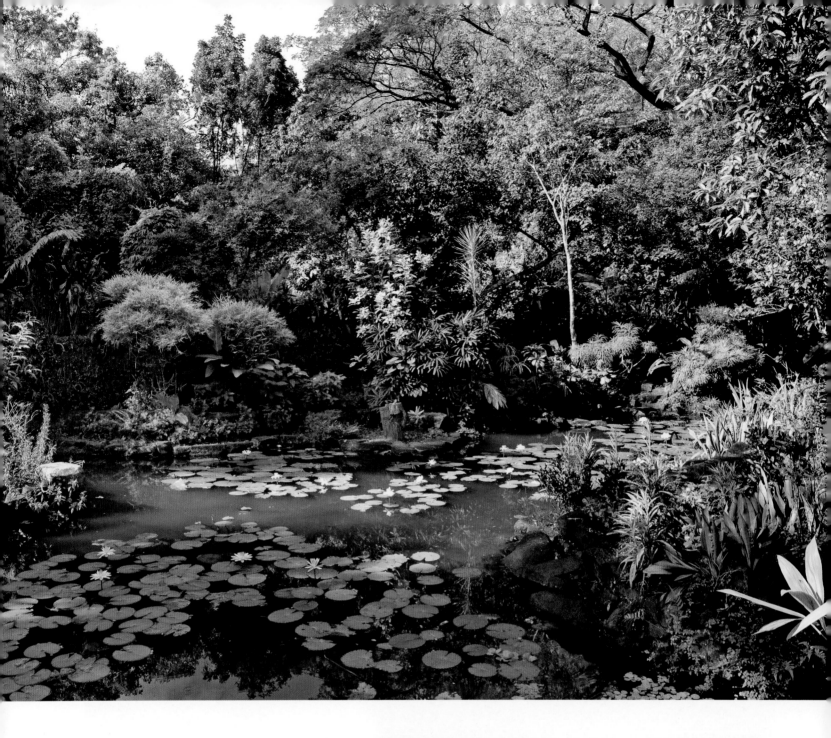

Above A stone-edged pond is the focus of a romantic tropical water lily garden imaginatively planted to simulate a wild and naturalistic garden. White Nymphaea *pubescens* and a pink variety called '*Sir Galahad*' thrive in the pond.

Right An organic wooden bench sits naturally within the sculptor's intuitive primeval creation. He says, "The garden is my highest achievement. It is my art philosophy coming true."

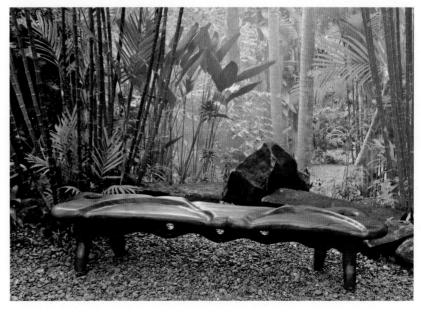

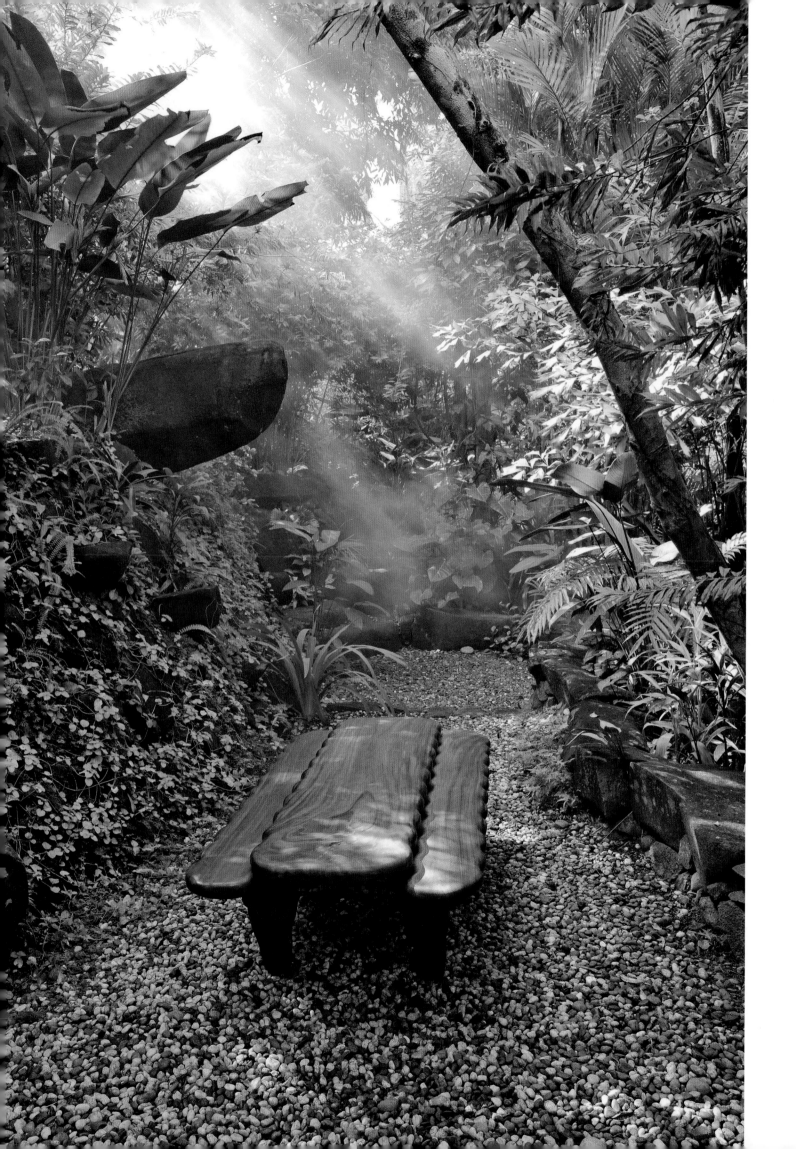

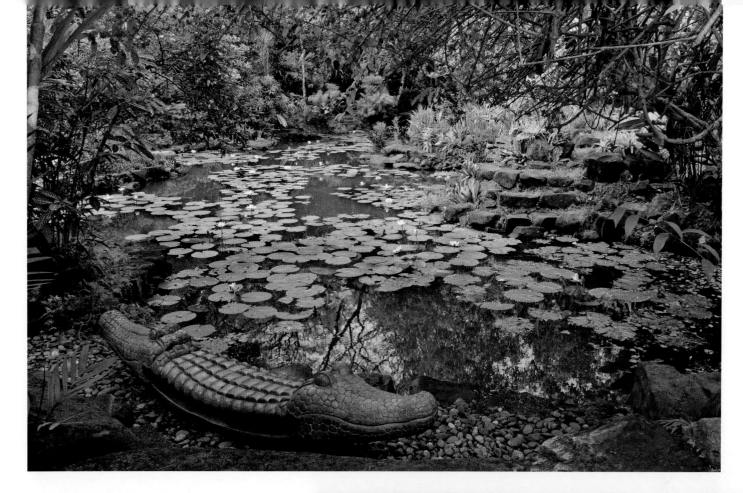

locally known as "stairway to heaven." It continues past a dramatic stonewall frieze designed by the owner and up a flight of stone steps to a woody glade bordered by betel nut palms and Heliconias. Comfortably set with tables and chairs, this space is used for entertaining since there is no house on the property. Down a slippery path of uneven stones on the right is the mandala garden, a space Araos created to serve as a peaceful and meditative environment where he could sit for hours to contemplate man's relationship to nature. The circular garden decorated with eight pillars fashioned out of old wood that he carved himself using mountain and river motifs is paved with gravel with a hole in the center. Spaces between the pillars afford the visitor different views of the garden.

Past the mandala is a circular sunken garden sometimes used for picnics and concerts, now carpeted with moss and self-sown Impatiens. The tapestry of contrasting textures and shades of green is continually traversed by winding paths of river stones embroidered here and there with moss and peacock ferns. Instead of grass or concrete, Araos covered the ground with gravel and river stones to allow rainwater to seep directly into the soil. Palms, bamboo and ferns abound in this tropical garden and are woven in dense combinations with Miagos and Alocasias. A Chinese hat plant (*Holmskioldia sanguinea*) provides an interesting distraction from all the green.

From the entrance, the path to the right leads to a studio where examples of the designer's furniture are on display. Just past the studio is a space designed as an outdoor theater. This section of the garden along with the *dapay*, a tribal gathering place for the elders (reminiscent of those

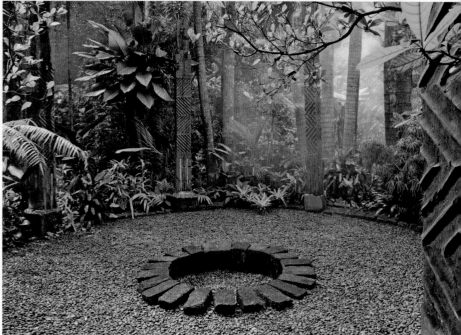

Opposite The artist's segmented table is set proudly by the "Galdugal," a vertical wall of rough-hewn basalt stones. The dark rocks jutting out of the hoary wall form a Cordillera-style "staircase", climbing along the slope to the next garden room.

Top The two-headed crocodile carved of Philippine hardwood represents the vicious two-faced politicians of this world. It sleeps through the night and day on the bank of "Laglagoon," the languid pond teeming with lilies.

Above The mandala garden is the only space with an architectural structure—eight carved posts on the perimeter surround a circle of cobblestones embedded at the center. It is said that spirits dwell here.

found in the Cordillera mountains) is a dry landscape of stones and rocks. A bushy *Plumbago auriculata* provides a pale blue note to the surroundings. The paths converge at a free-form lagoon, the focal point of this tropical paradise. Devoted to white and pink tropical water lilies, it is the highpoint of the garden's design. It was the first part of the garden to be developed, as it used to be a muddy, stinking quagmire.

Araos contoured the pond banks naturally using different plant configurations while ensuring spaces for open vistas. The pond's edges are planted with irises, Calatheas, *ti* plants and Alocasias combined with masses of Miagos and Raphis palms to give a textured, soft margin that merges seamlessly with the surrounding landscape. A *kamuning* tree festooned with Queensland tassel fern casts its shadow on the water. The still surface of the water, the careful choice of plantings at the water's edge and the restrained use of materials create calm and serenity. Here, along the lagoons' banks, the constantly shifting patterns of light and shade pull one into the garden, revealing paths that narrow and then open onto unexpected views; steps and curves that introduce new spaces, and secretive places to sit and enjoy the foliage and flowers.

An intuitive designer, Araos had strong ideas about how the garden should be developed. He had no master plan but he was sure that the design would bring the natural elements of earth, water, stone and plants into a harmonious whole expressing his very own philosophies about man and his relationship to nature. In this forever-evolving garden he has succeeded in doing just that.

Right A stand of bamboo by this pond is underplanted with *Xanthosoma lindenii 'Magnificum'* and *Ophiopogon jaburan*.

Far right A circular sunken garden carpeted with moss and peacock ferns is called the "Duplohan." It has a four concentric circled amphitheater for children; here young visitors congregate to socialize and dip their feet in the pond's waters.

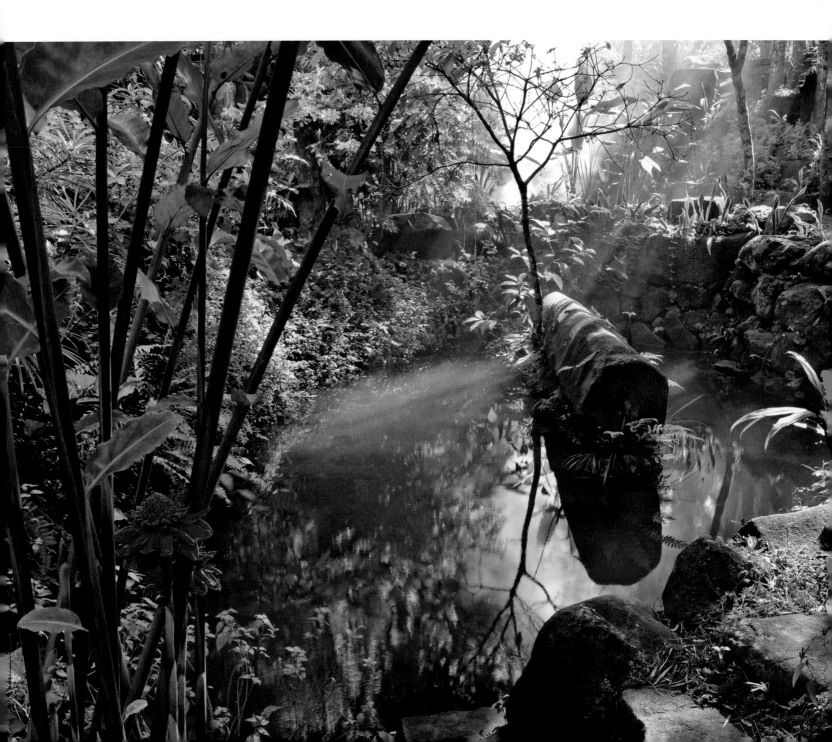

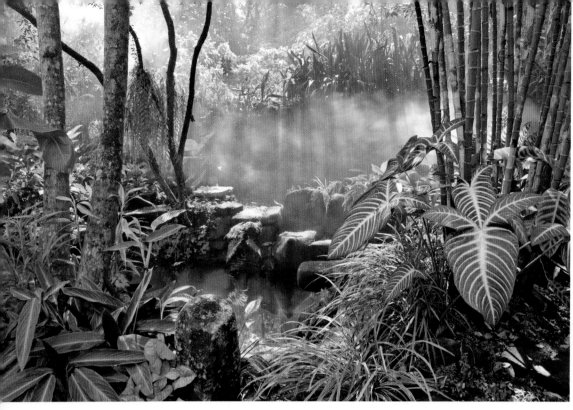

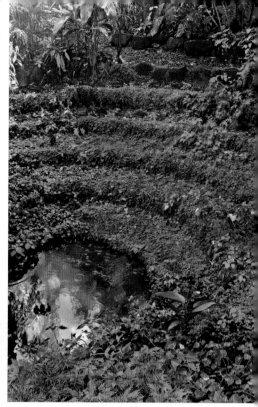

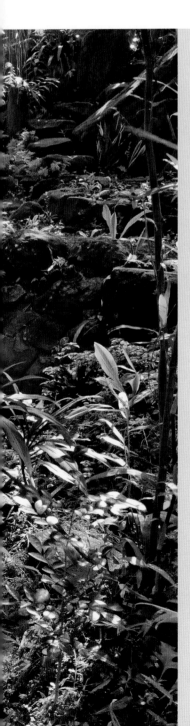

Left A solitary red torch ginger, *Etlingera elatior*, is the bright sentinel by the water source, a natural spring within the garden. One massive basalt boulder log remains in the pool, marking the genesis of the garden as sculpture.

Right The "Bagdan" is a natural stone stairway that connects different levels of the garden. The steps consist of seven elongated basalt stones ascending the garden path, sheltered by a blossoming *Freycinetia multiflora*.

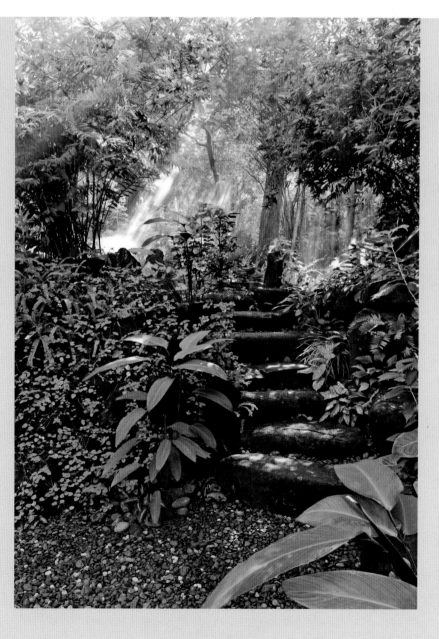

A JUNGLE GARDEN
Tagaytay City, Cavite

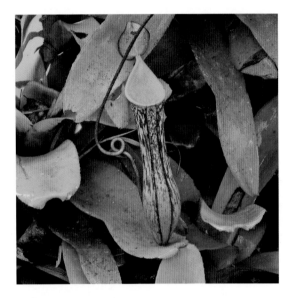

Passionate gardeners are known for coveting the most exotic and unusual plants. Collecting is a hobby shared by many and stories of keen gardeners and plant enthusiasts scouring the world in pursuit of the rare and extraordinary abound. Tucked away in the countryside of Tagaytay behind a tall nondescript wall is a rich garden filled with beautiful, naturalistic plantings that mirrors a woodland glade in the tropics. The owner, a modest and private country gentleman, has created a multifaceted garden mixing native species with ornamental exotics.

Over the years, this gardener's meticulous and keen eye for uncommon specimens has resulted in an intriguing collection that includes orchids, vines, Bromeliads and tree ferns. Some of the exotics and unconventional plants grown here may not be to everyone's taste and would not be suitable for ordinary backyard gardens, but they all have a distinct jungle appeal. In addition, there are also plants that many would regard as weeds, but in this tropical paradise shine like jewels.

Throughout the garden, a variety of trees provide both dense and dappled shade, with pools of light reflecting off the bold foliage of Philodendrons, vines and tree ferns creating an effect resembling a tropical forest. Your eye is constantly surprised with unexpected vistas, as landscaped areas merge with the wild. Winding paths thick with fallen

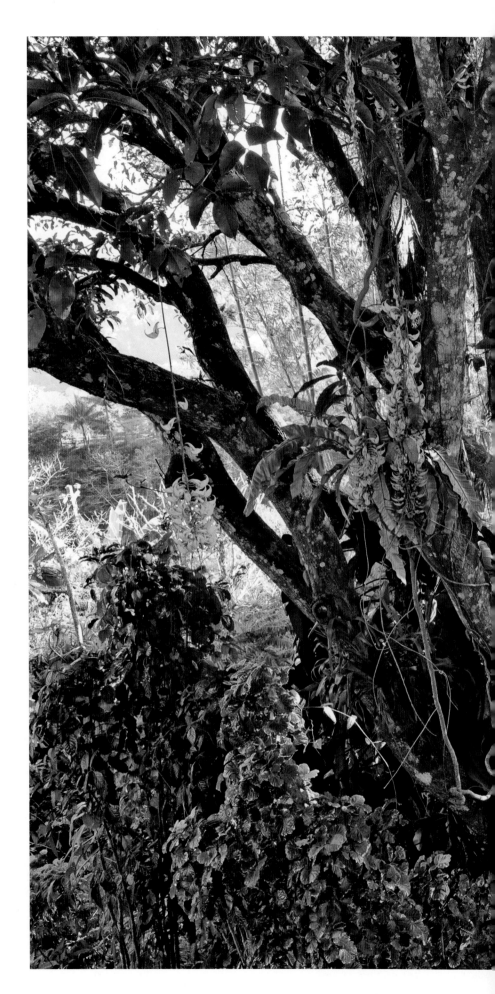

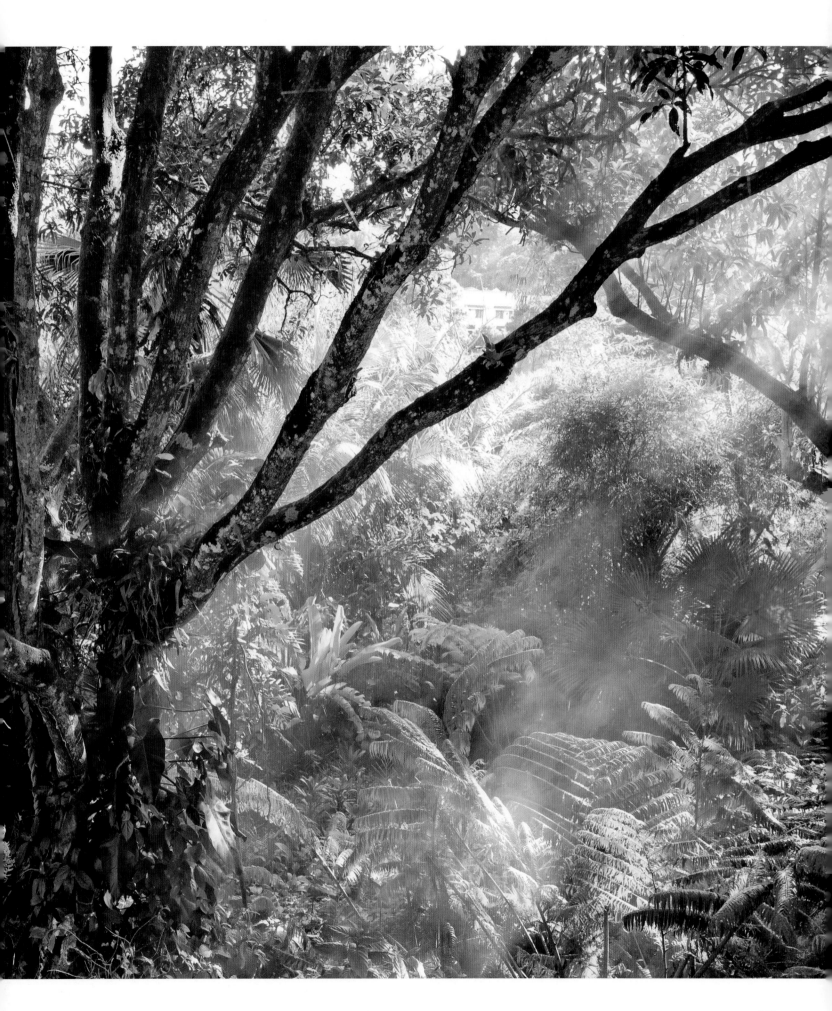

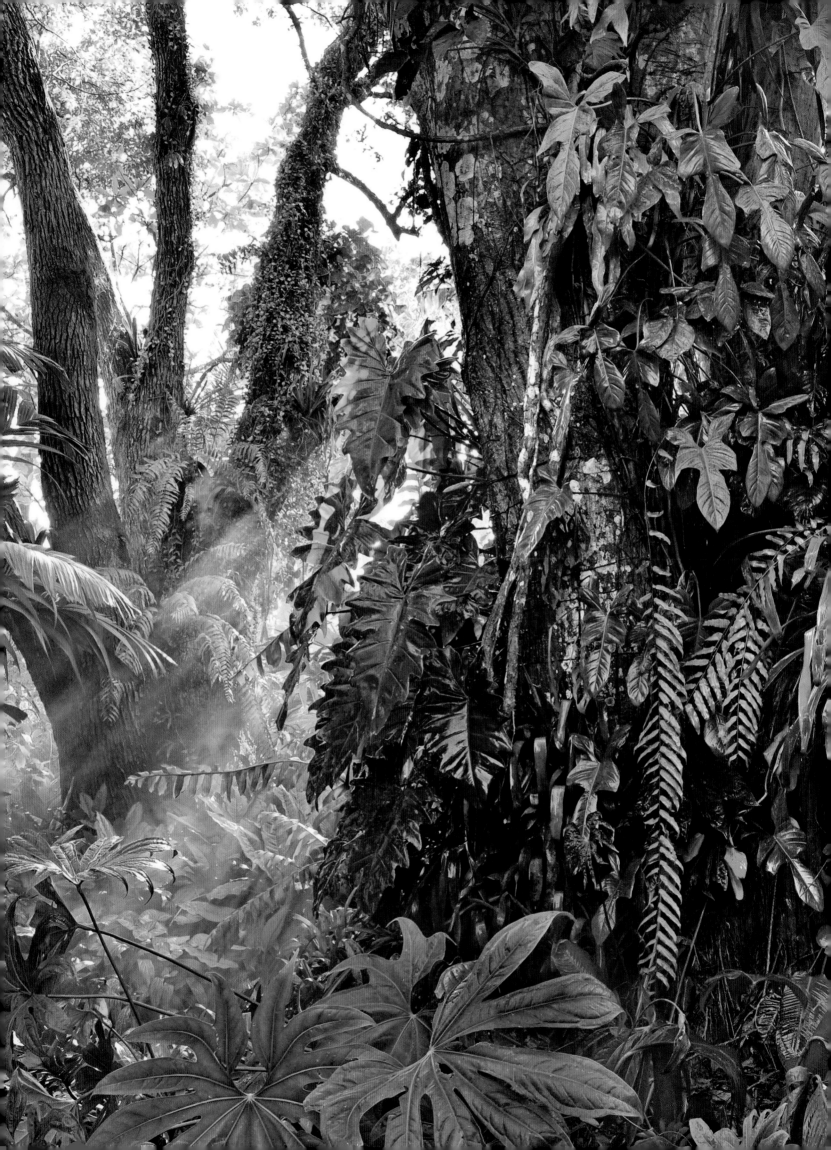

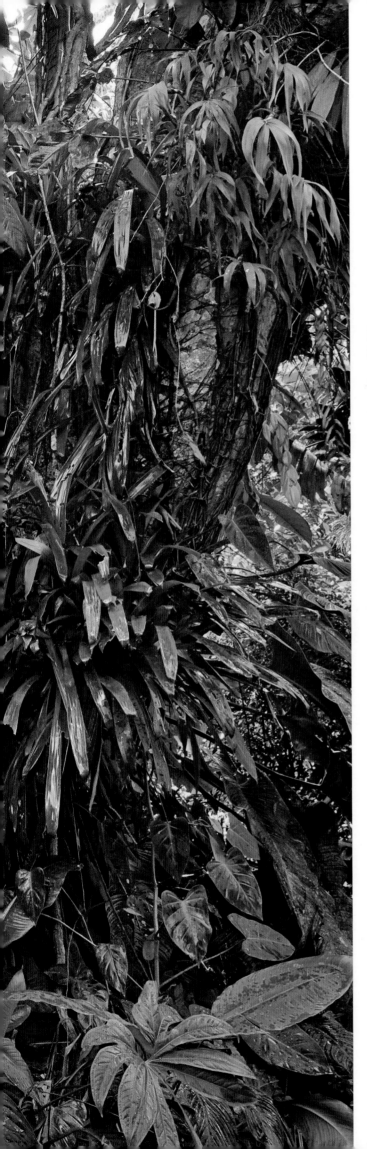

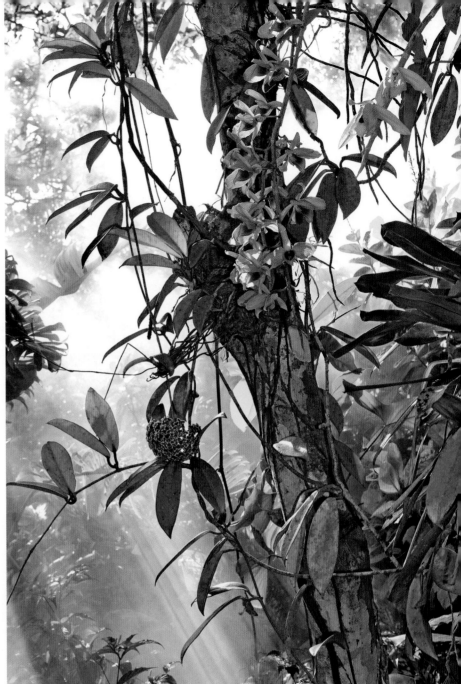

leaves weave through borders that include woodland flora, wetland species, native orchids and parasitic plants.

This garden recreates the marvel of coming upon botanical gems in their natural habitats or what the owner has created to look like natural habitats, that include native as well as non-native plants. Many parts of the garden look effortlessly natural despite containing ornamental plants that would not be found together in nature. The result is a garden that pays homage to nature yet also displays much gardening know-how and artistry. What makes it special is the mix of horticulture and ecology that has guided its development from the outset. The owner believes it is important to choose suitable plants for soil conditions and to pay considerable attention to their proper care and management to assure their survival.

As such, this natural jungle garden is pure enchantment and, for the owner who has endowed it with its magic, it is a crowning achievement.

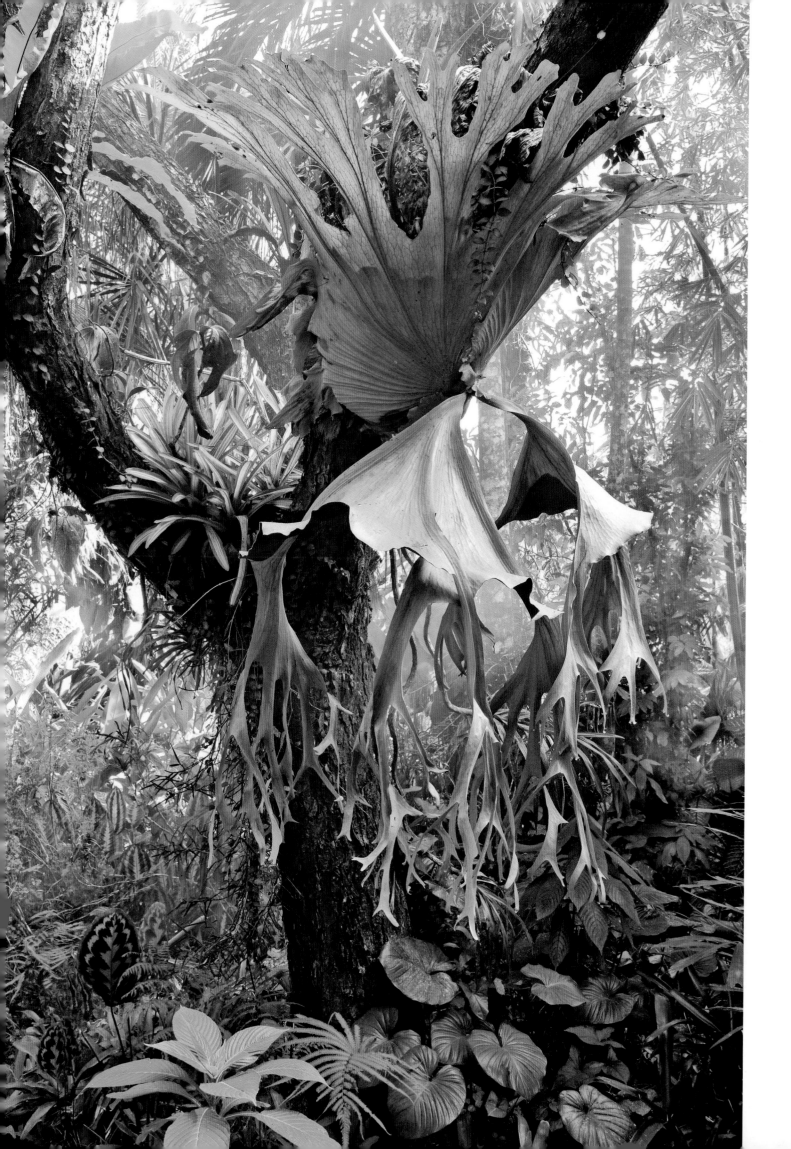

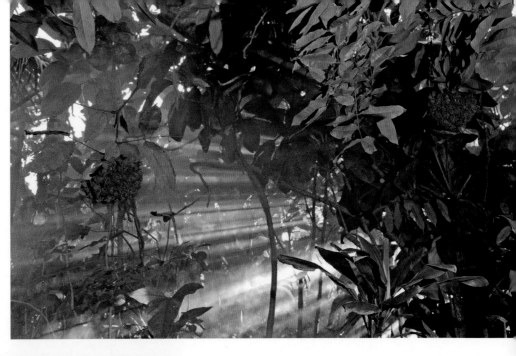

Page 84 Close-up of the pitcher plant, *Nepenthes* sp, a delicate climbing epiphyte usually found growing in high altitudes.

Pages 84–85 large photo Light bounces off the trunk and branches of a tree harboring a Philippine jade vine, *Strongylodon macrobotrys*.

Previous pages left An enormous tree provides dappled shade to Philodendrons, ferns, Bromeliads and Anthuriums.

Previous pages right *Hoya purpureo-fusca* and, above, the fragrant *sanggumay* orchid, *Dendrobium anosmum*.

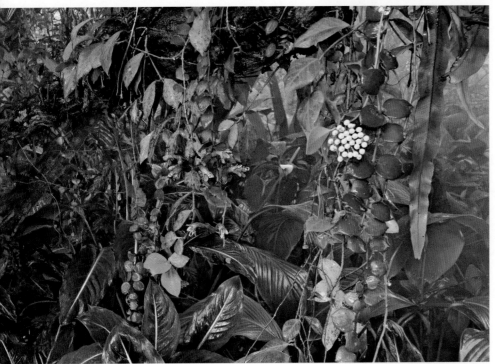

Opposite A giant staghorn fern, *Platycerium grande*, hangs from a branch. Coveted for its amazing size and form, it can grow to one meter (3 feet) in width.

Left A variety of epiphytic vines such as the lipstick plant, *Aeschynanthus speciosus,* and Hoya species mingle happily in this jungle-like garden.

Above The bright red flowers of the Rose of Venezuela, *Brownea grandiceps*, dangle from hairy branchlets bringing a cheery note to the surroundings.

Bottom left Vrieseas, native to South America are a recent introduction to the Philippines. A Bromeliad, they are named after a Dutch Botanist by the name of W DeVriese.

Bottom right Anthuriums are native to Columbia and have been successfully grown in many parts of the Philippines. Their flowers develop crowded in a spike on a fleshy axis, called a spadix.

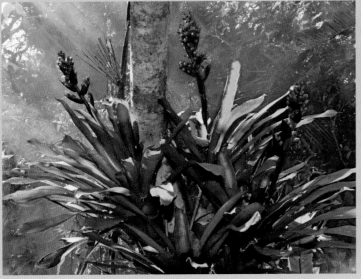

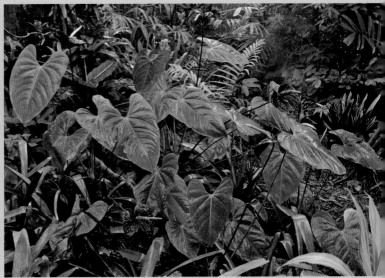

MEROS MOUNTAIN GARDEN

Alaminos, Laguna

Designed by Bill Lewis and Ely Bautista

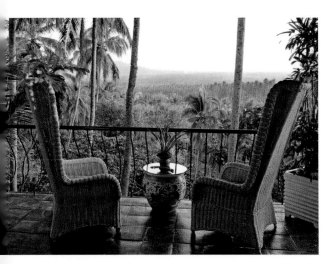

A sense of expectation begins when you turn off the main highway and start the long and dusty drive to this property through a plantation of coconuts. There is no house in sight for miles and you get the uneasy feeling that you are lost—until you catch sight of a solitary house half hidden on the side of a mountain. Octagonal in shape, the house and its garden occupy just a part of the 13-hectare (32-acre) site that Ely Bautista and Bill Lewis fell in love with after a long search. They had been looking for a suitable property to retire to after living in Canada and when they saw this piece of land they knew this was it. After building a modern multi-storey house, they decided on a garden that would integrate with the architecture and its eclectic collection of traditional and contemporary furniture.

Today, the garden, which they named Meros meaning "place" in Greek, has a tropical forest feeling and sublime views of distant mountains and the surrounding country-side. A spectacular *Amherstia nobilis* or Queen of Flowering Tree by the front door (right) is resplendent with coral flowers. The owners escort their visitors to the

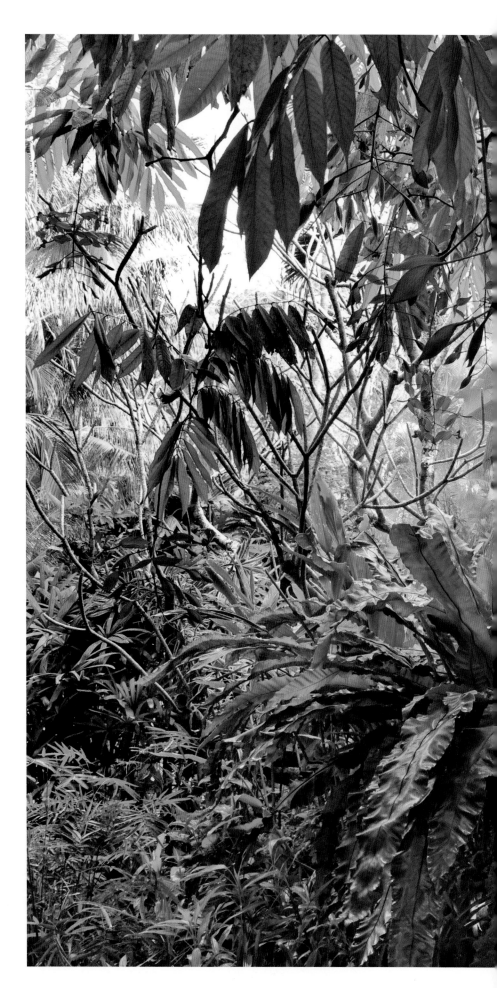

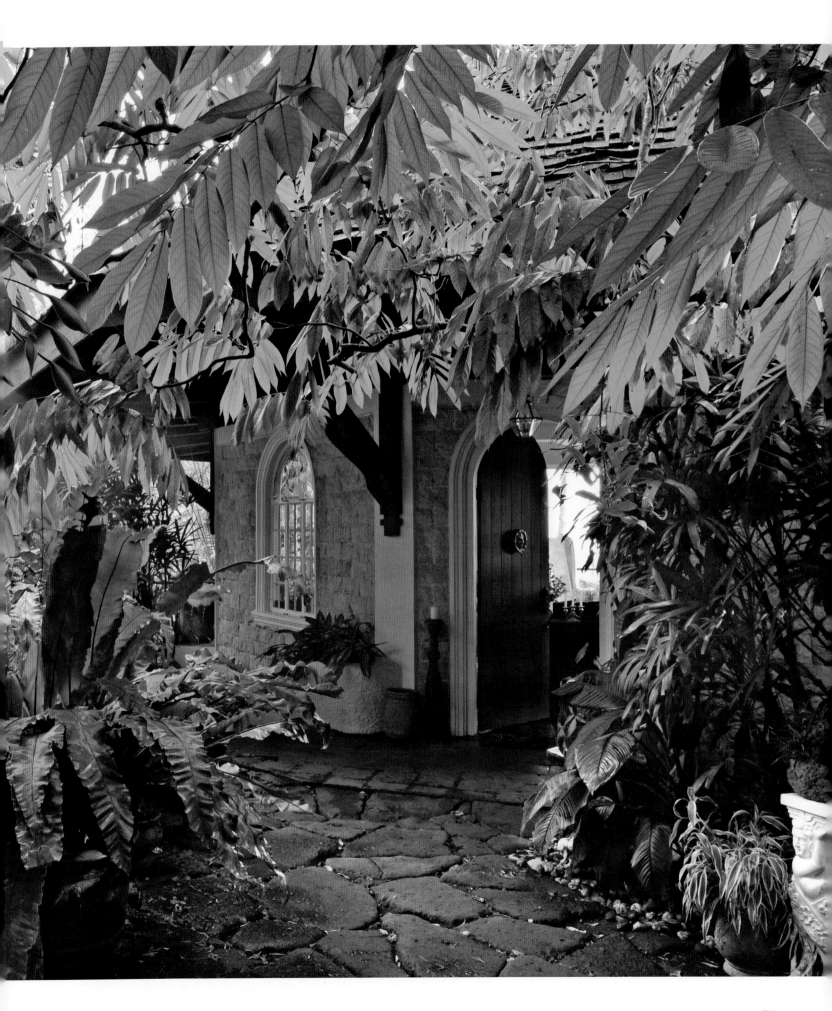

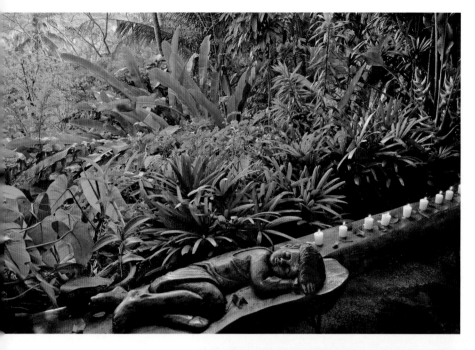

different areas of the garden down carefully chosen concrete and stone paths, past stands of Heliconias, into a grassy enclosure planted with a grouping of 'pregnant' trees, through a shady tunnel of Duranta, towards a 110-year-old Ifugao *dapay* house that was transported section by section to this aerie mountaintop from the Cordilleras.

Subtle landscaping, natural planting and a studied eye for decorative pieces are the key elements in the design of this modern tropical garden. All around it, the woodland that fringes the garden exerts a powerful presence and, from some points, the views are stunning. On the sunny side of the property, literally thousands of glorious Heliconias (15 varieties to date) and a number of ginger plants provide a stark contrast to the darkness of the forest of coconuts beyond.

At Meros, the owners have taken the powerful sense of place that is pervasive here and used it to create a private, serene and mysteriously sensual garden.

Previous pages main photo A spectacular *Amherstia nobilis* by the front door is resplendent with coral-colored flowers.

Previous pages small photo A balcony looks out onto sublime views of the coconut plantation and the surrounding countryside.

Above Sweet repose: A carved wooden bench with a sleeping boy is cradled by plantings of Rhapis palms, Philodendrons and Heliconias.

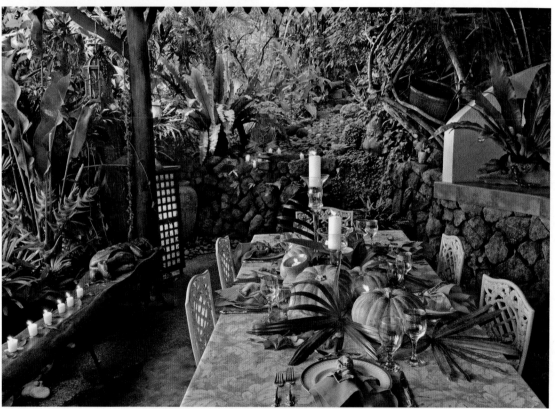

Above The dining table is set with local pumpkins and the flowers of *Amherstia nobilis*.

Right A Chinese deity stands guard beside an assemblage of tropical plantings.

Opposite The woodland that fringes the property exerts a powerful presence on Meros.

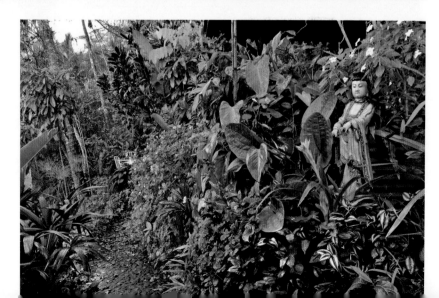

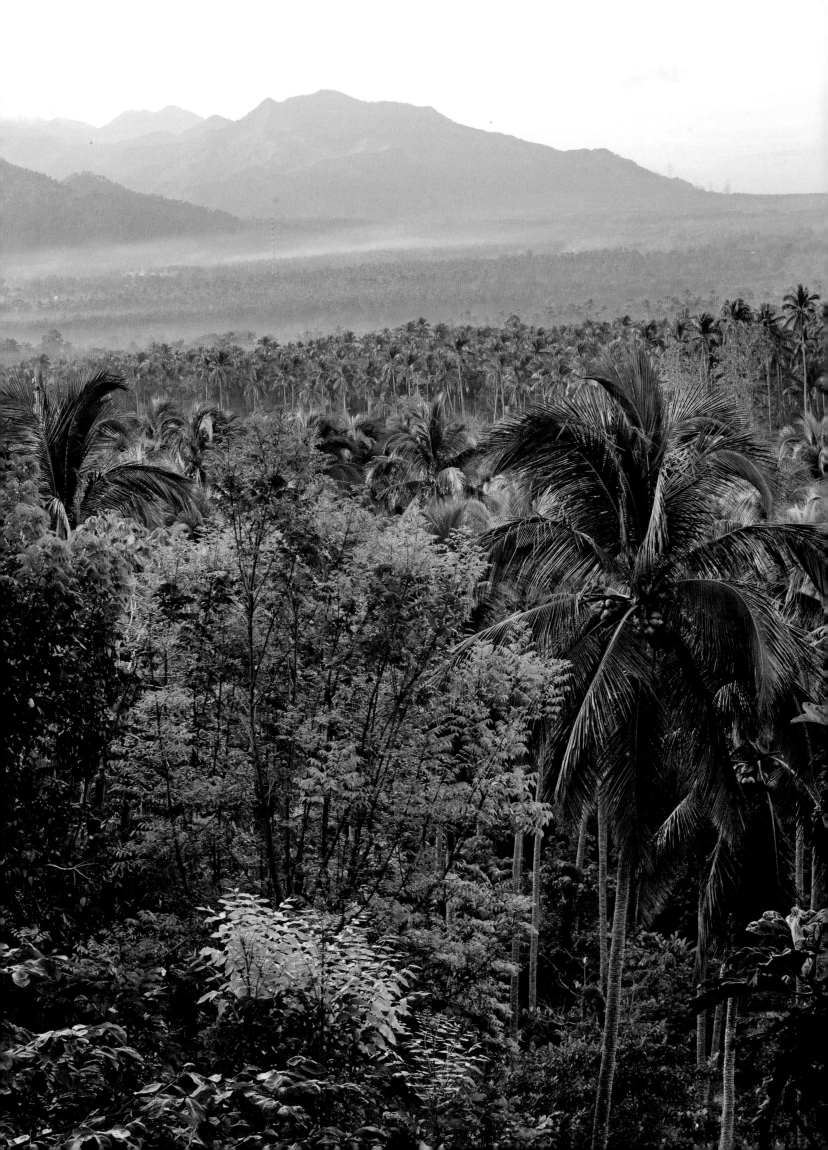

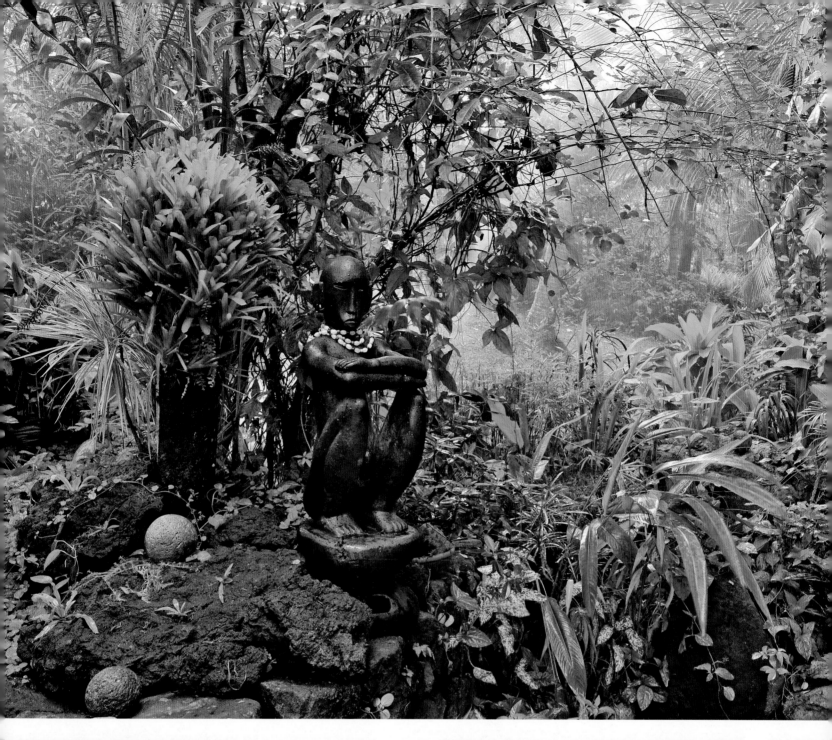

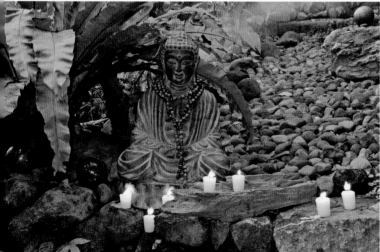

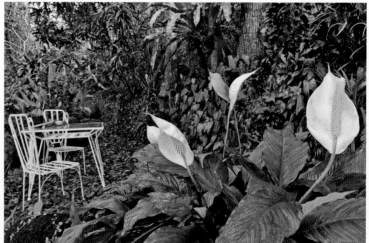

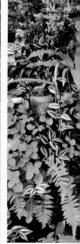

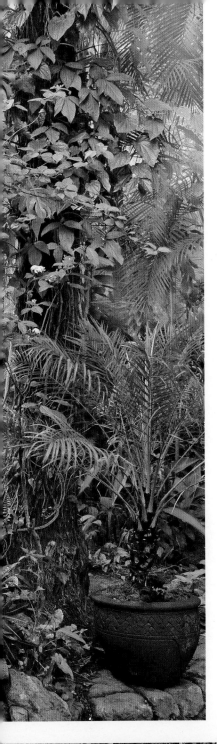

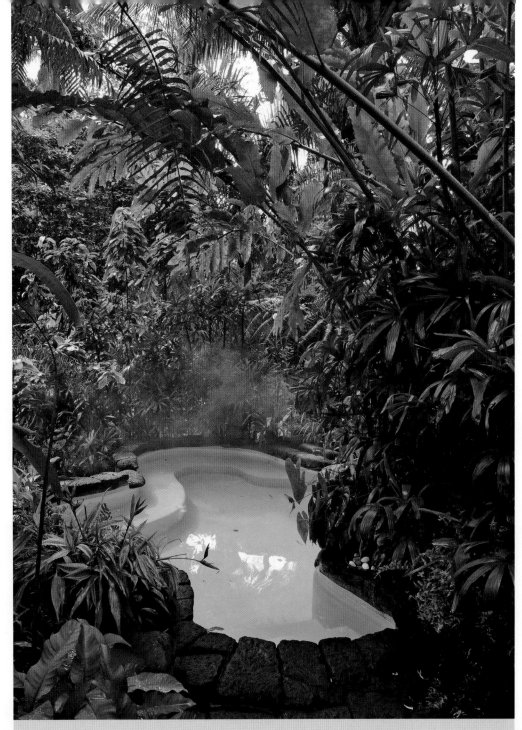

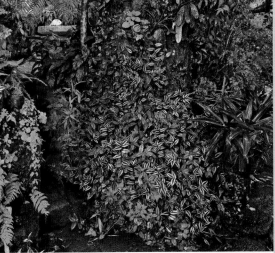

Top left A carved wooden figure of an *anito* (spirit) animates a corner of the garden.

Right This 100-year-old Ifugao *dapay* house was transported piece by piece from the Cordilleras.

Far left Flickering candles illuminate a Buddha on a rock shelf.

Middle left The striking *Spathiphylum commutatum* with its white spathe is indigenous to the Philippines.

Left Epiphytic ferns and a host of other air plants are at home in a rocky embankment.

Above Mist rises from a secluded pool sheltered by Heliconias, palms, Anthuriums and Hibiscus.

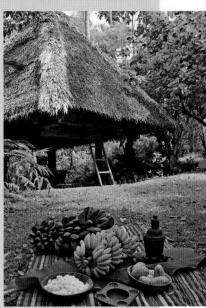

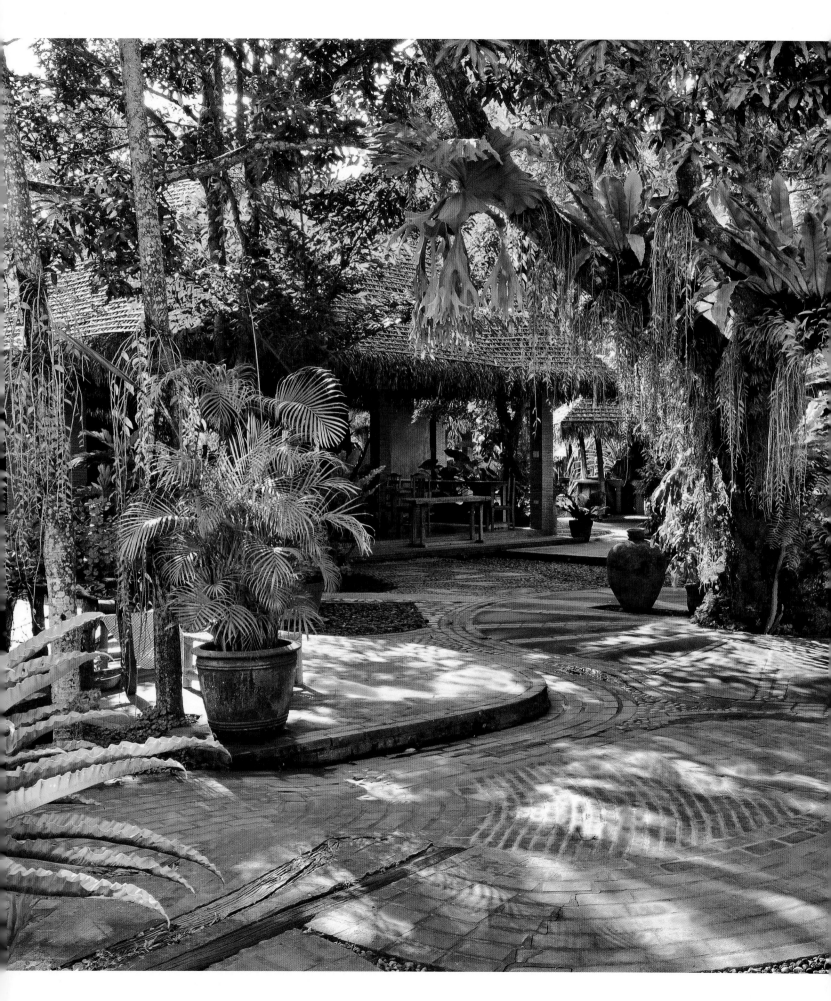

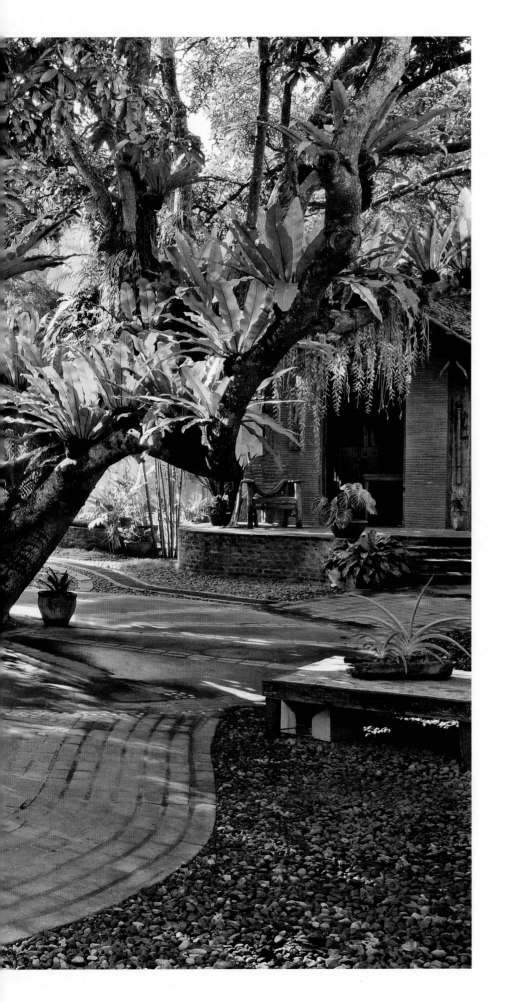

UGU'S POTTERY GARDEN

Tiaong, Quezon
Designed by Augusto Bigyan

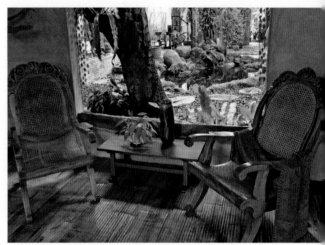

Patterned paths are all the vogue in modern gardens today. Likely as not, Augusto Bigyan is the name behind many of the walkways that grace the fashionable gardens not just in Manila but all around the Philippines.

Known to many as "Ugu", this artist/potter lives in a multi-dwelling compound in Tiaong, Quezon. A pink adobe house, cloaked with a magnificent red passion flower vine (*Passiflora coccinea*), welcomes the visitor to the property. Inside are 15 traditional Filipino-style pavilions, with intricately woven *anahaw* roofs and bamboo floors. One pavilion is used as a showroom for the owner's pottery and ceramics, another serves as a memorial for the owner's mother, while another is used for pottery lessons. The rest are rented out for seminars and events. The compound serves both as a restful retreat for tourists who visit the area and a laboratory for Ugu's growing brick and pottery business.

Injecting a contemporary twist to the vocabulary of traditional garden design, Ugu updated the surroundings of his traditional structures with some minimal yet focused plantings. A number of full-grown trees like

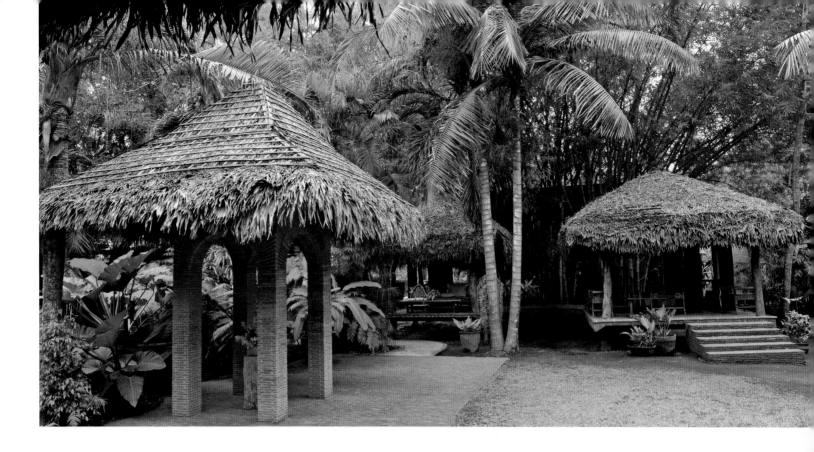

the mango that was already growing on the site from the beginning and stands of golden and Buddha's-belly bamboo heighten the spatial sensations of moving from brightly lit to darkly shaded areas. Sun and shade moving through the textured foliage provide continually changing patterns. Potted ferns and Philodendrons further help to define the different buildings.

An essential element in Ugu's garden, something that has become his personal signature, is the patterned paving. One is struck by the artful combinations of brick, tile and stone mosaics that draw the visitor's eyes to the different areas of the property. The paths of small marvels help manage movement and delineate space, creating rooms and boundaries and organizing views in the garden. The virtuoso play of contrasting materials subtly defines each space, changing with the circular flow around the garden.

The entrance to the garden is marked by a wide path of alternating brick and concrete with terracotta leaf and flower inserts. Black river stones seam the edges of the paths and create dramatic transitions to other paths, some made of concrete pavers with leaf motifs, others with ceramic tile and railroad sleeper combinations bordered with more terracotta designs of varying organic shapes.

Though relatively small in total area, the property seems much larger because of the imaginative layout that boasts many intimate spaces and a constant sense of surprise. With the use of a limited plant palette and the clever interplay of landscape with structure, Ugu has composed a garden that illustrates the strong relationship between an artist and his garden.

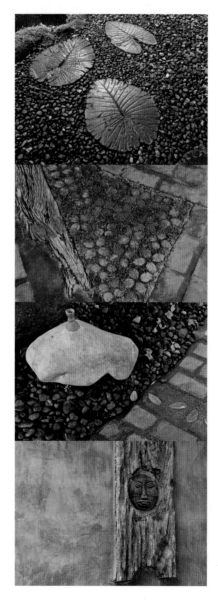

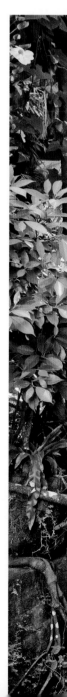

Previous pages main photo Unique, imaginative paving has become Ugu's personal signature. A sample of his work lies at the entrance of his multi-dwelling complex laid out around a tree clad with bird's nest ferns.

Previous pages small photo Pavilions furnished with Philippine vernacular furniture look out into the various garden areas.

Above Traditional Filipino-style pavilions, with intricately woven *anahaw* roofs and bamboo floors, comprise the multi-dwelling compound of potter, Augusto Bigyan.

Left Some of the imaginative uses of stone, brick and terracotta in Ugu's garden.

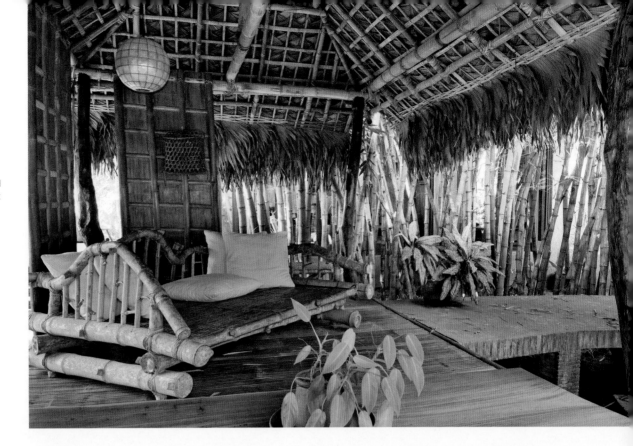

Right One of the pavilions for overnight guests: Its open structure encourages a unique back-to-nature experience.

Below Coconut trees dripping with epiphytes along with potted ornamental palms and bird's nest ferns enhance the walkways in the compound.

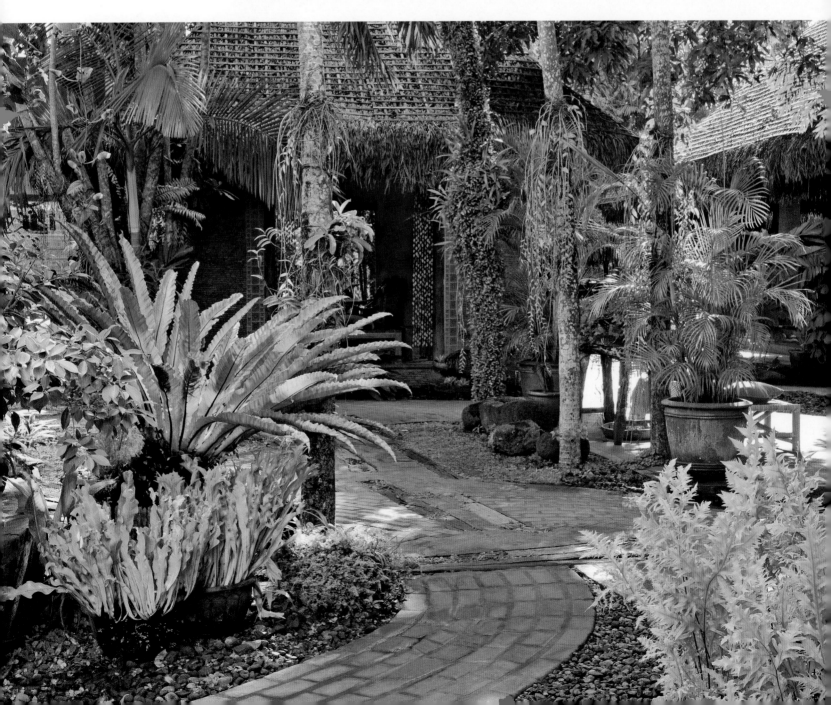

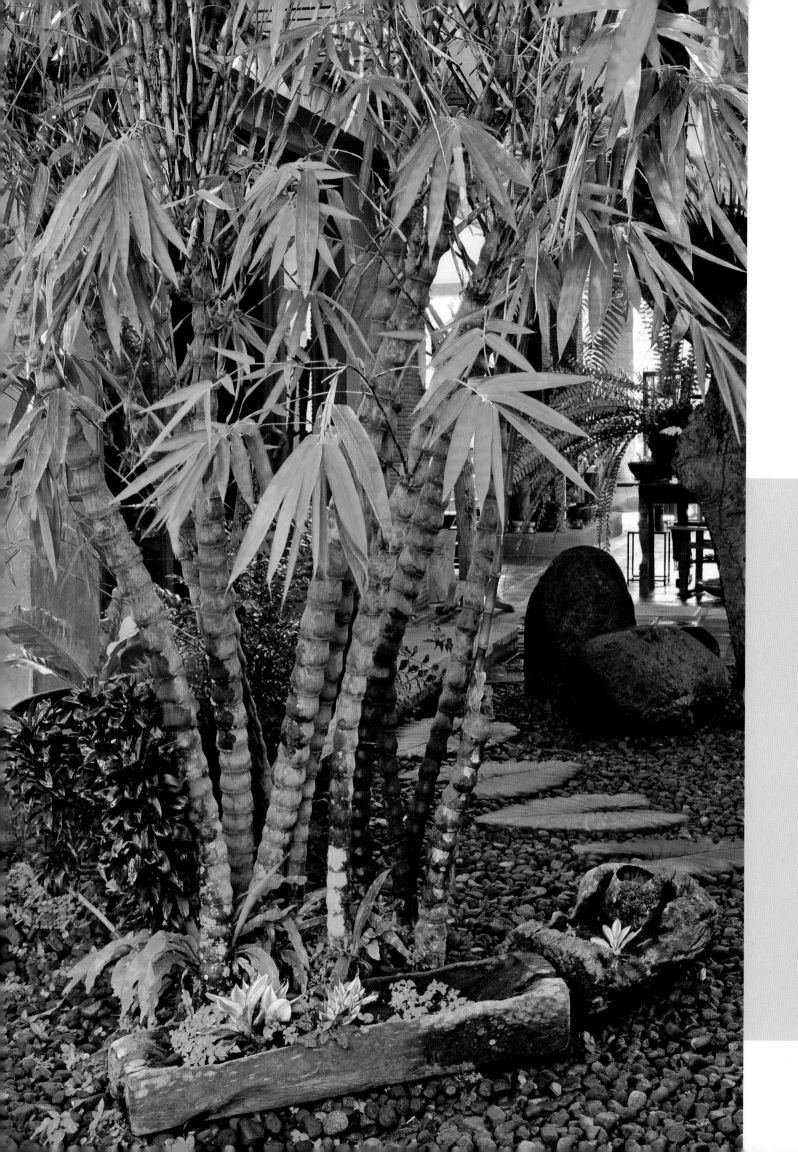

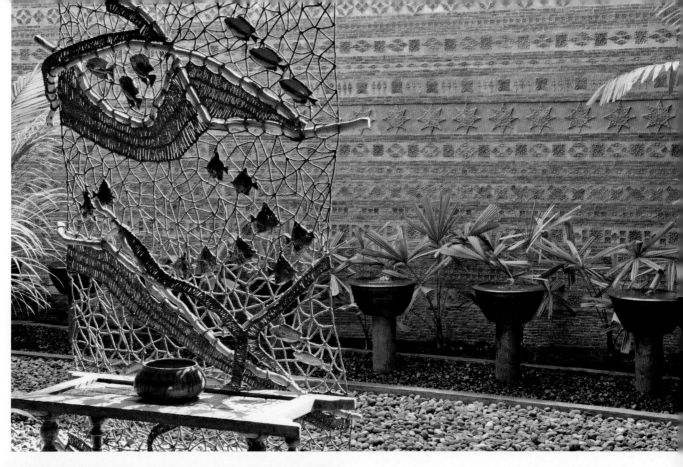

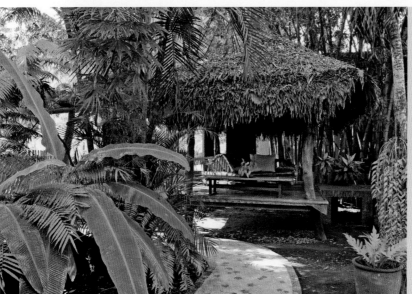

Above Two samples of the artist's work on display. A wall hanging fashioned out of rope with ceramic fish inserts hangs suspended against a lavishly decorated wall made of intricate terracotta cutouts in various geometric patterns.

Left The paved and gravelled paths help manage movement and delineate space in the garden.

Bottom Groves of the golden bamboo, *Bambusa vulgaris*, provide a screen for the various pavilions.

Left The bulbous culms of Buddha's-belly bamboo, *Bambusa ventricosa*, mark the entrance to the artist's showroom.

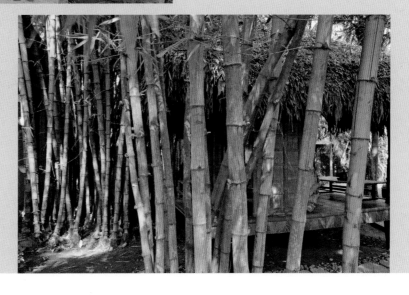

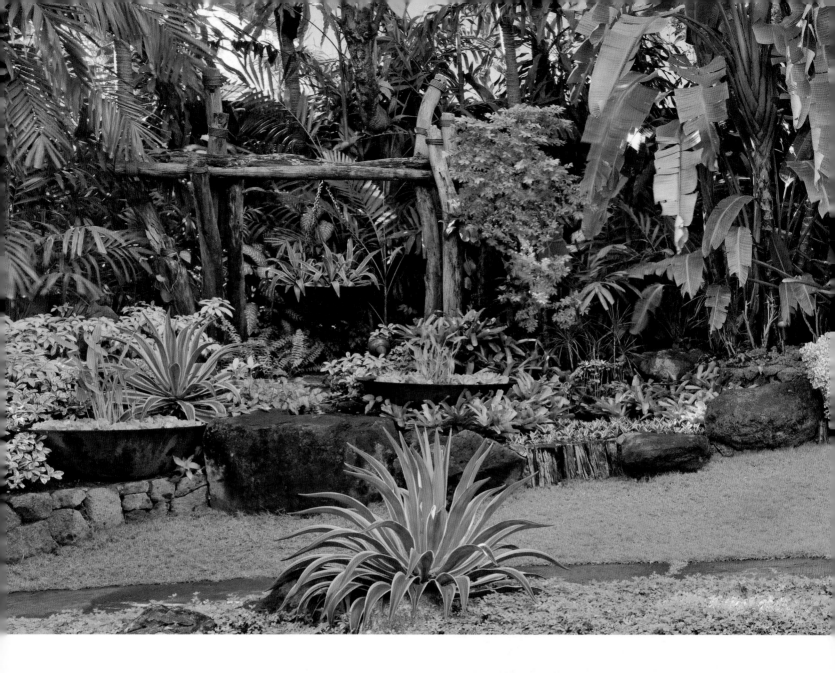

A TROPICAL OASIS

Forbes Park, Makati

Designed by Jojo Lazaro

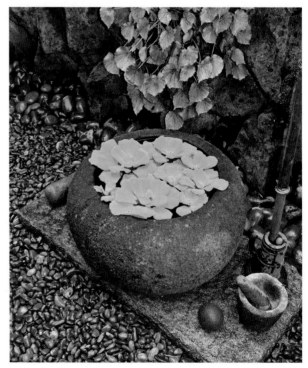

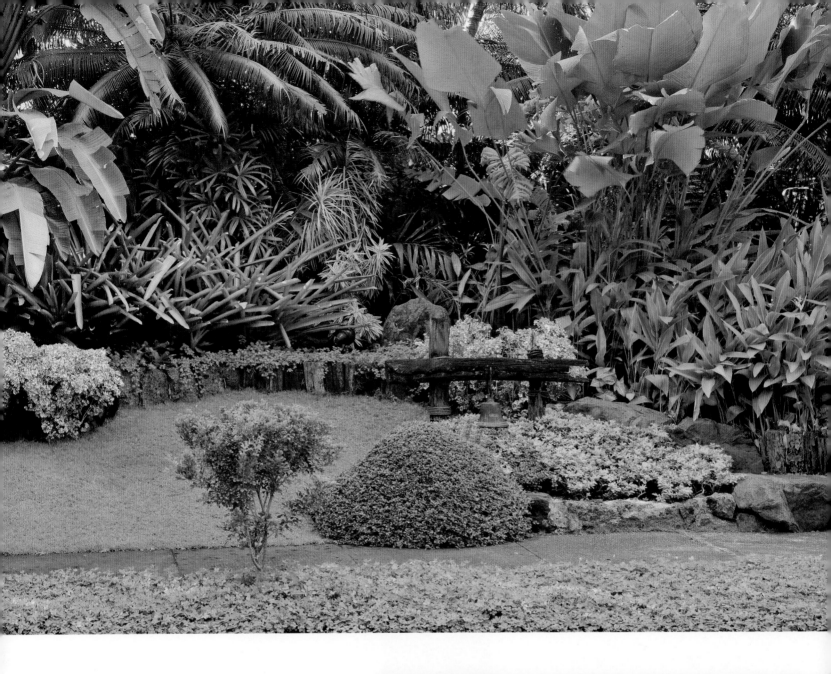

This multilevel home in one of the gated communities of Makati is a tropical oasis that serves as a refuge from the chaos of city life. From the sidewalk, a stunning composition of clipped Duranta mounds, interwoven with Cordylines and Bromeliads and decorated with bamboo poles and antique vats, is enough to make any passerby stop and take notice. The decorative elements lend a distinct Oriental flavor and set the tone of the garden that lies hidden behind.

Accessed via an iron gate, a small courtyard serves as a threshold into the quiet sanctuary beyond. Designed as a tiny Japanese garden with Ficus tree topiaries, Rhapis palms and peacock ferns, it serves as a boundary between the outside and inside realms. The garden behind is entered through the wonderfully romantic house whose openness to the garden contributes to its tropical ambiance. Tall folding shutters open onto the planted courtyard punctuated here and there with old sugarcane presses, stone lanterns and antique water jars. Here the design of Jojo Lazaro reveals a masterful use of space and materials.

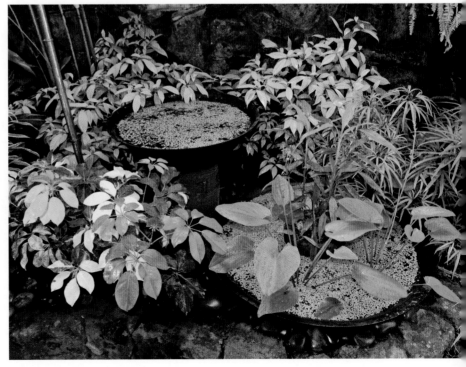

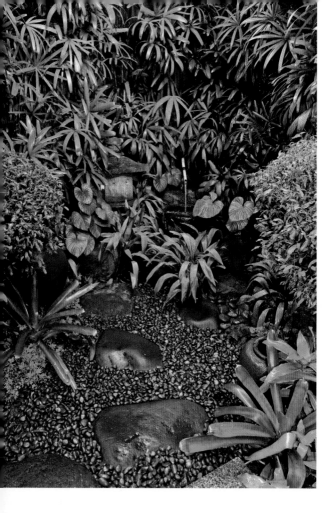

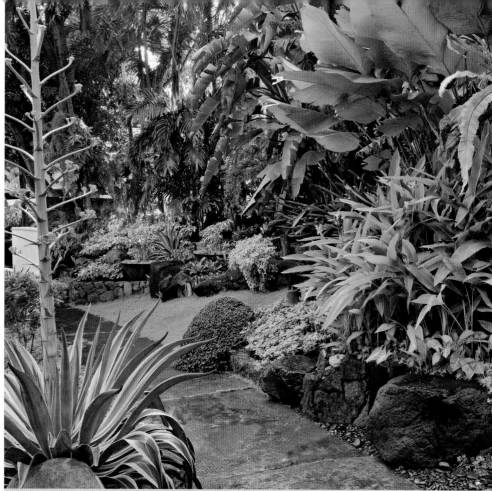

The relatively small garden seems much larger than its 200-sq-m (2,150 sq-ft) area, as Lazaro has created layer upon layer of interest, an important priority in a small garden. A variety of ferns cascades from the tall bamboo fence that borders the property along with steadfast climbers such as *Epipremnum aureum* and *Syngonium auritum*. Lazaro's first order of business was to plant fast growing shrubs and trees to provide shade over the more fragile plants in the garden. Palms create umbrellas for the Heliconias and Scheffleras that in turn shade and protect the understory of *Pilea nummulariifolia*, *Fittonia argentea* and *Selaginella cupressina* that blanket the garden floor. More ferns, Philodendrons, Bromeliads and Crotons mix with rare specimens of staghorn ferns and giant varieties of Japanese Anthurium. Splashes of color are provided by the maroon *Cordyline terminalis* enlivening the mostly green garden while leading the eye through the space that winds along the garden wall.

The owners, along with their designer, have created not just a tropical oasis here but a haven for all kinds of living things. Frogs, snails, goldfish, as well as butterflies and dragonflies, contribute to the delicate ecosystem created by this beautiful garden.

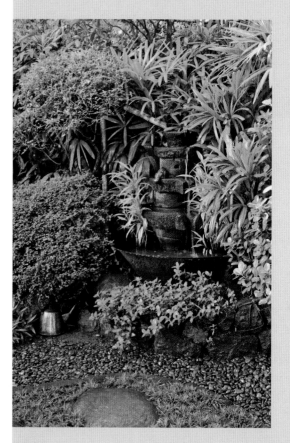

Previous pages top The stunning garden along the sidewalk is a magnificent display of layering and contrast.

Previous pages bottom left More contrasts: smooth river stones against rough stone wall and trough, bright green, velvety water lettuce against hairy, silvery Begonia.

Previous pages bottom right Two iron vats surrounded by *Schefflera arboricola* and *pandakaki*, hold Liya, *Lemna paucicostata*, a tiny, scale-like aquatic plant.

Above left A stone lantern lights up a corner of a small tea garden planted with Bromeliads, *Ficus benjamina* (weeping fig) and *Raphis excelsa*.

Above Another view of the sidewalk garden with lush plantings of bird-of-paradise, *Strelitzia reginae*, bird's nest ferns and clipped mounds of golden Duranta. To the left is an *Agave attenuata*.

Left A fountain fashioned out of stacked old sugarcane presses provides the soothing sound of water in this corner.

Right A variety of ferns and Bromeliads cascades down a rock wall complemented by plantings of Crotons, *Ficus benjamina*, *Schefflera arboricola*, and *Osmoxylon geelvinkianum*, below.

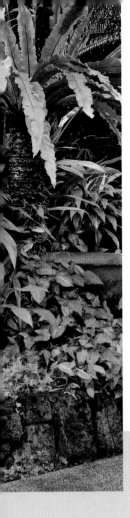

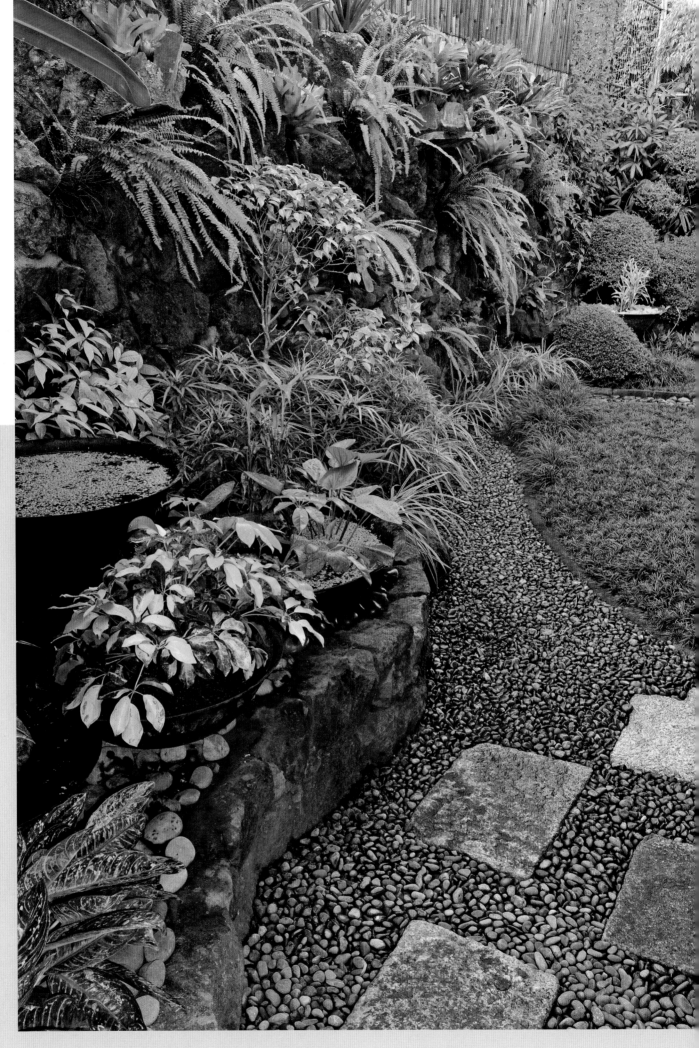

PATIS TESORO'S GARDEN
San Pablo, Laguna

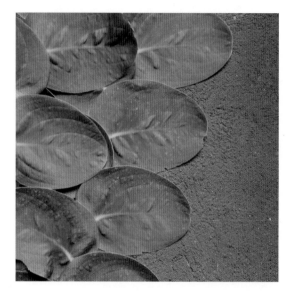

Hardwood trees dripping with Spanish moss (*Tillandsia usneoides*), graceful bamboo, some over 30 feet (9 m) tall, and lofty palms with outsized fronds, rustle in the gentle breeze screening Patis Tesoro's quiet sanctuary in Putol, San Pablo, Laguna. The house, designed along traditional Filipino lines, with a thatched roof and a series of indoor and outdoor areas separated by folding latticed doors with *capiz* shell panes, was inspired by the architecture of the area. The owner had envisioned a house that would be open and functional with a garden that was lush, wild and green.

Two decades on, the mature garden flows freely and embraces the two-story house on all sides. Complementing its native architectural materials, are towering golden bamboo, Indonesian bamboo, Buddha's-belly bamboo, black bamboo, and exuberant plantings of palm, Hibiscus, staghorn ferns and Dracaena. Majestic tree ferns mingle with Anthuriums and Alocasias. Cottage garden favorites such as Begonias and the Philippine *sampaguitas* (*Jasminum sambac*) join native wayside plants like Impatiens and common sword ferns.

Along the front entrance of the house, sliding *capiz* windows open to a verdant wall of tree ferns, climbing

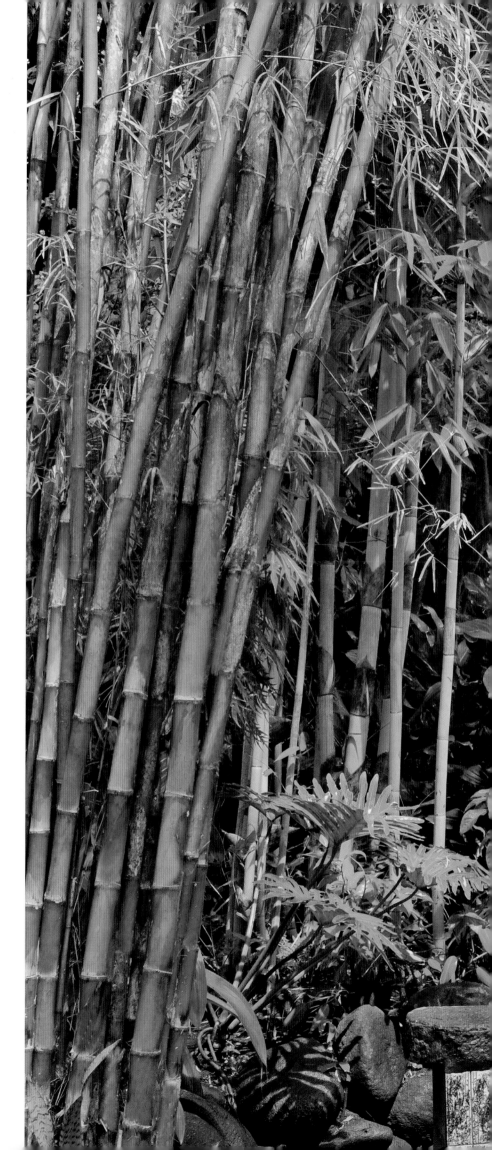

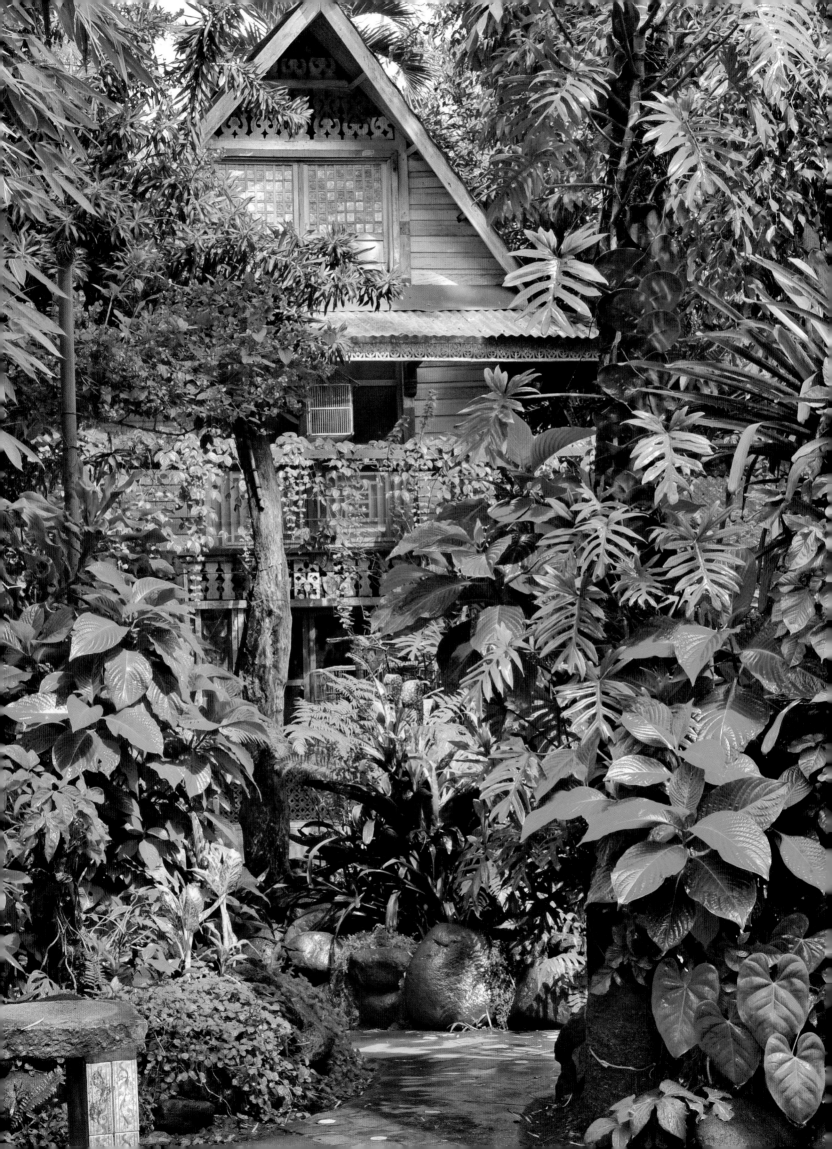

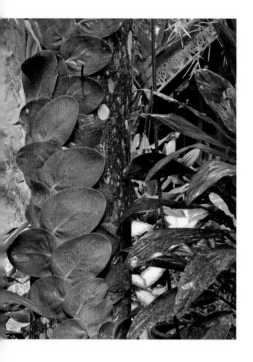

Philodendrons, Cordylines and Spathiphyllum. Tall stands of Heliconias cast filtered light over scallops of Anthuriums, lacy ferns and the evergreen *Monstera obliqua* that edge the pathways. In the front garden, spirit or *anito* stands made from dried coconut fiber are used as focal points to dramatize the lively compositions of Bromeliads and Mondo grass.

An inveterate collector, Tesoro's *objets trouvés* include rare garden antiques and architectural implements as well as old pieces of bric-a brac and discarded pieces of plumbing. In true Philippine spirit, she uses her recycled finds in innovative and unexpected ways, lurking as surprises amidst the foliage. Everywhere in this garden her manner of finding modern uses for old items has the brilliance of the obvious. "What draws me to an object is texture and form, and, because I am a gardener, I can look at a piece and see how it can become part of the garden," says Tesoro. "With the hope that in time, like the garden, it will have a life of its own."

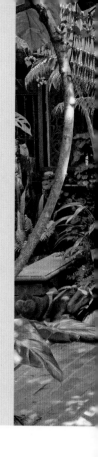

Previous pages large photo The lush, wild garden of Patis Tesoro in Putol, Laguna.

Previous pages small photo Close-up of the robust climbing shingle plant, *Rhaphidophora celatocaulis*.

Left The shingle plant on a tree trunk juxtaposed against a *ti* plant.

Right Tree ferns, Anthuriums, Alocasias and Philodendron provide an exotic backdrop to a cozy seating area under a canopy of flowering *Thunbergia mysorensis*.

Below left Antique finds in a corner of the garden.

Opposite below left The front façade is enlivened with a trellis dripping with *Petraeovitex wolfei*, a vine commonly known as Nong Nooch vine, after the Nong Nooch garden in Pattaya, Thailand, where it was first grown.

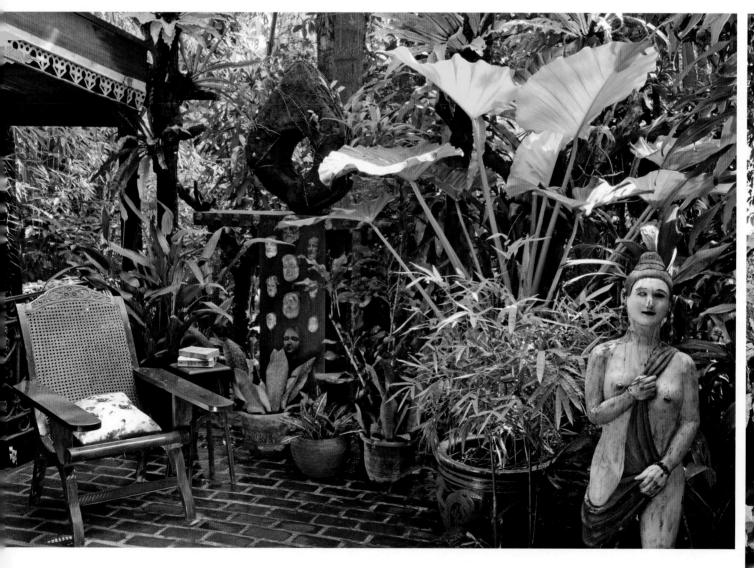

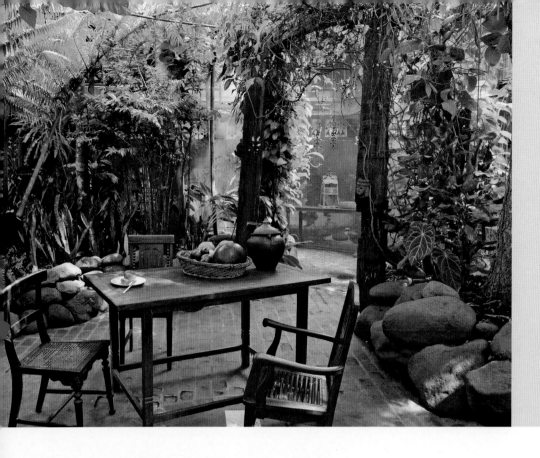

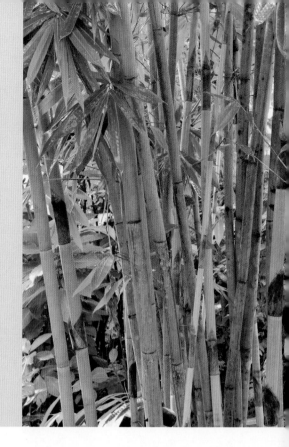

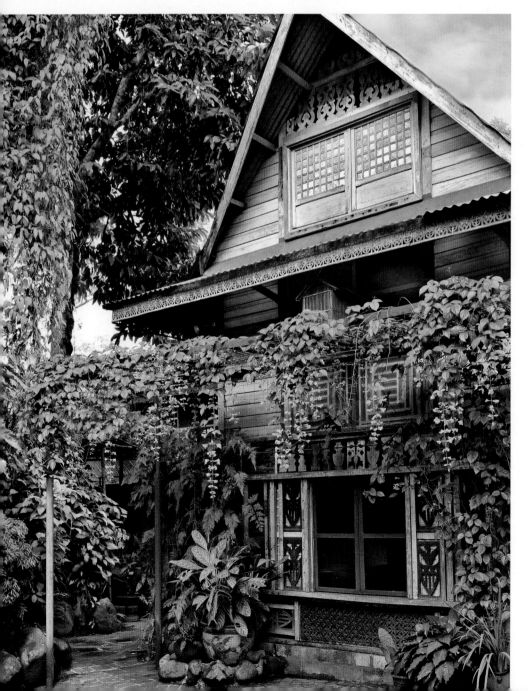

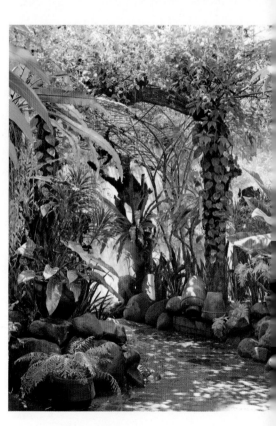

Top *Bambusa vulgaris*, otherwise known as golden bamboo, is just one of many different varieties of bamboo in this garden.

Above Vine laden tree trunks underplanted with Anthuriums provide sheltered walkways in this tropical country retreat. Here, a chinaman's hat or *Holmskioldia sanguinea*, a scrambling shrub, blooms with red flowers above.

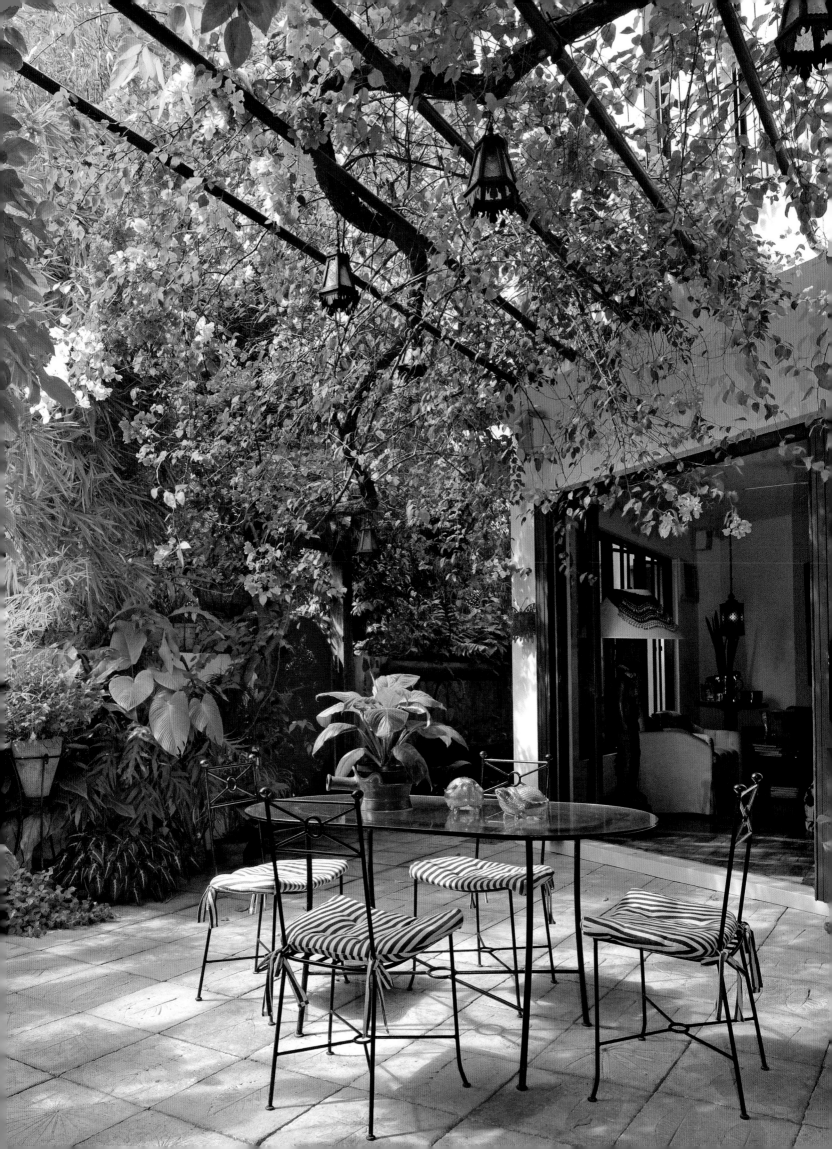

GARDEN OF BUTTERFLIES

Ayala Alabang

Designed by Emily Campos

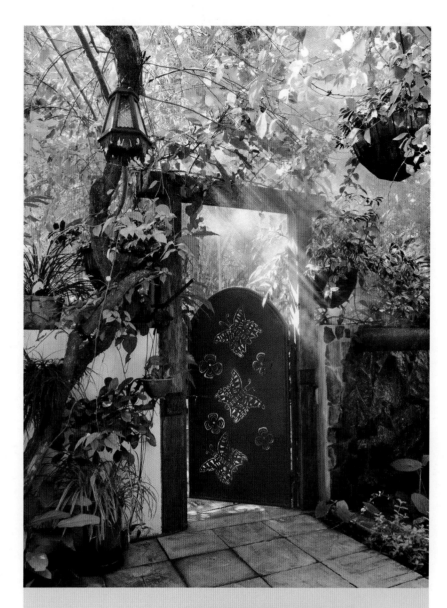

Located in the gated community of Ayala Alabang is the property of Emily Campos, an erstwhile homewares exporter who most recently switched to designing bags. The 200 sq meter (2,150 sq ft) garden replaced an old house and garden and, today, has grown to surround the new house, creating a series of "rooms."

The walled enclosures form and knit together the structure of the garden. The master plan was achieved by creating these "exterior garden rooms" which facilitate easy circulation around the property. The structure engages the imagination and enchants the eye as one makes one's way through the enclosures. Each room is unique with its own plants, garden ornaments, tables and chairs; all provide places where one can sit, eat and relax.

A butterfly theme resonates within the garden. You find the ephemeral creature as wall fixtures, hanging as mobiles and in fabrics, further reinforcing the tropical mood. A courtyard just off the living room, resplendent with pink and white Bougainvillea, is shady and cool. The vigorous climbing Bougainvillea, a prominent feature of the garden, grows on an adjacent mango tree. During the construction phase it was painstakingly diverted from the site, then slowly guided back to the trellis when the construction was complete. Now, it provides flower power to this predominantly green garden.

The owner is very much a hands-on gardener, all the time adding and subtracting to her collection of plants. She is quick to point out that a garden should maintain interest throughout the growing season so tropical stand-bys like bamboo and palms are mixed with outstanding foliage plants like Anthuriums and Philodendrons and texturally impressive grasses and ferns. The garden has served as a laboratory for trying and propagating plants, which she loves to share with her gardening buddies.

Almost other-worldly, this garden is reminiscent of the magical Oriental gardens of old; divided by arcades and green walls, its enclosures make nature feel at home.

Opposite A courtyard ablaze with pink and white bougainvillea just off the living room serves as an extension of living and dining areas.

Above A metal gate with butterfly and floral cutout designs leads to the garden beyond.

Right A little side garden with a water feature can be viewed from the living room.

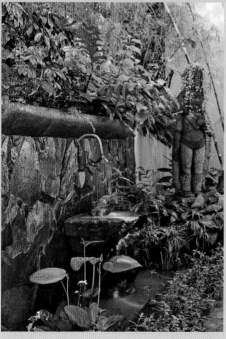

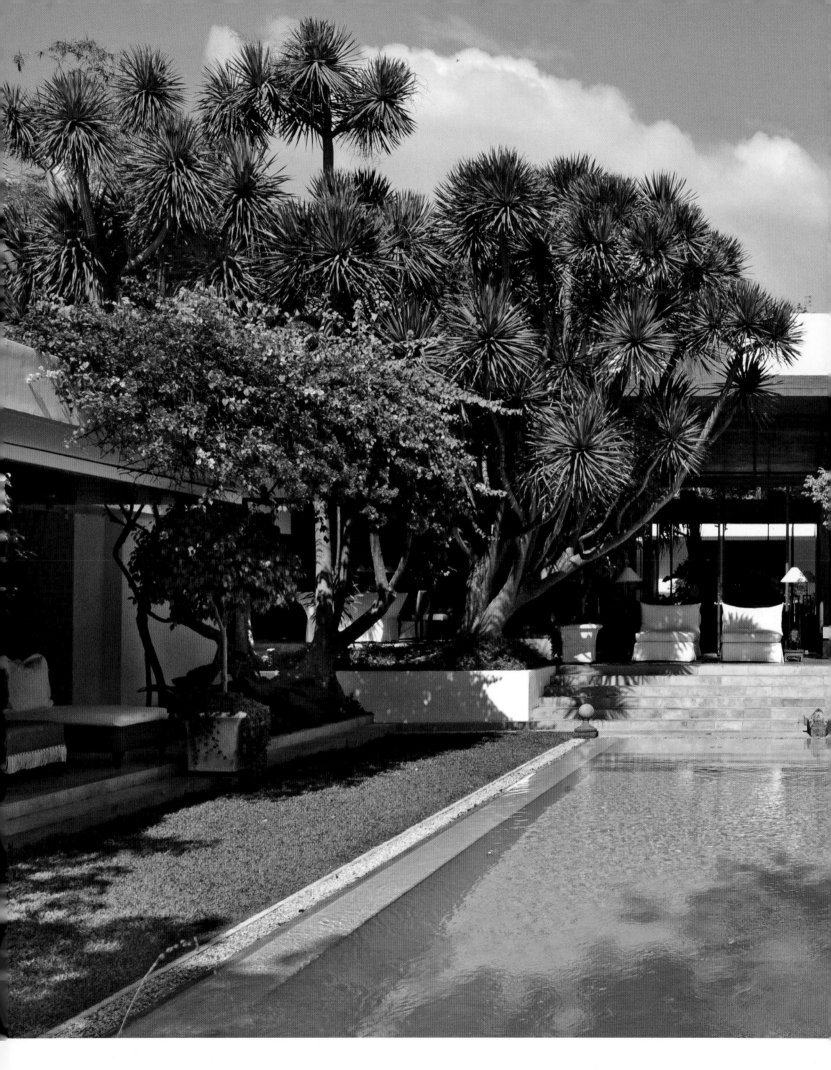

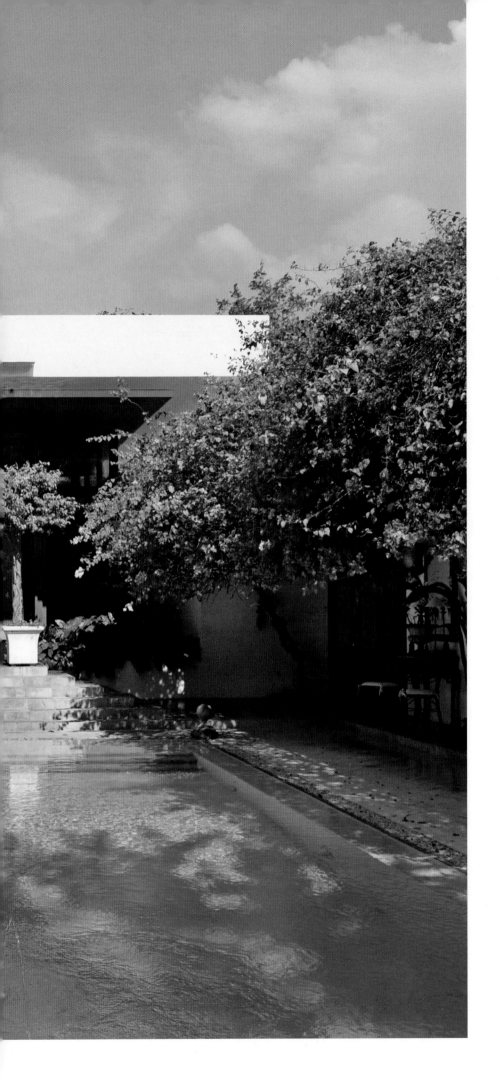

POOLSIDE PROSCENIUM

Forbes Park, Makati
Designed by Ponce Veridiano

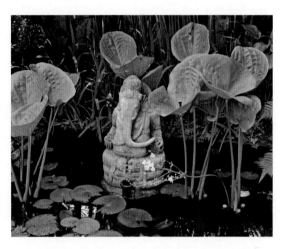

A union of indoor and outdoor living, this garden-oriented house can best be described as transparent. Built of concrete and glass, everything in this modern house conspires to direct one's attention to the outdoors. The u-shaped structure that houses the bedrooms on one side and the den and guest room on the other side looks out onto a garden dominated by a rectangular, turquoise pool. A focal point of the garden, this prominent water feature was carefully designed to sharply mirror the architecture of the house and its surrounding trees and to contrast with the other dark reflecting ponds on the property.

A paving of French limestone connects the pool with the garden and when the tall, pivoting glass doors are open, the outside and inside merge, thereby allowing movement from the water garden at the entry of the house to the living room, from the living room to the pool, from the den to the garden. Pocket gardens poised off the library and dining room also bring the garden inside and extend the interiors outward.

The garden-loving homeowner and her landscape designer, Ponce Veridiano, chose the color, plants and landscape materials to produce a flowing, interconnected series of spaces. Certain Veridiano trademarks are visible here: the use of clipped box balls of Fukien tea and Eugenia scattered about the garden, winding paths that weave alternately through dense plantings and sunny spaces, and sweeps of a single color that allow the eye to

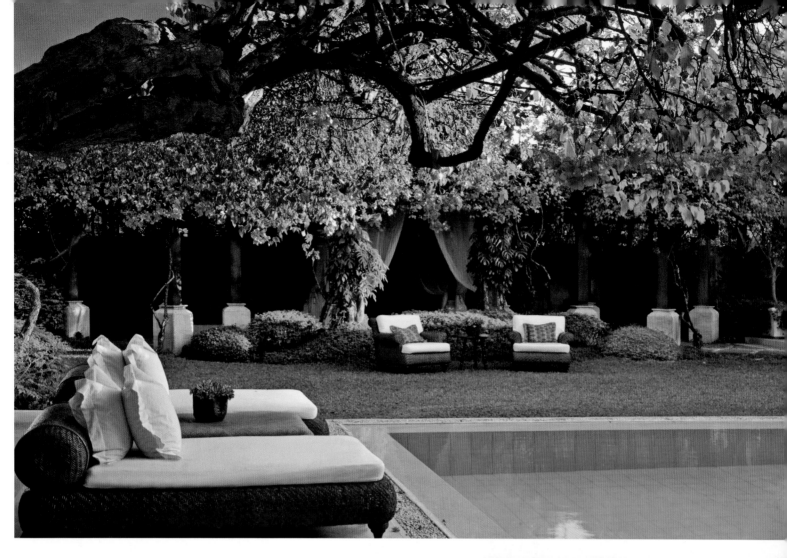

rest. Palms, Dracaéna, Heliconias and mature trees along
the perimeter wall screen the property from nearby houses.

As well as being appropriate to the sense of place
and providing a habitat for wildlife and otherworldly
creatures (yes, there is a resident "faerie" here named
Federico with his own spirit house), the wall of green
anchors the house. For the hardscape, the pair chose
white pebbles, *piedra China* and limestone. The distinctive
paving allows for a crisp, highly polished look and serves
as a great foil for the verdant greenery. All the natural and
man-made elements unite into a harmonious whole.

In this compact, yet powerfully designed garden,
the owner and designer have tackled the challenges of
breaking down barriers and choreographing movement
through space—and have succeeded with flying colors.

Above A well-established pink
Bougainvillea cultivar provides
shade to various seating areas
around the sparkling pool.

Right The house of Federico,
resident "faerie", presides over
a limestone patio enlivened with
Ficus, Heliconias, Draceana, bird's
nest ferns and clipped balls of
Eugenia and Fukien tea.

Bottom left and far right
Scupltural effects are provided
by exposed roots growing on a
wall of the entry courtyard and
dramatic foliage of Philodendron
planted underneath some tree
trunks by the pool.

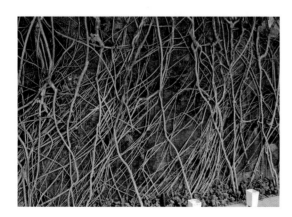

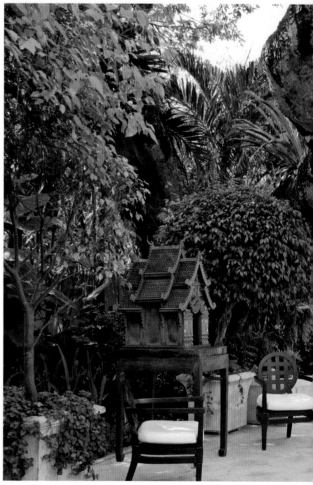

Previous pages main photo
The focal point of the garden, the rectangular turquoise-blue swimming pool, sharply mirrors the surrounding trees.

Previous pages small photo
A stone statue of Ganesh dominates the small ornamental pond.

Right A curtain of Bougainvillea shades a pair of poolside loungers. The Bougainvillea, a semi-woody climber native to South America is now one of the most popular ornamental plants in the Philippines.

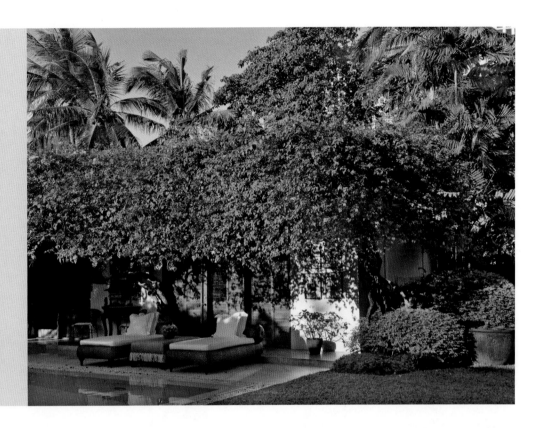

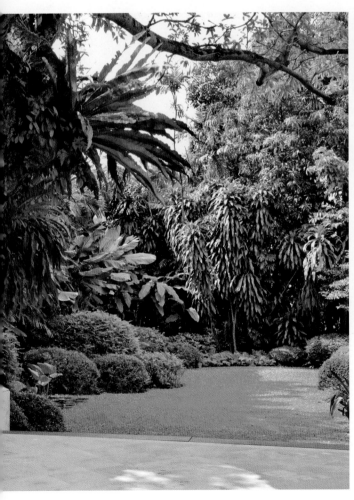

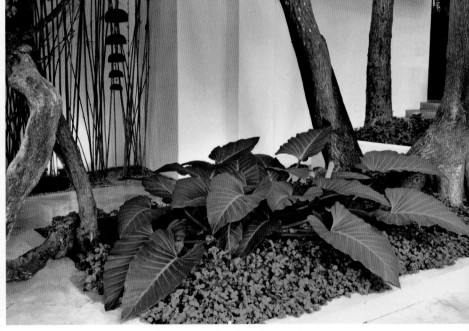

AN ARTIST'S ROOFTOP GARDEN

Tandang Sora, Quezon City
Designed by Bobby Gopiao

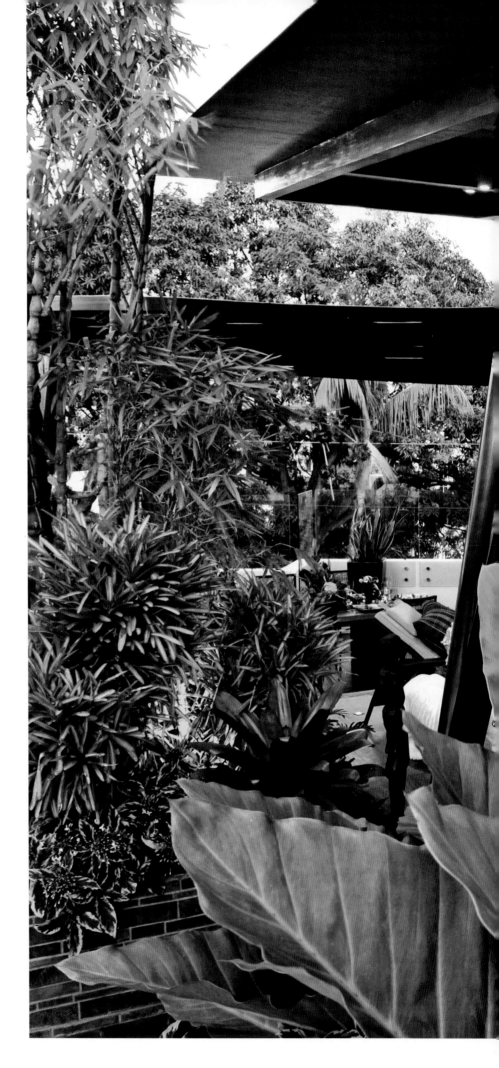

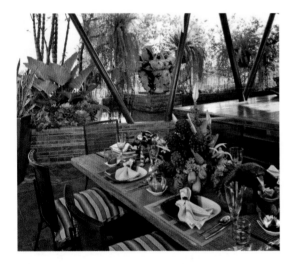

The roof deck garden of contemporary artist Ronald Ventura, is situated atop his three-story studio home in Quezon City. From the street looking up, the Artist's Deck, as it is called, is topped by a "beehive" roof of yellow fiberglass. Landscape designer Bobby Gopiao designed the 270 sq-m (322 sq-yard) open-air roof deck. The designer, inspired by the hyperrealist artworks of his friend, wanted something modern yet functional where Ventura and his wife could entertain their friends.

He divided the space into two areas—a raised, covered platform with a teak floor flanked by a pond on one side to serve as the living and dining room, and a tiled open space designated as the skylight terrace. Steel-plated roofs supported by iron posts lead the eye through the space to highlight the wooden deck's dramatic structure. Thick beds with Buddha's-belly bamboo, underplanted with Vrieseas and variegated Cleredendrons and punctu-

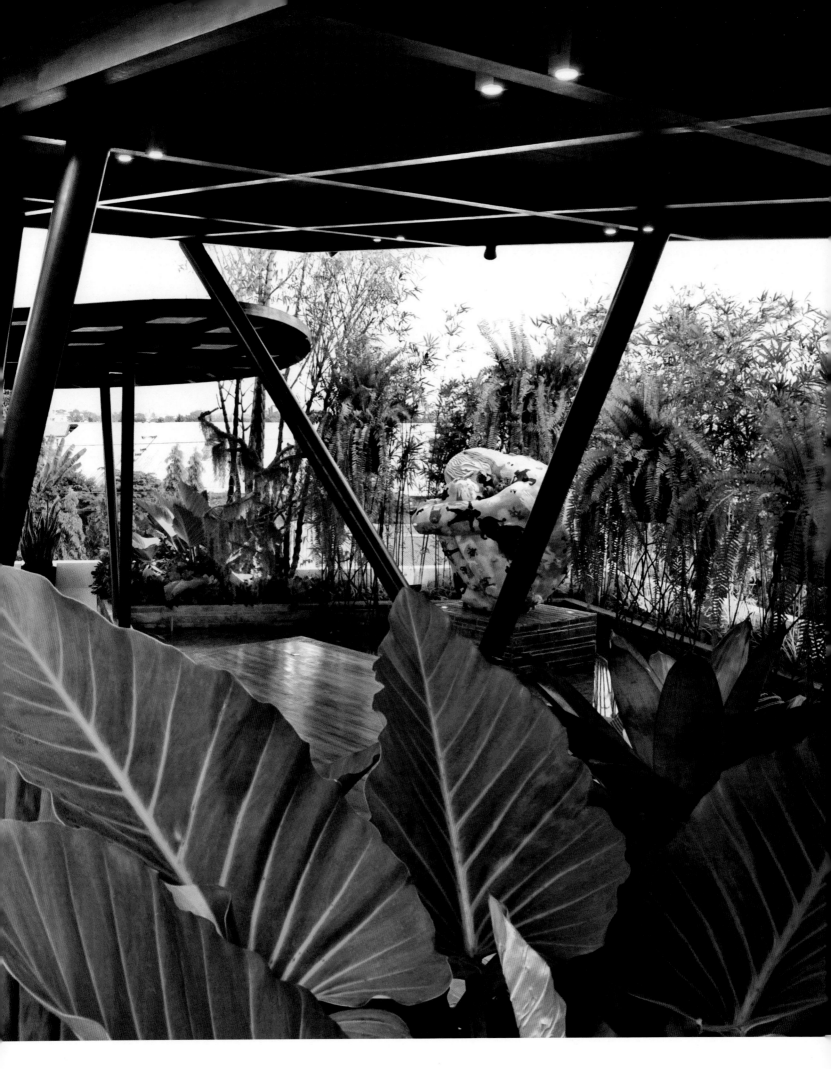

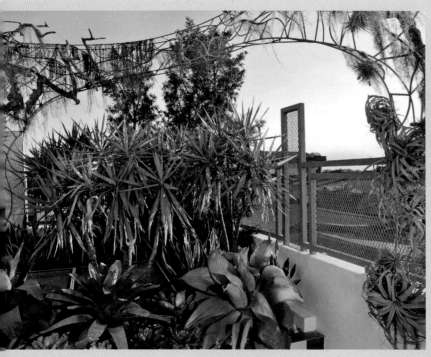
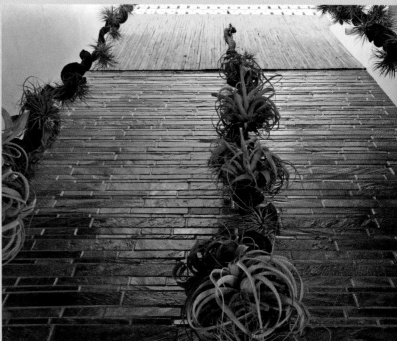

Previous pages main photo
The artist's deck and garden, shown here with its two contrasting roof treatments. The pond with central sculpture is surrounded by feathery bamboo and ferns.

Previous page small photo
The roof garden affords ample space for dining alfresco.

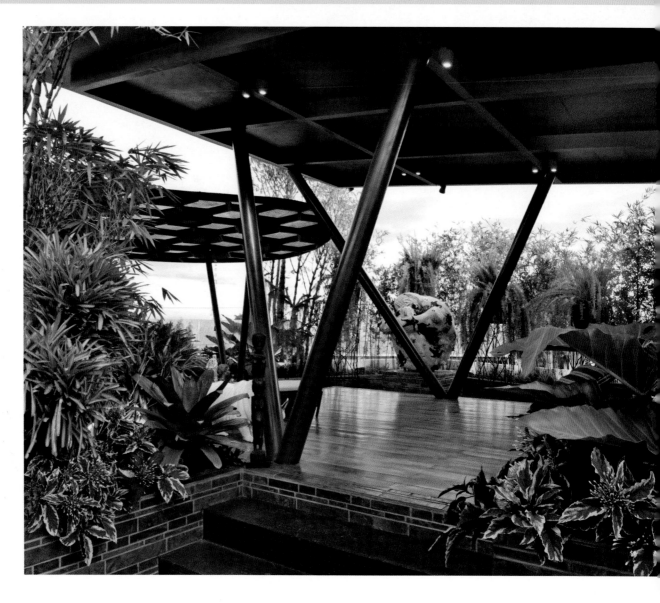

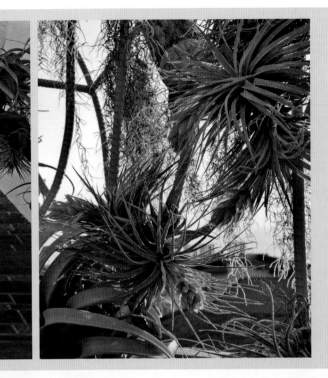

ated with *Imperialis rubra* and a gigantic Philodendron mark the entrance to the roof garden space while green, feathery bamboo screens the high deck from outside view.

Three wrought iron stands hold up cascading Peruvian ferns over the pond and frame the imposing male nude sculpture crouched into a ball. This modern art piece, a self-portrait of the artist, dominates the pond and is one of the focal points in the garden. Glass panels printed with images from the artist's library serve as graphic accents and separate the dining from the living area.

Just off the living/dining area is the outdoor terrace. Open to the sky with a checkerboard floor (a homage to details in Ventura's early paintings) this space is planted with graphic and sculptural specimens—Bromeliads, false Yucca, and Maguey (Agave sp). Continuing the slightly surreal theme, a dramatic trellis, fashioned out of twisted wrought iron spiked with the ephiphyte Tillandsia, lends just the right abstract flavor to the surroundings. Designer Gopiao calls this "the arid side of the deck; it's bolder and more dramatic especially at night."

Far left Sculptural plantings of false Yucca, Bromeliads and Maguey border the outdoor part of the roof terrace.

Left center Recurved, silvery-gray rosettes of *Tillandsia duratii* hang like garlands over the artist's home from the skylight terrace above.

Left Exotic air plants, *Tillandsia bergeri*, with small, stiff, gray-green leaves and showy pink bracts, cling to the trellis.

Below left A metal-framed wooden roof supported by iron posts highlights the rooftop deck's dramatic structure.

Below A dramatic screen and trellis fashioned out of twisted iron bars and spiked with Tillandsia separates the outdoor terrace with a checkerboard floor from the raised covered platform with a teak floor.

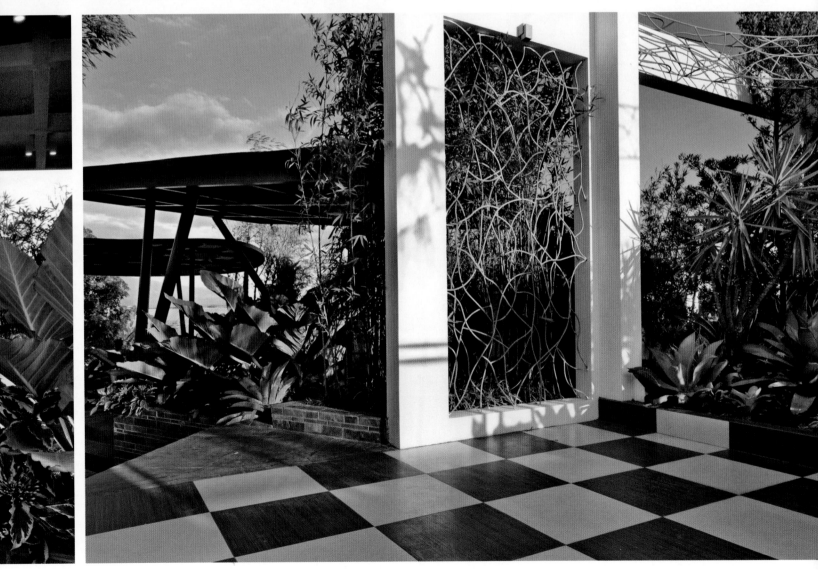

BONSAI GARDEN
Greenhills, San Juan, Manila
Designed by Bobby Gopiao

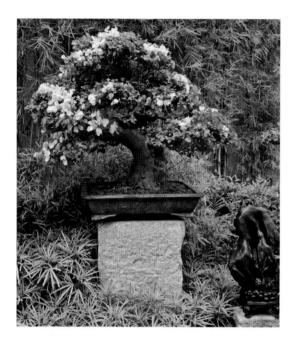

Bonsai is the Japanese art of cultivating trees and shrubs in pots to create art forms by a special technique of wiring and pinching of the branches. Encapsulating aspects of art, history and gardening, this ancient form of arboriculture is attracting a legion of fans. The owner of this garden, a man of refined taste, had over the years developed a fascination for bonsai. As his passion grew, so did his desire to have a garden where he could indulge his interest in these amazing dwarfed specimens. Enlisting the help of landscape designer, Bobby Gopiao (also a bonsai collector himself), he requested a design for a small garden behind his modern house to showcase his growing bonsai collection. Together they created what can best be described as a little "jewel of a garden".

Appropriately, tall graceful stands of bamboo screen the perimeter wall of the property, giving the surroundings an inately Asian ambiance. From the minute you step into the garden—accessed via a gravel path of white stones—you feel you have entered a place of calm and serenity. The lovely bonsai collection, individually potted to show each species' particular characteristics, shines in its Japanese garden setting. Stone lanterns enhance the Oriental feeling and establish a sense of place, while stone and wood plinths act as bonsai supports.

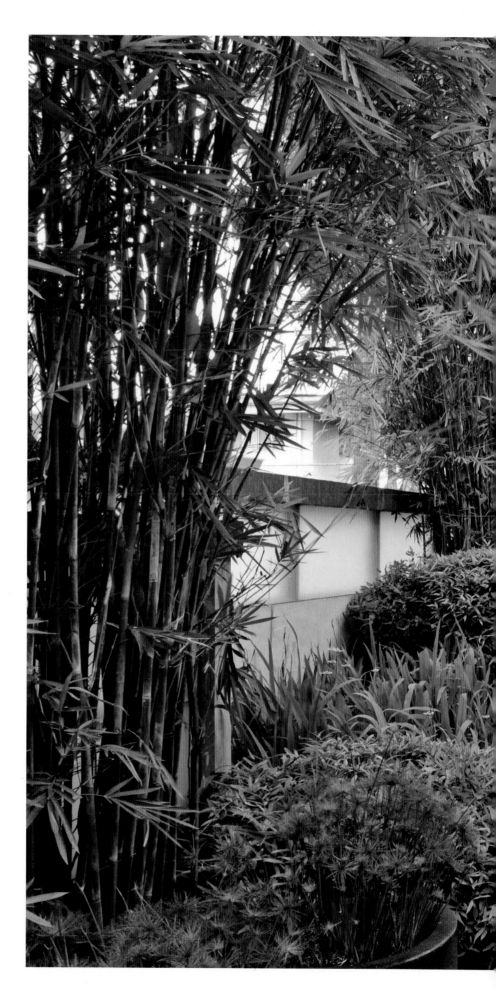

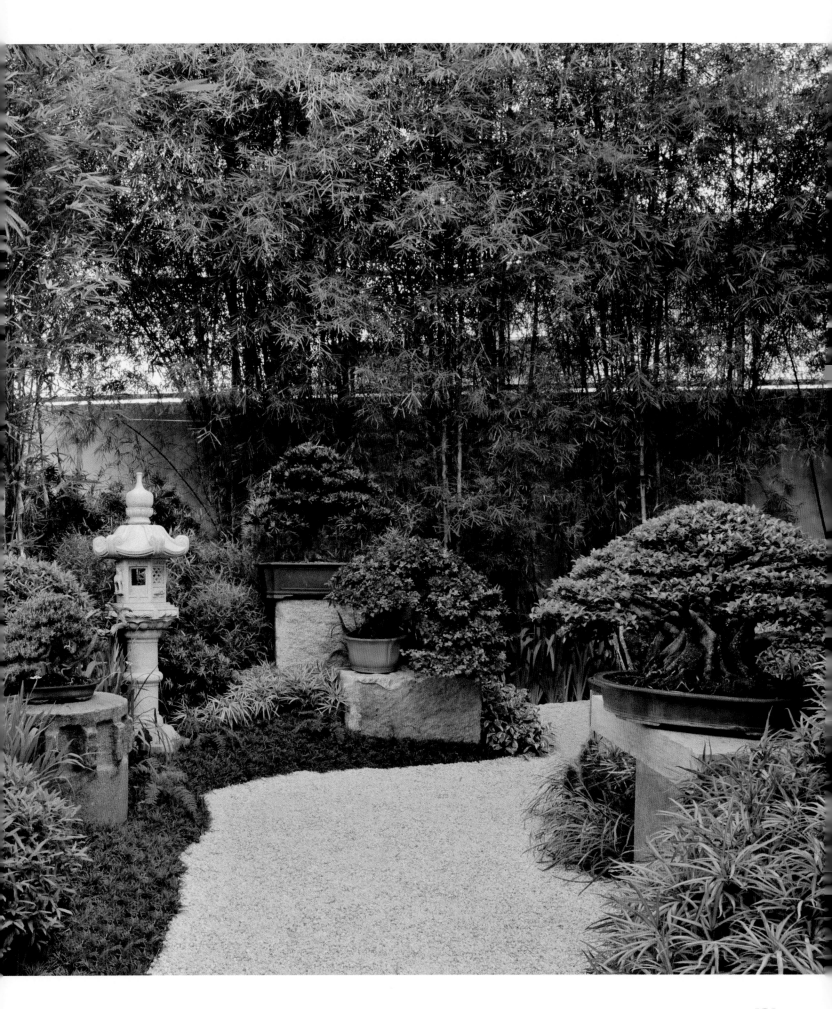

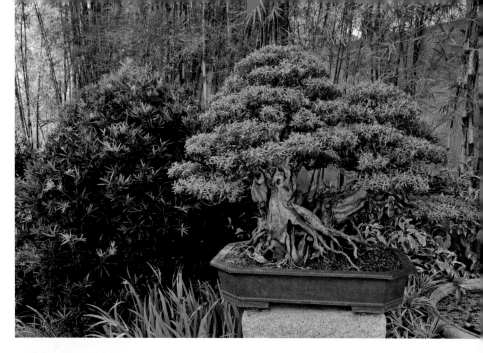

Artfully poised along the narrow path, bordered by ornamental grass and architecturally clipped shrubs of Podocarpus and Eugenia, the various bonsai specimens compete for attention. Around a bend, at the far end of the garden sits a native *bantigue* (*Pemphis acidula*); usually found growing in coral rocks in the Philippines, it is just bursting into flower. Just below is a ravishing orangey-pink bougainvillea, also in flower.

Though Japanese in inspiration, with a number of very costly and highly collectible bonsais from Taiwan, many of the specimens are native to the country. This exquisite walled garden displays a keen sense of Philippine rectitude and resilience.

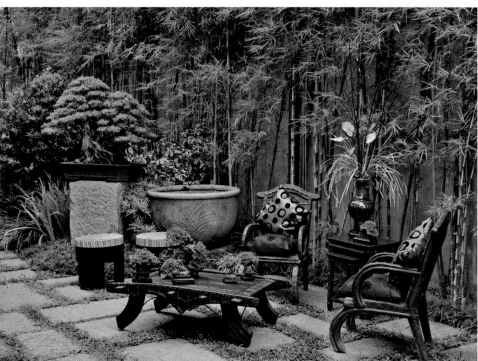

Previous pages main photo The lovely bonsai collection, individually potted to show each plant's particular characteristics, shines in its Japanese-inspired garden setting.

Previous pages small photo A pink and white Bougainvillea bonsai in flower sits above a bed of *Osmoxylon geelvinkianum*.

Opposite Two elegant bonsai specimens are displayed on *kamagong* stands along with an oriental jar in a corner of the owner's home. The tall stand houses a silver leaf bonsai from the Eloganeous species while the short stand has a *Lantana camara*.

Left Tall stands of graceful bamboo screen the perimeter wall providing an Asian ambiance to the surroundings.

Above A particular favorite, the *Pemphis acidula*, which is native to the Philippines is prized for the rugged character and shape of its trunk.

Bottom left A favorite amongst bonsai specialists, this *Serrisa foetida* is a handsome specimen. The Serissa produces numerous small funnel shaped flowers, hence its common name "tree of a thousand stars."

Bottom right To keep his Bougainvillea bonsai in flower, the owner of this bonsai collection makes sure that the soil is nearly always dry. As with the normal sized Bougainvillea, this specimen does not like to be over watered.

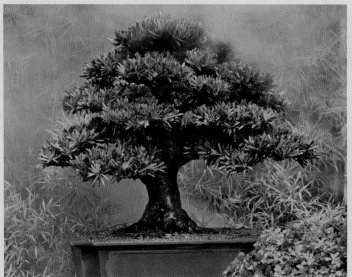

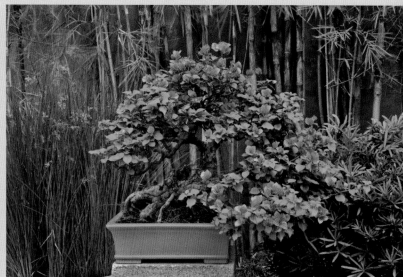

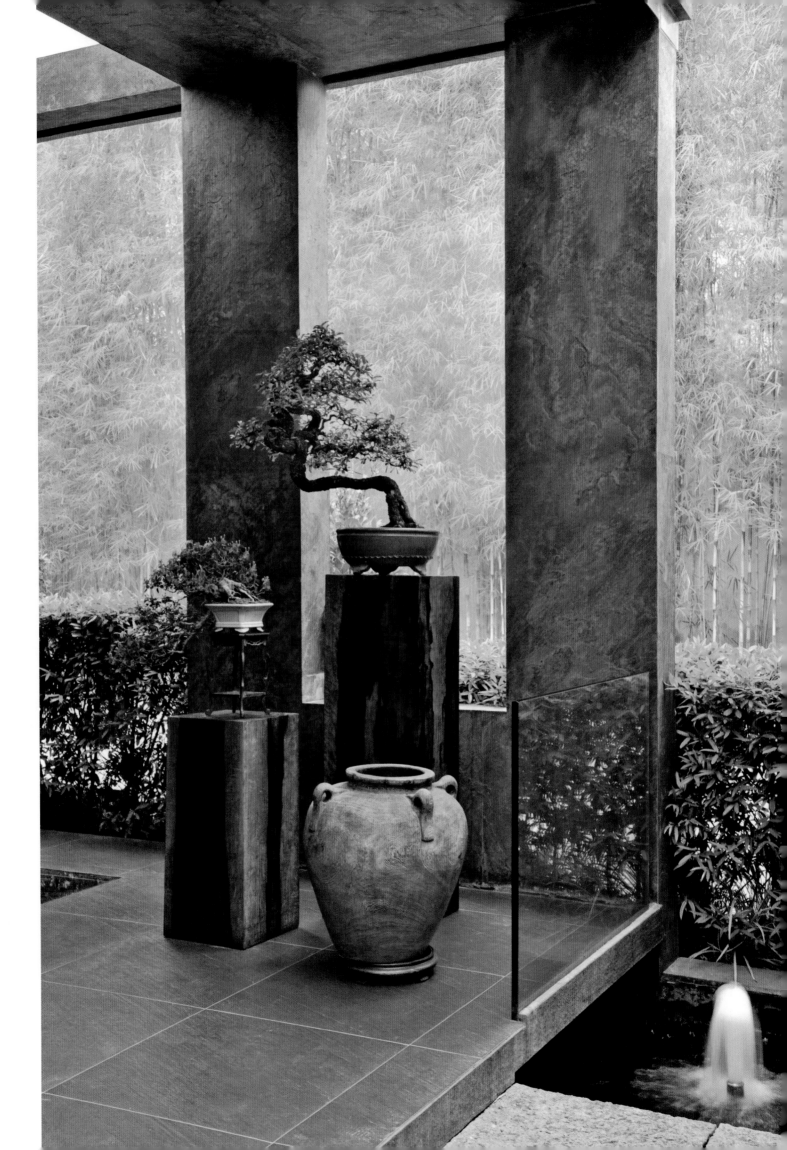

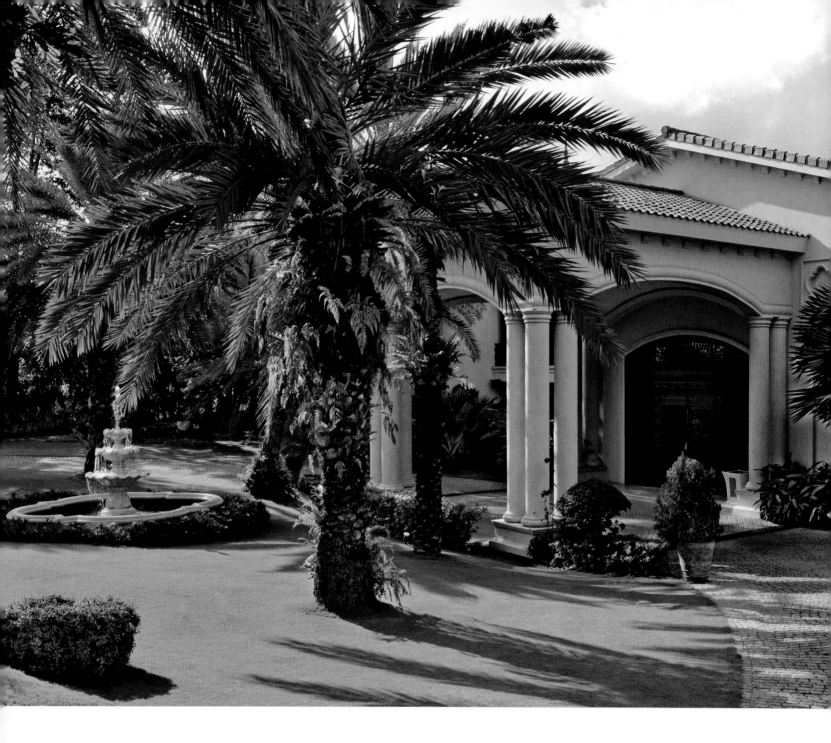

A PALM LOVER'S GARDEN

Maria Luisa Subdivision, Cebu
Designed by Jaime Chua

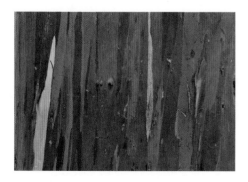

A long paved driveway takes the visitor into this large, sprawling property enclosed by a fine hedge. In the heat of the day one delights in entering this oasis of calm. The garden is awash with the sound of water from a fountain, which greets you as you approach the house, rendering a soothing spell on your mind and body.

The landscaping scheme designed by Jaime Chua is centered around a classic Mediterranean villa set on a gently rolling manicured lawn punctuated with formal beds of clipped shrubs and ornamental borders. A variety of palms dots the landscape and enhances the tropical character of the garden. These solitary eye-catchers lead your eye through the landscape. A major component in the garden, they comprise: sugar palms (*Arenga pinnata*), royal palms (*Roystonea regia*), majestic fan palms from Madagascar (*Bismarckia nobilis*) and African oil palms (*Elaeis guineensis*), native to West Africa. These tall specimens

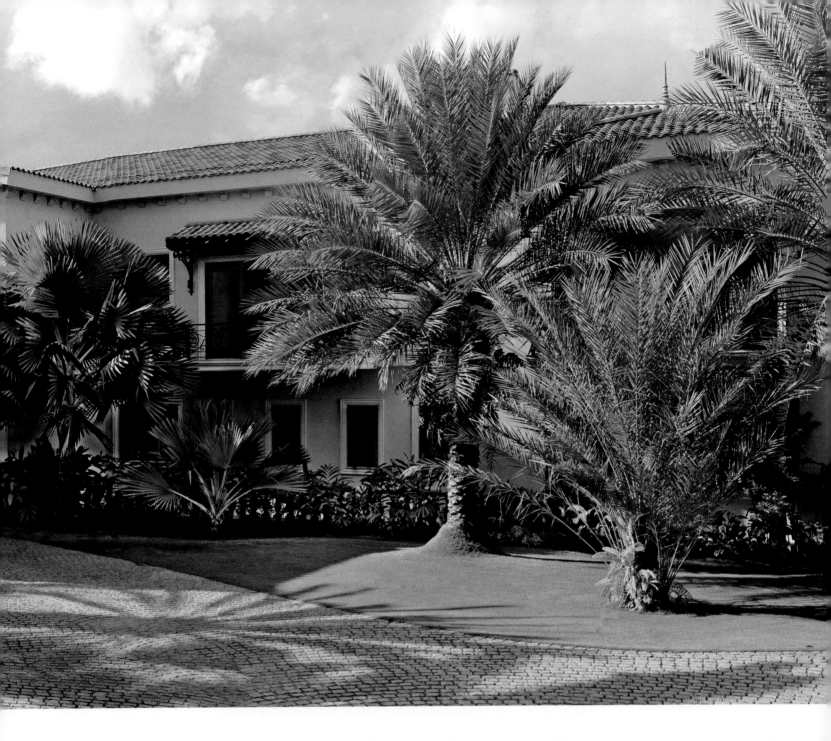

Above A grand Mediterranean-style villa greets the visitor at the end of a long bricked driveway.

Right The gleaming turquoise pool is one of the focal points of the garden.

Opposite below Close-up view of the bark of an Australian Eucalyptus tree.

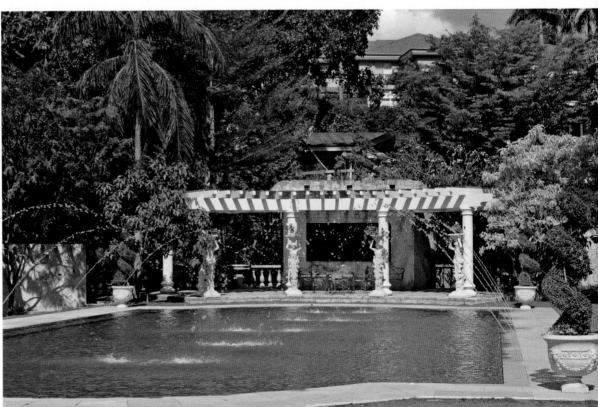

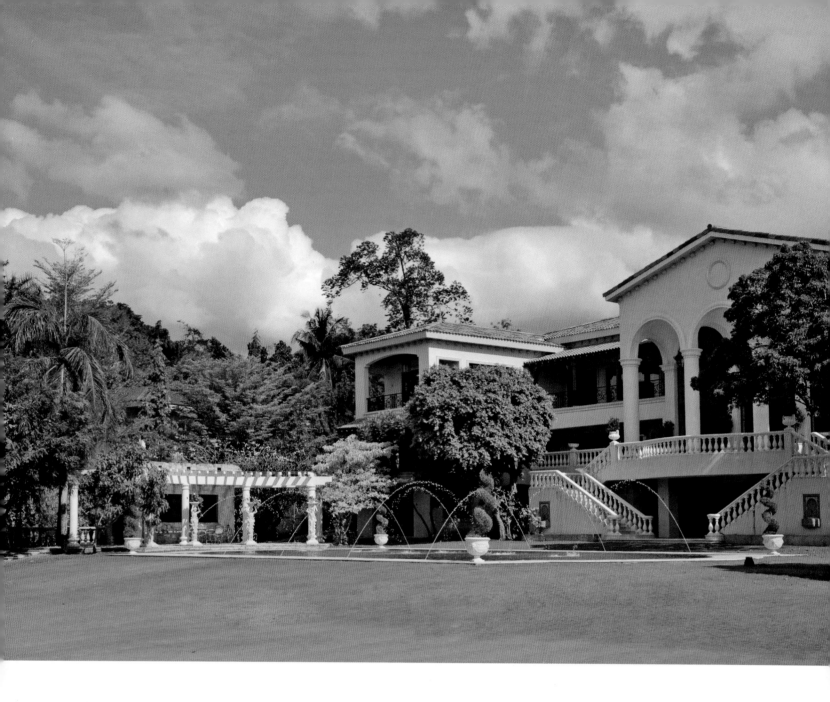

with ringed trunks and feathery fronds are the source of palm oil and are not commonly found in this part of the country. The owner loves to recount how he has spent years collecting and propagating his palm collection.

The rear façade of the house extends out to a large and elegant terrace with a balustrade that looks out onto a magnificent pool with jets of sparkling water. Down one side of the horseshoe-shaped staircase is a limestone pavilion with a pergola that provides shade and space for entertaining. The graceful structure frames a posse of classic statues of Grecian maidens pouring water into the pool. Jets of water from the pool's outer rim shoot into the air mimicking the vertical lines of frangipani and Australian eucalyptus trees.

The design of this relatively new garden remains faithful to a formal style and provides a panorama both true and borrowed; all sorts of architectural elements help to knit the garden's structure with the house.

Above A large and elegant terrace with a balustrade looks out onto a magnificent pool with jets of sparkling water.

Opposite top A three-tiered fountain and a collection of palms including African oil palms contribute to the exotic tropical character of this garden.

Opposite bottom left Clipped rounded shrubs provide sculptural contrast against a vertical hedge.

Opposite bottom center A walkway cloaked in pristine white and scented *Thunbergia fragrans* exudes romance.

Opposite bottom right The ocher-colored house replete with arches and balconies is glimpsed through an African oil palm underplanted with Heliconias.

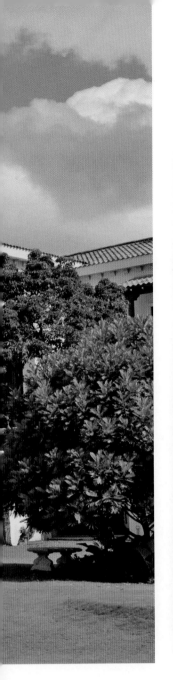
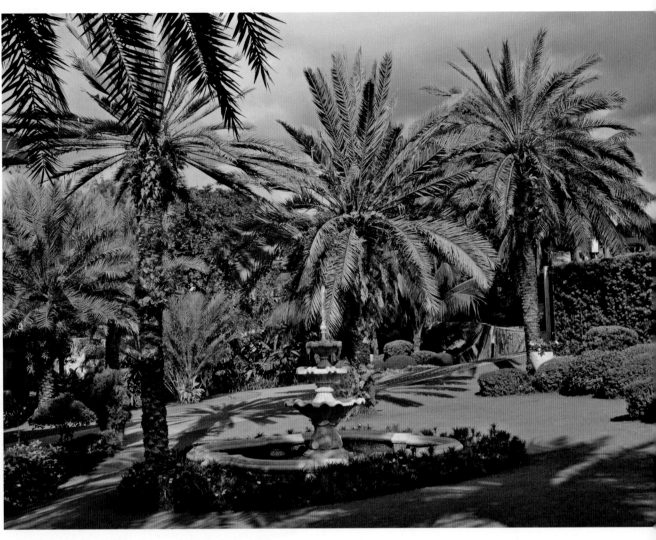
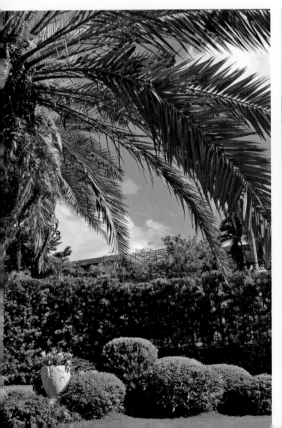
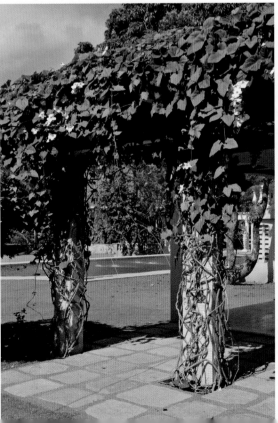
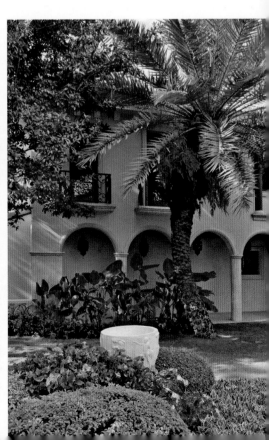

TESSA VALDES WATER FOUNTAINS

Forbes Park, Makati

Designed by Frank Borja and Shirley Sanders

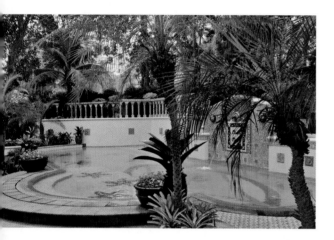

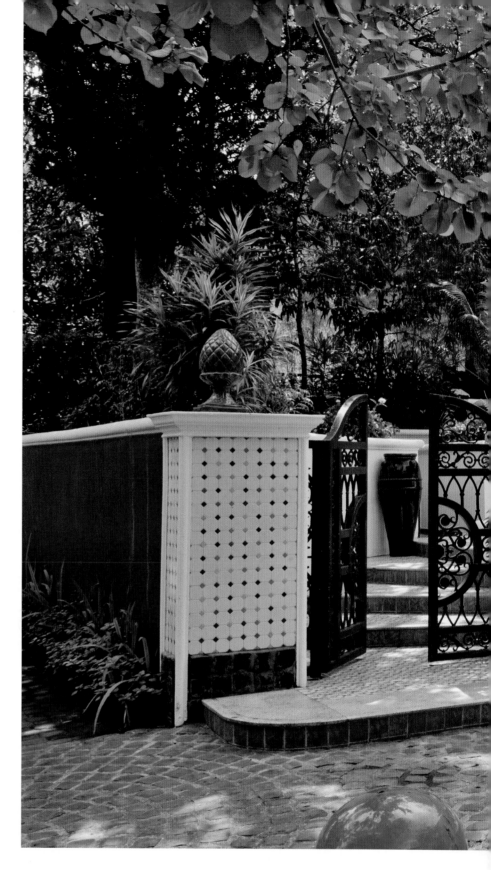

While on a grand tour of Venice with her husband, Tessa Valdes discovered the architecture and gardens of the Italian Renaissance and, like many others, found inspiration in the water gardens and enriched façades of the Italian villas she saw. She returned to the Philippines and built a neo-Gothic Venetian-style mansion in the leafy enclave of Forbes Park in Makati.

About six years ago, she approached landscape designer Frank Borja to help her complement the architecture with a garden design. Together they decided on a multi-tiered fountain up front and a large patio with a swimming pool with a fountain out back. The patio, though Italianate in feeling, features the colors of Spanish and Portuguese ceramics.

Some three years later, garden landscaper, Shirley Sanders, was brought in to supervise the plantings. The spirit is of a *jardin exotique,* one planted with a variety of exotic tropical specimens such as ferns, Bromeliads and palms. The palm was a clever choice because of its size and its power to suggest exotic lands. On each side of the swimming pool are colorful pots filled with flowers of the season. Visible from many parts of the house, the trefoil-shaped swimming pool is an impressive sight. The grandiose water feature presides over the patio, the focal point of the garden.

It should be mentioned that this water-themed garden is not meant to strike strong architectural chords but is rather playful, seeming to treat its design and ornamen-

tation more from a dramatic perspective. The approach is distinctly theatrical (like its owner who happens to be a television personality) with its balustraded walls and niches. Similarly, the water feature in the front delights passersby with the sound of water.

The sound of splashing water and dripping fountains enlivens the Valdes garden and echoes throughout the entire space. The owners and their designers have tried to stimulate the imagination as well as the physical senses by evoking an exotic faraway land.

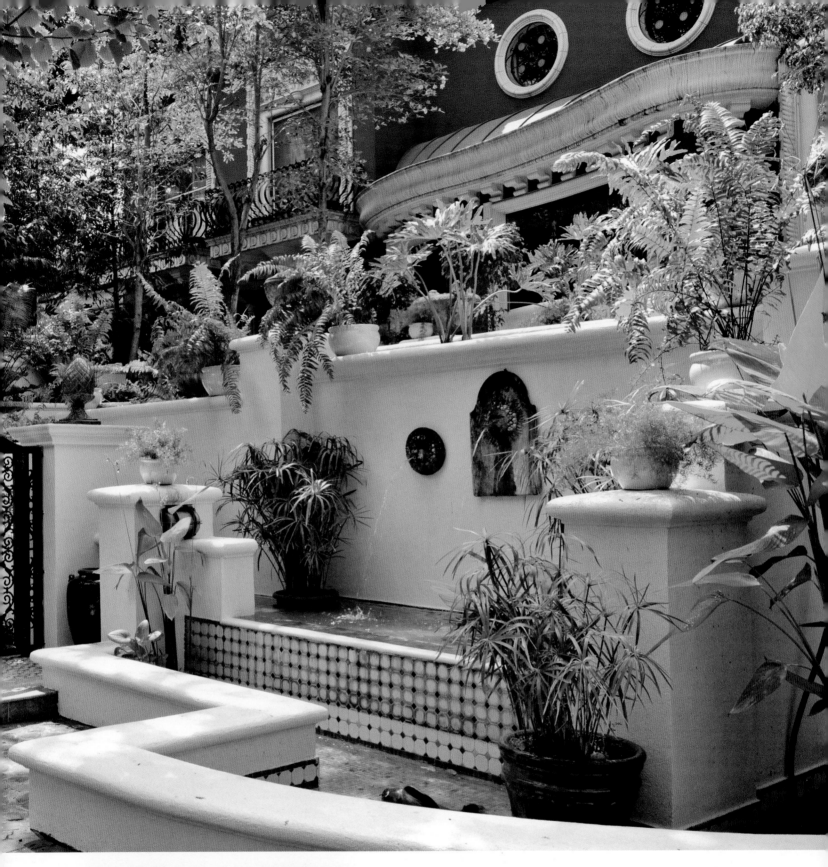

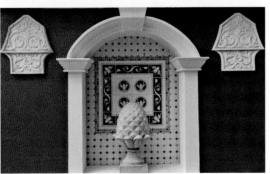

Above A tiled fountain fronting the street decorated with potted Philodendrons, ferns, umbrella plants and blue ceramic pots delights passersby with the sound of splashing water.

Opposite The *jardin exotique* at the back of the house features a trefoil-shaped swimming pool.

Left A tiled niche on the wall decorated with an acorn finial.

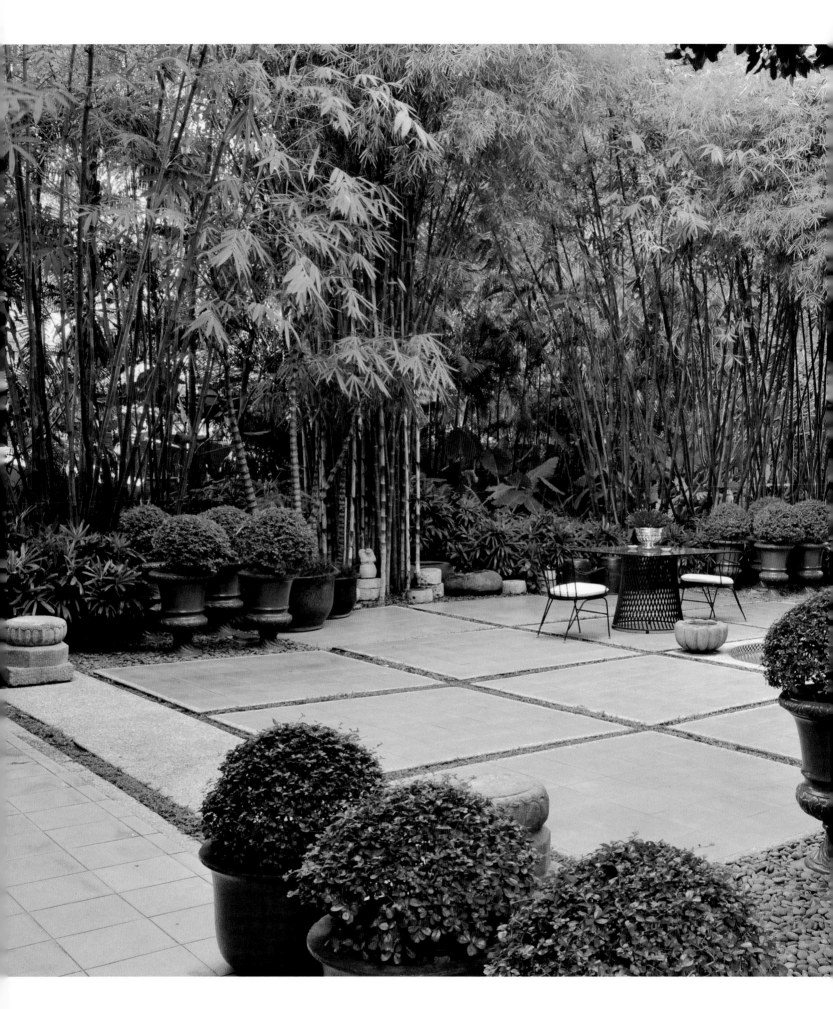

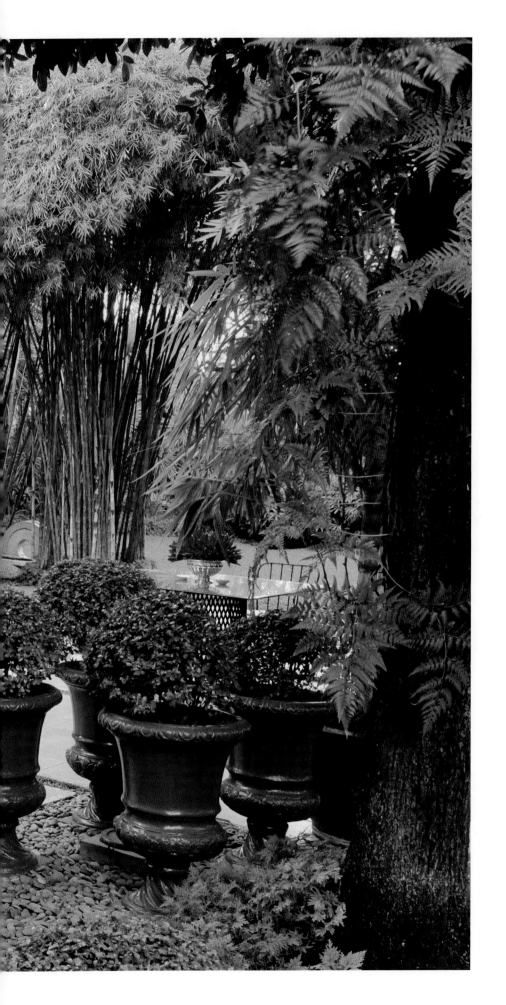

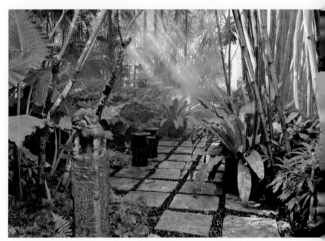

Ramon Antonio is a proponent of the chic, urban look for city gardens that highlights clean lines, manicured lawns and rigid paving. His work reflects the crossover between a Philippine tropical planting tradition and an architectural awareness of space. His attention to detail, both in planting and hardscape materials is attributed to his Modernist background which unites a strict formality with exuberant but carefully planned drift plantings. His design philosophy is sometimes expressed by creating a simple, often large, grid of planting enclosures that he calls "garden rooms." He constructs them individually, and then allows for rhythm and repetitions to develop inside them.

His own garden in Dasmarinas Village, Makati, is an example of this garden room idea. The house opens onto a patio with wide *piedra Pinoy* pavers seamed with grass and a small sunken pond with a fountain in the middle. The garden is cut by a strong central axis that shoulders date nut palms, Plumeria and Cordylines as well as fruit trees such as *chico* or sapodilla (*Manilkara zapota*), *santol*

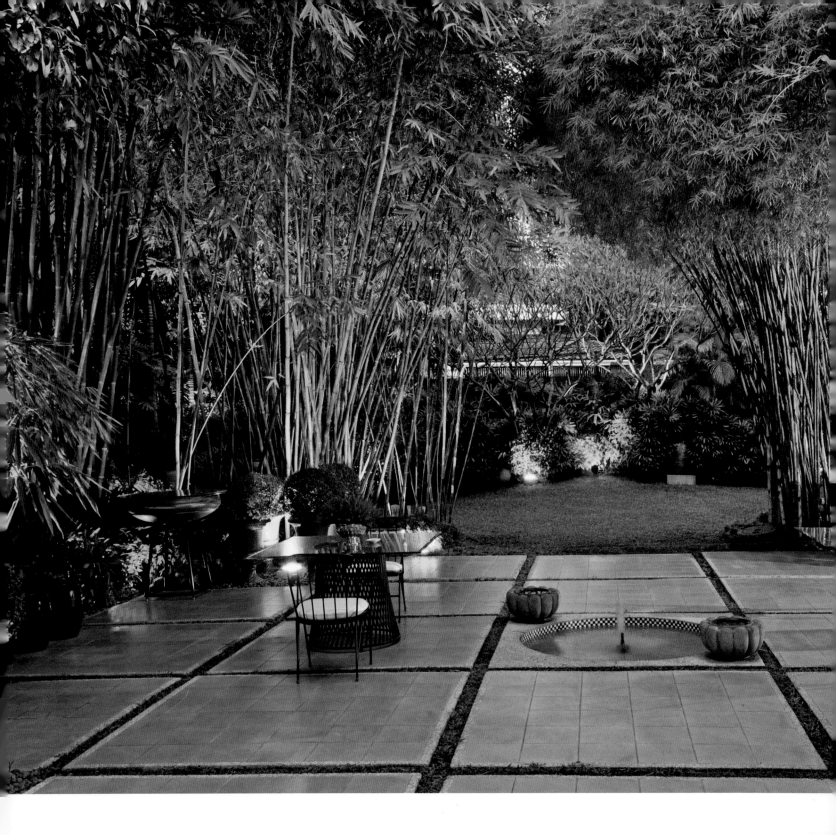

(*Sandoricum koetjape*) and *makopa* (*Syzygium samarangense*) which provide shade from the sun. Box balls of Fukien tea in urns march across the paved terrace defining the enclosures. They contrast with dense plantings of Rhapis palms and giant stands of lacy bamboo that sway in the wind disrupting the garden's modern lines. Keeping within the Philippine tropical vernacular are Alocasias, bird's nest ferns, Aglaonemas and Bromeliads providing the strong textures that keep everything in line.

Color other than green is kept to a minimum and is provided by bowls of brightly colored cut flowers that decorate the tables in the patio. (A sense of impending chaos within a general order, an apparent design trend in modern gardens today is palpable here.) The green garden rooms lead one to the other, and depending on the time of day and the theme of the space, they change in mood and material. Each enchanting enclosure is intense with garden seats, lanterns, ornamental pots, jars and stone fragments, yet, somehow remains focused and interesting, with all components in sync.

Above The house, dramatically lit at night, opens onto a patio with wide pavers seamed with grass and a small sunken pond with a fountain in the middle.

Right A seated Buddha high-lighted by decorative woodwork provides a serene note.

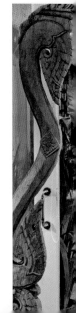

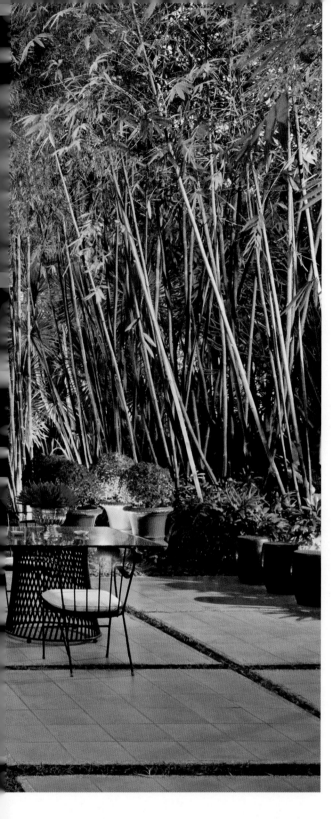

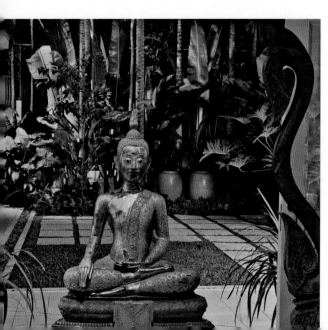

Previous pages main photo
Giant stands of bamboo along with clipped balls of Fukien tea in urns frame and define this airy "garden room."

Previous pages small photo
Alocasias, bamboo, bird's nest ferns, Rhapis palms, Aglaonemas and Bromeliads provide textural and botanical interest.

Below Round capiz lanterns illumine the garden at night heightening the sense of drama within the different enclosures.

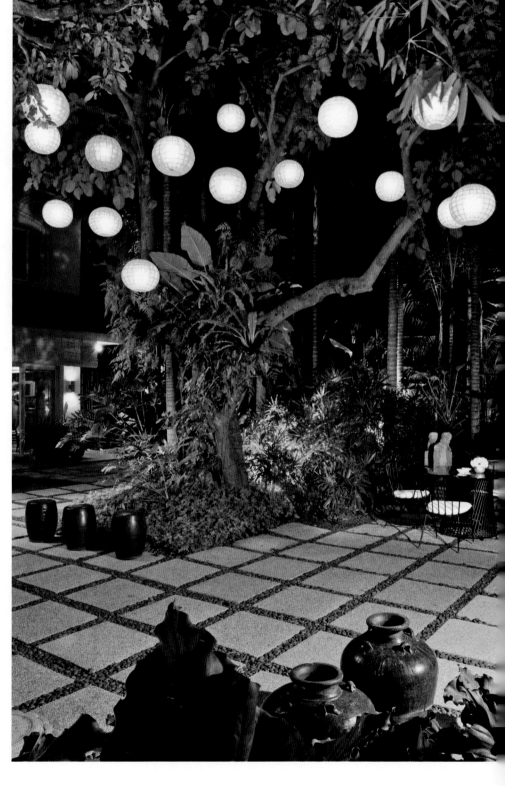

RAMON ANTONIO'S "GARDEN ROOMS"

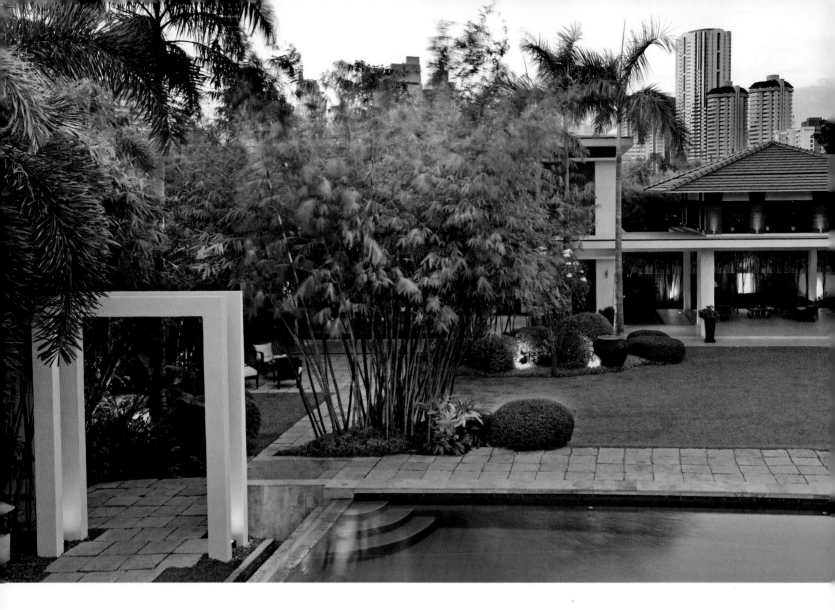

A SECOND ACT

Dasmarinas Village, Makati

Designed by Ramon Antonio

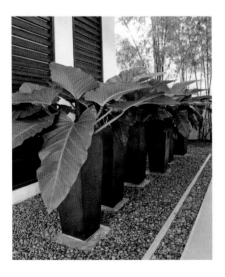

Ramon Antonio designs with an architect's eye for space and a gardener's passion for plants. The ability to integrate the dualities of architecture and landscaping has made him one of the most sought-after designers of suburban and city gardens. When asked by an old client to make additions to an existing house and garden he had previously designed after they had purchased an adjoining lot, Antonio responded by building a concrete and glass house with a garden of pleasing proportions and just the right modern elements.

The front drive is flanked on one side by sago palms and an elegant stand of bamboo, making for an imposing entranceway. From here, you climb a stairway of black granite lined on each side by uniform plantings of *Ficus triangularis* to approach the house. Tall shiny black jars stand sentinel on a moat-like feature by the front door. The sight of water with brightly colored koi welcomes you. Fine textured pole bamboo (one of six varieties in the garden) was used to create a fence of green against the concrete wall that surrounds the property.

The design is minimal here, with a limited color palette ensuring a satisfying sense of quiet. Plantings are composed of subdued tones; green dominates, but is punctuated here and there with touches of white Plumeria, orange

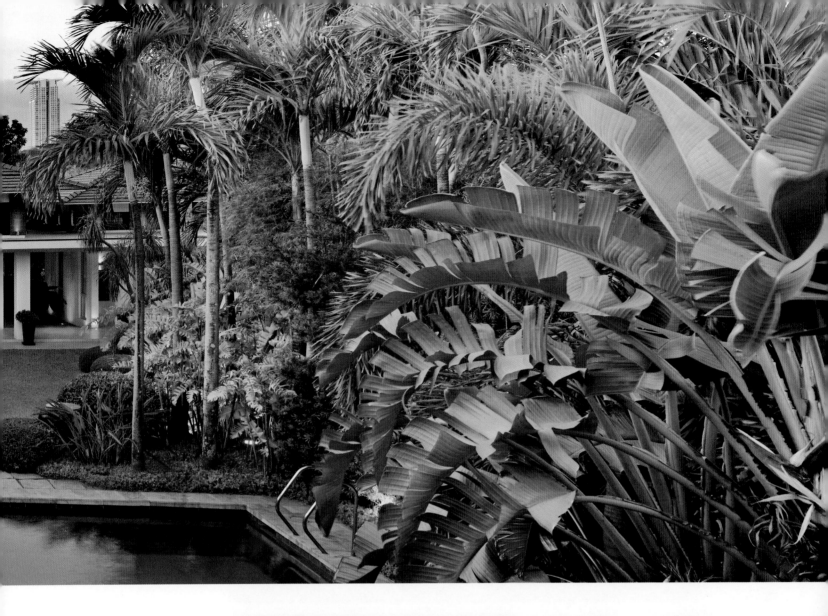

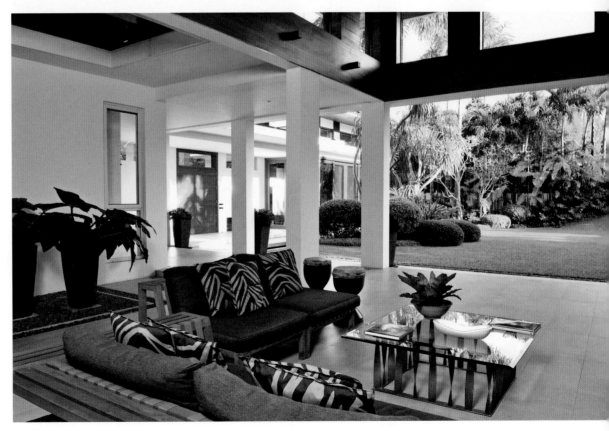

Above The new addition viewed from the pool framed by plantings of bamboo, royal palms (*Roystonia regia)* and banana-like bird-of-paradise, *Strelitzia nicolai.*

Opposite Tall, shiny black jars planted with a Philodendron hybrid stand on a bed of gravel creating an interesting focus in the *lanai.*

Right The spacious *lanai* with comfortable seating provides an inviting spot from which to view the garden.

Ixora under bamboo, and red ornamental gingers by the pool. This is a design where shape is more important than color. Elsewhere, Antonio acknowledges tropical tradition by ensuring ample outdoor living spaces that serve to connect the different areas.

The site slopes down steeply from the old house to the new, so to ease a runoff problem a trench lined with black river stones was installed at the edge of the lawn where it meets the new house. The result is practical, attractive and modern. The stone-lined canal bed directs water away from the house allowing slow filtration into the ground.

Though modern and sleek, there is a real feeling of intimacy here, a sense of living in the garden, which is the aim of every good designer in the tropics.

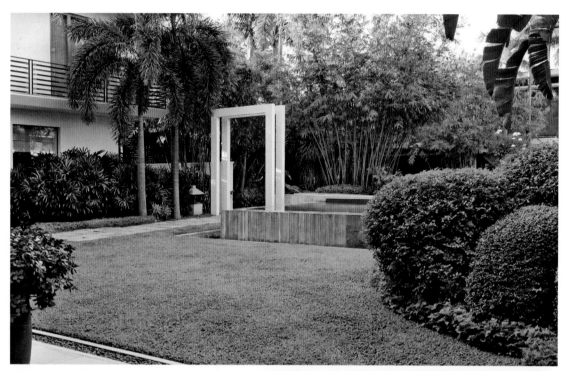

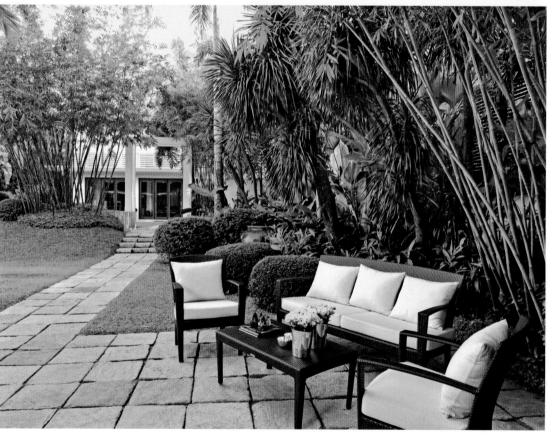

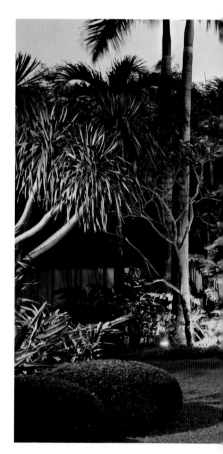

Left A modern white arch flanked by two royal palms marks the entrance to the pool area.

Below left Plantings of bamboo, Dracaena, Heliconias and Fukien tea soften the hard edges of stone and concrete in this seating area.

Right Stately royal palms, *Roystonea elata*, Heliconias and an evergreen shrub screen the perimeter wall and cast shadows over the rectangular swimming pool.

Below Dramatically lit at night, the site slopes down gradually from the old house to the newer house down below.

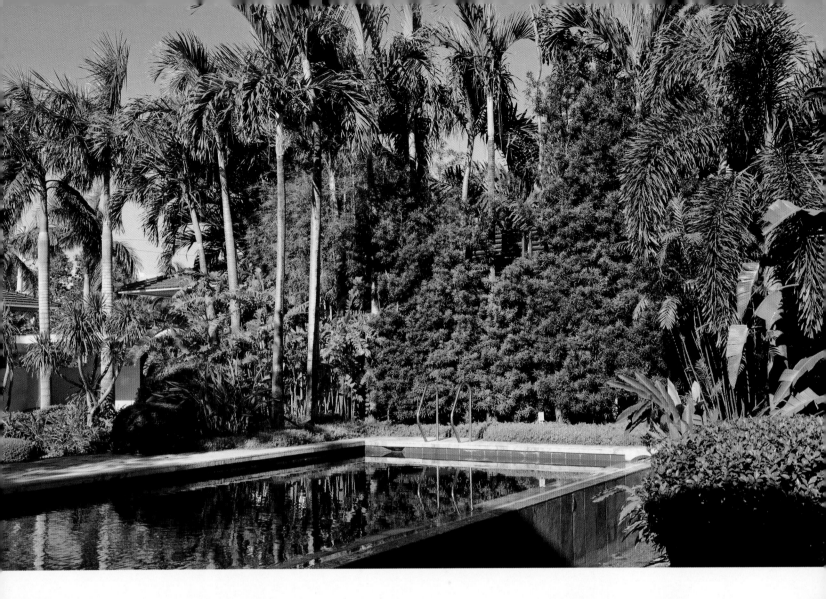

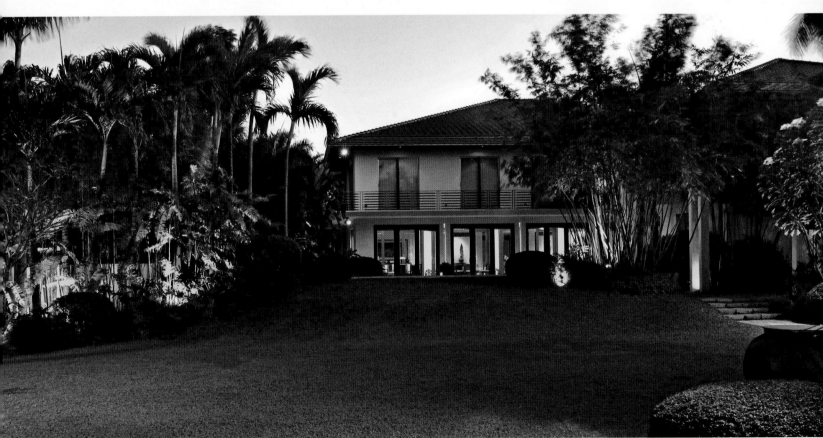

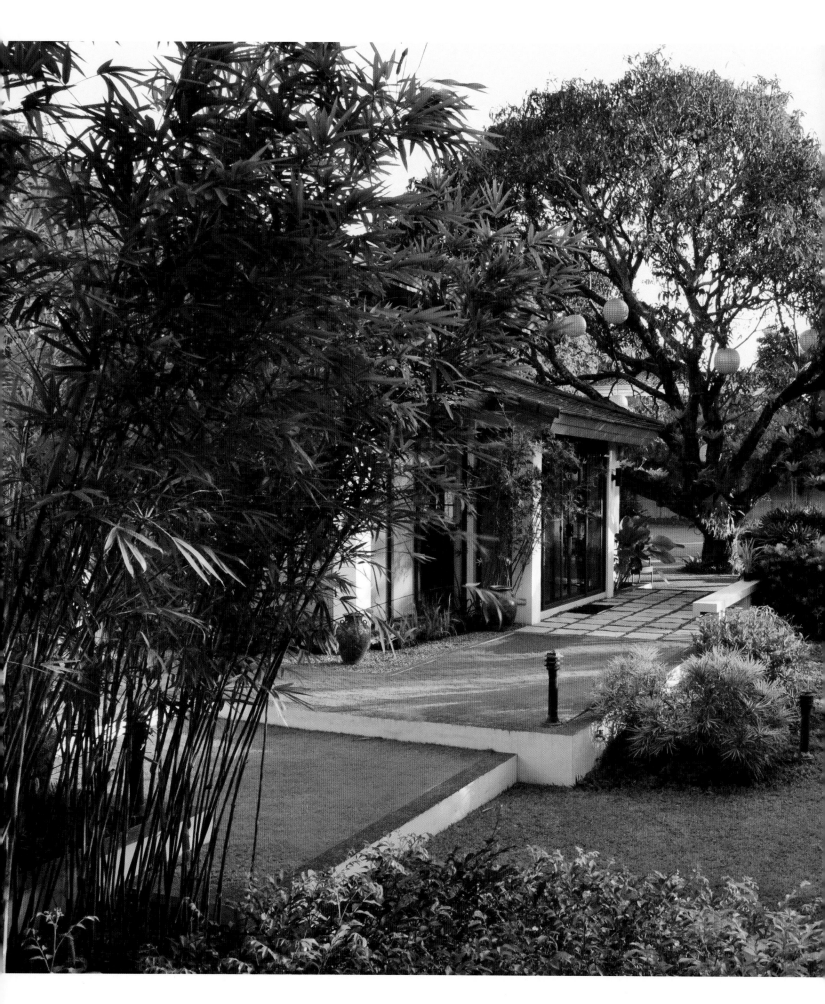

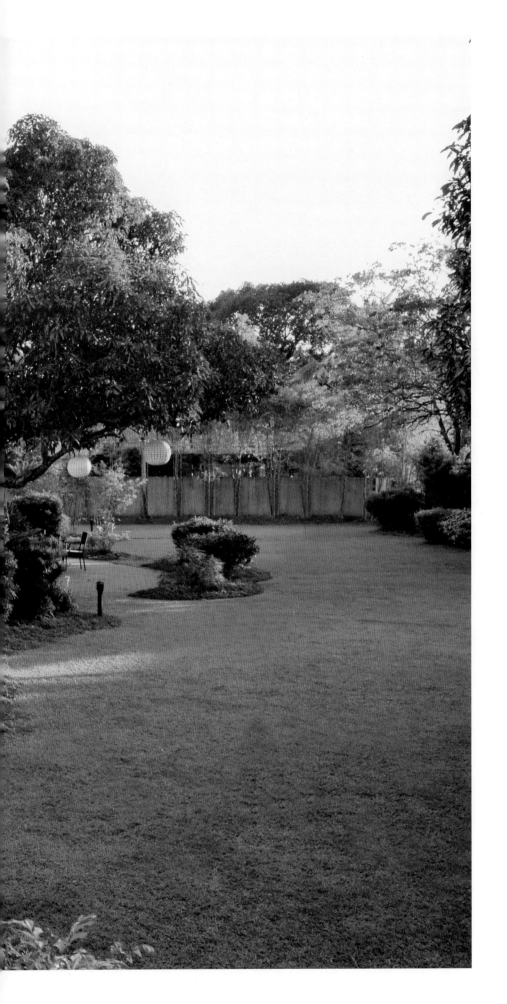

ALABANG MODERN
Ayala Alabang
Designed by Frank Borja

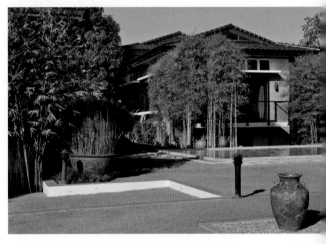

Grid-pattern gardens designed for people and their "leisure needs" rather than plants are a modern idea. One challenge of residential landscape design today is not only creating aesthetically pleasing environments but integrating into them outdoor living elements, such as decks, grills and spas. As more and more people utilize their outdoor spaces for entertaining and recreation, the hardscaping (use of hard materials such as stone, concrete, gravel and wood to connect spaces) becomes the backbone of the design that holds the garden together.

Frank Borja's love of plants and stylish functionalism appealed to the contemporary tastes of the owners of this suburban garden, as did his modern sensibility born from years as a landscape designer for the prestigious firm Belt Collins. Employing the principles of repetition, contrast and color, he was able to transform the nondescript property into the modern, functional garden it is today. First, Borja softened the house's architectural edges with carefully chosen plantings of bamboo and palms. He kept many of the existing mango trees to provide shade and stability to the borders. Then he installed a light-diffusing

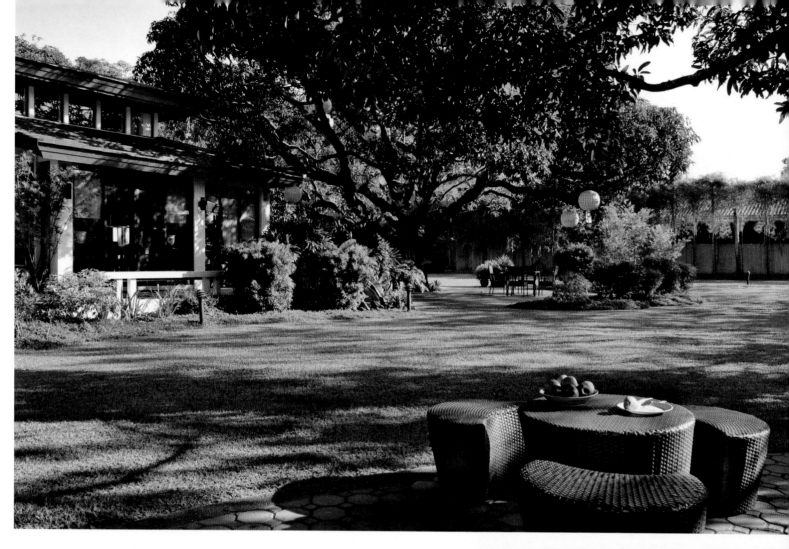

perimeter wall of pale brick and white slatted panels.
Lastly, he refashioned the concrete driveway into a grid
of tiles so it would hint at the graphic paths of pavers
he used throughout the garden. Borja, who grew up in
Guam, and worked for a landscaping firm in Hawaii for
many years, drew on a tropical planting tradition that
combines textures and shapes to plant a harmonious mix
of attractive foliage plants.

This modern garden contains everything you need
for recreation: an outdoor barbecue, a lawn for the
children to play on and comfortable places to dine and
entertain in. There is even a spa garden just outside the
master bedroom, below the rectangular pool, enclosed
with the same walls as used in the house and with a
perimeter of bamboo to nestle the structure into the
rest of the garden.

With its dramatic outdoor living space, incorporating
cooking, living and dining areas, and low maintenance
yet exotic planting, Borja and the owners have managed
to create a garden packed with practical style but with
the luxurious feel of the outdoors.

Above This modern garden has
everything: a lawn for kids to play
on, comfortable places for entertaining and an outdoor barbecue.

Right There is also a pool and a
spa garden just outside the master
bedroom. Plantings of bamboo ease
the structure into the rest of the
garden.

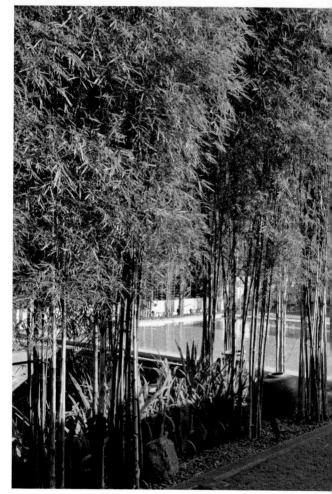

Previous pages main photo
Plantings of bamboo soften the architectural edges of the property while established mango trees provide stability to the borders.

Previous pages small photo
The hardscaping is the backbone of the garden's design. Hard materials such as stone, concrete, gravel and wood connect the various spaces in the garden.

Right and below right Grey graphic paths of pavers are used throughout the garden to connect spaces and hold the garden together.

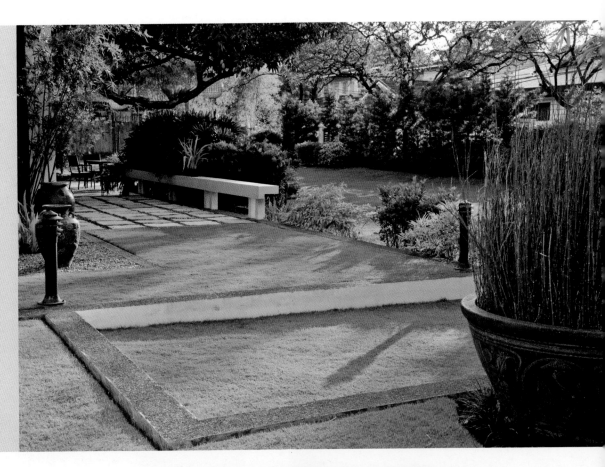

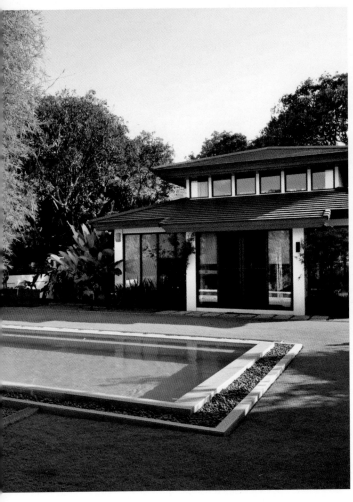

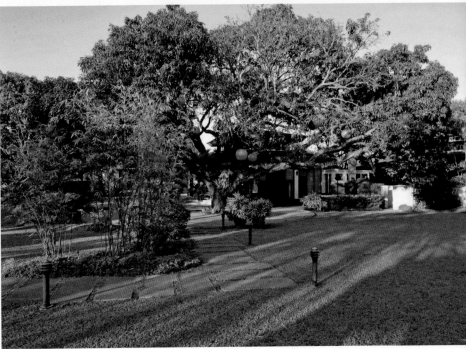

ZEN SERENITY

Urdaneta Village, Makati
Designed by Michelle Magsaysay

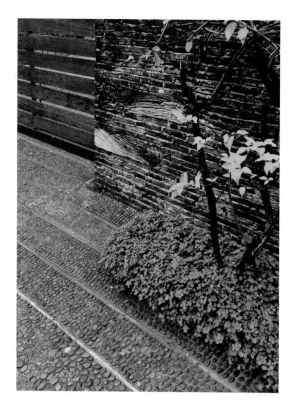

A modern garden in the tropics can be more than just clean lines, carefully maintained lawns and repetitive plantings. Elements such as stone, water and texture can be incorporated to greatly enhance the garden's design. Stone can be used to define spaces and subtle shifts in ground level. Contrasting qualities of light can be brought about by a diversity of textures in the carefully chosen plant material. Water can be used to transform surfaces and fill spaces with sound.

Entering the Alejandrino garden from the street, you are welcomed into an intimate courtyard paved with dark, fine gravel. The elegant space, fringed by delicate bamboo, is punctuated by two pieces of stone lending it an Asian ambience. Water reverberates through the space from a fountain, cascading into a rectangular basin dominated by a *kapal-kapal* tree (*Calotropis gigantea*). A native of the desert, this medicinal plant thrives on sand and has showy lilac flowers. There are also plantings of *Cyperus papyrus*, a sedge that was used by the ancient Egyptians as paper.

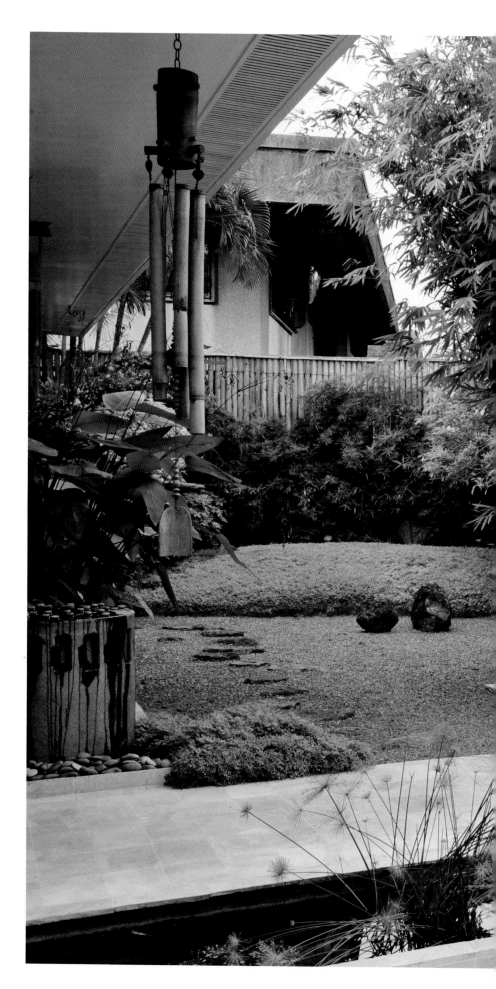

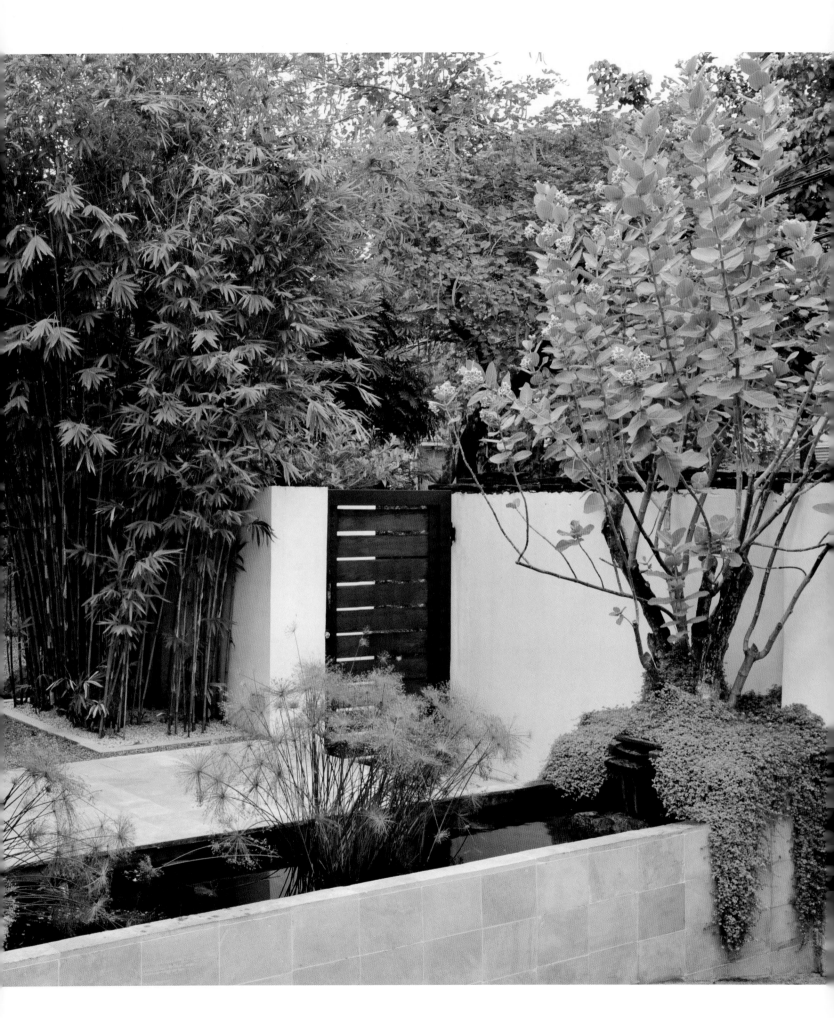

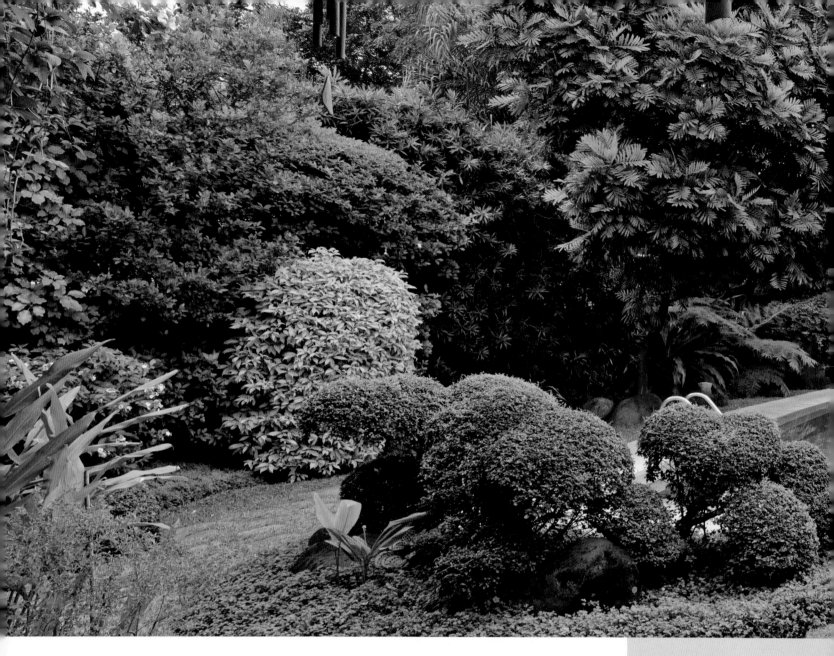

As you proceed beyond the courtyard, you enter a lush narrow garden bordered by an assortment of palms, ferns and Heliconias. This space is dominated by a Japanese fern tree (*Filicium decipiens*) that provides shade to the pool area. Plantings of variegated *Excoecaria cochinchinensis* against a dark green hedge at the far end of the pool catch the light. Along one side of the house are a striking pink Plumeria and a *Cordyline australis* dripping with orchids and under planted with clipped box forms of Fukien tea.

Paths of stone and a varied paving palette of pebbles, gravel and bricks sewn with grass create elegant transitions between spaces in the garden. The use of color other than green was intentionally toned down to maintain a sense of quiet. The predominantly green garden enjoys touches of a limited color palette of white—with white orchids hanging on the trees, a splash of blue in the side yard and a pink garlic vine trailing up the *lanai*.

Overall, the modern garden exudes serenity and calm. Credit must go to both the designer and the owners who have not been hampered by the limited space; rather, they have used scale to endow the garden with an appropriate reverence.

Previous pages main photo A bamboo wind chime welcomes the visitor into an intimate court-yard fringed by delicate bamboo

Previous pages small photo A brick paved wall with wooden inserts provides an interesting detail by the front gate.

Above A stunning fern tree, *Felicium decipiens*, on the left of the pool contrasts in height and texture with the clipped shrubs of Fukien tea in the foreground.

Right A paving palette of fine gravel and stone creates elegant transitions between spaces in the garden.

Right middle Water trickles off a round boulder decorated with river stones.

Far right *Duranta repens* provides a blue note in the garden.

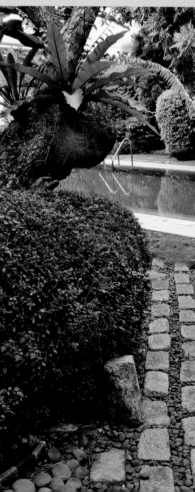

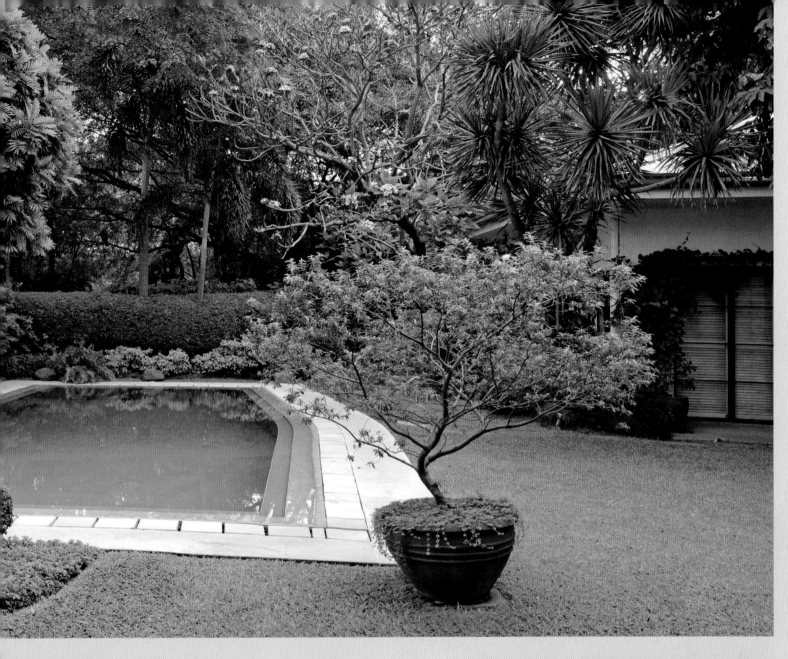

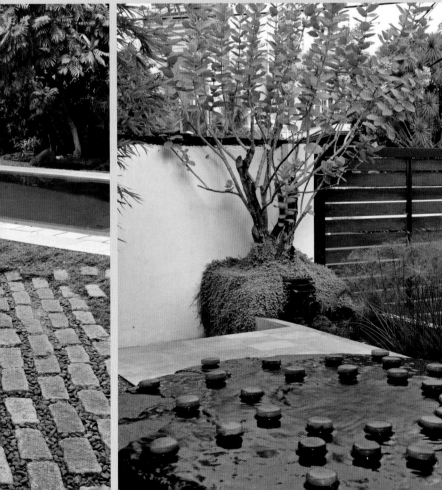

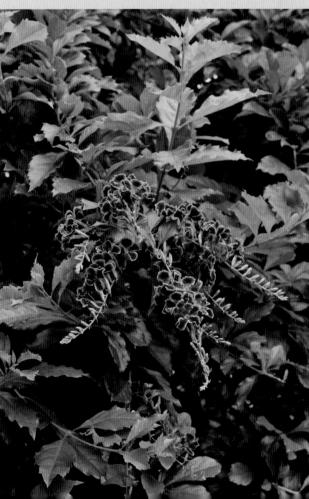

ANDRES WATERFALL GARDEN

Libis, Quezon City

Designed by Rading Decepida

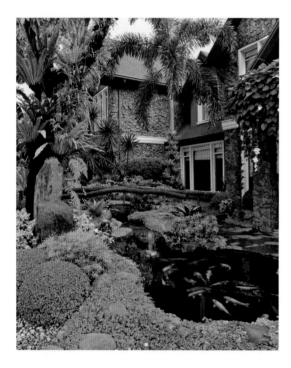

The owners wanted a garden that would embrace the house on all sides and contain water features that would add soothing sounds and sparkling sights to the property. The task fell to Rading Decepida, a self taught landscape designer, who rose to the challenge by creating a garden designed for the senses.

To eliminate noise from the street, Decepida installed a pond spanned by a bridge at the front of the house. The constant trickle of flowing water muffles the sound of traffic and heightens the sense of place. The pond edges are planted with irises, Euphorbia and creeping morning glory and, together with masses of Miagos and spike moss or Selaginella, they provide a textured, soft margin.

An iron gate by a side entrance leads to a secluded garden where a tall Yucca towers over boxed Podocarpus at the entrance. A path picked out in round cement pavers and springy moss takes you around the space. The border that runs along the perimeter of the property is thickly planted with a variety of plants with contrasting shapes and textures. The diversity of the plant textures

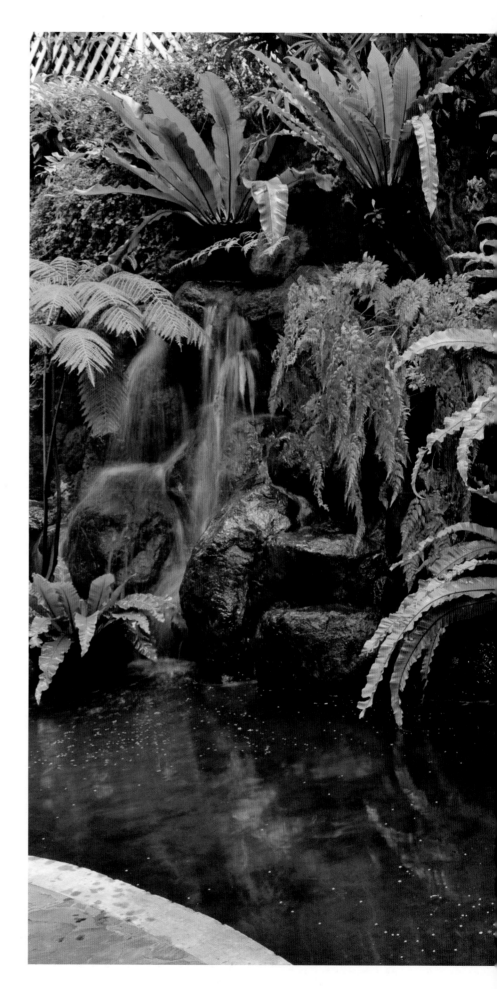

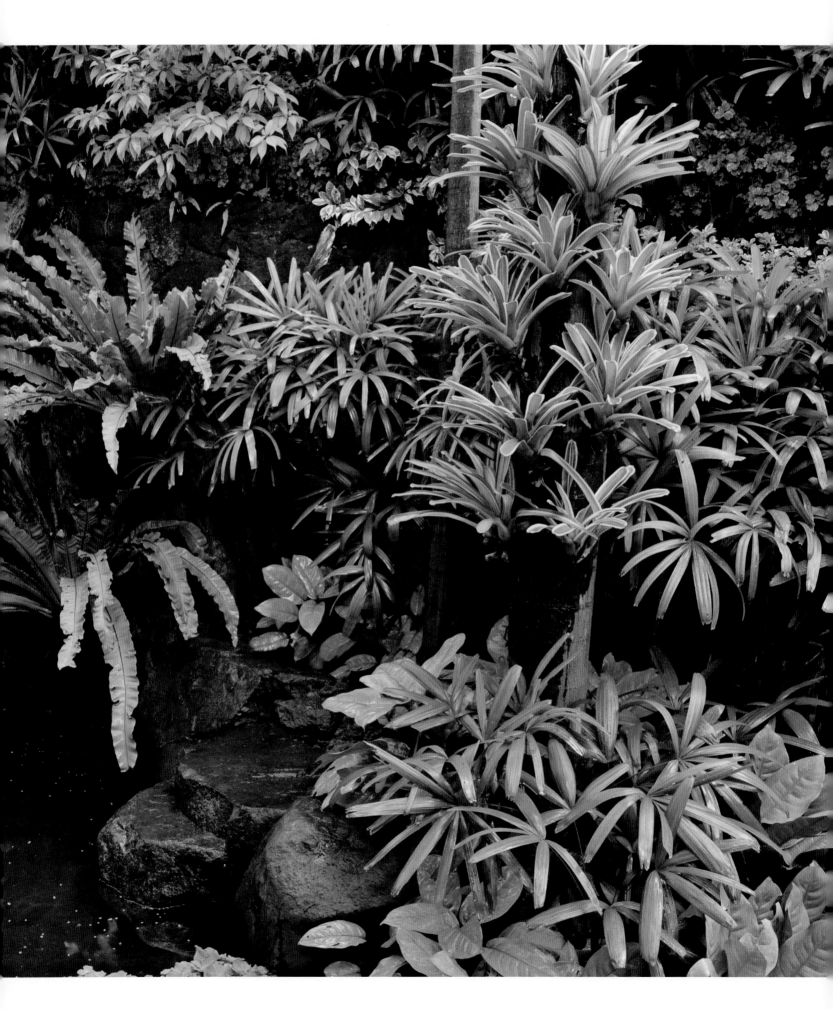

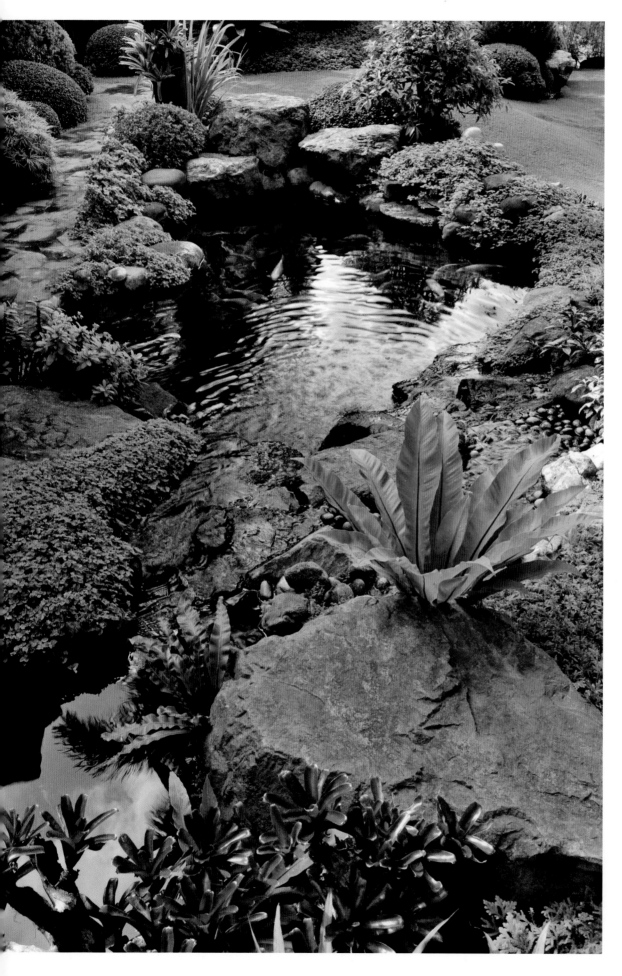

Previous pages main photo
A stunning waterfall with lively
compositions of bird's nest ferns,
Vrieseas and *Rhapis excelsa* is the
central focus of the garden.

Previous pages small photo
A view of the house from the
street with the koi pond in
the foreground.

Left An artful natural koi pond
edged with Selaginella, creeping
morning glory, bird's nest ferns
and colorful Vrieseas in the front
garden drowns out traffic noise
from the street.

Opposite top A bed of river
stones snakes along the edge of
a border planted with miniature
ornamentals and a variety of
tightly clipped shrubs.

Opposite right *Excoecaria
cochinchinensis*, locally known as
picara, drapes over a tiny pond
covered with an aquatic floater,
Pistia stratiotes.

Opposite far right A waterfall
provides dramatic impact at the
far end of the garden.

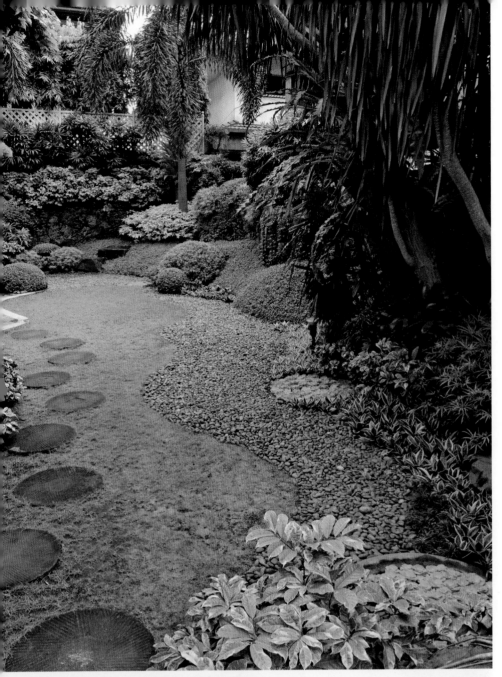

results in varying qualities of light. From the living room that looks out into the garden, one notices the lacy foliage of Selaginella lying underneath the silvery green leaves of *pandakaki* that is overshadowed by the marbled leaves of *picara*.

The sculpted style of this garden begins with the arranged marriage of stones and greenery. The clipped boxed forms of Fukien tea and *kamuning* provide solid stability to the border, while a procession of low growing *Excoecaria cochinchinensis*, *Sansevieria trifasciata* 'Hahnii' and Aglaonemas leads up to taller plantings of foxtail palms, Podocarpus and *Dracaena reflexa* 'Song of Jamaica'. Decepida's deft hand is also evident in the carefully studied compositions of plant textures derived from the juxtaposition of different varieties of Bromeliads, golden Miagos and a variegated *Polyscias balfouriana* cultivar with flowering specimens of Euphorbia, Spathiphyllum and Anthuriums.

To maximize the existing space in this garden of intimate dimensions, the designer selected plantings primarily for their form, shape and texture, with the latter (the quality, shape and feel of the foliage) as the key design tool. The central focus is a stunning waterfall, situated around a bend at the end of the garden. Best appreciated from the dining room, it provides dramatic impact with its assemblage of rocks and boulders from the province of Bulacan and the town of Antipolo and lively compositions of bird's nest ferns festooned with rabbit's foot ferns, *pandakaki*, Rhapis palms and tree ferns.

The strong architecture, dramatic waterfall and balance of verticals and horizontals define this compact, modern garden—but it is its textural quality that sustains it.

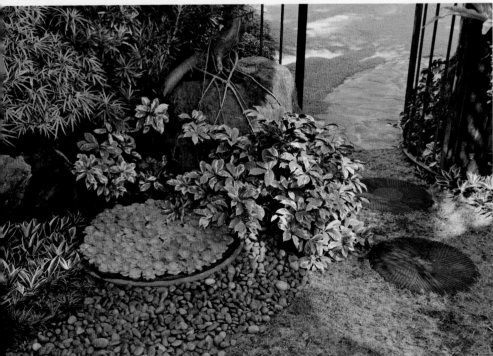

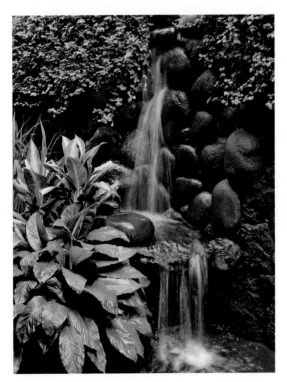

ARANETA'S MANGO TREE GARDEN

Ayala Alabang

Designed by Toni Serrano Parsons

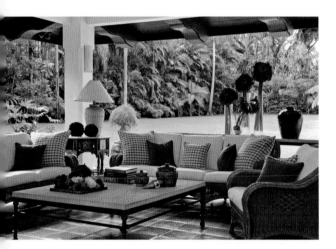

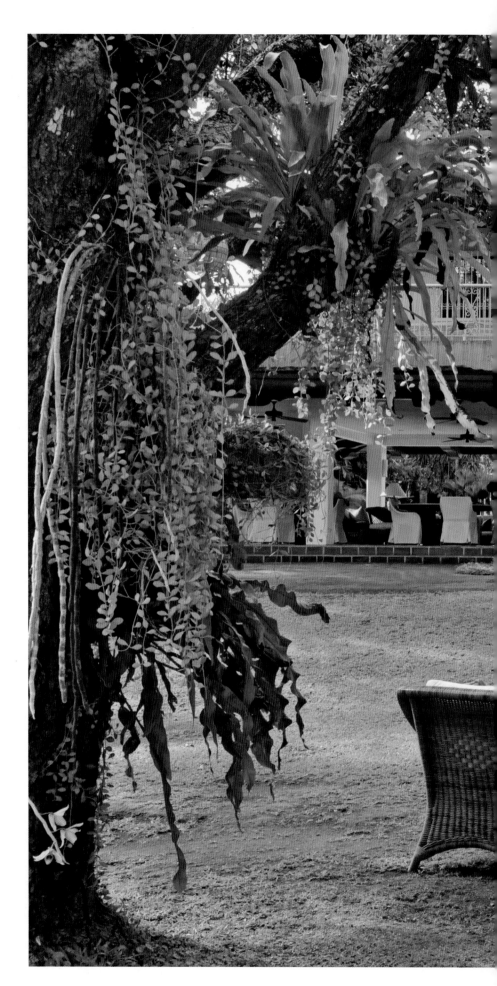

The feel of this property is that of a large country house with a definite Philippine air characterized by an eclectic collection of antiques and artifacts. Daily life revolves around the *lanai* that looks out into a garden with a spacious lawn and magnificent greenery. A screen of trees around the property hides nearby houses. Twenty eight years in the planting, the garden was a collaborative effort of the owner Baby Araneta, her mother, and her sister, Toni Parsons—all gardeners and plant enthusiasts.

At the center of the lawn, visible from many parts of the sprawling house, is a collection of very old mango trees, host to an amazing collection of bird's nest ferns dripping with common Dischidia. Often found in gardens in the Philippines, these valued fruit trees are the focal point of this particular garden. A seating arrangement under one of them acknowledges and reinforces the sense of place in this tropical garden.

A tropical border snakes along the whole perimeter of the property: Planted with impressive groups of tall tree ferns, Heliconias and Alocasias, it is also home to clumps of variegated *picara* planted amongst Ophiopogon grass and Rhapis palms which contrast in texture and shape with Miagos, *Osmoxylon geelvinkianum* and *ti*

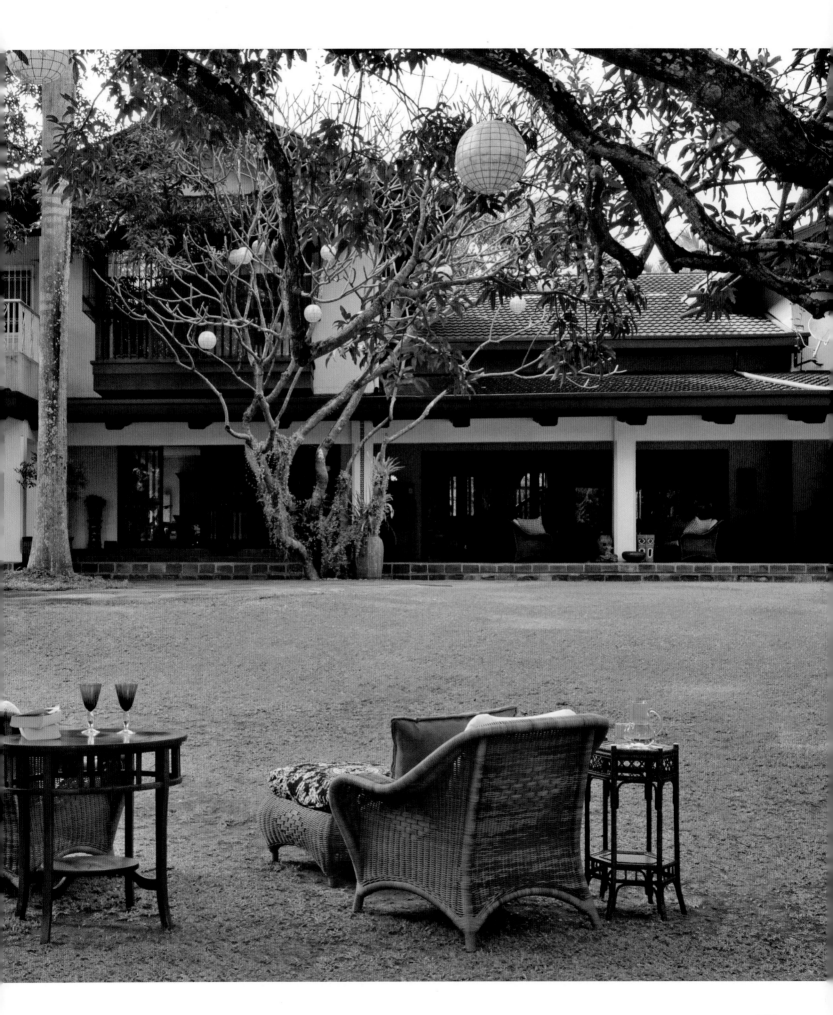

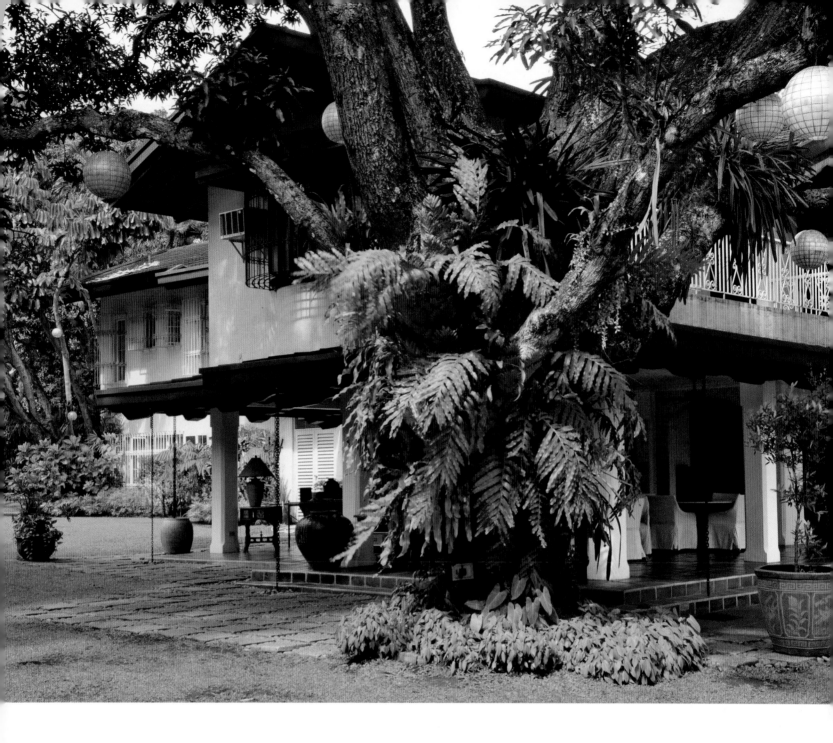

plants. The full-grown trees and palms serve as wind-breakers as well as canopies for the thick underplant-ings of bird-of-paradise, ferns and Dracaenas. Frangi-pani or Plumeria, known locally as *calachuche*, provide height and sculptural form while *Saraca thaipingensis* lends splashes of vibrant orange color. Lush groupings of bird's-nest ferns, spider lilies and Scheffleras define the structural layout of the garden.

It is worth mentioning that Toni Parsons is a noted floral designer who offers unusual and difficult-to-find designer plants to the public. She has brought her artful aesthetic to both this garden and her business, where she imports and sells specialty plants. Her inven-tory includes topiary trees, orchids from Hawaii and Bangkok, forced bulbs from Holland as well as other standard ornamentals that she cultivates in her nurseries in Alfonso, Cavite.

Previous pages main photo
A bird's eye view from the garden of the sprawling *lanai* that wraps around the Araneta's home.

Previous pages small photo
Daily life revolves around the spacious open-air *lanai* decorated with Toni Parsons' contemporary floral creations.

Right The densely planted tropical border that snakes along the perimeter of the property.

Far right The white columned portico at the front entry is crowned by an enormous hang-ing basket of bird's nest ferns, *Asplenium nidus*.

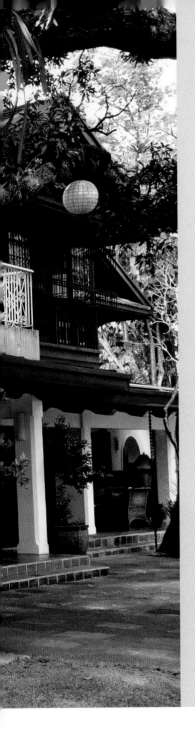

Left Another old mango tree this time weighed down with *Goniophlebium persicifolium*, an epiphytic fern. The fern is endemic to the Philippines and has very long stalks.

Right The lemon-yellow house's windows fashioned with white wrought-iron grillwork overlook a courtyard paved alternately with black river stones and *piedra China*.

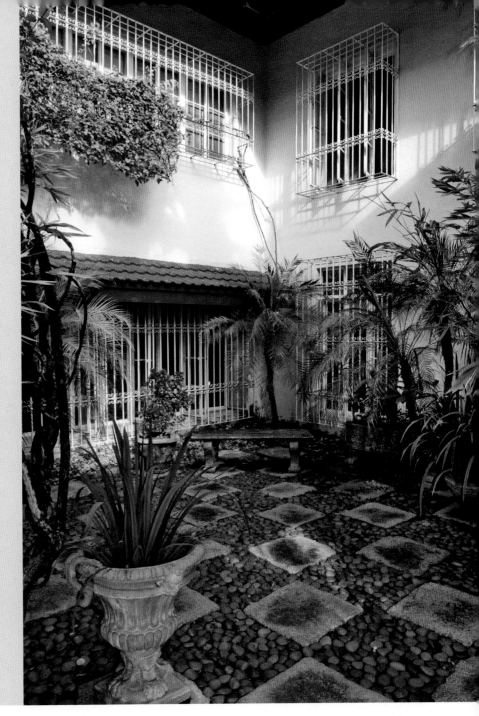

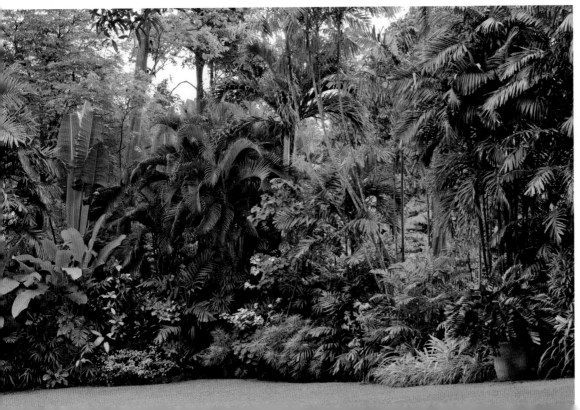

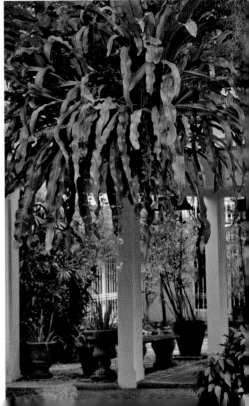

AN ART COLLECTOR'S GARDEN

Forbes Park, Makati
Designed by Ponce Veridiano

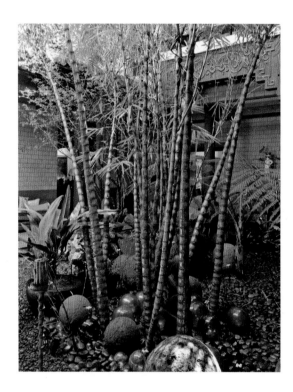

For an art loving couple, Ponce Veridiano created a lushly planted garden that relies on a framework of densely planted borders to give architectural coherence and flow to the design. For the Oriental-style house, he chose an exotic planting scheme that incorporates attractive and fast-growing plants. He knew that a small garden like this would have to rely on a strong framework to balance the bold architecture of the house.

Veridiano's first task was to fill the borders with a sweep of ornamental specimens such as palms, ginger and bamboo while using mature trees to provide stability to the borders. To avoid rigidity, he focused on the owners' favorite plants: *Saraca thaipingensis*, *Ixora finlaysoniana* Wall. ex G. Don, Plumeria, ferns and Cycads and kept to a palette of vivid greens. Thoughtful plant groupings emerge in the borders: *pandakaki* against variegated Scheffleras, sculpted Fukien tea with Bromeliads, Buddha's-belly bamboo under planted with Episcia and Zamia.

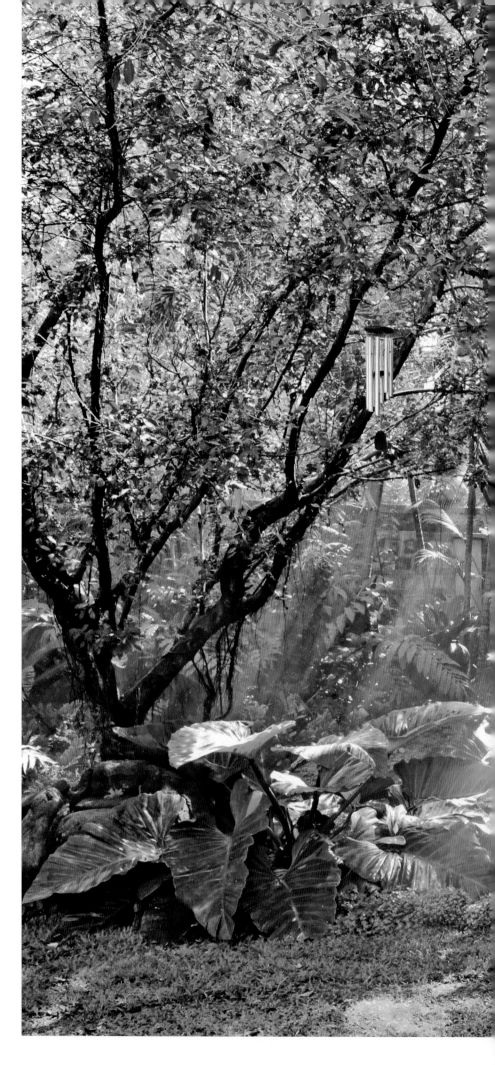

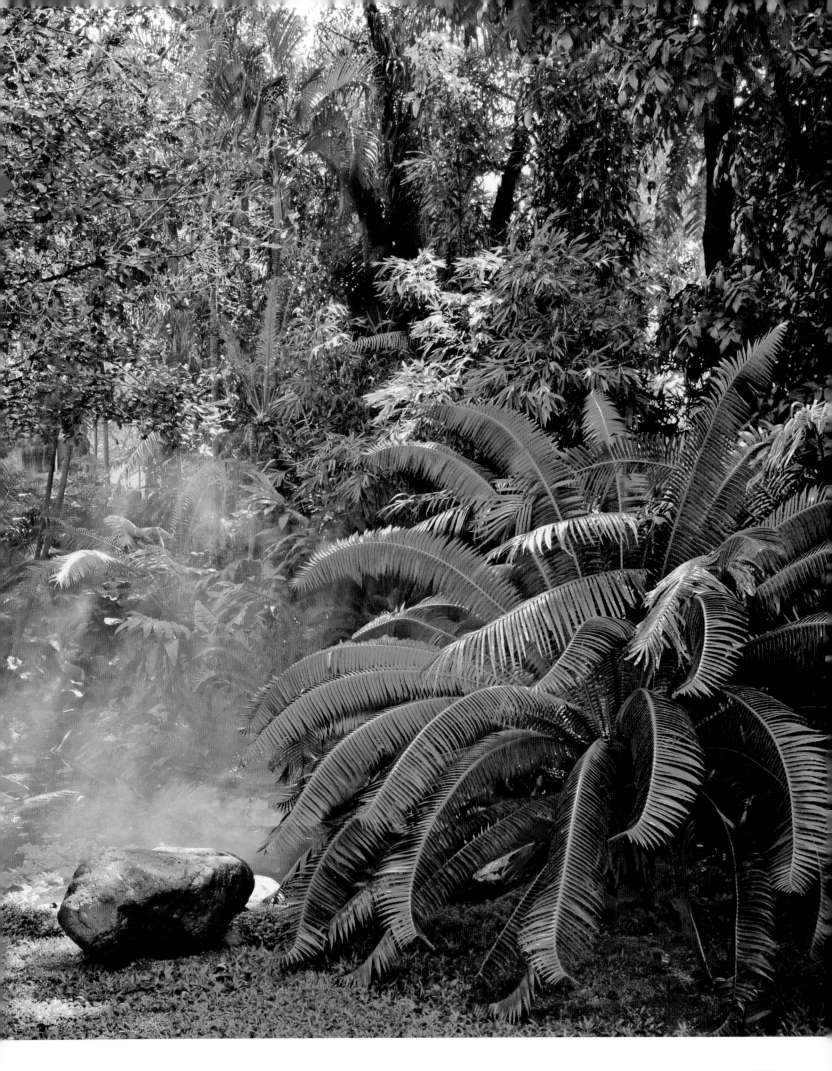

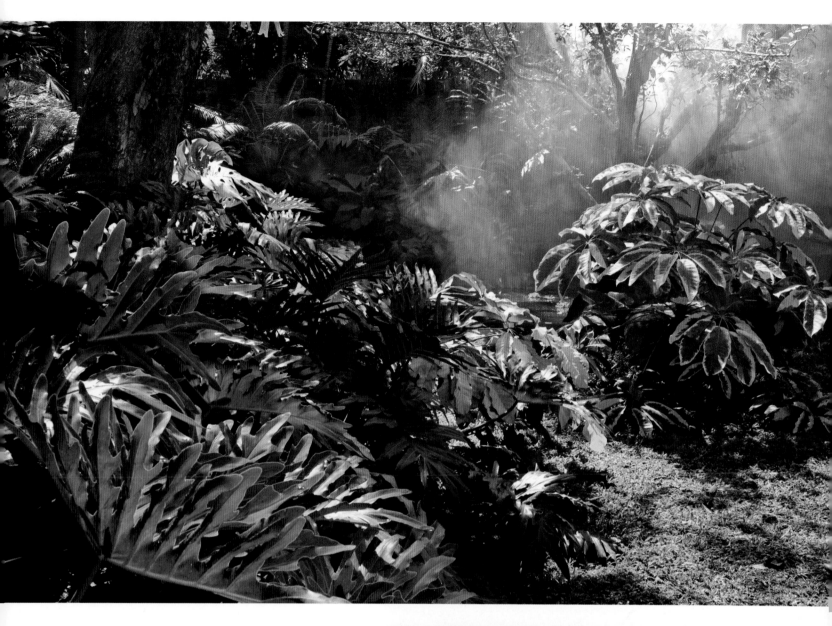

Constantly shifting patterns of light and shade pull
one's eye into the dramatic, exotic garden. Much of it
can be viewed from the expansive living room and the
wonderfully eclectic dining room through tall, glass
sliding doors. The panorama is of stately trees dripping
with *Tillandsia usneiodes* and a richly layered understory
of shrubs and ornamentals. From both rooms, one can
look out into the lawn vista animated by lively creatures
—live ones as well as those cast in stone. A pond, half
hidden on one side by massed groupings of Scheffleras
and Philodendrons, enhances the tropical feeling.

Inside, a gravel-covered courtyard is planted with tree
ferns, bamboo and Philodendrons and decorated with
glass buoys and *anito* statues. It helps to bring the outside
in and serves as a welcome focal point for the house.

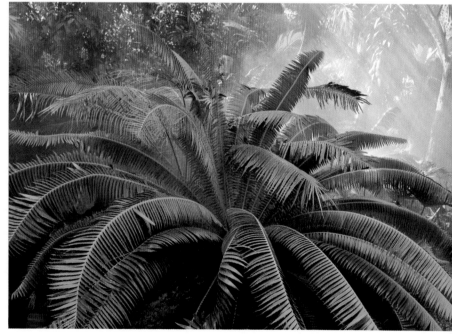

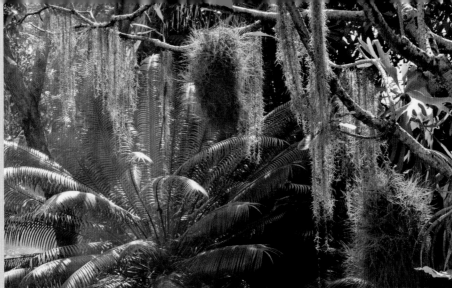

Previous pages main photo
A combination of mature trees and carefully chosen ornamental specimens, such as the prehistoric looking Cycad on the right and the Philodendron on the left, provide this garden with a rich tropical flavor.

Previous pages small photo
Yellow and green Buddha's-belly bamboo, *Bambusa ventricosa*, looms over stone and glass decorative elements in the gravel covered indoor courtyard garden.

Opposite top *Philodendron selloum* and *Schefflera arboricola* 'Hongkong Variegata' make lively displays in this tropical sanctuary.

Opposite bottom Similar to a palm but in actual fact a Cycad, *Dioon spinulosum* is a recent introduction to the Philippines and is still quite rare in gardens.

Right top The bare branches of a frangipani tree play host to epiphytes such as the hair-like *Tillandsia usneoides* adding drama and mystery to the setting.

Middle right and far right
The different shapes and textural qualities of the various specimens such as the Cordylines on the left and Tillandsias on the right, soften the hard edges of stone and create interest in the garden.

Bottom Colorful koi enliven a moat-like feature at the entrance.

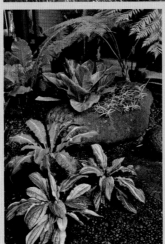

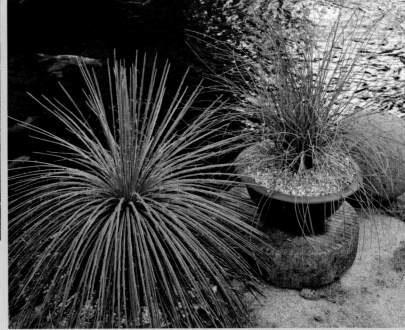

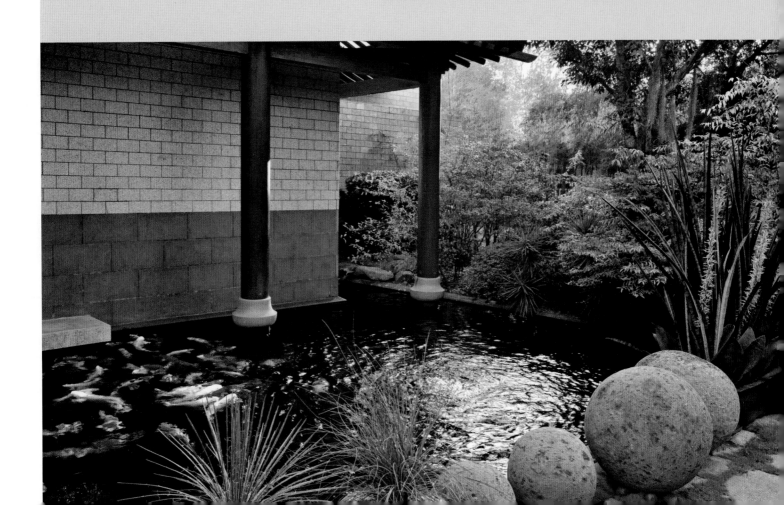

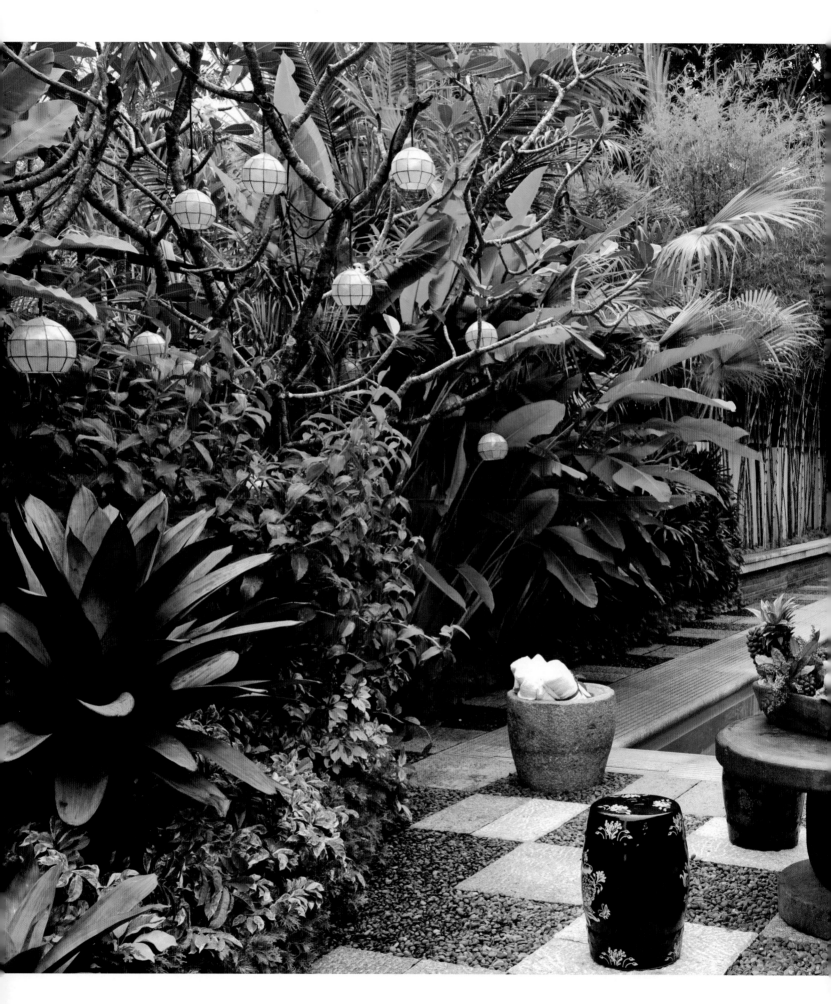

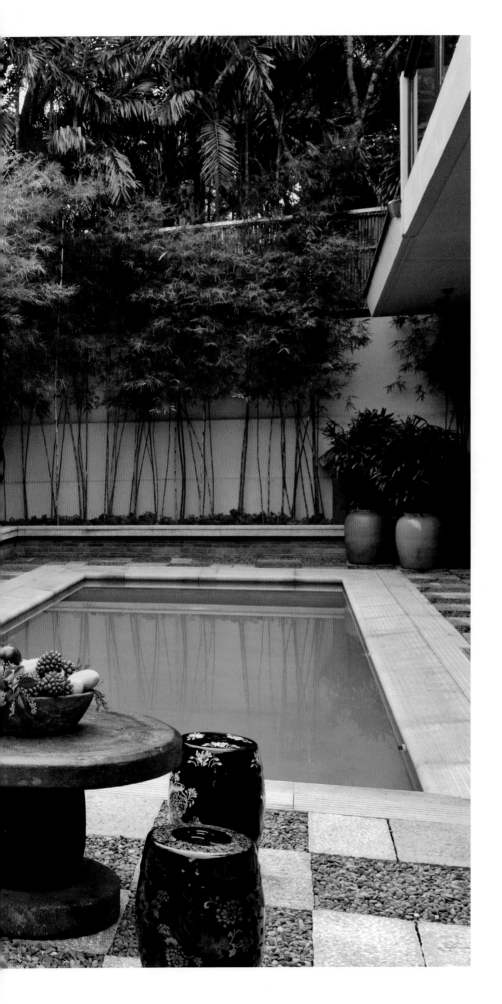

A CHIC SUBURBAN GARDEN

Ayala Alabang
Designed by Bobby Gopiao

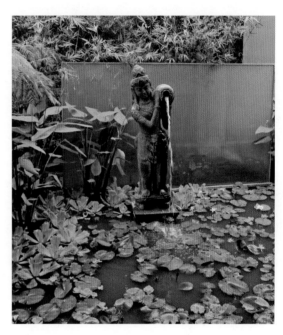

No Filipino garden is complete without the presence of water. This stylish garden, situated in one of the posh suburban enclaves of Manila, has a number of attractive water elements that are integral to the design. In fact, they form the main focus of the sublimely tropical setting.

The owners' interest in a water theme prompted them to create a pond to define the character of the garden and act as a haven for wildlife. They knew that even a small area, such as the one they had in mind, would attract frogs, dragonflies and a host of water loving birds. Set in an open part of the garden which receives a lot of sunshine, it is oxygen rich with clean and clear water and a range of aquatic plants; these comprise a combination of rooted and rootless floaters and submerged oxygenating plants. Plantings of bamboo, tree ferns and irises on its fringes give it a tranquil and serene quality with a decidedly Oriental feel.

Today, the sound of water pervades the garden and draws you to its source. The lovely square pond enlivened with tropical water lilies and water lettuce and punctuated at one end by a statue of a woman carrying a jar is the

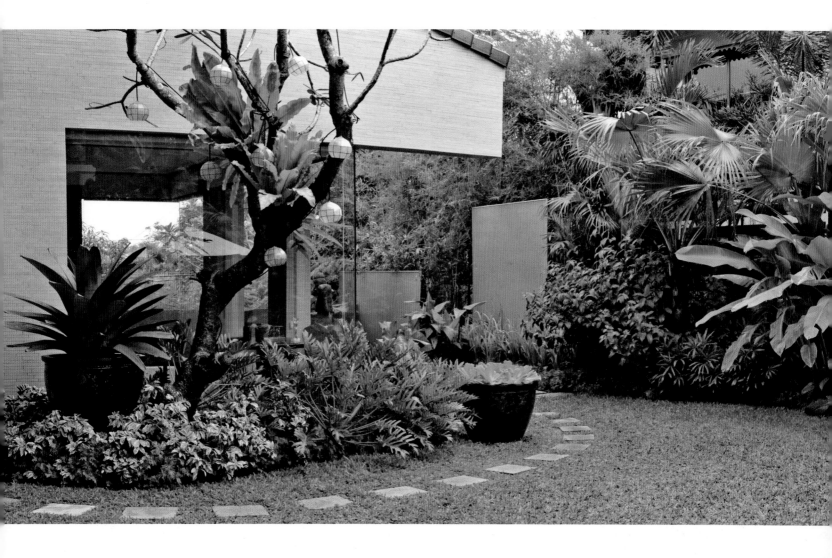

culmination of the owners' dream. Glass panels that add another dimension and make the pond look bigger provide a contemporary touch.

Around the corner is a second water feature in stark contrast to the ornamental pond—a rectangular swimming pool set on a checkerboard paving of gravel and tile. Contemporary in style, it mirrors the sky above and allows for elegant entertaining with an attractive seating area and sophisticated plantings. A screen of bamboo at one end and plantings of Australian fan palms, Heliconias, Rhapis and Plumeria on the other end ease the pool into its setting.

Elsewhere, garden ornaments and a variety of stone paths reinforce the garden's design while giving focus to other planted borders. Towering palms and a choice selection of trees such as Plumeria and mango provide height and contrast in shape and size with the shorter specimens of stepladder spiral ginger, Heliconias and Aglaonemas. Some plants are given special treatment such as *Excoecaria cochinchinensis* which is used extensively in the garden—in the border around a bend under a huge potted Bromeliad with *Philodendron selloum* and Selaginella; on the grassed bank by the driveway with

tree ferns, Miagos, Rhapis palms and Plumeria; and along a brick wall planted with Podocarpus and Selaginella. In the long border that runs along the perimeter wall, the repeated groupings of Australian fan palms, Heliconias, Aglaonemas, Rhapis palms and Bromeliads contribute to a naturalistic effect as well as provide color and texture.

Nevertheless, it is to the water features that we always return: providing sparkling effects and life to this garden, they also give it a timeless quality.

Previous pages main photo A rectangular swimming pool set on a checkerboard paving of gravel and tile is designed for elegant entertaining.

Previous pages small photo A lovely square pond planted with water lilies and water lettuce is graced with a statue of a woman carrying a jar.

Top Repeated groupings of Australian fan palms, Heliconias, Aglaonemas and Bromeliads add texture to the border by the perimeter wall.

Right The pond was designed to be a haven for wildlife.

Far right The fine, delicate texture of the Cyathea, *Osmoxylon geelvinkianum* and *Polycias balfouriana cv* offset the hard shiny surface of brown clay jars.

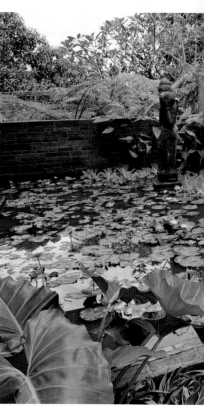

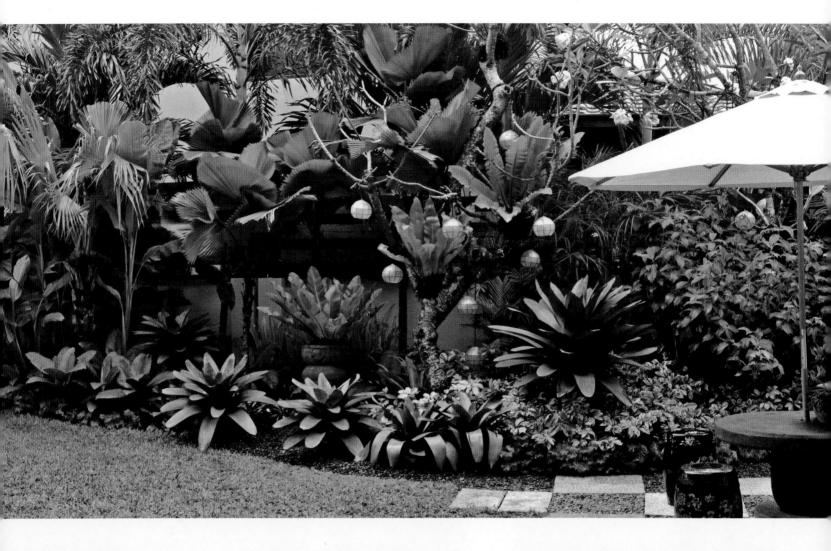

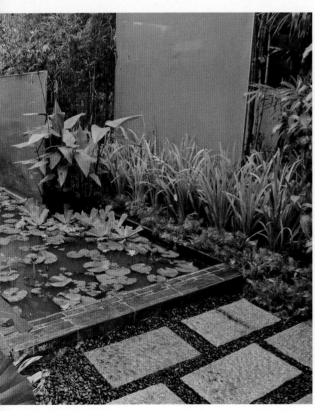

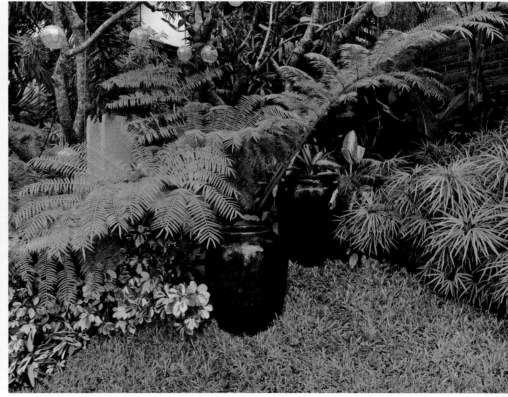

BOBBY GOPIAO'S GARDEN
Loyola Heights, Quezon City

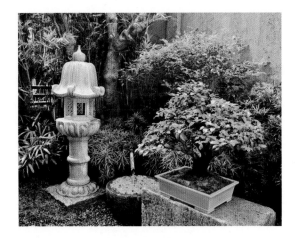

Hidden behind huge, double wooden gates in a dusty, noisy street in Quezon City is the home of Bobby Gopiao, landscape designer and president of the Philippine Bonsai Society. Once inside, all sense of being in an urban environment vanishes. Instead, one gets a feeling of having wandered into a woodland forest.

On the right, a bank of ferns blankets an entire wall. There are giant bird's nest ferns and fishtail ferns, ribbon ferns, maidenhair ferns, rabbit's foot ferns, fork sword ferns and common sword ferns. Natives of the forest, they seem to have adapted to their new habitat quite well. On the left, hidden behind a green staircase is a secret garden. Designed as a boundary between the outside and the inside, one can take a contemplative pause here before entering the house.

A path of river stones and *piedra China* pavers leads to a tea garden screened by date palms and thick plantings of Rhapis palms and Podocarpus. Two huge stone lanterns lend an Oriental touch. A recirculating pump directs water into a stone basin through a bamboo spout and

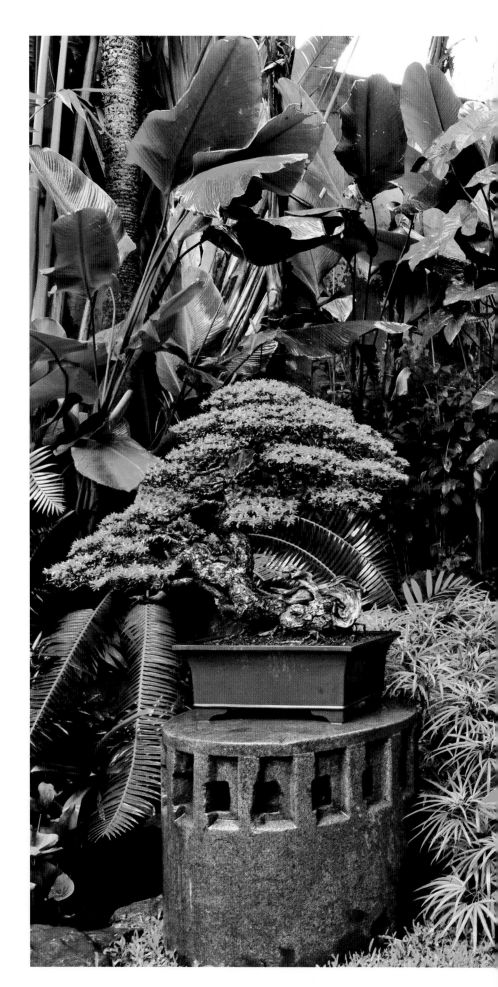

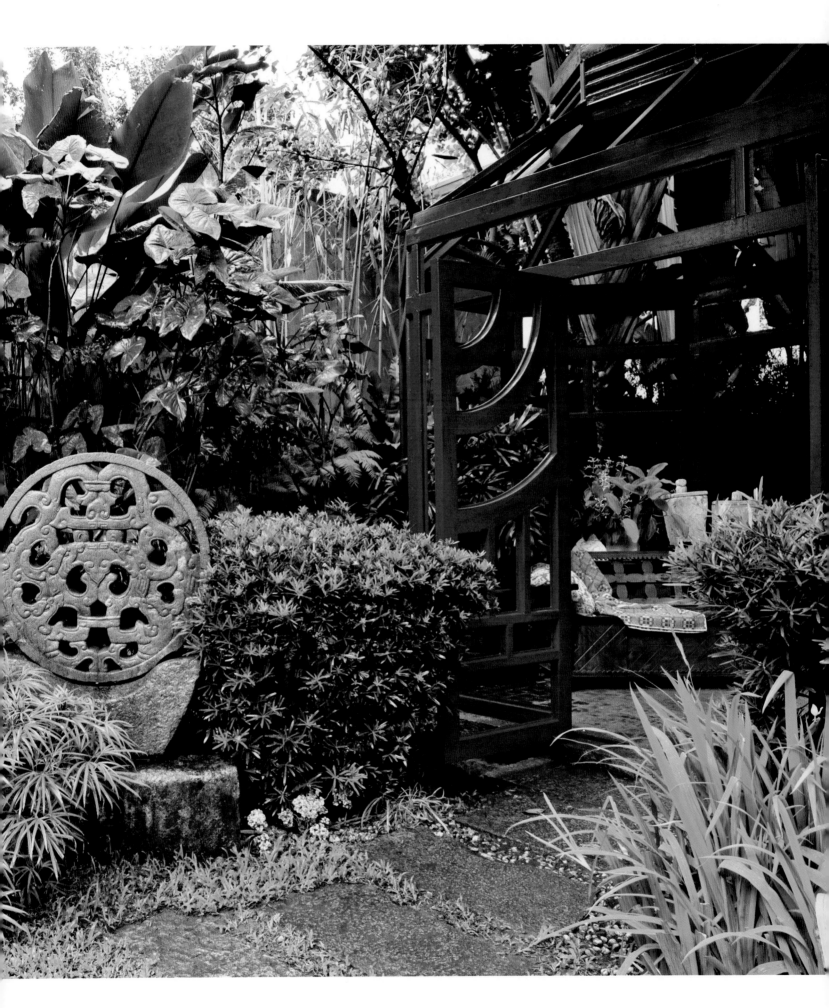

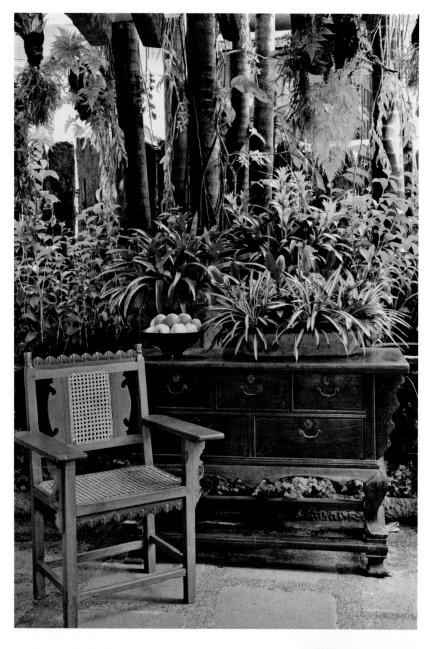

instills the space with a welcoming sound. Juxtaposed against a massive stone sculpture are some examples of the owner's bonsai collection planted on ceramic trays and set on top of boulders. There is a Bougainvillea in flower and a *bignai* tree *(Antidesma bunius)* along with two amazing specimens of *mansanita (Ziziphus mauritiana)*, and an Elaeagnus tree from Taiwan.

The main garden is approached through the house that is tastefully furnished with Spanish antiques and Philippine contemporary art. Tall glass windows with intricate wrought-iron grillwork look out onto a side garden luxuriantly planted with Aglaonemas, Heliconias, Anthuriums and Alocasias. Giant bird's nest ferns frame a flowering *Dendrobium anosmum*, while potted Philodendrons and Bromeliads in huge ornamental jars anchor a multifarious assembly of plants. Off the dining room is a *lanai* that serves as a visual link between the house and garden.

A wide tiled path leads to the focal point of the garden, a red glass pavilion. In the dappled sunlight, sheltered by towering rambutan *(Nephelium lappaceum)*, golden bamboo, Washingtonia palm, *Ficus triangularis*, fragrant frangipani and Traveler's palm, it is an awesome sight. The pavilion, informally decorated with a combination of antique and modern furniture, was added seven years ago along with a pond and a waterfall. The water features heighten the sense of place, which the owner likes to describe as "heavy tropical meets Oriental modern." A magnificent grouping of *Medinilla magnifica* with its thick, leathery leaves and pink and purple bracts, draws the eye to the interesting collection of Cycads, Miagos, Alocasias and peacock ferns around the pond.

In addition, more bonsai specimens are displayed elsewhere in the garden and on a second-floor balcony, while numerous architectural appointments—stone mills, antique jars and statues—further highlight the garden's sense of drama.

Previous pages main photo "Heavy tropical meets Oriental modern" is how the owner describes his garden. Oriental elements include this red pavilion, statuary and the bonsai specimen.

Previous pages small photo A Japanese stone lantern and an ornamental jar fountain with bamboo spout stand beside a bonsai specimen in the tea garden.

Above Pots of Vrieseas and Neoregelia adorn an antique chest of drawers.

Right An imposing stone sculpture, an old agricultural implement, marks the entrance to the red glass pavilion.

Opposite Sunlight streams through assembled groupings of *Medinilla magnifica*, bird's nest ferns and Bromeliads in the pond.

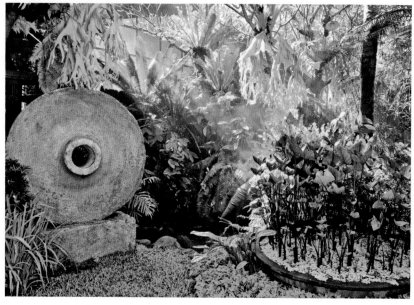

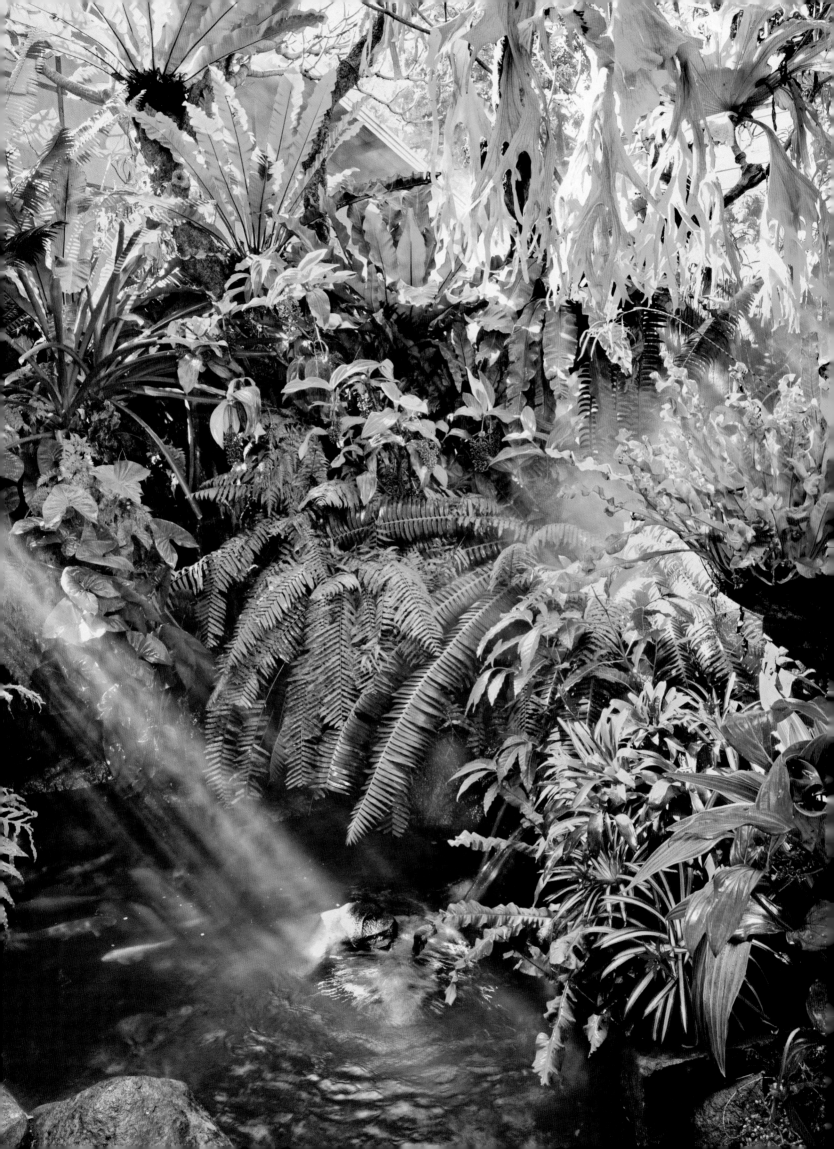

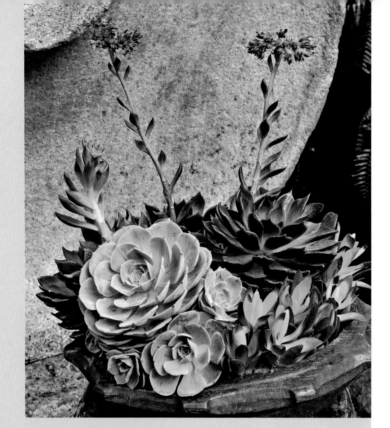

Left A sweet arrangement of Echeverias. This genus of succulents is becoming popular in modern gardens because of its ever-changing, colorful and dramatic foliage.

Below A dramatic composition of potted bird's nest ferns, bamboo, Heliconias, spiral ginger and *Osmoxylon geelvinkianum*.

Right The side garden seen through grilled fretwork from the living room.

Bottom Decorative pots and statuary contribute to the richness of this wildly eclectic garden.

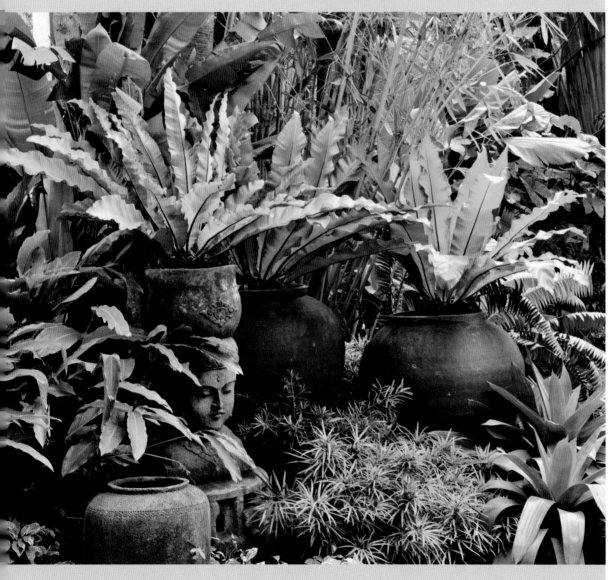

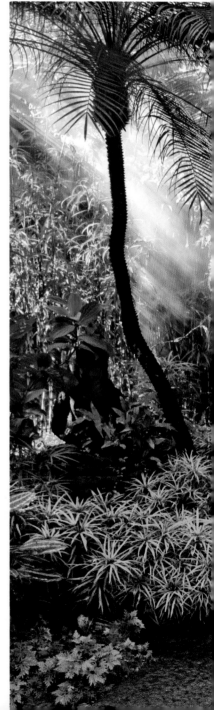

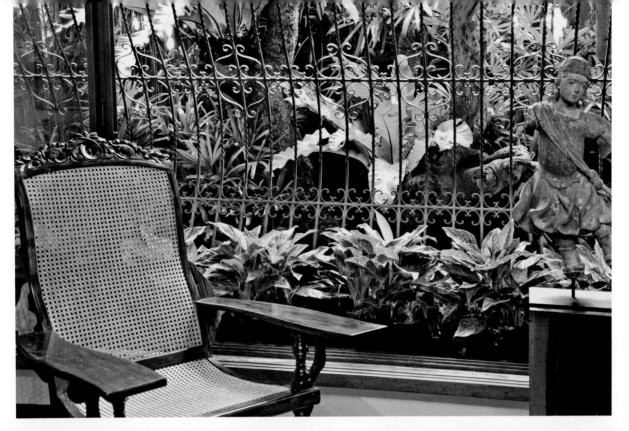

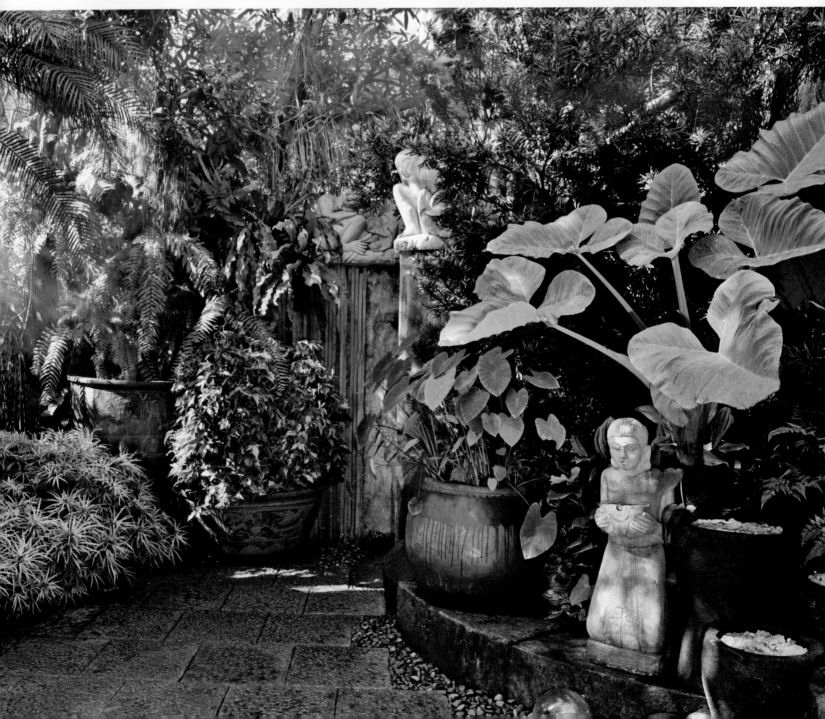

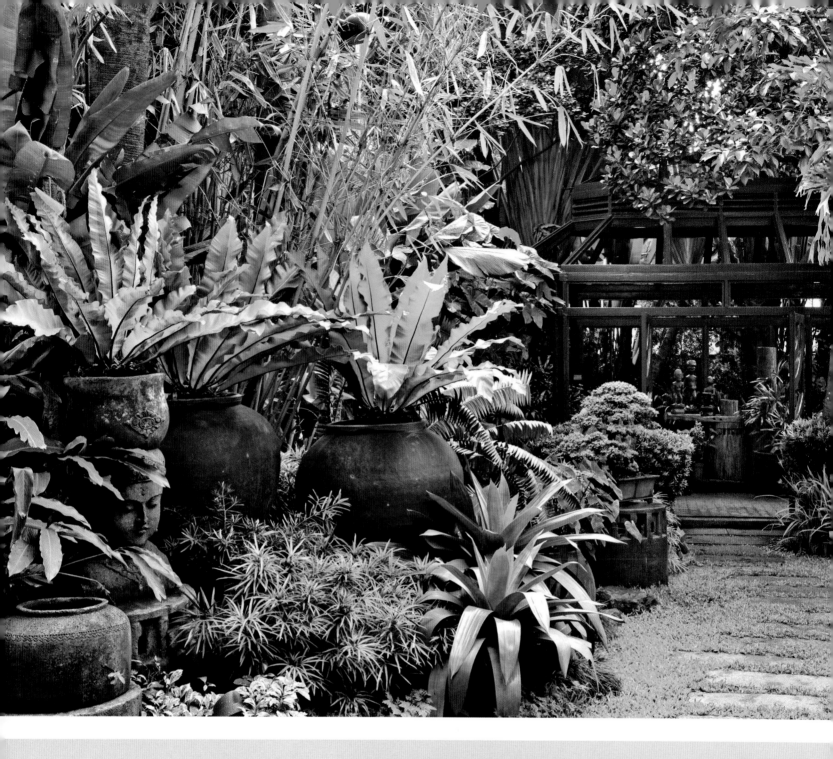

Above The focal point of the garden is a bright red glass pavilion furnished with antiques and native artifacts.

Right Detail on the weathered front gate.

2nd right In the tea garden foot path, imaginative pavers with geometric forms are set in a bed of pebbles.

3rd right An overall view of the tea garden.

4th right Bonsai specimens in the tea garden are juxtaposed against some stone sculptures; the arrangement harks back to ancient Chinese ideas of symmetry and order.

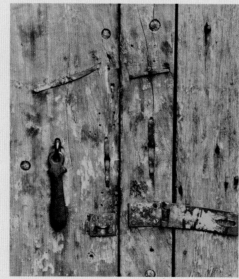

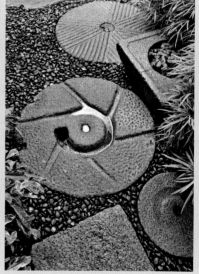

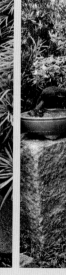

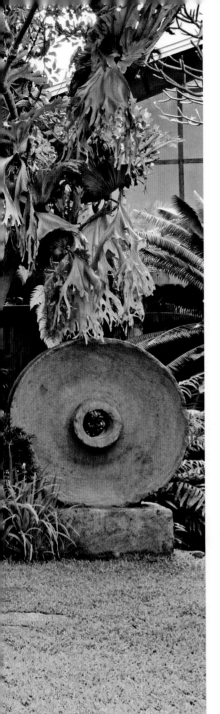

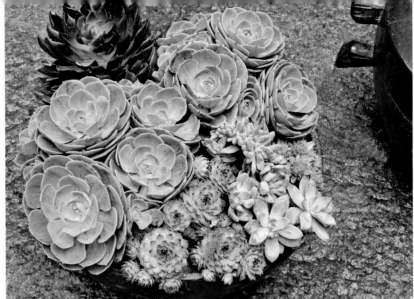

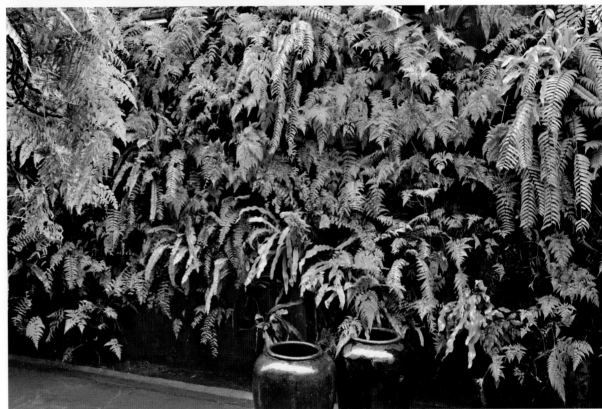

Left A pretty potted assortment of succulents has a sculptural quality.

Below A tapestry of ferns on a side wall by the driveway is accompanied by two oversized ceramic jars.

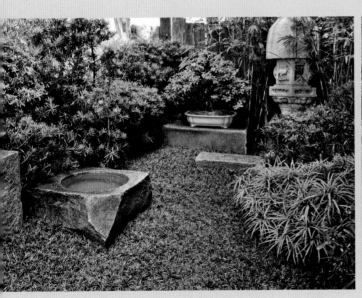

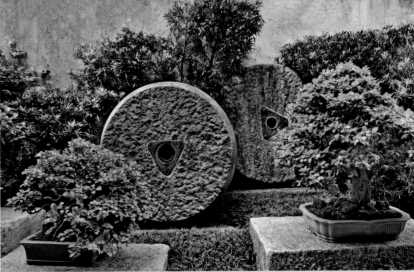

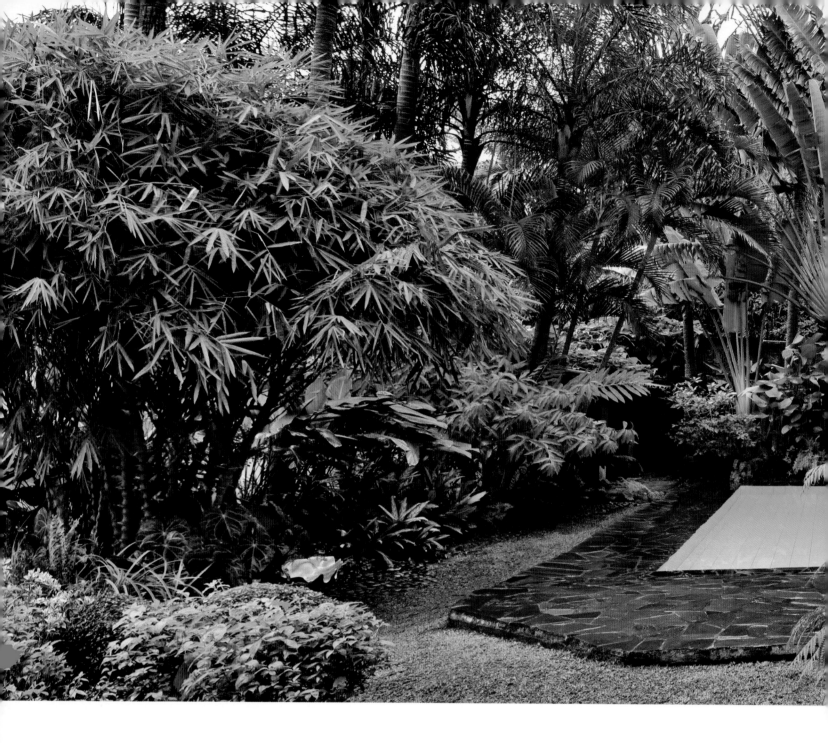

OLBES POOL GARDEN

Dasmarinas Village, Makati

Designed by Michelle Magsaysay

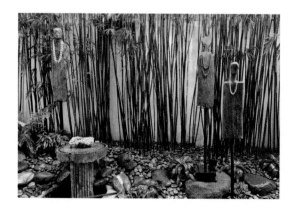

At the Olbes home, a spacious *lanai* serves as the visual link between the house and the garden, enouraging the landscape to become part of the house. Garden walls are dressed with bamboo, Cycads, Rhapis palms and Mussaenda. Fukien tea, clipped to emphasize its sculptural qualities, provides a formal note at one end of the garden while an arresting tableau composed of ball-pruned Ficus, driftwood with Vandas and Phalaenopsis, and a potted Bangkok *calachuche* dominates a sidewall. These latter flowers provide color and texture with mounds of Ophiopogon grass and variegated boat lily (*Rhoeo spathacea*).

The owners and their designer also reserved special places for water, with a pool area marked by an elegant stand of bamboo. Paved with flagstones and surrounded by plantings of traveler's palm, Buddha-belly bamboo, bird's nest ferns along with stepladder spiral ginger, Alocasias, Yucca and Rhapis palms, it is a brilliantly concealed surprise. Ferns add a complementary note of pale green color and delicate texture.

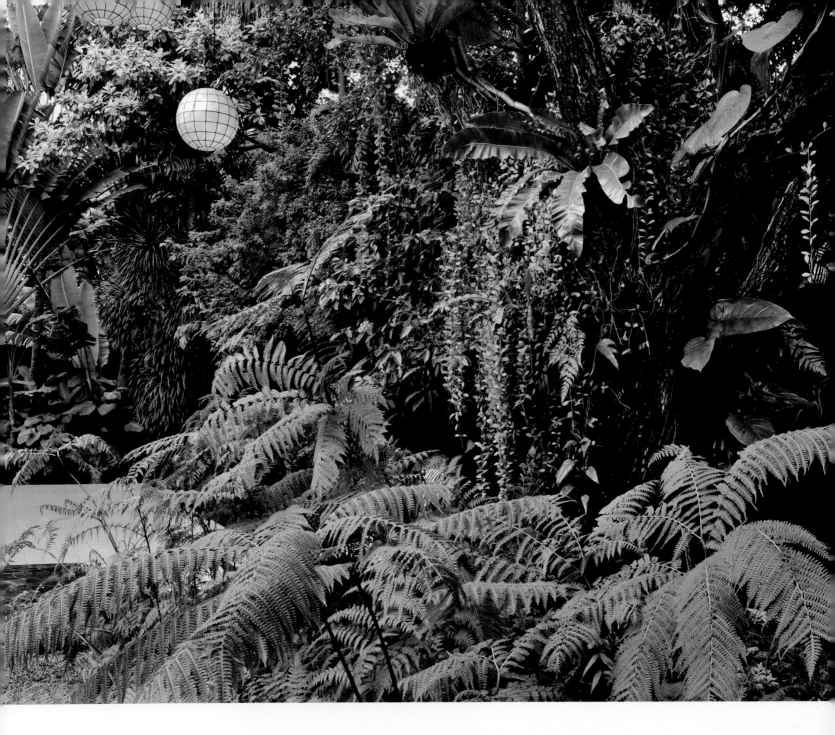

Above The highlight of the garden is the pool area hidden around a bend. Lush with various palms, bamboo, a variety of ferns and a couple of traveler's palms, *Ravenala madagascariensis*, it is accessed through steps of railroad timber.

Opposite bottom Samples of the owner-designer's work are displayed in a courtyard garden planted with bamboo and Bromeliads.

Right One side of the house is sculptural with ball-pruned Ficus, Vandas and Phalaenopsis on driftwood stands, a dwarf Bangkok frangipani, golden Ophiopogon grass and variegated boat lily, *Rheo spathacea*.

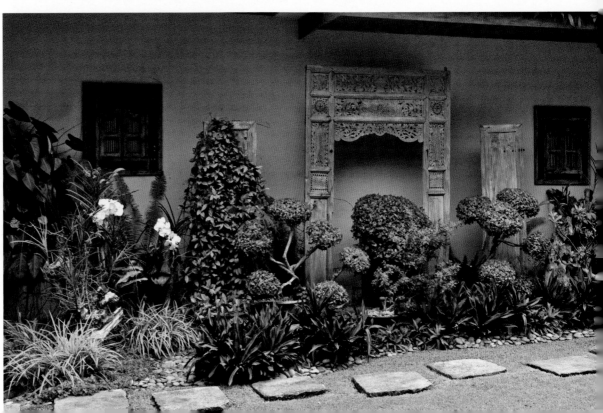

ABOITIZ GARDEN
Maria Luisa Subdivision, Cebu City

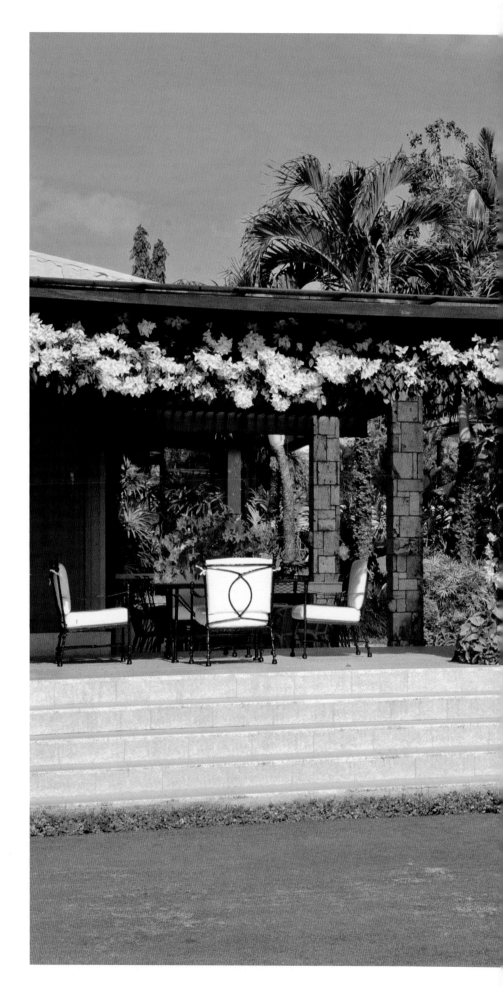

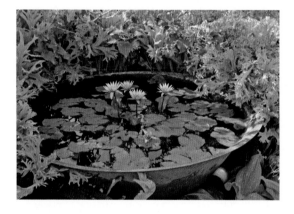

You drive up a narrow lane bordered by Bougainvillea to a charming wood and brick home located in one of the exclusive gated communities high above Cebu City. The property, belonging to Annie and Louie Aboitiz, sits on a raised bank built from Mactan stone. All around and below, a cascade of white Bougainvillea commands your attention. You gaze down on a waterfall of flowers and admire the floral tapestry that drapes over the wall. Looming above is a stand of Plumeria trees, now festooned with white blossoms filling the garden with a heady, voluptuous fragrance.

The side of the garden adjacent the house is even more remarkable: Here, a grouping of royal palms provides architectural interest and also gives shelter to a wide array of plants. A *lanai* is resplendent with the same white Bougainvillea cultivar from Singapore that greeted you at the gate, but now trained as a vine on wooden posts. Nicely furnished with wrought iron furniture with white cushions, this is the threshold of the garden.

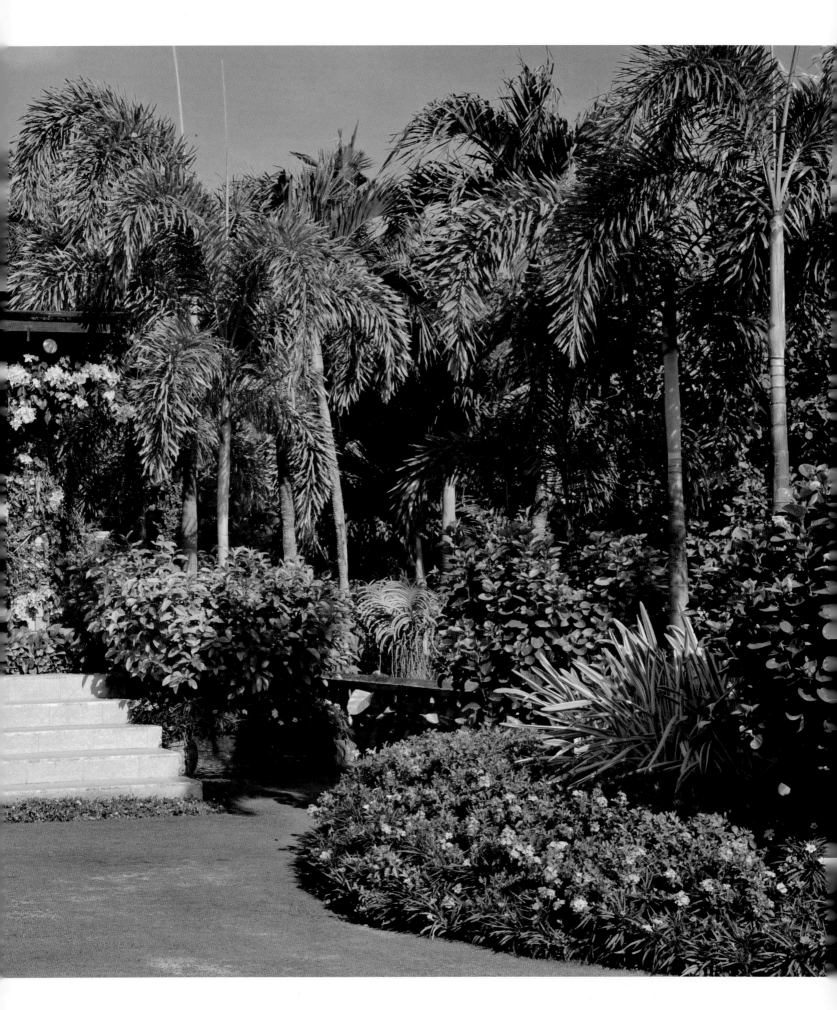

From here you can go down the limestone steps that lead to a manicured lawn bordered by flowering specimens of Plumbago and shrimp plant.

White Bougainvillea in ceramic pots further reinforces the predominantly white color theme of the garden. Both the soil and climate can be challenging in Cebu with a dry season that can be hot, dry and windy on occasion, thereby calling for a limited plant palette. Bougainvillea, a thorny, semi-woody climber with long drooping branches and small flowers, works well here as it does best in full sun and needs little water. Ranging in colors from red, pink, yellow, purple to white, it is native to South America and was named after the first Frenchman to cross the Pacific, Antoine de Bougainville. Today, the Bougainvillea has become one of the most popular plants in the Philippines with numerous cultivars grown throughout the country.

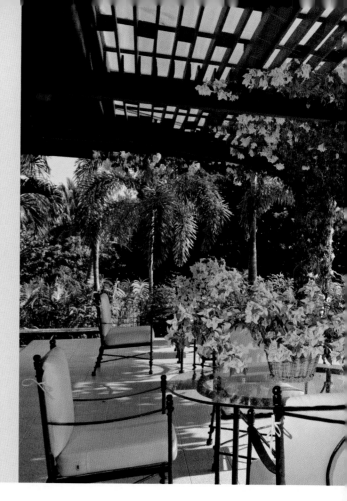

Previous pages main photo
An inviting veranda tastefully furnished with wrought iron furniture with white cushions serves as the threshold of the garden.

Previous pages small photo
An iron vat filled with tropical water lilies.

Right The white theme of the garden is echoed in the cushions on the wrought iron chairs as well as in the Bougainvillea floral arrangement on the table.

Below Towering palms hover over a driveway screened by a pink and white Bougainvillea hedge.

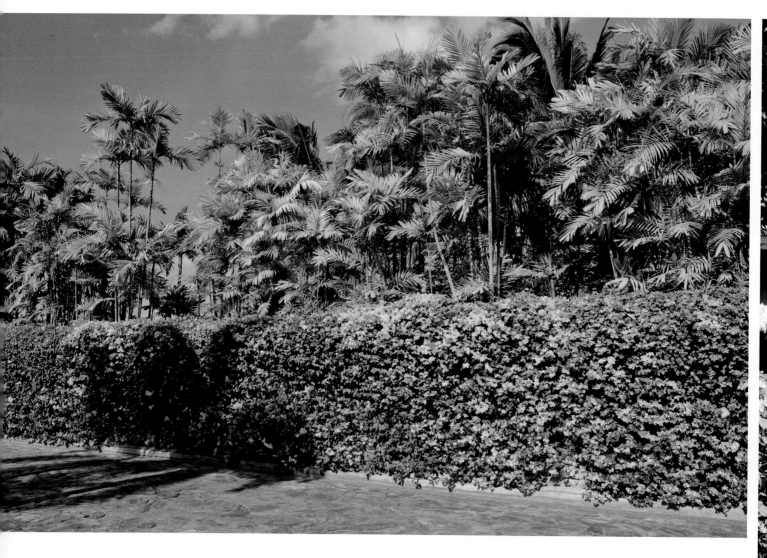

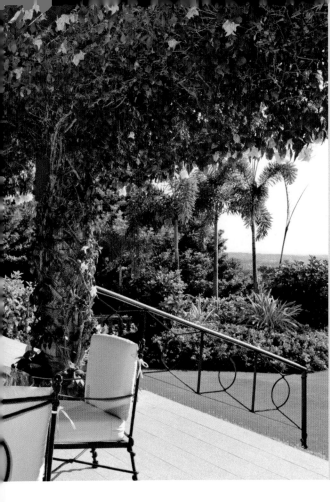

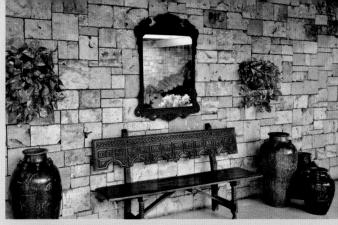

Right top and middle Oriental jars and white Bougainvillea in ceramic pots enliven the veranda.

Bottom Flower laden frangipani trees (Plumeria sp) loom over a cascade of white Bougainvillea.

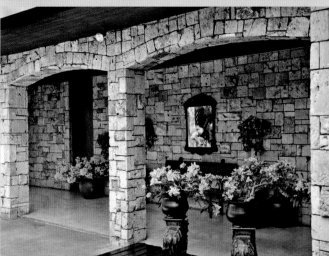

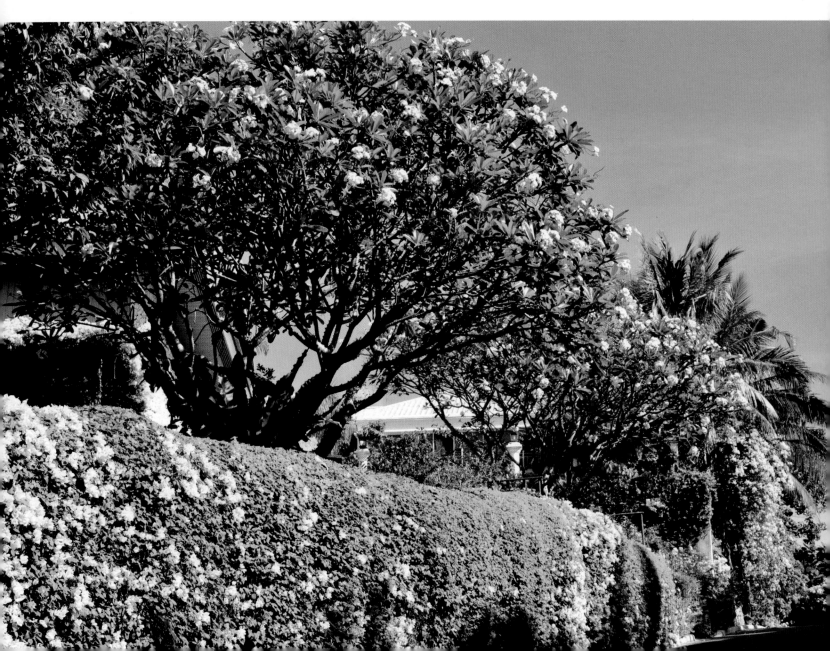

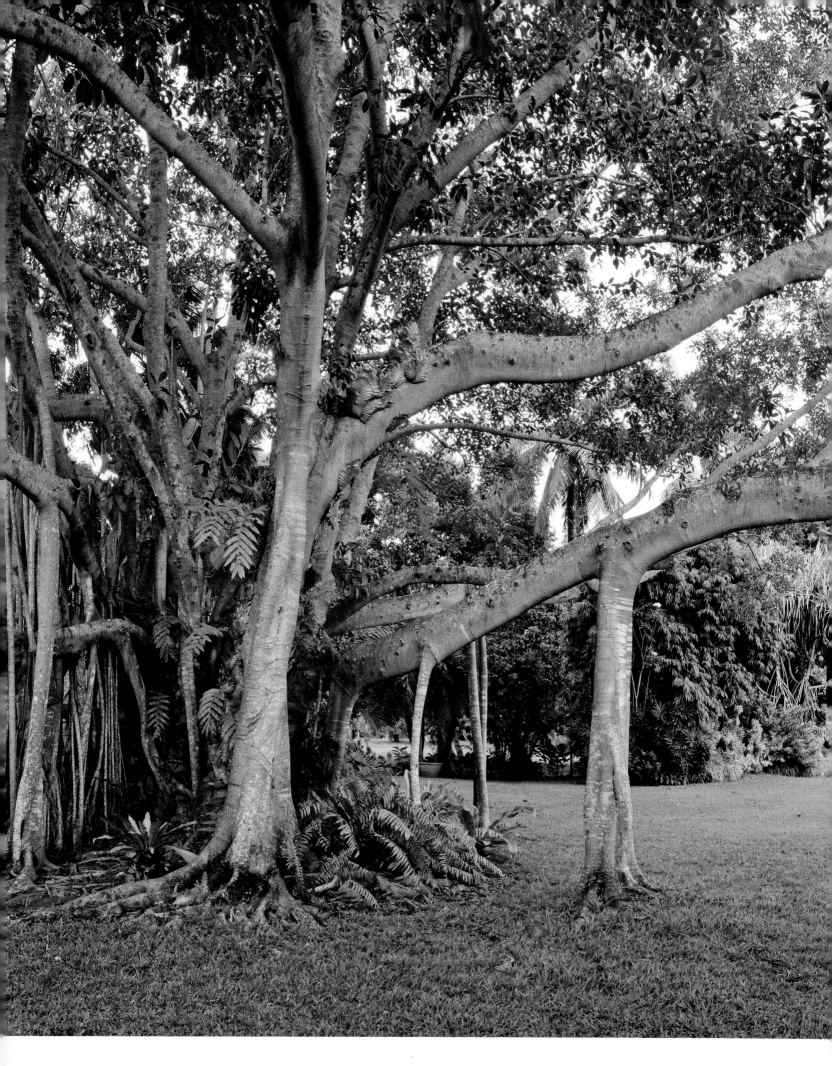

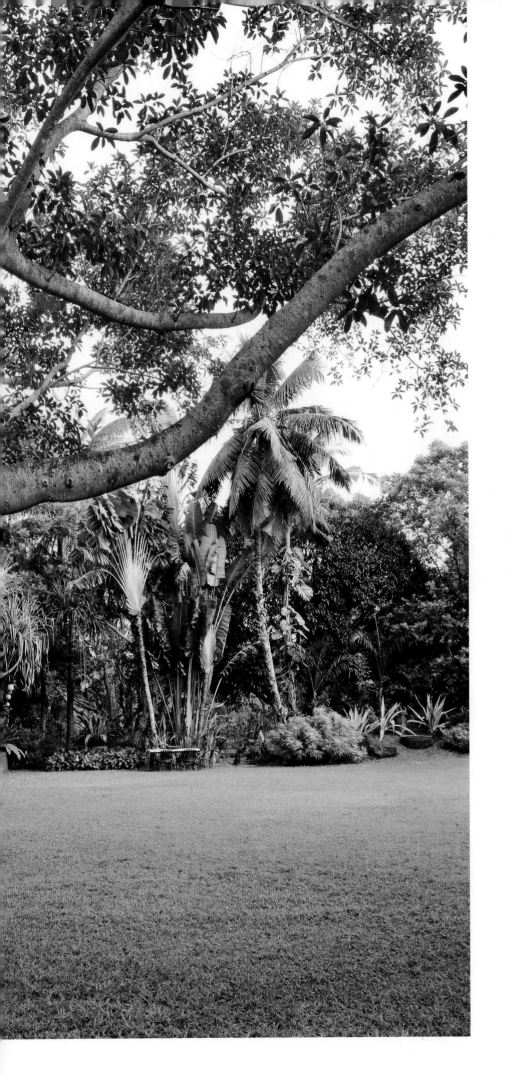

HACIENDA BALBINA
Bacolod, Negros Occidental
Designed by Shirley Sanders

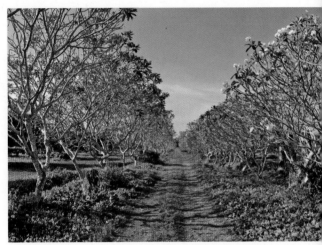

In this garden, one feels the vastness of the landscape: there are a number of magnificent old trees including a focal rubber tree, a lavishness of plantings, and a massive amount of space devoted to lawn. Home to a family estate or hacienda and located on land blessed with a generally pleasant climate, an abundant water supply and rich volcanic soil, it is an ideal garden environment.

The gardens, which include orchards, orchid borders, a chapel garden and a large ornamental pond were designed in collaboration with landscape designer, Shirley Sanders. The lady of the house, Gretchen Oppen Cojuangco, a woman with a deep feeling for plants, wanted a garden that would reflect her enthusiasm for naturalistic plantings and her environmental consciousness. A zigzag of Plumeria trees mimics the curve of mountains in the distance, while a palette of many different greens echoes the color of the vast plains of sugarcane that lie beyond the garden. Both native and indigenous plants line the garden's perimeter, softening the transition from

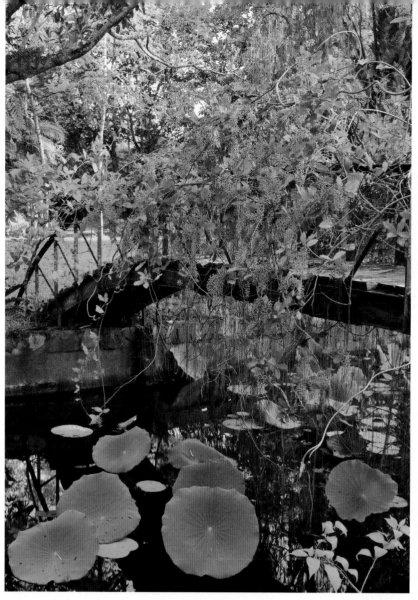

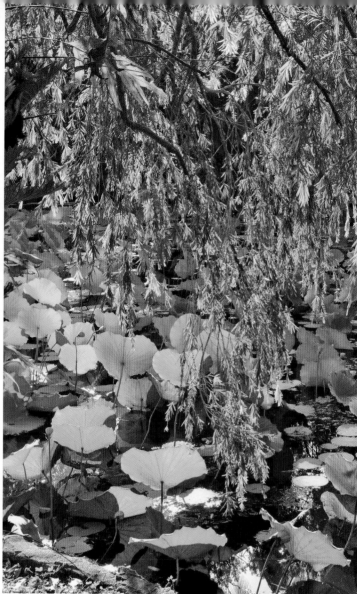

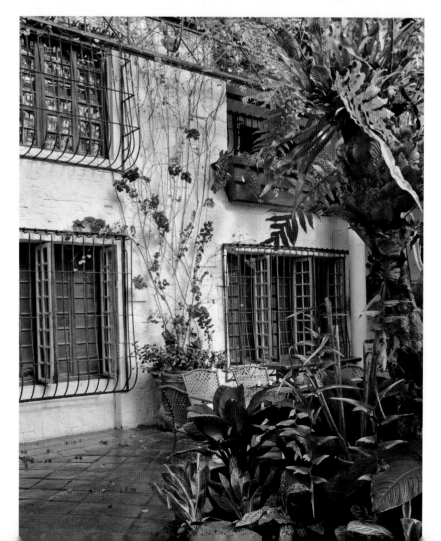

formal to natural landscape. Drifts of orchids bring to mind the endemic species of the rainforest.

Beyond the pool, the garden opens into several areas connected by a series of wide-mown paths. One of the focal points is a chapel cloaked with the creeping fig or *Ficus pumila*. It's a small replica of the owner's parish church in the outskirts of Manila and is bordered with plantings of *Osmoxylon geelvinkianum* and Mussaenda.

The crowning glory of the garden, however, is a breathtaking ornamental pond, framed by undulating green walls of Chinese bamboo and carpeted with a dense mat of lotus, *Nelumbium nelumbo*. Curvilinear in shape, its banks are planted with several weeping Japanese willows and coconut palms. Arching over is a bridge made from railway sleepers and festooned with blue *Petrea volubilis* blooms. In high summer, the middle of the pond is lush with billowing papyrus and the dark green blades of cattails that come up to its edge. One side is planted with *Jatropha* 'Shanghai Beauty' with under plantings of *Lantana camara,* both of which lend color and add oomph to the border of mostly moisture-loving plants.

Clearly the soul of the garden, this amazing water feature is now home to a thriving population of koi, salamanders, frogs and insects.

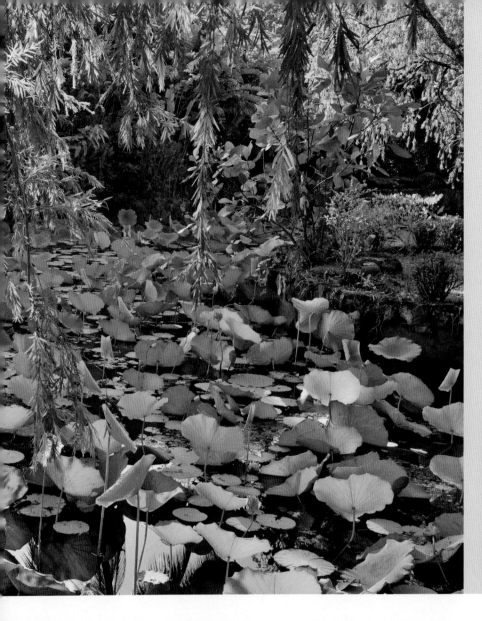

Previous pages main photo
An impressive giant rubber tree,
Ficus elastica.

Previous pages small photo
An alleyway of frangipani trees.

Far left, below and bottom
The purple wreath vine, *Petrea volubilis*, dangles over the lotus pond. This twining vine has rough green leaves, but is popular because of its spectacular clusters of purple flowers that can attain one foot in length.

Left Branches of the weeping bottlebrush tree, *Callistemon viminalis*, sway over a magnificent pond filled with water lilies.

Opposite bottom Brightly colored Bougainvillea, orchids and Heliconias brighten a court-yard with brick flooring.

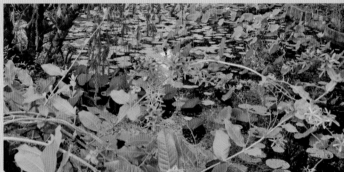

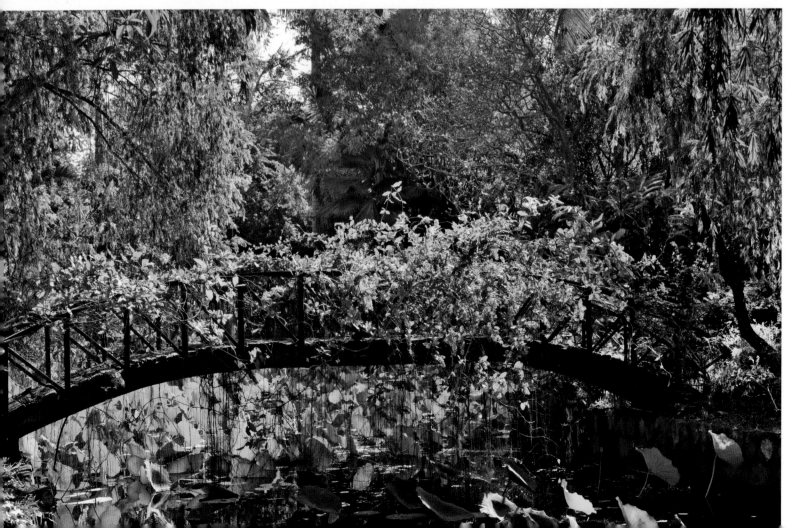

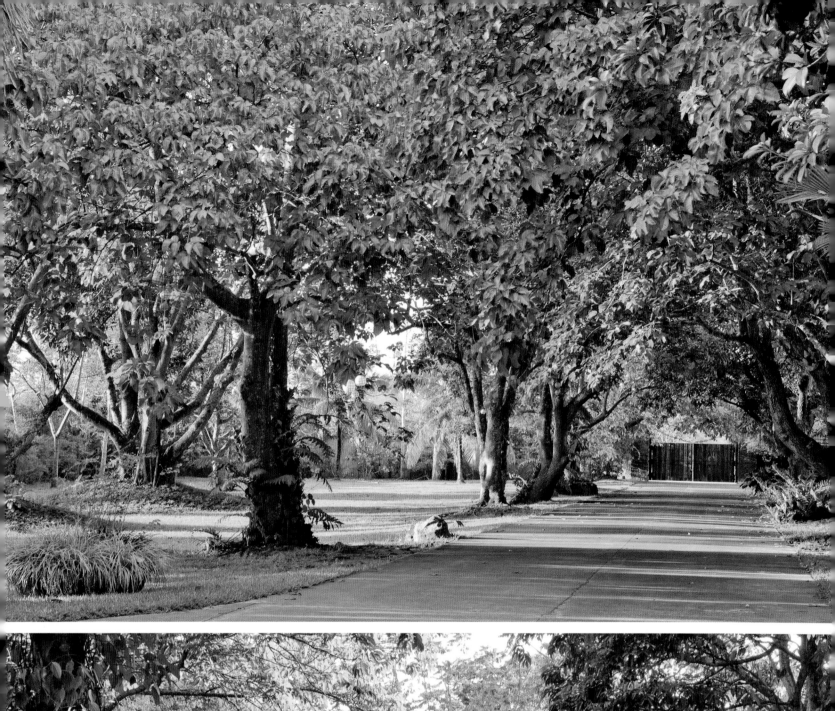
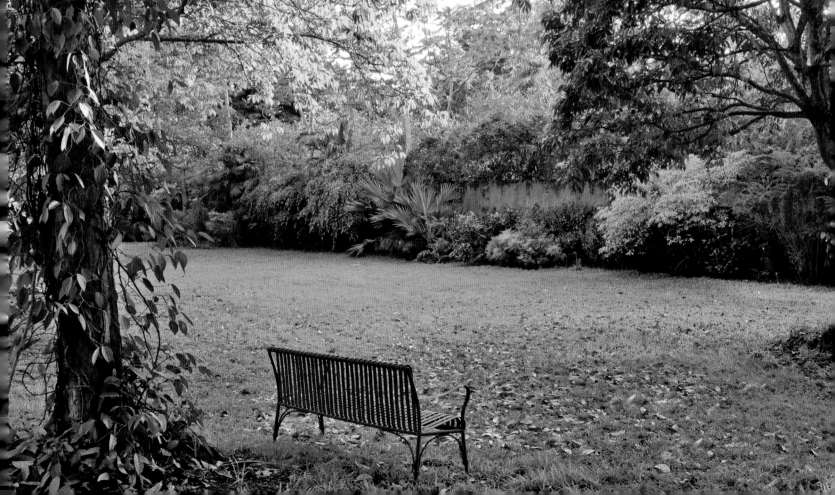

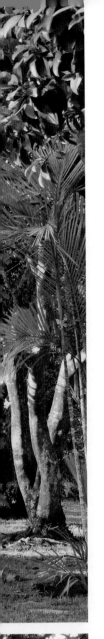

Left A driveway is lined on both sides by *santol* trees, *Sandoricum koetjape*.

Right top An antique planter's bench awaits company beneath an archway in the courtyard.

Right middle A fine example of layering in the border. Marble-leaved *picara* in a pot stands out in a bed of green colored plants.

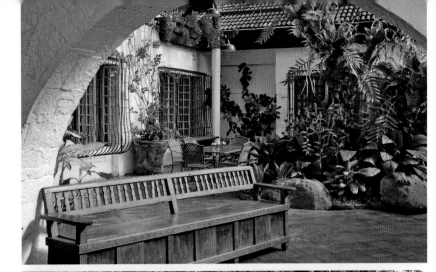

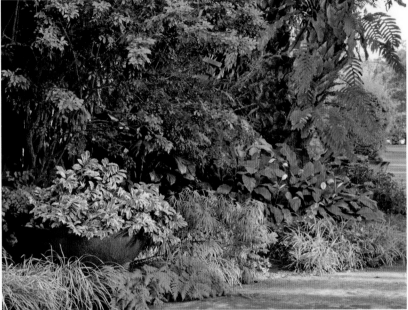

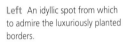

Left An idyllic spot from which to admire the luxuriously planted borders.

Right Irregularly shaped stone pavers seamed with grass lead to the breathtakingly awesome *Ficus elastica* which is native to tropical Asia.

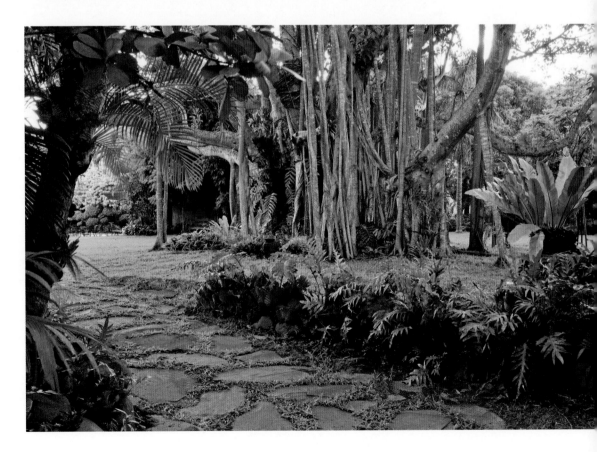

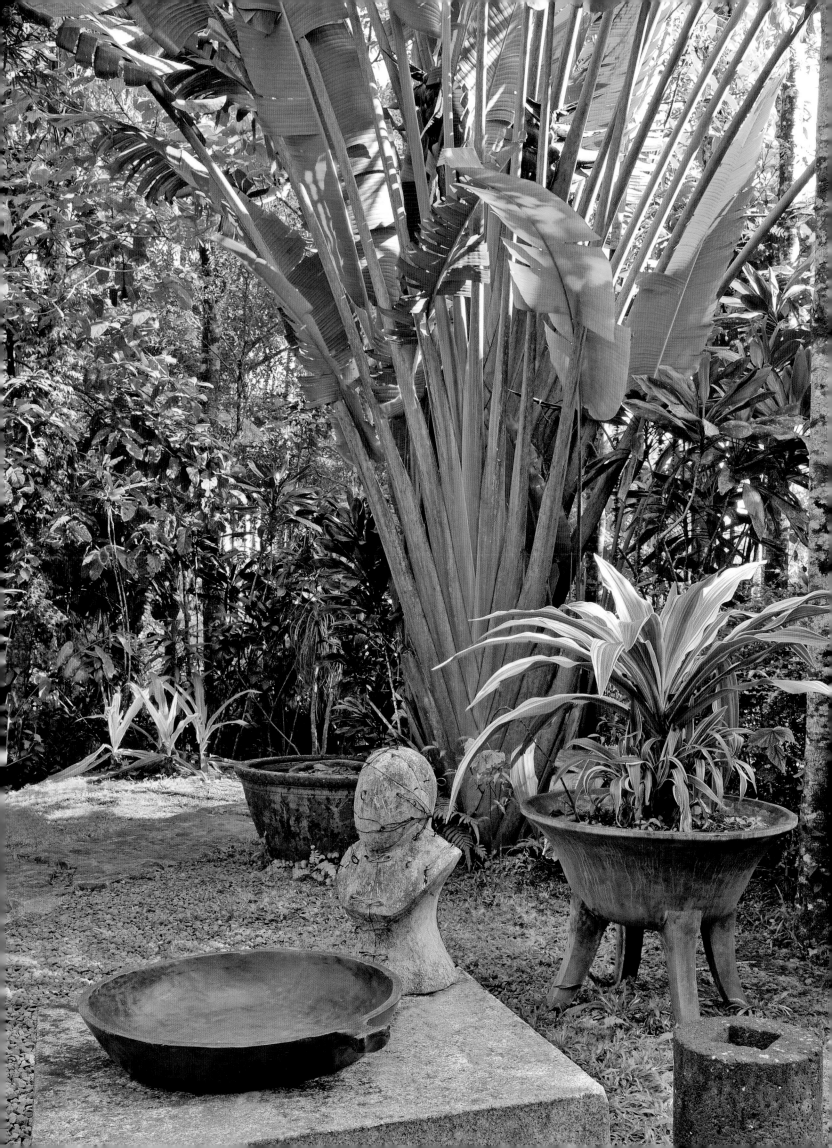

ERNEST SANTIAGO'S GARDEN

Lucban, Quezon Province
Designed by Ernest Santiago

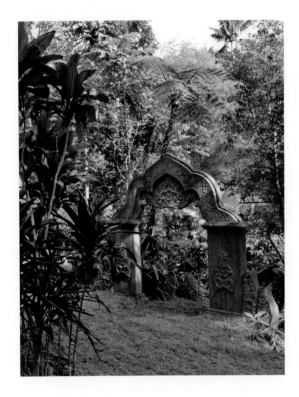

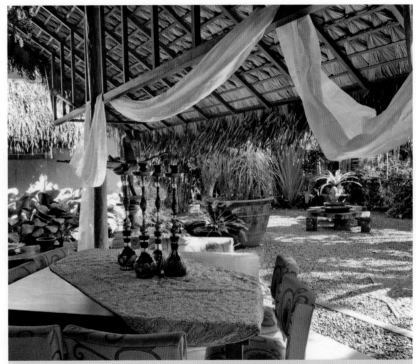

One of the late Ernest Santiago's most significant projects was his own garden in Lucban, Quezon. Lush and green, thanks to the abundant supply of water in the area, you can feel nature's sensuous spell here. The use of natural elements in the different pavilions that compose the multi-dwelling compound and masses of luxuriant plantings ensure that the focus is on the outdoors.

A *lanai*, comfortably furnished with both antique and modern furniture, looks out onto the garden which is enlivened with stands of bamboo and native trees and dense plantings of a wide variety of ornamental plants. A series of gravel and concrete paths provide a structural framework for exuberant plantings of Heliconias, bamboo and ornamental gingers. The dramatic landscaping also includes a spirit house, a large dining pavilion and a thatch-roofed gazebo adjacent a water lily pond at the bottom of the property.

Opposite A traveler's palm, *Ravenala madagascariensis*, presides over some of the owner's collection of ornamental jars and sculptural pieces.

Above A piece of cloth drapes over a colorful dining set in the *lanai* of the late Ernest Santiago.

Right This outré red rose chair is a floral "Tribute to Ernest;" created by good friend and fabric artist Romy Glorioso, it lends a touch of whimsy and fun.

Above left Deep in the Lucban garden stands this unusual archway—once part of the set design of the film "Apocalypse Now", filmed in Santiago's home town of Pagsanjan.

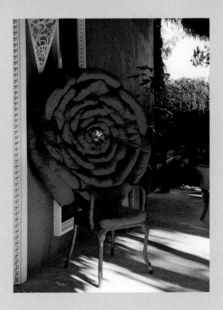

An ardent collector of architectural salvage materials and local artifacts, the fashion designer and landscape artist Santiago wittily employed his finds to achieve a sense of drama in his surroundings. A stone arch once used on the set of the movie "Apoclypse Now" currently serves as the entrance to an allée of "hot" burgundy-red *ti* plants that leads to the spirit house. Elsewhere, there are stone mills, columns and arches in surprising locations, as well as colorful banners that provide bolts of strong color.

The clever gardener's hands-on approach goes beyond the architecture of the property. From the twinkling lights interspersed with shells that dangle from the trees to the pots fashioned out of coconut husks that hold Bromeliads, to the flower filled troughs that scent the paths, everything bears the owner's stamp.

Water is a recurring theme. Small surprises hidden in the greenery are water-filled jars that hold fish and various aquatic plants. At the entrance, a rill, finely edged in con-crete with a paved flagstone surface, hums with the sound of gently trickling water. Flanked by dramatic borders of Spathiphyllum, red ginger, tree ferns and Begonias, it is used to heighten the sense of place. Another water feature, possibly the central focus of the garden, is the breath-takingly beautiful natural pond at the bottom of the property. Reached via a winding path that descends gradually past a majestic stand of bamboos, this is clearly one of the most desirable features a garden can possess, not only for the wide variety of plants it supports but also for the indigenous wildlife that it attracts. The pond, dominated by white water lilies, is alive with fish and birds as well as dragonflies and white herons. Frogs are present in good numbers as are the fireflies that light up the pond at night.

Rustic, yet modern and playfully exotic, this garden is a fitting tribute to its creative, resourceful and highly original designer. Although only two years old, it seems to have grown in admirably.

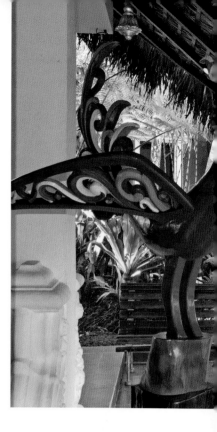

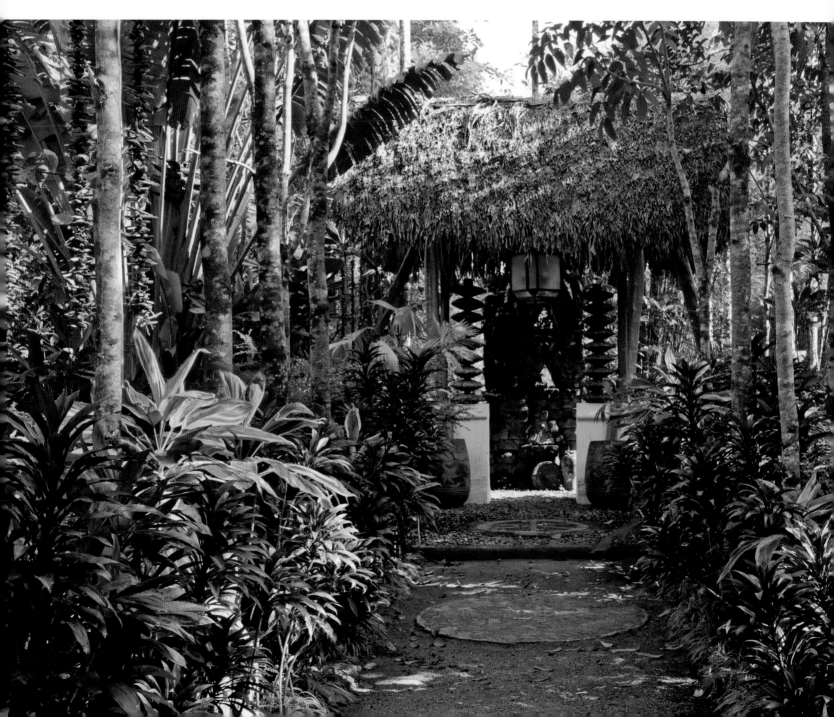

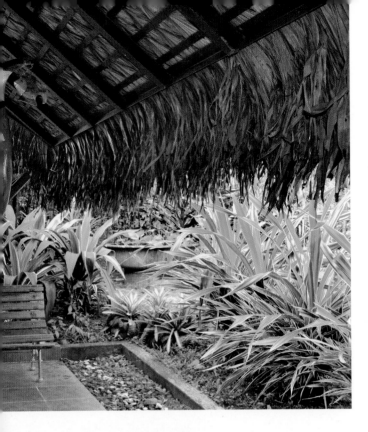

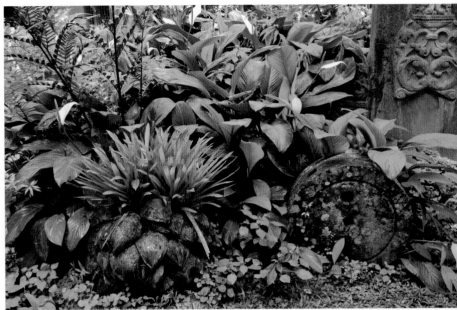

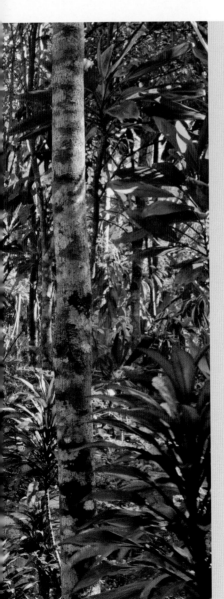

Above left A modern carving of a *sarimanok* (phoenix bird) decorates a corner of the main dining pavilion.

Above right A small garden vignette features a plant container fashioned out of coconut husks planted with Bromeliads and a stone ornament swathed in greenery.

Left An allée of burgundy-red *ti* plants, *Cordyline fruticosa*, leads to a thatched-roofed spirit house with a stone altar.

Right Decorative stone pieces as well as unusual objects are used around the garden to surprise and delight the eye.

Bottom right Colorful detailing on this semi-enclosed bathroom pavilion shows how no design detail is left to chance.

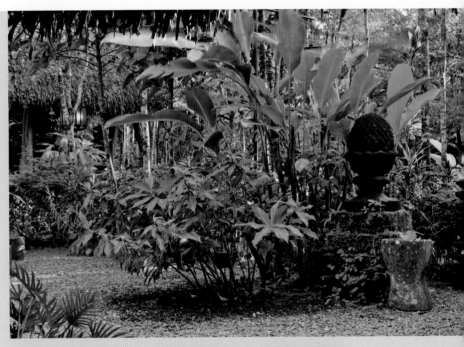

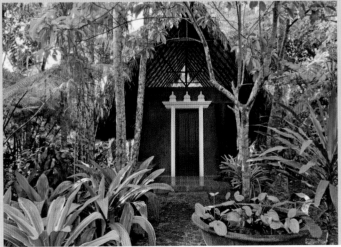

GEERTZ MOON GARDEN

Tagaytay City, Cavite

Designed by Peter Geertz

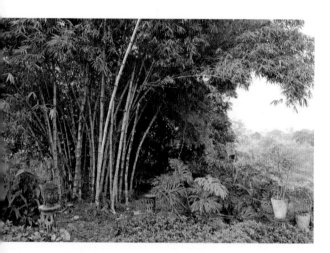

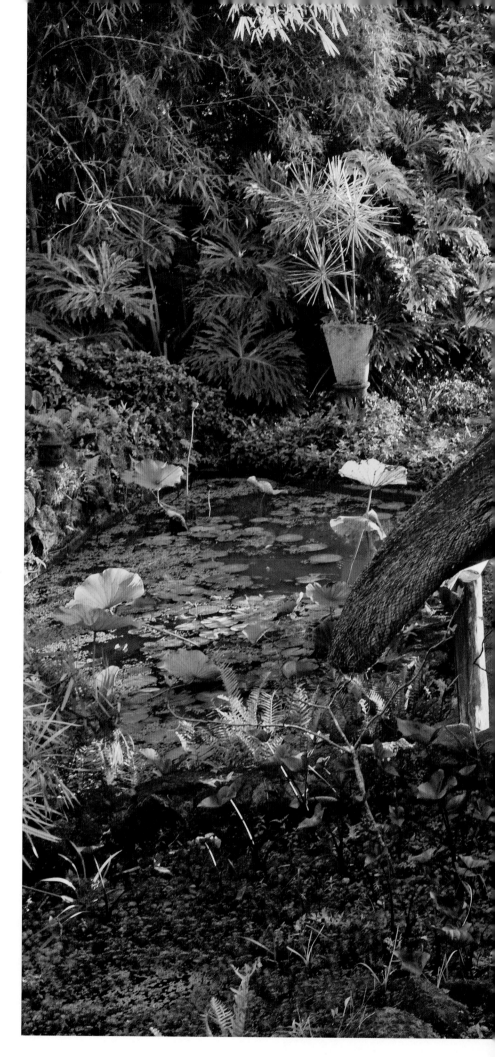

Peter Geertz, a Belgian veterinarian, came to the Philippines to study the swine virus but a surprising string of events turned him from a vet into a restaurateur cum gardener. The rich volcanic soil of the area inspired him to create the garden/restaurant of his dreams; called the Moon Garden, it is a romantic magical place, filled with scented and luminous flowers.

The garden braids a tropical planting tradition with natural woodsy elements in a modern setting. In the entry courtyard a long pergola built from tree trunks shoulders an amazing collection of vines. Draped with the celadon-colored jade vine, *Strongylodon macrobotrys*, and white, blue and orange-yellow Thunbergia, it leads you to the main restaurant pavilion and garden beyond. Mexican flame vine flowers clamber over the unusual looking *Aristolochia sturtevanteii* and white *Thunbergia fragrans*, while enchanting, pink Congea and *Holmskioldia sanguinea* in both yellow and orange contribute to the colorful assembly. A number of open-sided thatch roofed Ifugao dwellings (right) built by Eugene Canson also enhance the exotic feel of this garden.

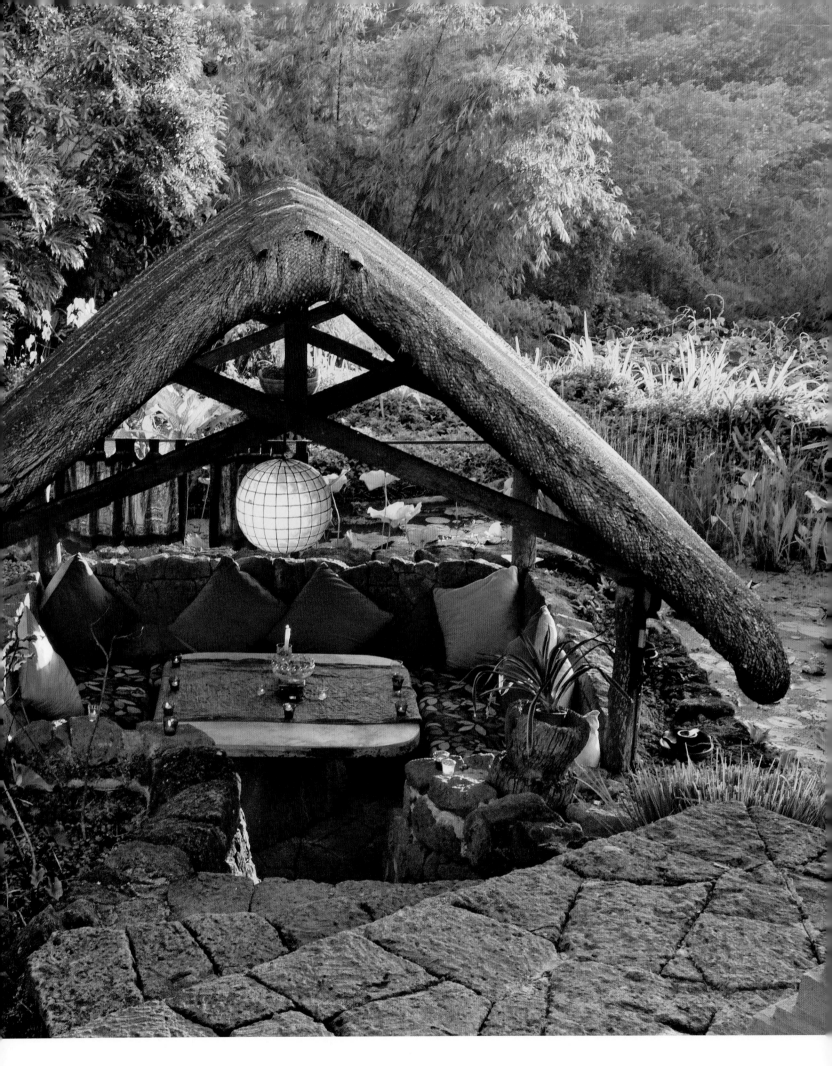

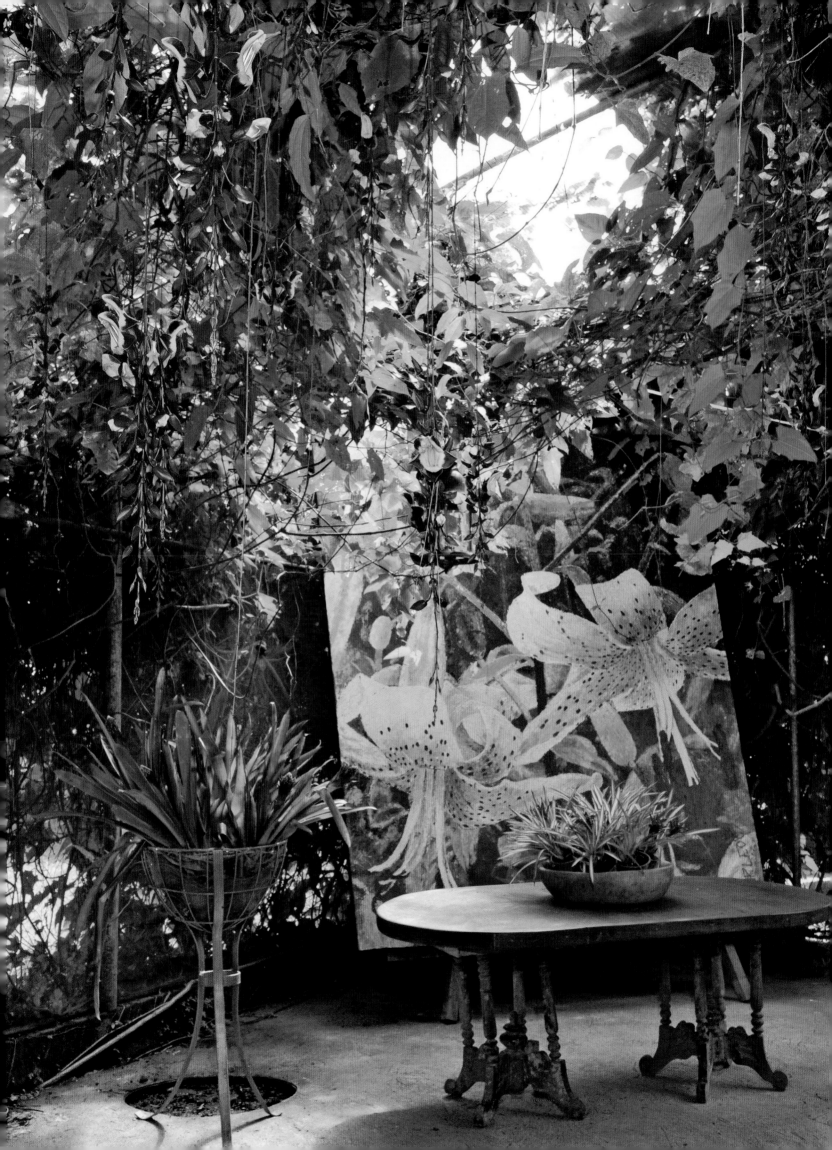

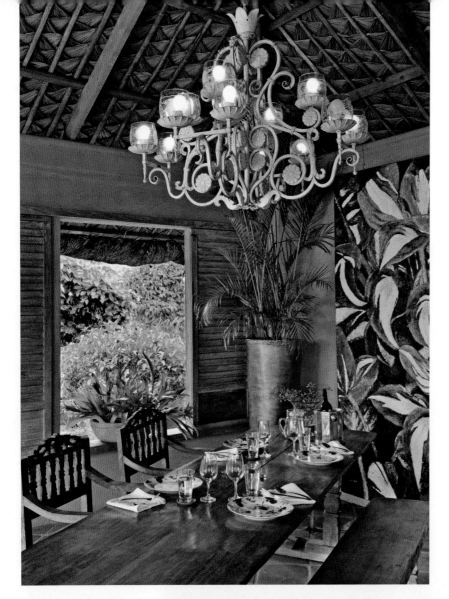

The view of the central garden from the main pavilion is of two ponds edged in stone against a backdrop of Heliconias, sugar cane, *Caesalpinia pulcherrima*, bamboo and Philodendron. The pond, richly planted with tropical water lilies, irises, lotus and *Thalia dealbata* with pendulous clusters of dark blue flowers serves to mirror the changing sky. A mango tree grown purely for ornamental purposes separates the ponds, both of which support a thatched Ifugao dwelling. Paths fashioned out of a porous stone called *escombro* connect the main pavilion to the pond structures. In atmosphere, the garden is romantic without being too obvious. One senses a practicality to it because it has to stand up to the harsh elements imposed by the rugged terrain of the area.

The design of the garden operates on two levels: the "real" garden, with the actual architecture and plantings, and the image of a garden, as seen in the large canvases of flowers by local artist Tony Empleo that are prominently displayed throughout. In this garden of pure romantic feeling and thought, you can dig deeply to unmask the layers of contrast and moving symbolism.

Previous pages main photo
An Ifugao hut fashionably set for dining sits on a lotus pond richly planted with tropical water lilies, irises, lotus and *Thalia dealbata*.

Previous pages small photo
Stately golden bamboo, *Bambusa vulgaris*, heightens the sense of place of this magical setting.

Left A spectacular *Thunbergia mysorensis* frames an oil painting of a lily, the golden yellow of its showy flowers highlighting the bright yellow color of the flower in the painting.

Above A huge contemporary botanical oil painting graces the main dining pavilion with picture windows showing vignettes of the garden.

Right The "real" garden and the "imagined" garden side by side. The large paintings of flowers are by local artist Tony Empleo.

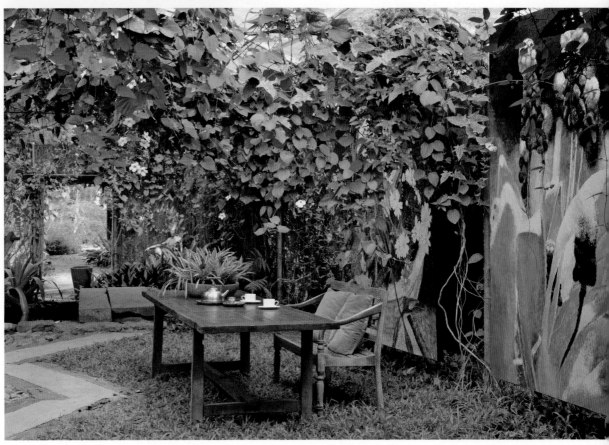

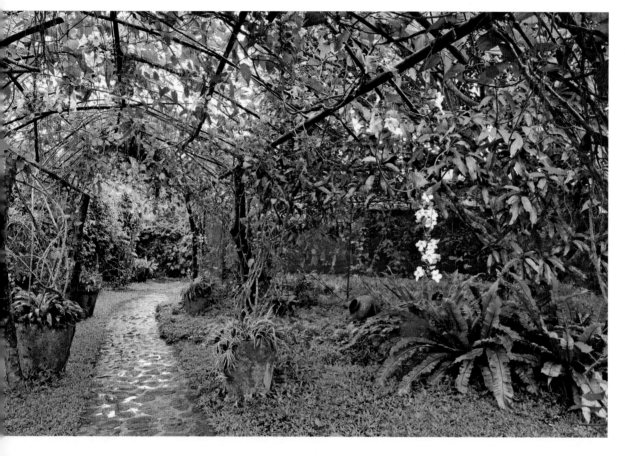

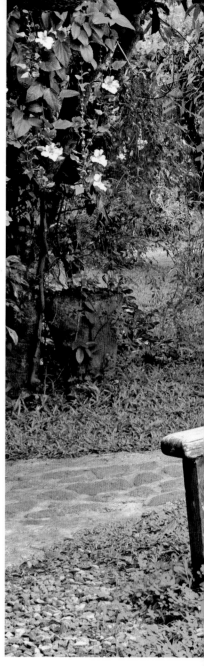

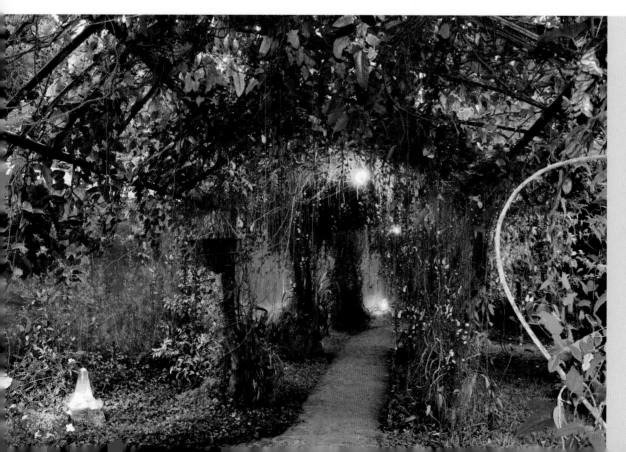

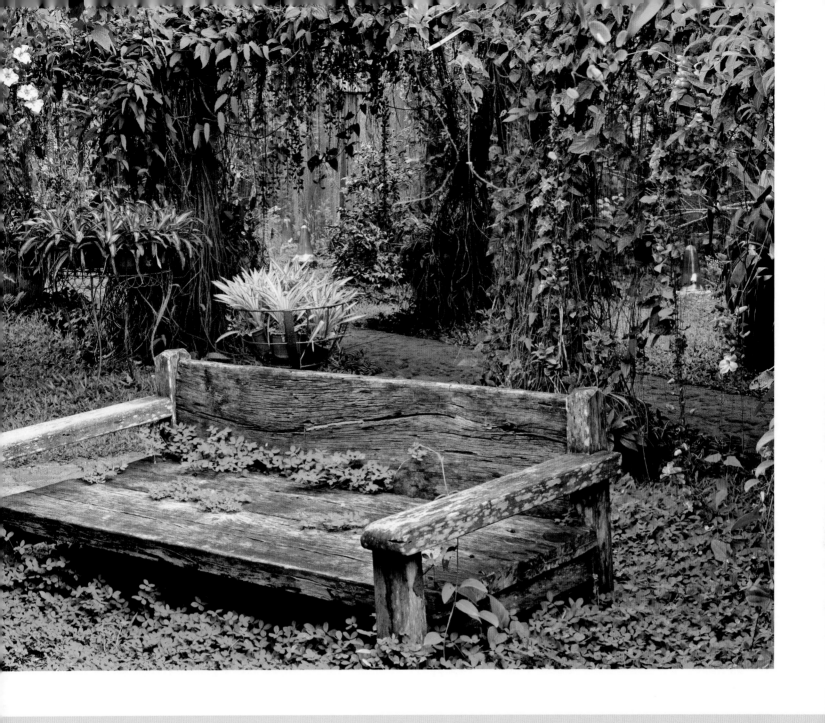

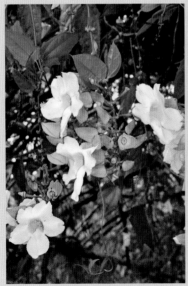
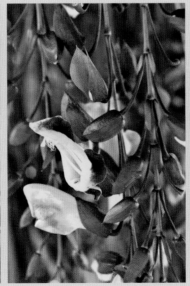
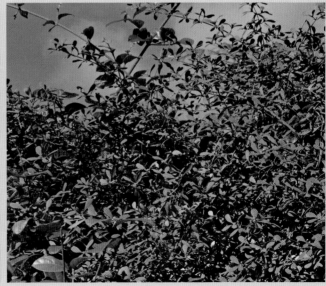

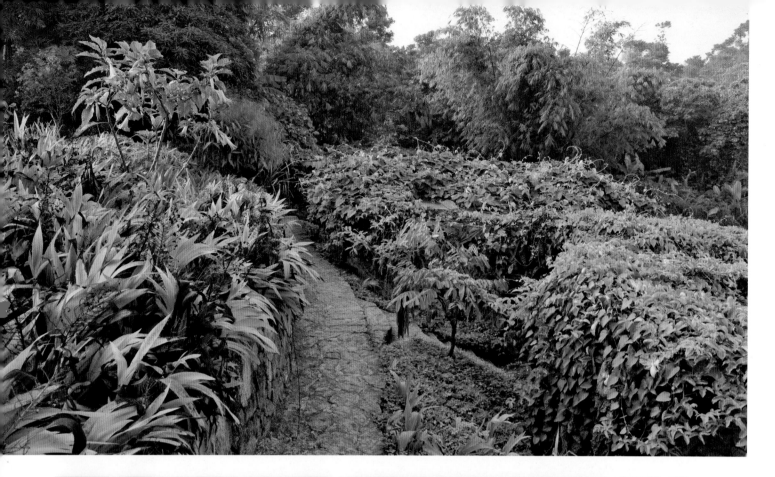

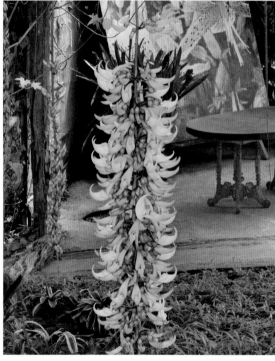

Top A solitary *Brugmansia sua-veolens* waves its beautiful pink trumpet-like flowers above a bed of spent irises.

Above Close-up view of *Strongy-lodon macrobotrys*, the Philippine jade vine; a deep blue-green, it resembles the color of jade.

Right *Brugmansia suaveolens* is also known as angel's trumpet, due to the shape of its sweetly fragrant pendulous flowers. It lends its own distinct silhouette to the surroundings.

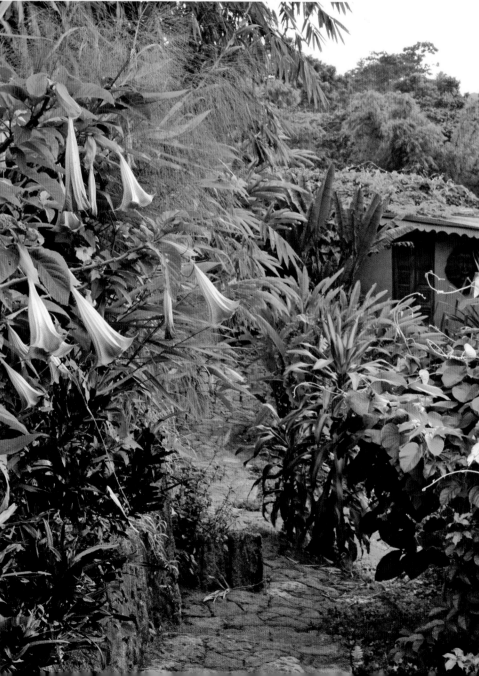

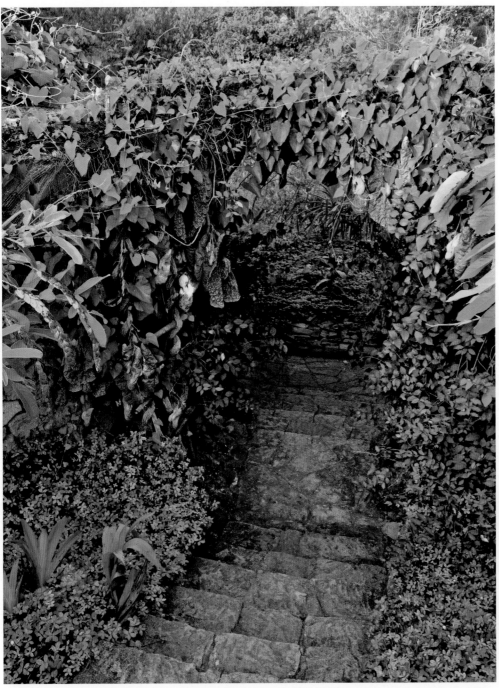

Left An arbor decked with *Aristolochia sturevanteii* provides shelter to a passageway. The genus Aristolochia comprises over 500 species, but the climbers are the most prized for their heart-shaped leaves and unusually shaped tubular flowers.

Below Close-up of the strange looking Aristolochia vine. It is often called Dutchman's pipe for obvious reasons.

Bottom right and left The bright pink flowers of Congea draw the eye to the tunnel of vines beside it.

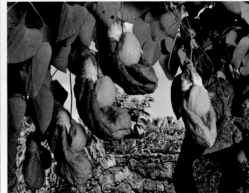

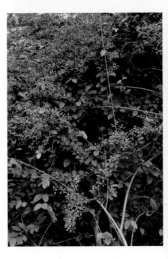

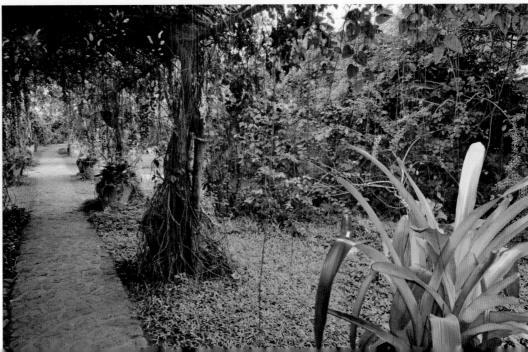

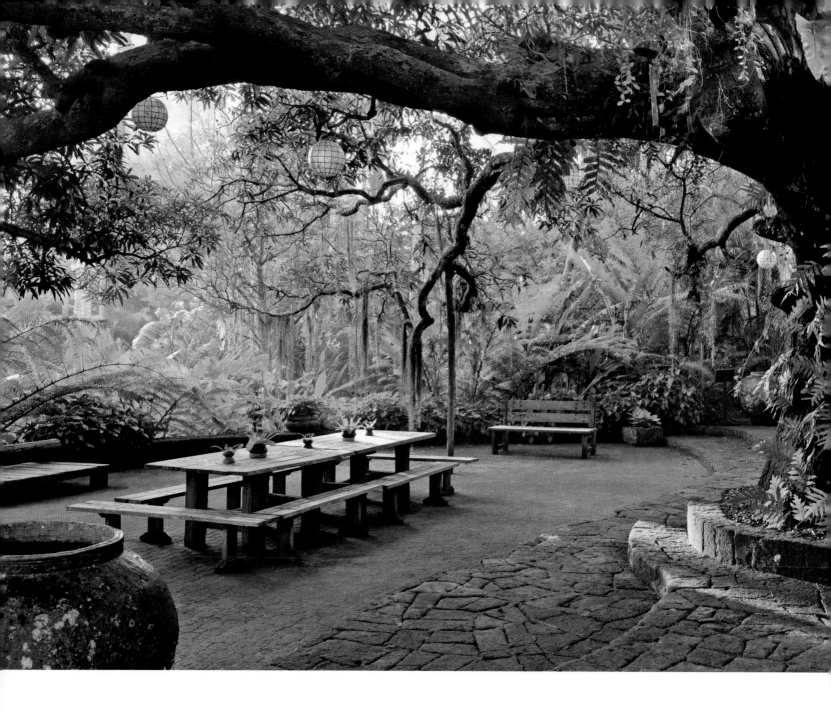

THE FARM AT SAN BENITO

Lipa, Batangas

Designed by Eckhard Rempe and Thorsten D'Heureuse

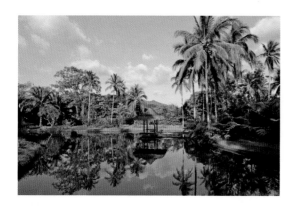

Ferns, mainstays of the tropical garden and long relegated to the background, are emerging from their supporting roles at the Farm at San Benito, a luxurious, modern spa in Lipa, Batangas. Here, they thrive in the damp shade and rocky crevices and enjoy star billing. Dainty rock ferns, powder blue ferns, staghorn ferns, common sword ferns, glossy bird's nest ferns, and last but not least majestic tree ferns, enliven this tropical paradise.

Ferns are happiest in the shade, with loose wet rich soil and good drainage. There are 26 endemic species of the tree fern (Cyathea) in the Philippines. Locally called *pakong buwaya*, they can grow up to 10 feet (3 m) tall with stalks spanning 35 feet (10 m). Some of the oldest plants on earth, they provide the Farm at San Benito with a unique sense of place.

The Farm, a center for holistic healing and wellness, just a short distance from Manila, has the feeling of a secret grove. Coconut palms under planted with mixed ferns fringe the border of the property. Once inside,

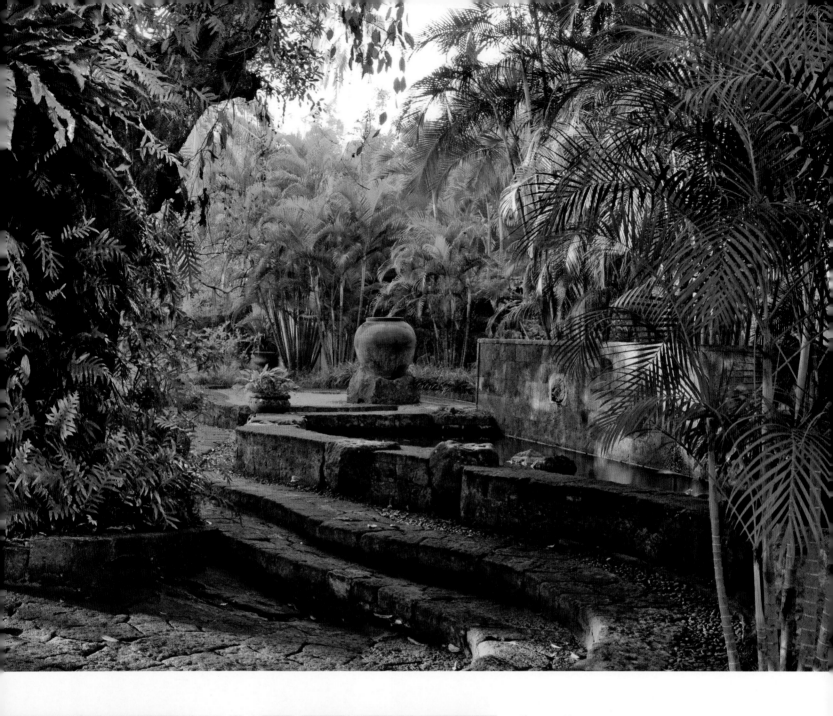

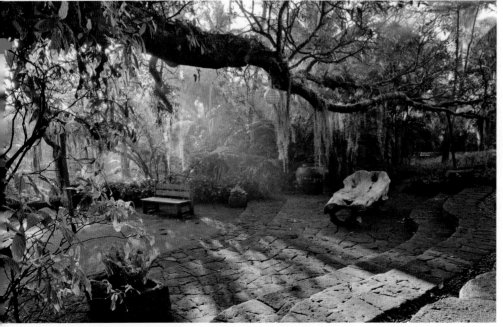

Above An old mango tree cloaked with epiphytic ferns casts its shadow over a moss carpeted courtyard.

Opposite bottom A vast lagoon mirrors the sky and surrounding vegetation. The design of the pavilions is reminiscent of Balinese temple pavilions that seem to float over the water.

Left The imaginative use of garden ornaments such as stone lanterns, antique water vessels and rustic driftwood furniture conveys a close kinship with the natural world at The Farm.

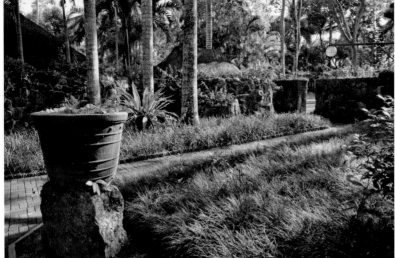

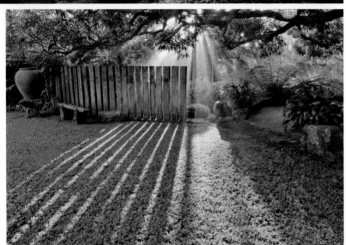

magnificent specimens of tree ferns provide height and dramatically enhance the various villas and treatment rooms. In combination with Philodendrons, butterfly and traveler's palms, and a variety of ground orchids, they create a symphony of green that intensifies the serenity of the place. One can wander and explore what lies behind every turn in the greenery from a network of walking and jogging paths powdered with the spores of giant tree ferns.

Striking water features are evident throughout the grounds. Tiny ponds were created to mirror the sky and reflect the verdant scenery, while an Indonesian theme is evident in the use of water as a meditative element (the design of the pavilions by the main lagoon is reminiscent of Balinese temple pavilions that seem to float over the water). To reinforce the spirit of meditation and calm, a palette of peaceful greens was used with accents from fragrant Plumeria and colorful Bougainvilleas. In addition, an imaginative use of garden ornaments, such as stone lanterns and antique water vessels, as well as rustic, sturdy furniture conveys a close kinship with nature and the great outdoors.

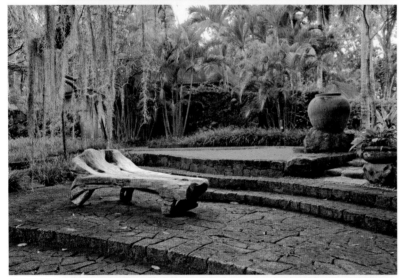

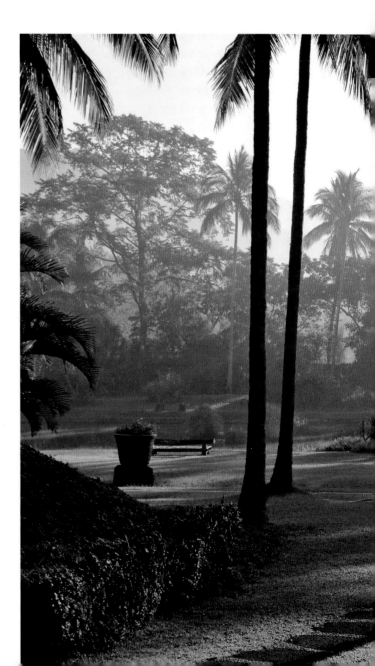

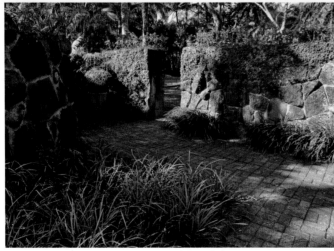

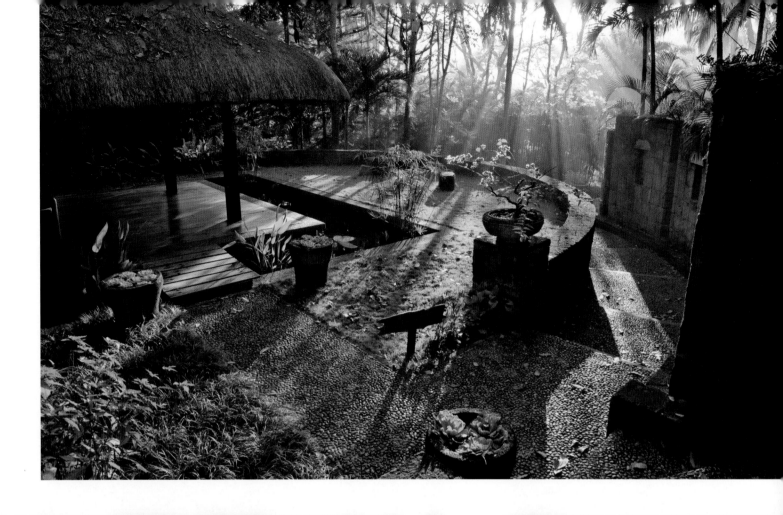

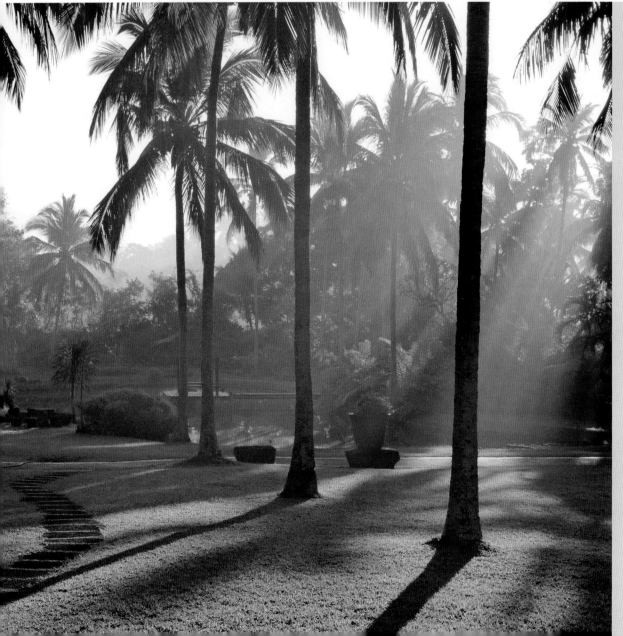

Above A palette of peaceful greens reinforces the spirit of meditation and calm around the yoga pavilion. Color comes in the form of a potted Bougainvillea.

Opposite top to bottom One can wander and explore what lies behind every turn in the greenery from a network of walking paths.

Left Tall elegant coconut palms, *Cocos nucifera*, dot the landscape. The Farm was originally the site of a coconut plantation.

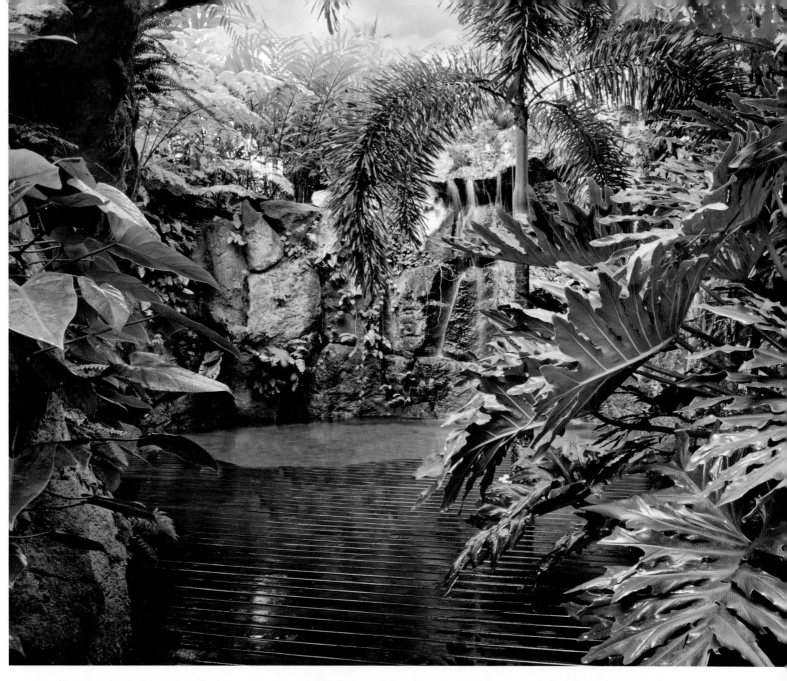

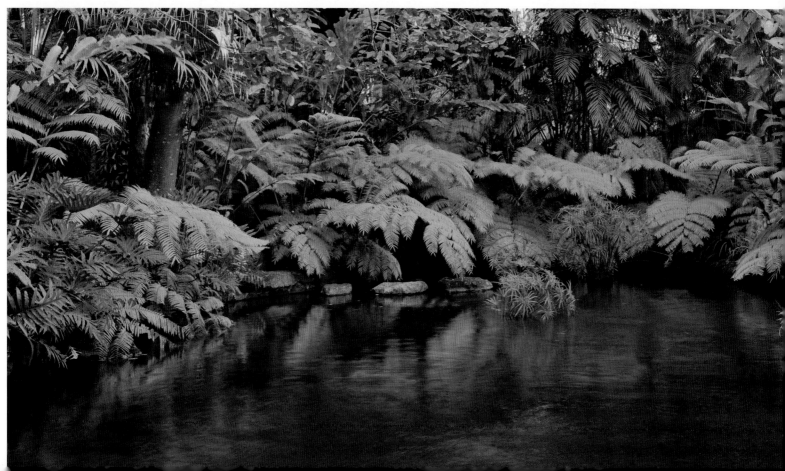

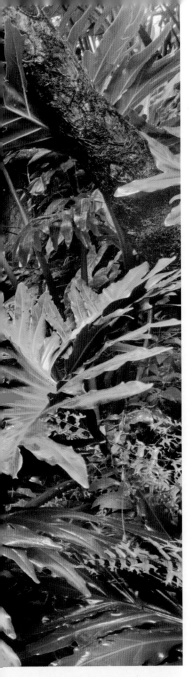

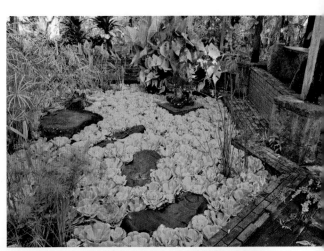

Left One of several secret bathing pools with a waterfall is hidden behind lush tropical greenery.

Left bottom Tree ferns, Cyathea, provide The Farm with a unique sense of place. They can grow up to 10 feet tall with stalks spanning 30 feet.

Right A dense mass of water lettuce, *Pistia stratiotes*, blankets an ornamental pond.

Below *Tilliandsia usneoides*, an epiphytic Bromeliad, adds an eerie effect to this tropical setting.

Bottom The spa's infinity pool looks out onto a majestic view of the surrounding countryside.

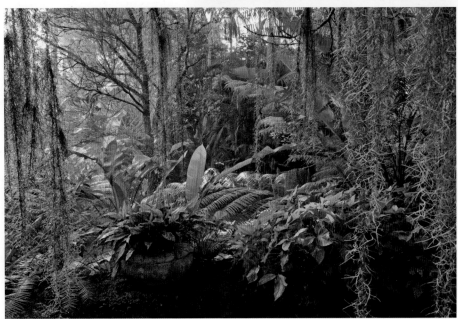

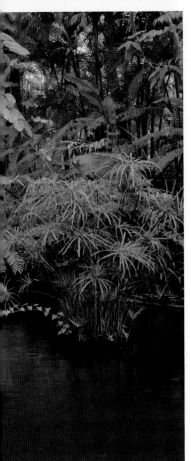

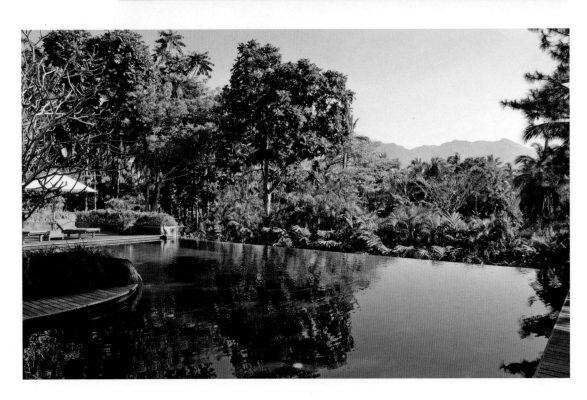

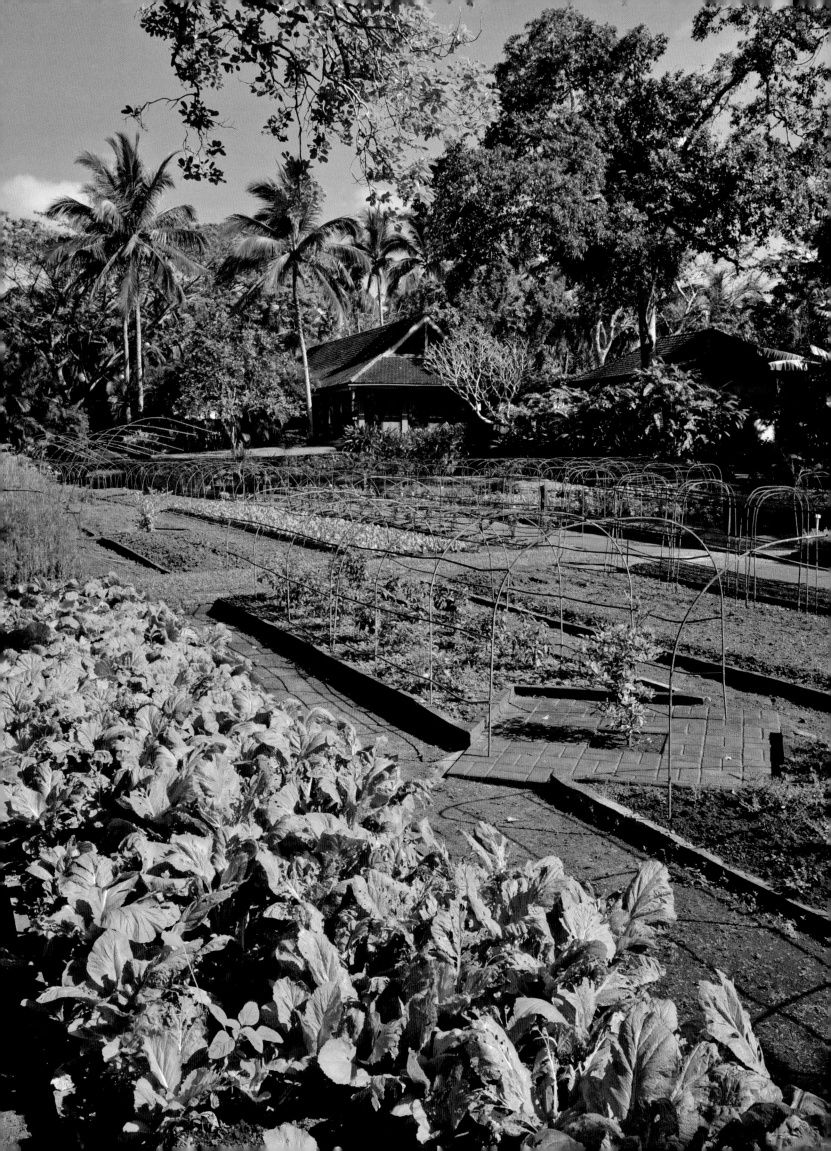

ORGANIC GARDEN AT SAN BENITO

Lipa, Batangas

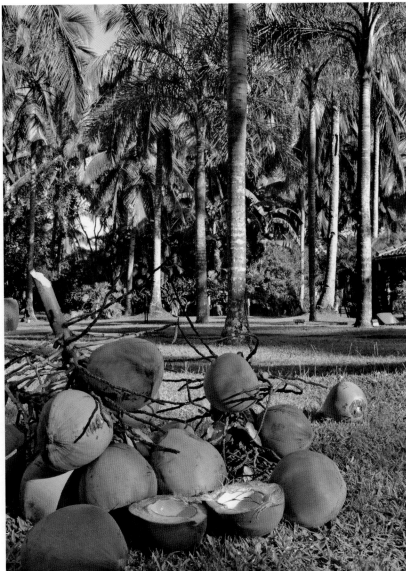

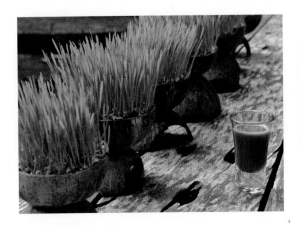

Two gardens, one just below the Alive Restaurant and a new kitchen garden alongside the spa, provide the majority of fresh produce that is harvested daily at The Farm and used in its menu preparations and spa treatments. In the kitchen garden beside the restaurant, a variety of salad greens and herbs such as tarragon, chives, mint, basil, and oregano are grown in neat beds divided by stone pavers. Favorite crops include cucumber, eggplant, Baguio beans, radish and cabbage. Wheat grass is propagated at a nearby shed. At the newer, more rustic garden started in November 2009, are more vegetables and herbs planted along with flowers used in the spa's colorful mandala arrangements.

According to Elmo Bado, head of landscaping at the Farm, the property's vegetable garden subscribes to a totally organic method of gardening. Only organic compost—prepared by putting together discarded plant material, grass clippings and kitchen scraps and then allowing bugs and worms to do the rest of the work— is used to fertilize the vegetables and herbs. Carbon is

Opposite A variety of salad greens and herbs is grown in neat beds in the kitchen garden.

Above left Wheat grass is propagated and grown in a shed adjacent to the kitchen garden.

Above and right A large part of The Farm is still devoted to coconuts whose fruits are used not only for food but for spa products such as soaps and oils. They subscribe to a non-dairy food program that use substitutes such as coconut and soy milk.

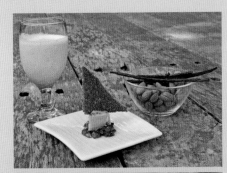

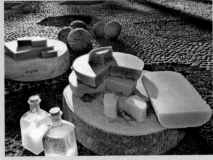

released from the decaying leaves and straw and nitrogen from the grass clippings and kitchen scraps. From time to time, organic materials are added as they become available and the piles are turned regularly to speed the process until everything looks like dark, rich soil. Diseased vegetable vines as well as animal fats and waste are avoided to prevent contamination and unwelcome pests. Bado makes sure there is always a steady supply of compost for use in the gardens of The Farm.

He also adheres to a biological pest control program that is in total harmony with nature, using only natural insecticides made from trees and vines. A solution is made from the dried fruit and runners of the *bayating* vine (which is plentiful in the property) and sprayed on the plants. The same is done with the leaves from the *Albizia procera* tree, which is combined with hot chile to make a very effective insecticide.

A tree and medicinal plant expert like his late father and grandfather before him, Bado came to The Farm from the University of the Philippines in Los Banos where he specialized in the study of forest based medicinal trees, herbs and grasses. An Igorot by birth, he grew up in the Visayas where he learned traditional farming practices as a young man. He is quick to extol the virtues of the *pako* or fiddlehead fern (*Athyrium esculentum*), an edible fern grown in the garden and one of the favorite salad components on the restaurant's menu, and the roots of the cogongrass (*Imperata cylindrica*), both of which he says are powerful antioxidants.

Bado has also implemented a program to educate the gardeners not only about the indigenous and endemic plant specimens at The Farm but also about harmful gardening practices such as the *kaingin*, the indiscriminate burning of plants for clearing purposes that has destroyed many valuable plant specimens in the country.

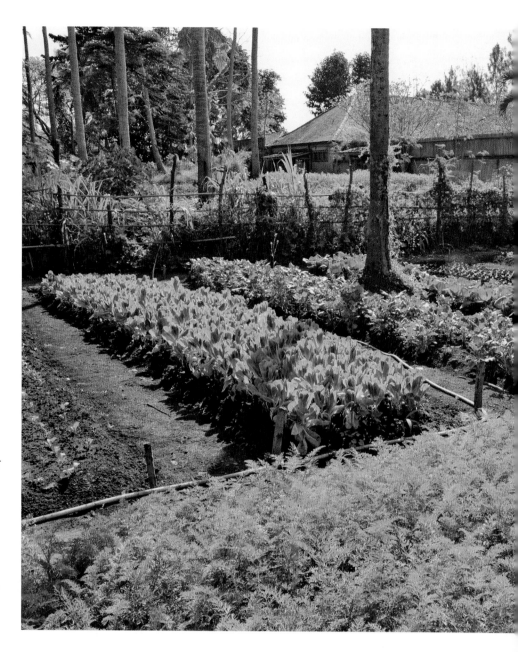

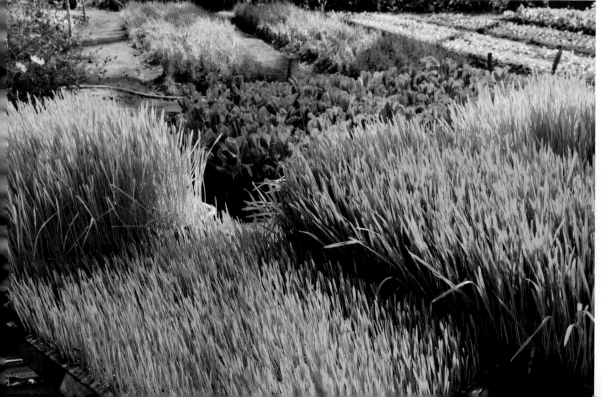

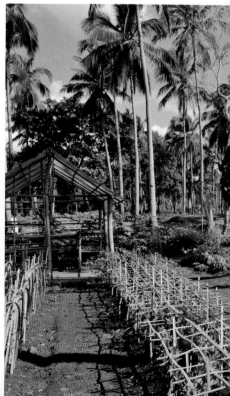

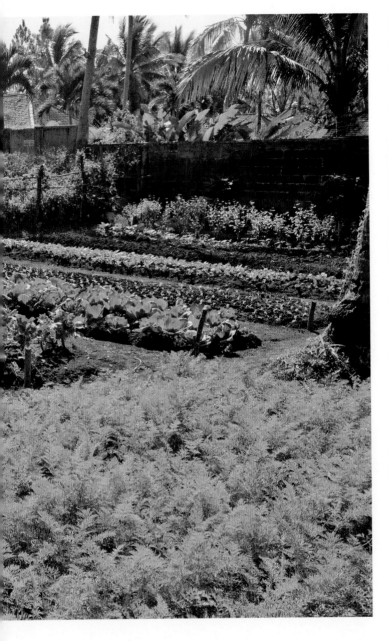

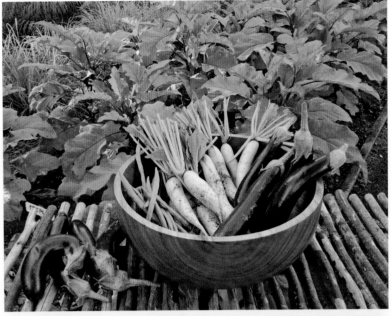

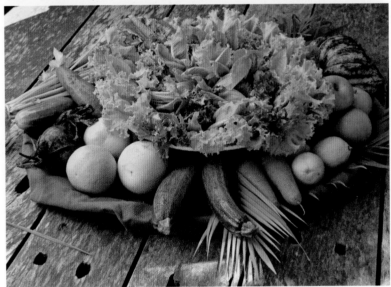

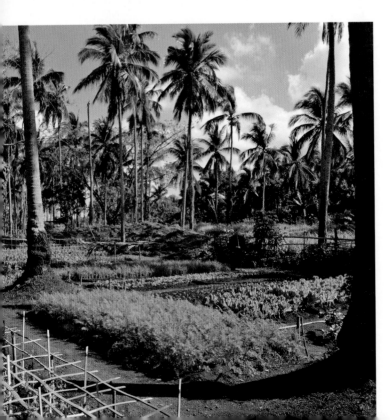

Above left The new vegetable garden beside the spa.

Far left Wheat grass in trays ready for use.

Left Bamboo stakes are used to prop up the young plants in the nursery.

Top Newly harvested radishes and eggplants.

Above A bountiful harvest of salad greens, cucumbers, yellow and green zucchini, beets and carrots.

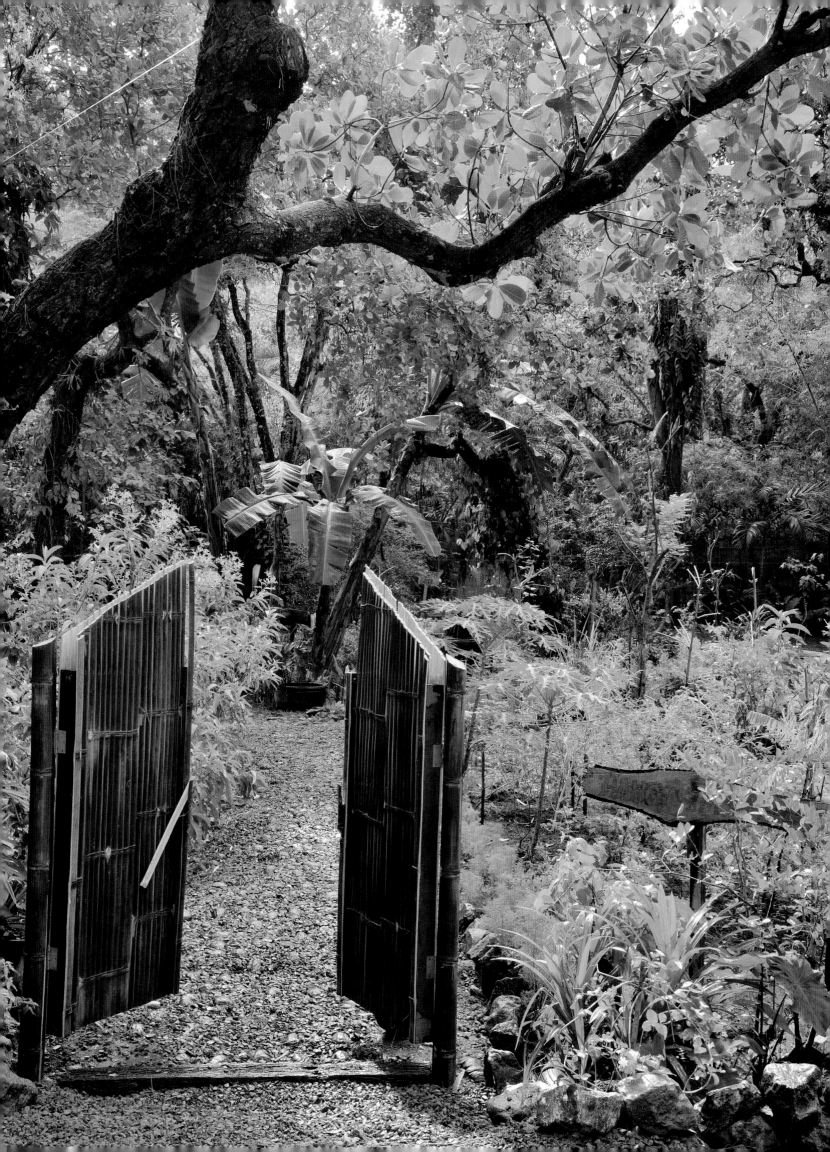

FLOR'S HEALING GARDEN

Antipolo, Rizal
Designed by Flor Tarriela

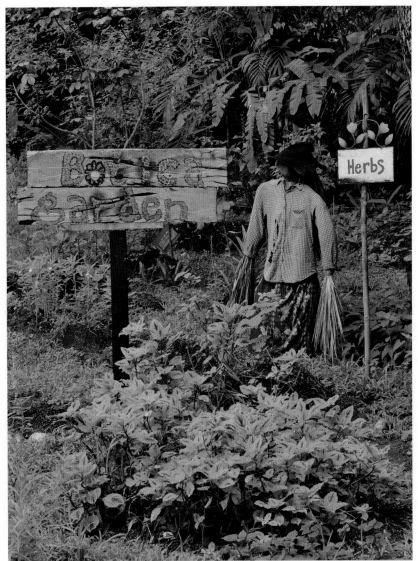

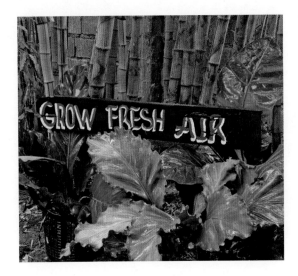

In the hot dry hills of Antipolo just east of Manila, Flor Gozon Tarriela has developed a richly planted experimental garden in total harmony with nature. It is filled with native trees, ferns, homegrown vegetables and herbs, as well as a selection of ornamentals suited to the climate and soil of its location. This is a garden that celebrates life, nourishment and healing, where families go to learn how to stay in touch with the earth through the plants and vegetables growing here. Parents and their children visit for the pleasure of touching, smelling, observing and gathering flowers as well as watching nature at work.

The garden is laid out on different levels and divided into separate areas, with each area identified by a sign bearing its name. The herb garden marked *Pang Asim* (For Souring) is planted with Philippine herbs used as flavoring agents. Among the specimens here are guava, coriander, lemongrass, mint, screwpine and *Averrhoa bilimbi*, a small tree grown for its juicy, acidic, yellow-green fruit. Not far away is the Kitchen Garden planted with eggplant, sweet potato, cashew and wild Fukien

Opposite The herb garden called *Pang Asim* is planted with Philippine herbs and plants used as flavoring agents.

Above left Grow Fresh Air is for ornamental plants that can be brought indoors.

Above The Botica Garden is devoted to medicinal plants and aromatic herbs grown for home remedies for common ailments.

Right top The attractive fruits of the cashew tree, *Anacardium occidentale*.

Right below A spiky soursop, *Annona muricata*.

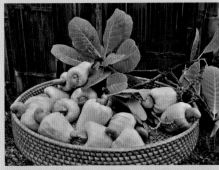

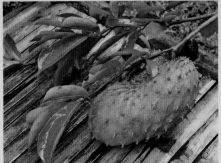

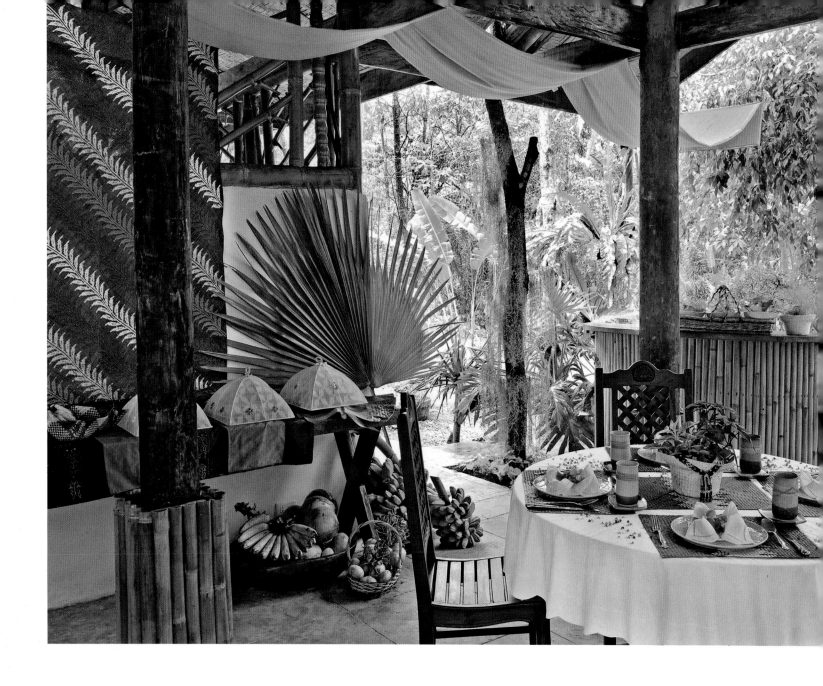

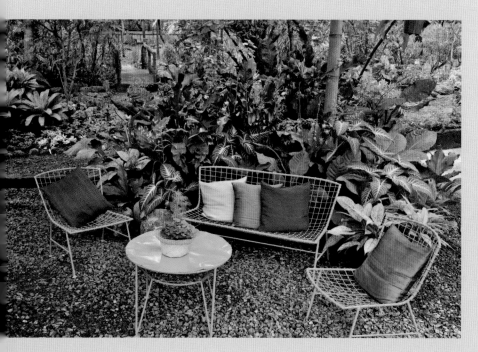

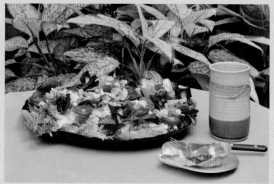

Above The colorfully appointed dining pavilion.

Left A Mickey mouse plant, *Solanum mammosum*, makes for interesting conversation in a seating area.

Below The specialty of the house, a festive homegrown salad that includes the colorful flowers of blue ternate, *Clitoria ternatea*, Katuray, *Sesbania grandiflora*, and Cadena de amor, *Antigonon leptopus*.

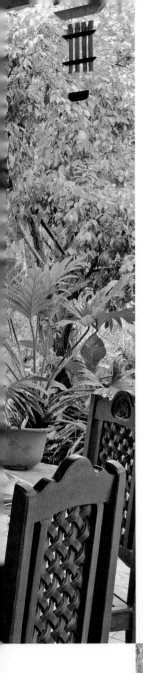

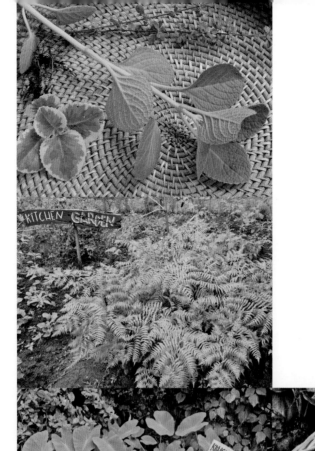

Left, anticlockwise from top to bottom A selection of delicious healthy herbs and vegetables all organically grown: sprigs of oregano; an edible fern, the fiddleleaf; *kangkong* or swamp cabbage, popular in Chinese cuisine; sweet potato, *Ipomea batatas*.

Bottom A lovely spot from which to view the impressive cashew tree on the right.

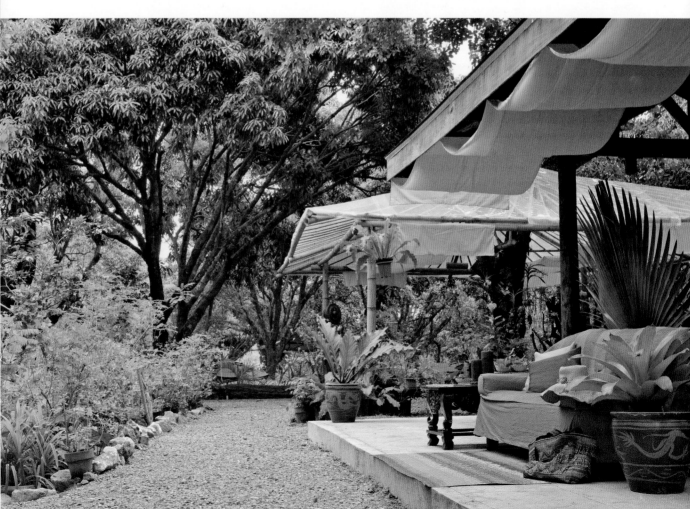

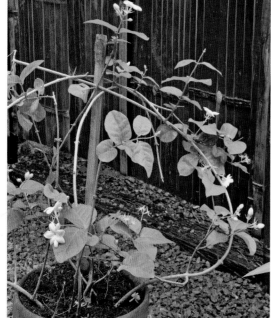

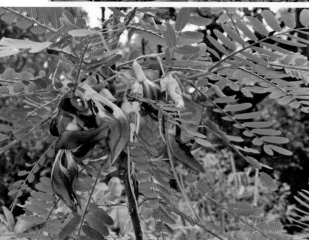

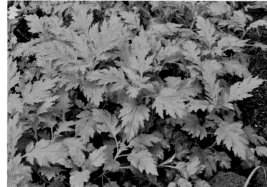

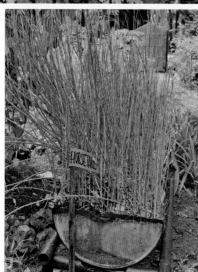

tea. Tarriela has devoted a special area, aptly named Botica Garden, to medicinal plants or "weedicinals" as she likes to call them. In addition to medicinal plants, she grows aromatic herbs for home remedies such as marsh mint (*herba buena*), oregano, Coleus (*mayana*), and Chinese honeysuckle (*damong Maria*). There is also aloe vera (*sabila*), pennyworth (*gotu kola*) and camphor (*sambong*). By contrast, the area with a wooden sign that reads "Grow Fresh Air" is assigned to ornamental plants that can be brought inside the house. "Bring the plants indoors!" she exclaims, "They absorb carbon dioxide and release oxygen into the air." She enumerates about 50 plants that serve this purpose.

A particular interest of Tarriela's is the "Square Foot Garden" (which is really more like a meter) where she demonstrates the cultivation of organic edible gardens in the backyard. A gardener and teacher, Tarriela is intent on spreading the gospel of self-sufficiency and productivity. According to her, a one square-meter garden, planted well and cared for properly can sustain an entire family. An adjunct to the homegrown garden is the "Double-deep Dig" garden designed for raising root crops in one-foot deep holes.

Although the Healing Garden is founded on a great deal of applied knowledge and experience, what makes it unique is the mix of horticulture and dedication that has guided Tarriela's philosophy of "No Filipino should go hungry" and "Mother nature will provide" from the outset. The result is a garden that provides an inspiring experience of nature as well as a display of horticultural ingenuity and productivity.

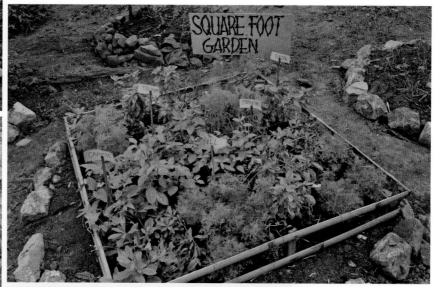

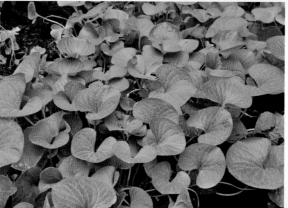

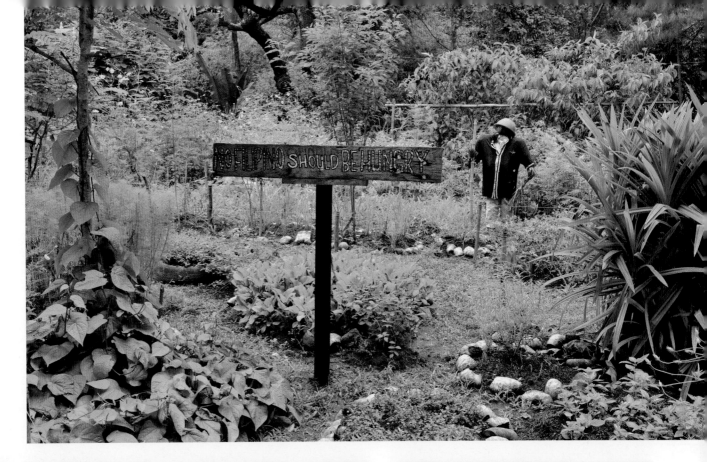

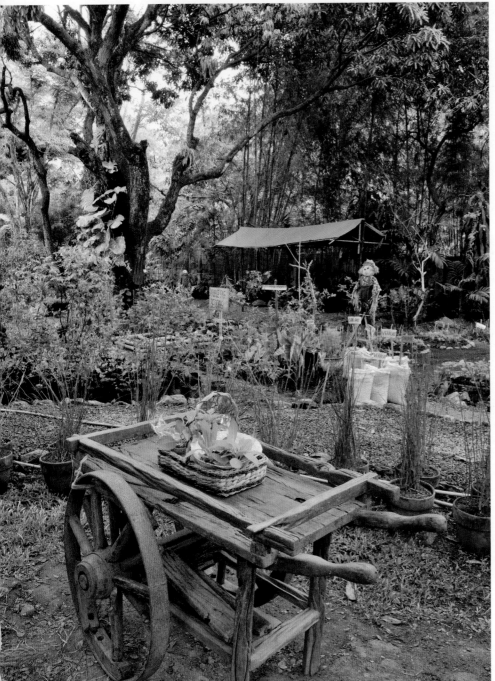

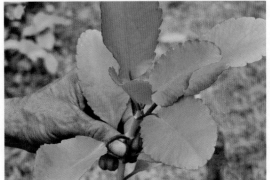

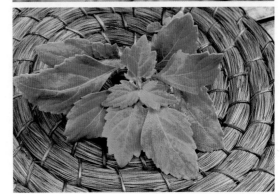

Top A scarecrow helps to drive away unwanted visitors in the Square Foot Garden.

Left The Double-deep Dig Garden is designed for raising root crops on one-foot-deep holes.

Above middle Leaves of the poetically named *katakataka*, *Angelica bryophyllum pinnatum*; believed to be an effective anti-inflammatory, it is part of the medicinal plant collection.

Above A sprig of patchouli (Pogostemon sp) sits on a woven basket. Patchouli is a bushy herb in the mint family, best known for its heavy perfume.

209

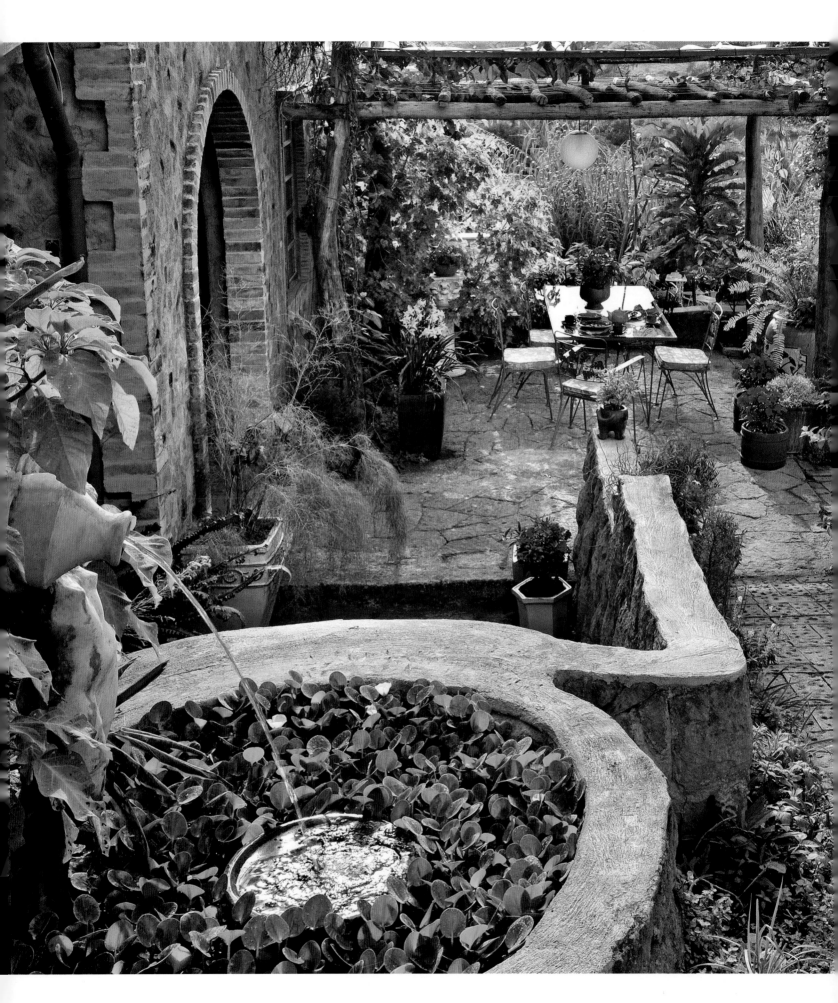

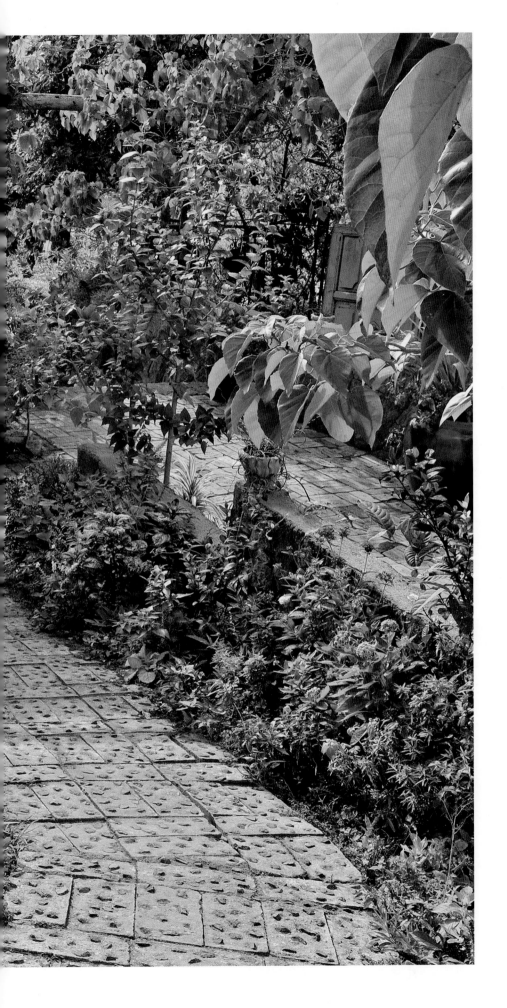

THE ADAMS HERB GARDEN

Tagaytay City, Cavite
Designed by Neil and Marcia Adams

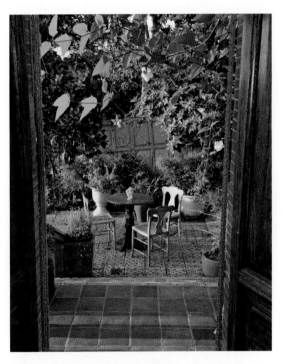

In the ruggedly beautiful town of Tagaytay, past meadows of wild sunflowers and miles of dirt road, lies a garden that has been a labor of love for owners, Englishman Neil Adams and his Filipina wife, Marcia. They have created a wildlife-friendly garden of edible herbs and flowering plants in the vernacular of the modern cottage garden. Days here are filled with usual garden business—birds tugging at wiggling worms, bees buzzing in and out of flowers, and frogs lazing in warm pools of water.

An architectural framework of stone walls, terraces and paths defines this garden's structure and reinforces the sense of space. The planting style throughout is an intermingling of native and non-native species, which are allowed to self-sow and compete with each other. And should a war of the species occur, there is a wide variety of foliage plants to provide the necessary textural link to relieve the tension and rigidity that may arise.

Visitors enter the garden from the top of the hill past the main house on the right and the first of several

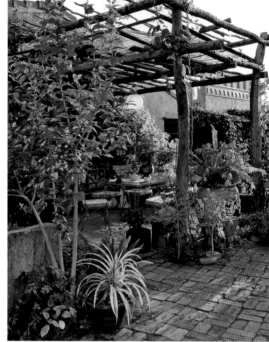

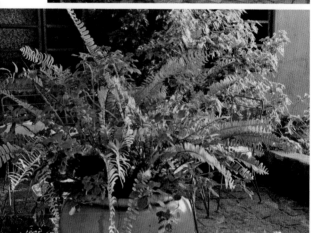

trellised terraces on the left. Here, an open structure, furnished with informal chairs and tables, has vistas of the surrounding gardens and sugar cane fields, and acts as a relaxed entertainment venue. Down a flight of stone steps is a small potager garden with a growing collection of herbs and vegetables. Beyond, a concrete path set with river stones takes the visitor to a restaurant at the bottom of the property.

On either side of this path one notes informally mixed borders. Flowers are here not just to be admired but also to attract pollinators, in particular insects. The owners have consciously included herbs and wild flowers in the beds, fully aware of the benefits of the symbiotic relationship between plants and insects. Herbs such as oregano, thyme, sage and borage, attract butterflies and bees by the dozen, as do the plantings of lavender. Rosemary is an early nectar source, while chives are also popular with pollinators. Mint can be an invasive plant but is full of the sweet ambrosia that insects love.

The Petrea vine-covered terrace that serves as the entrance to Marcia's Restaurant is a delightful wooden arbor that acts as a shelter for potted plants of Impatiens, Cymbidiums and ferns. An *Abutilon pictum* 'Thompsonii' or flowering maple with its variegated leaves punctuates a corner, while vintage wrought iron furniture, brightly painted in primary colors, lends a retro-modern accent. A nearby fountain shrouded by a yellow flowering Datura provides the trickling sound of water, while borders lining the path spill over with Pentas, Dianthus, candytufts and jasmine.

By using a wide variety of flowering plants, the owners have created multiple viewing vistas; the difference in flower size, color and leaf form provide visual interest. At turns, the garden is flamboyant and reverent, bold and restrained, all the while filled with many whimsical touches and always in tune with nature.

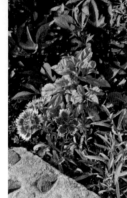

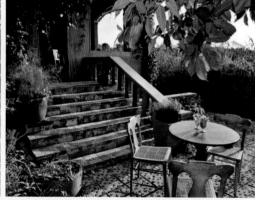

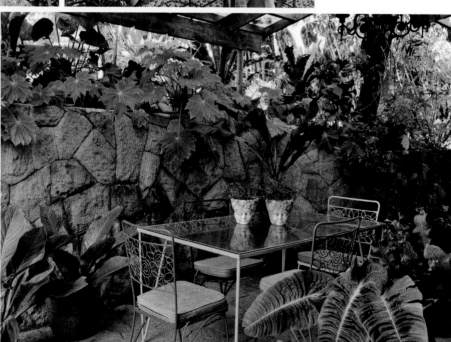

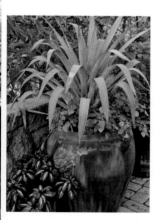

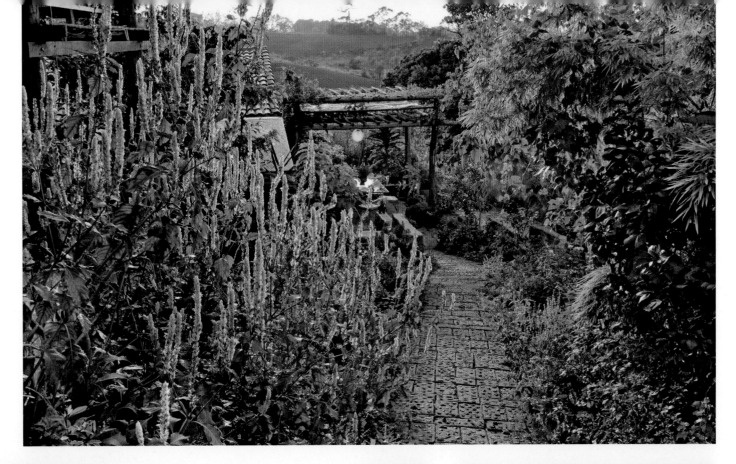

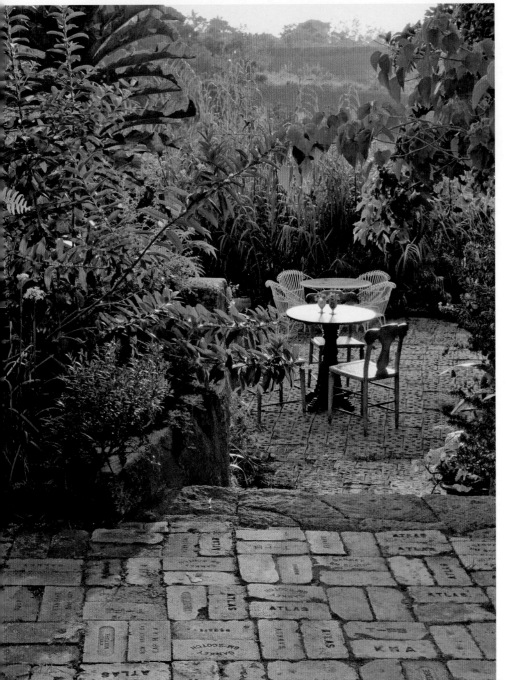

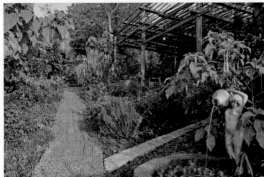

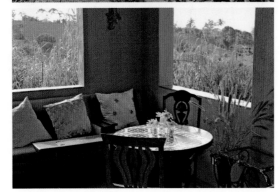

Top Informally mixed borders of flowering plants and edible herbs attract a wide variety of insect pollinators to the garden.

Left Sunset casts a golden glow over the garden and the surrounding countryside.

Above The restaurant and its garden offer the flexibility for a wide variety of events with vistas of the vegetable and herb borders and the sugar cane fields beyond.

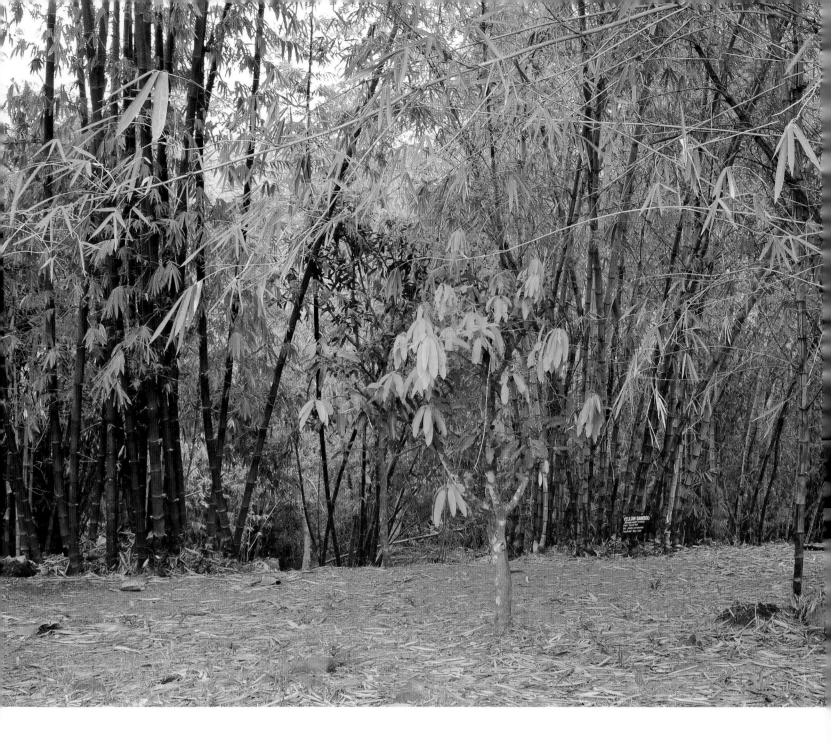

CAROLINA'S BAMBOO FARM

Antipolo City, Rizal

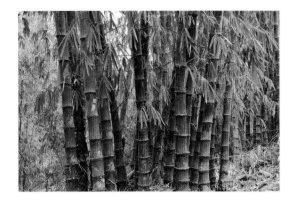

Few materials used in garden design are as versatile as the ubiquitous bamboo. Delicate yet strong, in colors ranging from pale to dark green, olive green to gold, nothing says "Asian" or "tropical" more than bamboo. Multi purpose in use, it always raises the Asian ambiance in a landscape or home. No one knows this better than Carolina Gozon Jimenez, who has loved bamboo since she was a child. As director of the Carolina's Bamboo Farm, she has been championing the virtues of this member of the grass family (yes, bamboo is a grass, not a tree!) for a long time.

Carolina's Bamboo Farm is located just outside Manila in the city of Antipolo. Nestled in a clearing surrounded by groves of bamboo, it is hard to miss. Worn paths blanketed with bamboo leaves lead to open clumps of *Bambusa vulgaris*, to potgrown clumps of Buddha's belly and to more open clumps of feathery bamboo. In this bamboo paradise, the owner raises and propagates at least 27 varieties of bamboo and sells up to 10,000 seedlings per year.

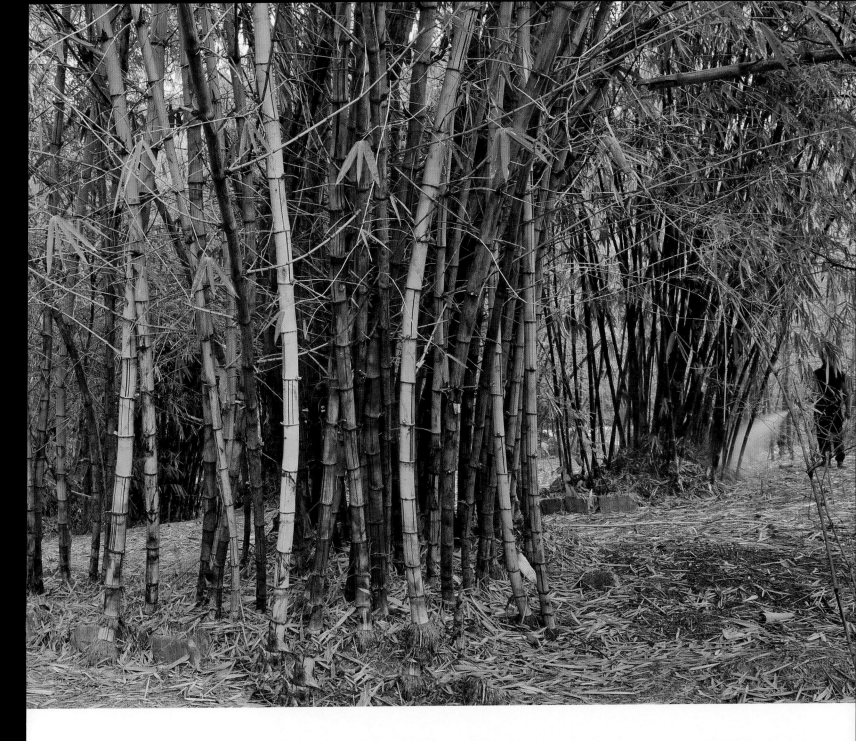

Above An expansive grove of golden bamboo, *Bambusa vulgaris*.

Opposite bottom The silvery brown bearded culms of the *Dendrocalamus asper*, an east Indian bamboo, is cultivated for its edible shoots and use in construction. It can withstand cold temperatures and has been known to withstand frost in colder zones .

Right Delicate, yet strong, the bamboo's color can range from pale green to dark green to olive green to gold. In foreground are green culms of Bambusa sp.

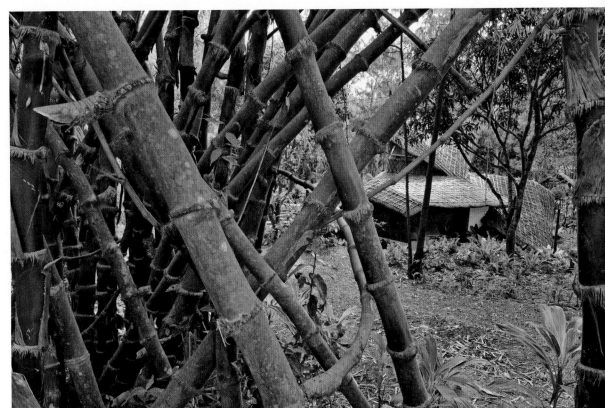

To educate people about bamboo, Jimenez conducts annual workshops on its environmental and practical uses. She believes that bamboo has the answer to many of our environmental problems since it prevents soil erosion, is an effective air purifier and conservator of minerals in the soil and, as the fastest growing grass on earth, it absorbs more carbon dioxide than any other plant species in the botanical world.

Along with her workshops are demonstrations that feature a new type of *bahay kubo* (native hut). Sporting a unique "hyperbolic paraboloid" roofline that extends three levels, with a cantilevered staircase at the center and a spacious interior space with three rooms, it was designed by architect Angel Lazaro from the United Architects of the Philippines. The house is 75 percent bamboo and costs only P25,000 to make.

In gardens, bamboo tolerates neutral to sandy, loamy soil. Most varieties are native to China and were introduced to the Philippines at various times throughout history. Of the 1,250 species existing in the world, 48 can be found in the Philippines. More than a few are on display here.

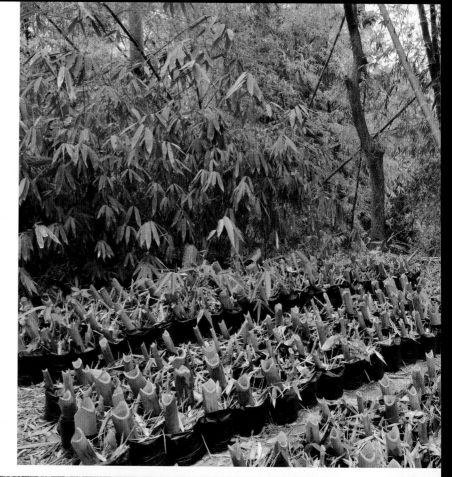

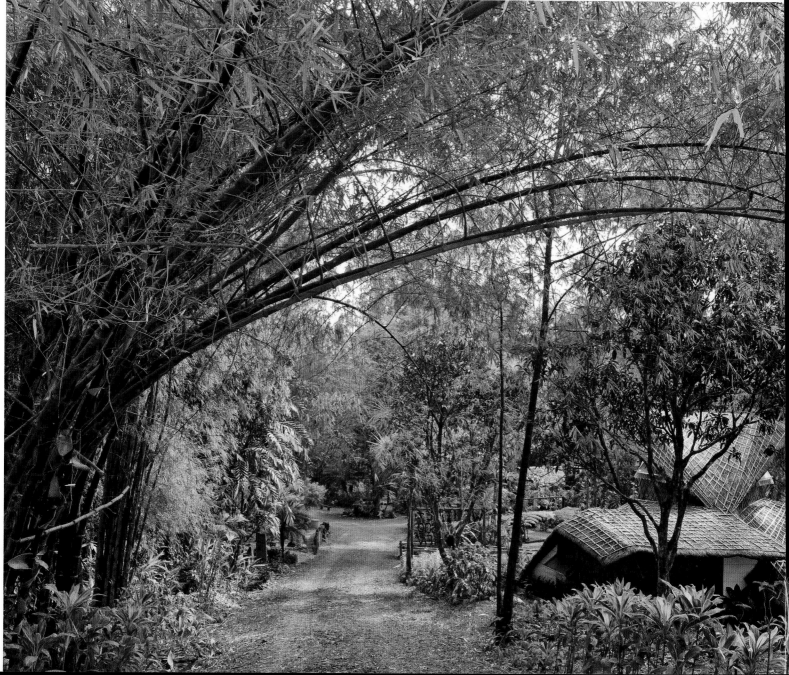

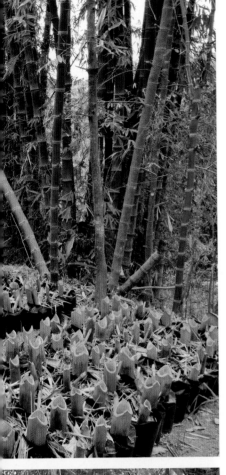

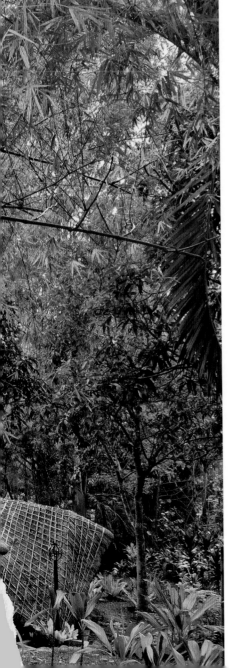

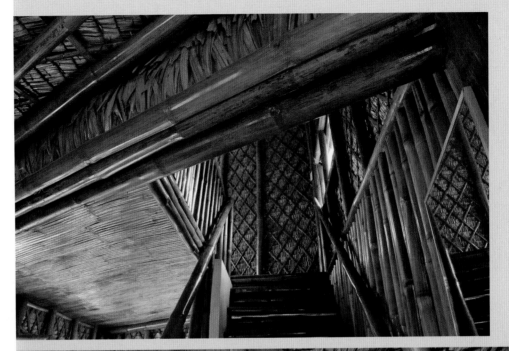

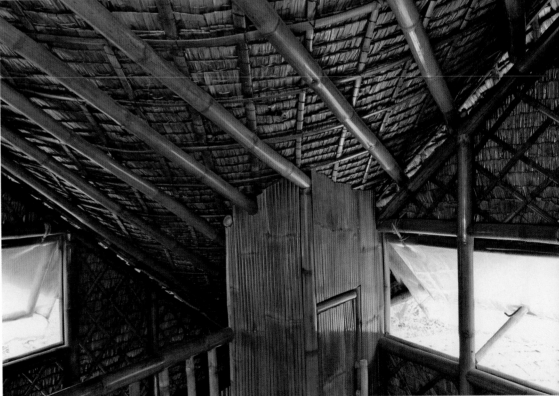

Opposite top A propagation area that illustrates how fast bamboo grows. Jiminez notes that bamboo can provide food, secruity and livelihoods for Filipinos.

Opposite bottom An exterior view of the new *nipa* hut with its hyberbolic paraboloid roofline.

Top and above A close up look at the interior details of the modern *nipa* hut which combines bamboo as well as *nipa*, *Nypa fruticans*, whose leaves are used for the roof and walls of the simple abode.

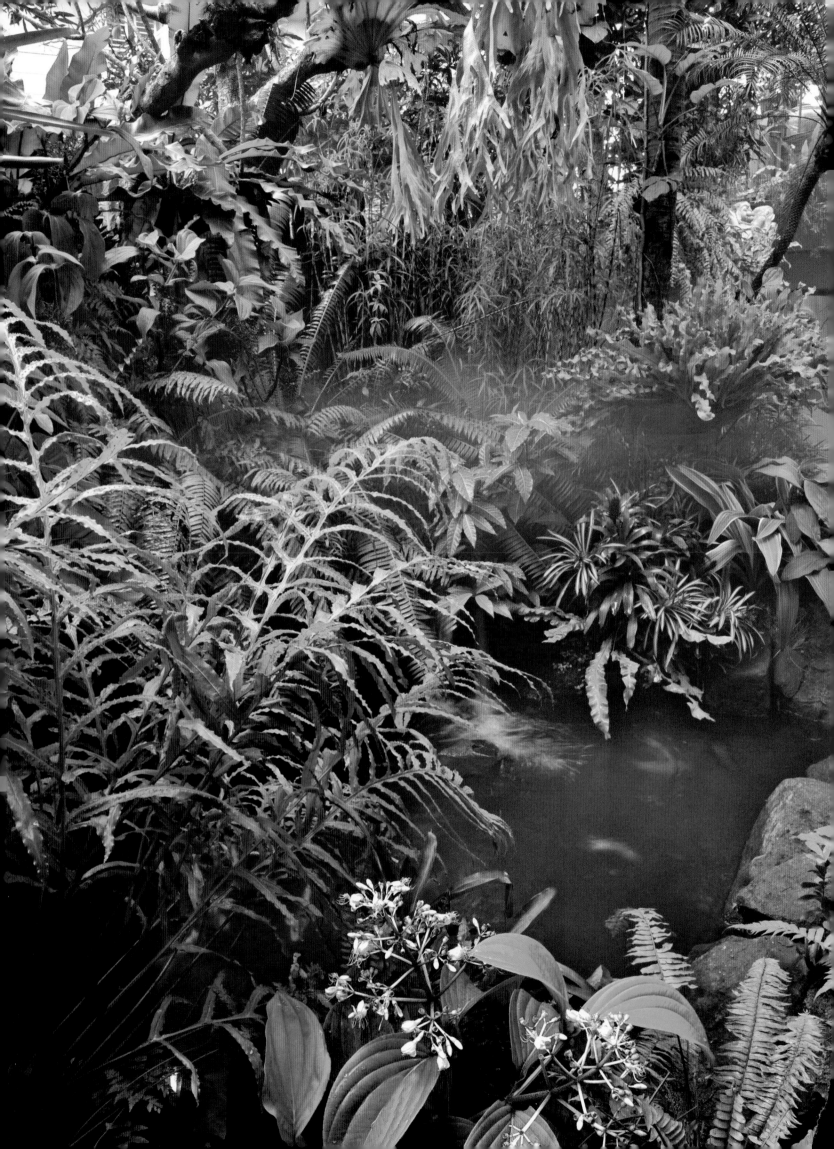

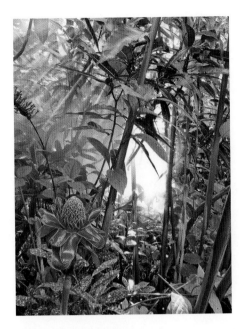

DESIGNER
PROFILES

Roberto P Gopiao
Passionate landscaper-gardener

One of the most versatile garden-designers in our diverse collection is Roberto "Bobby" P Gopiao. He grew up among the trees and gardens of Pampanga, where he developed his passion for horticulture, before migrating to Quezon City. After a college degree in business management from Ateneo de Manila, he took up Landscape Architecture for two years at the University of the Philippines, before deciding it would do him good to have hands-on-the-soil experience to do landscape design.

Gopiao's first major job was as the "landscape enhancer" of the Puerto Azul Leisure Complex in Ternate, Cavite, as mentored by architect Gading Hofilena. After serving as a project director for the company for two years, Gopiao went on to design landscapes for the Villar group of companies, including Cotton-woods, Maia Alta, Valenza and Rio Grande Villages. He has designed landscapes for leisure complexes such as Canyon Ranch and Subic Yacht Club; and for golf and country clubs at Eastridge, Riviera and Wack-Wack West.

Gopaio has also worked on residential projects for such well-known clients as Freddie Garcia, Henry Hagedorn, Eduardo Espiritu, Alfonso Yuchengco, Marlyn Go, Beaver Lopez, Dra Loi Ejercito and National Artist Ben Cabrera in Baguio.

Gopiao's greatest passion and expertise lies in bonsais. He has been president of the Philippine Bonsai Society since 2003; has won many prizes in international competitions; and has influenced many clients to engage in this creative nature art. With an abiding interest in antiques and modern art, the versatile Gopiao takes a fresh, creative approach to each individual project.

Roberto "Bobby" P Gopiao
168 B Gonzales St, Loyola Heights, Quezon City, RP
tel/fax nos: +63 2 920-9349
email: r_gopiao@yahoo.com
website: www.bobbygopiaolandscapes.com

Frank Borja
Environmental designer

As an environmental planner and landscape consultant for the past 21 years, Frank Borja has worked on multiple projects of the Leisurely Lifestyle Kind. He has created large public landscapes primarily around hotels, resorts and high-end residential communities —in Hawaii, Guam and the Philippines.

Borja graduated in Environmental Planning and Design, with an emphasis on Landscape Architecture, from Arizona State University, USA. His early work experience covered the Pacific Basin and the south-western USA—the very driest desert areas of the States. It was the later projects, under the architectural firm of Belt Collins, that took him back to tropical Asia and the Pacific from where he had originated. In the design of landscapes for golf courses and resorts, Borja has advised on tropical plant use for Asian soil.

Twelve years ago, Guam-born Borja and his wife Lori started their own DQA Environmental Design company, specializing in landscapes and interiors for high-end hotels and resorts. He creates sprawling environments and leisurely spaces around buildings, using paths, ponds, pools and pavements—trimmed with classic or traditional green soft-scapes amid modern features.

The landscape consultant also designs landscapes for private residences in Makati and Alabang. Borja has done distinctive home landscapes for such individualist owners as Tessa Prieto Valdes, Carmelita Matta, David Lim, Eric and Phyllis Tensuan, Mrs Steven Sy, and Mrs Annabel Wisnewski.

Franklin "Frank" G. Borja
DQA Environmental Design, Inc.
101 Aguirre Street, Legaspi Village, Makati City
tel no: +63 2 750-2021 – 750-5012
fax no: +63 2 812-8917
email: dqaenv@yahoo.com

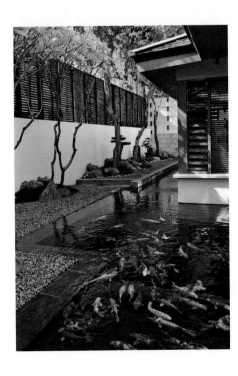

Yuyung LaO'
Master garden artist

Yuyung LaO' is the over-educated landscape artist in our array. He started work as a mining engineer, then withdrew out of boredom to "just grow plants". He evolved from miner to plant-lover to plant-addict, and finally to landscape artist, at the top of the heap in the mid 1990s. He credits one mentor: "My guide is Mother Nature."

LaO' became an intuitive plantsman by collecting grasses and traveling far afield to seek out unusual species. He recounts: "I got truly addicted to plants in the mid '80s and became part of the plant-crazy clique of Dr Vicente Santos, senior physician at PGH and avid plant collector running a farm in Lucban, Quezon. Dr Santos *obliged* us acolytes to visit him once a week—so we could share all his discoveries of exotic plants."

LaO' meticulously studied the habits and tolerance of plants and deliberately chooses low-maintenance plants for his gardens. He joined Manila's big garden shows in the '80s and has won the Best-in-Show Award 18 times. From there, he was invited to create friends' private landscapes. He excelled in ornamental street-side and pocket gardens— looking like sculpted stage settings.

"I considered doing landscapes like fashion designs," he says. "I always looked for new plants, new designs, latest trends . . . I was first to use the big carabao jars and giant *kawa* (cooking vats), and bring massive angular boulders into the gardens. I also made my own accessories to blend with the natural plants . . . My projects always have a wow factor."

LaO' had great visions for the landscaping art; at one stage he adopted some apprentices, seeking to pass on his skills—"until money-grabbing turned their heads." Nowadays, he tends to keep a low profile, though his great skill and talent is well known overseas. At home, Yuyung LaO' remains one of the low-key masters in the country.

Yuyung LaO'
Philippines

Jun Obrero
Natural forest gardener

Jun Obrero had always a heart for wild forest plants, even while he dabbled in gardening at an early age. He took up architecture

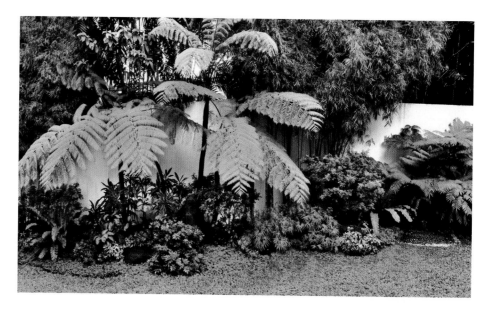

in 1974, worked as an designer in the Middle East for several years, then studied Commercial Nursery Management in San Antonio, Texas, in 1998. Back home, he moved into "miniature landscapes" in 2001, teaching bonsai arts to plant-lovers, and winning the plant exhibition in Intramuros, Manila. In 2002, an old friend from bonsai classes asked him to help her nephew, Antonio Escalante, to create a "big tropical landscape" for his new fine dining restaurant in Tagaytay. The chef Tony and the landscape-maker Jun made great waves for food and gardens together.

Another major project in Tagaytay was the meditative forest-park of Balai Taal, the residential compound of Marivic Concepcion. Of this, the forest-man Obrero says: "I brought ferns, trees and streams back to the almost destroyed environment!". This was followed by Jon Concepcion's vacation house garden in Nasugbu and Senator Miguel Zubiri's gardens in Calatagan—large tropical landscapes on the Batangas coastline.

Aptly, it was through Antonio's Fine Dining in Tagaytay that Rockwell President Nestor Padilla sought out its forest-garden designer; and Obrero started doing urban landscapes for Rockwell Land, his top client today. Obrero's signature style called All-Natural Gardens was established there. Developed around the idea of "bringing nature into the city," Rockwell officials wanted "to mix the greens with the blues," and to promote a different taste in city landscapes. When Jun Obrero applies himself passionately to a new environment, his city gardens are naturally done, not manicured—and he never loses the forest-loving touch.

Jun Obrero
Riverside, Bgy. Pansol, Balara, Quezon City
tel no: +63 939 806-6416
email: tess.obrero@yahoo.com

Jaime Chua
Cebu's own landscaper

As the first recognized landscaper of Cebu, Jaime Chua is a conscientious garden maker with a background in architecture. He trained in the management of plant nurseries, then obtained upscale garden landscaping experience in Cebu City, his hometown.

Chua's interest in gardens developed during his architectural studies at San Carlos University, Cebu. His thesis considered various greenhouse designs for the maintenance of Philippine orchids and he continued his

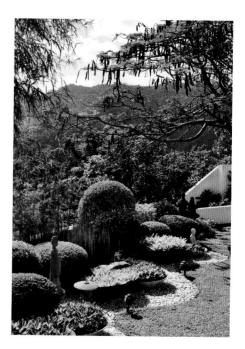

academic path by training in the production management of plant nurseries in the Netherlands. On his return, he opened a large plant nursery and personal garden in Busay, north of Cebu. There Chua keeps a picturesque farm nursery, landscaped with his favorite Asian tropical plants—bamboo, palms, and different varieties of Heliconias.

Since 1987, Chua has provided Cebuano residents with varied garden styles—Asian tropical, Asian Zen, Mediterranean and Philippine tropical, to name a few. His list of clients in the Maria Luisa and North Town Subdivisions includes such distinguished names as Lhuillier, Lu Ym, Aboitiz, and Arculli; Berenger, Caballero, Ong, Cokaliong, Tiu, Cullens and Darza.

In the commercial sector, Chua has worked on landscaping and garden beautification for Cebu Marriot Hotel, Paseo sa Ramon, Banawa, Cebu and, lately, the Suluban project in Bali, Indonesia.

Jaime Chua
9 Guadalupe Heights Village, Cebu
tel no: +63 32 346-2768
email: me_jai1010@yahoo.com

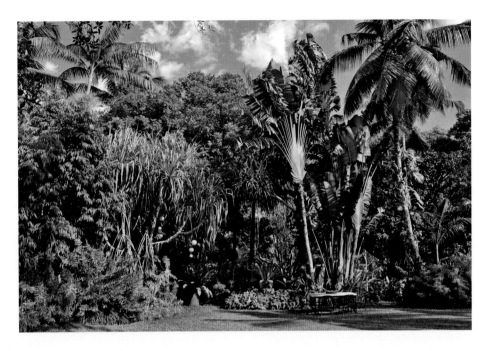

Shirley B Sanders
Friendly tropical gardener

Landscape-artist Shirley Bringas Sanders makes friendly tropical gardens. "I rarely refer to my works as formal gardens of particular styles. They are just planned environments providing pleasant surroundings." Her landscapes focus on colorful native species, informal compositions, and folksy artifacts. They aim to be easy, low-maintenance affairs; when a corporate garden needs support, she provides the service to keep it blooming.

Sanders designs gardens with Filipino *halo-halo* consciousness and a bias for native plants. Her icon Burle Marx, father of modern landscape design in Brazil, favored "jungly gardens with a nationalistic spirit, making use of the country's vast botanical resources." Sanders follows this idea, trying "to create the effect of a lush island paradise within one's home."

Her early exposure to plants derived from her mother's backyard; their plants were always the envy of passersby. The filial daughter studied medical technology, though she longed to be out with the plants. Sanders soon "left that world of illness" and opted for a life outdoors—making gardens. In the '80s, she volunteered to design rich friends' gardens, and soon launched her own business with natural instinct and great people skills. She established plant nurseries and operated with "fast-track" reliability. Her big break came in 1989, when a publisher from Hong Kong publicised her works in a glossy book, thereby raising Sanders' profile. She now takes on more commercial and corporate projects too.

Gardens by Sanders Inc (GBSI) has been making environments for 30 years and is listed among the top five landscapers in the country. Today, GBSI runs big plant nurseries spread on four islands—with the irrepressible lady gardener jetting among ongoing projects. But still, Sanders relishes the small home jobs—creating pleasant environments for all—and remains partial to the friendly tropical garden that requires little maintenance.

Shirley Sanders
Gardens by Sanders Inc (GBSI)
Mandaluyong, Manila
tel no: +63 2 917 839-2619

Jerusalino Araos
Sculptor as Gardener

Jerusalino Araos is a sculptor who translates experience into garden landscape. As a poet once wrote, "Araos plotted his garden as a paean to the myths and visions of a highly personal ideology . . . The result is a continuing feast of revelation for all the senses." Down on the ground, Araos is a consummate artist: sculptor, writer, teacher, gardener, designer, builder; a rebel and intellectual of wit and a creator of sculptures as gardens.

In 1999 he bested 340 entrants in an International Public Art Competition—by designing "an interactive sculpture as garden that contributes to the healing of national wounds." The prototype of that artwork is today a 700-square-meter garden carved onto a subdivision lot in Antipolo—a living sculpture, nurtured just for itself. More than a collation of plants around a lagoon, the garden is a social gathering place, a grouping of small gardens or "garden rooms", interconnected by a pathway of basalt stones. The adjoining

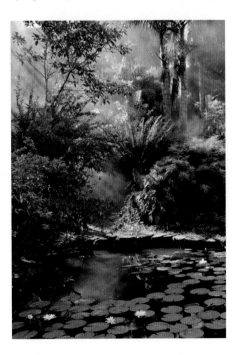

rooms form an undulating shoreline around a large lotus lagoon, the garden's heart. The pond is for wandering and musing; a mirror to reflect on trees—or selves.

Araos believes that "a garden must be derived from a spirit of religiosity or spirituality—or else it is just *agriculture*—a functional space, to feed people." He goes on to explain: "All my gardens are materialized visions of my desire to transcend common experience." His nature essay and "living sculpture" comprises social spaces that serve the rituals and ceremonies of life: "My garden is a 'place of power', it has its own sense of place and space."

Araos himself is as colorful as his gardens. He studied journalism in Silliman University, Negros, then lived a checkered life as iconoclast artist and social activist. He exhibited artworks in the top galleries; was named an outstanding sculptor in the ASEAN region; and did the first-ever living artist's solo show at the National Museum. He writes columns on design and architecture; lectures in humanities and conducts art-workshops at the University of the Philippines. He wrote a book on his Antipolo garden—which has been nominated for a national award.

Several of Araos' sculptures as garden or public art landscapes thrive well at the UP College of Fine Arts; the Department of Natural Resources, QC; and in Fort Bonifacio Global City in Metro Manila.

Jerusalino Araos
UP Village, Diliman, Quezon City
tel no: +63 921 258-5532
email: liwa_araos@yahoo.com

Rading Decepida
Decorative garden designer

When asked to design a modern garden for small urban lot, landscaper Decepida follows a precise and intelligent design "style". He creates decorative garden spaces around the home, from front to back, with at least one water feature. "A small pond placed by the façade for feng shui purposes is my signature." He wraps the house with grass lawns, plus rock or boulder accents; does elevations to soften the landscape and create views for the home; and plants high against the walls for privacy.

Conrado "Rading" Decepida is a self-trained, self-motivated landscape designer. He originates from Marikina and graduated in BS Commerce in 1986 at San Beda College

Manila. He now lives in Antipolo City. After four years in the banking industry, he realized he just loves to create gardens.

To get on-the-job training in landscaping, Decepida apprenticed for two years under Yuyung LaO', the most prominent garden artist at the time. He learned to assemble urban landscapes using selective plant and soil materials, along with water ponds, wildlife props and accessories.

In 1990 he started his own business, creating decorative gardens in Manila and the Visayas. His home landscapes "maximize the things in nature and create inspiring outdoor spaces ... spaces that encourage my clients to slow down and enjoy the more important things in life." He aims to design gardens that inspire people "to take respite, to seek quiet solitude and time with family and friends." Needless to say, most of Decepida's clients have rediscovered the joys of staying at home.

Rading Decepida
Vermont Park Subdivision, Antipolo City
tel no: +63 917 850-2973; 02 212-0376
e-mail: ricci_dcpd@yahoo.com

Toni S Parsons
Florist cum garden designer

One of the first female landscapers in town, Toni Serrano Parsons was a jet-setting fashion model of the 1960s, who created tropical landscapes for plant-crazy friends in the '70s. In the '80s and '90s, Parsons evolved from avid plant-collector to friendly landscape creator and stylish wedding florist.

"My idea was to bring natural tropical landscapes from the countryside into urban lots," she describes her work ethic. Then, putting her money where her mouth is, she "very simply" pulled together a classic tropical border garden for her sister Baby Serrano Araneta's hacienda-like landscape in Alabang, Muntinlupa. Then, for Klaus Freund—who dealt with silk flowers—Parsons composed a jungle garden that felt like a natural tropical rainforest in its heyday.

By the mid '90s, when her landscaping business began to overpower her family life, Ms Parsons downsized her large-scale business into one that specializes in floral arrangements for buffet tables and wedding pews. She has recreated herself as a natural floral stylist, saying: "Floral arranging is just landscaping on a small scale!"

Toni Parsons was a sporty *collegiala* from St Scholastica and St Theresa's and an haute-couture model long before the plant-bug bit her. In the '80s, she was genuinely into plants—the sole female in the plant-lovers' clique of Dr Vicente Santos in Lucban, Quezon.

By the '90s she turned her gardening thumb toward producing sumptuous wedding events. Toni Parsons became, simply, the finest floralist for all rites of passage.

Toni Serrano Parsons
517 Flower Company, 517 Remedios St, Malate, Manila, RP
tel no: +63 02 832-7276
email: flower_517_company@yahoo.com.ph

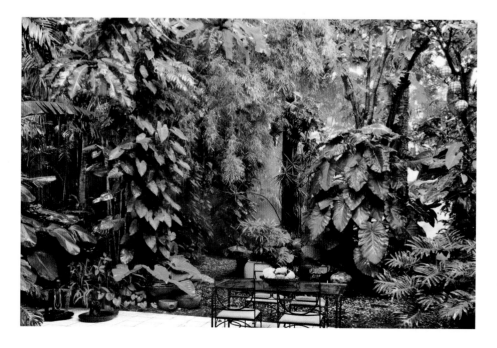

Ponce Veridiano
Tropical modern landscaper

The modern minimalist landscaper today is Ponce Veridiano from Laguna, the River Province. His manicured garden style is seen frequently among up-scale residentials: fine lawns are rimmed with topiaries and tiny leafed bushes, layered before backdrops of bamboo or tall palms. His urban landscapes are built on a limited palette of shades of green, like nature paintings suspended over the land.

Though Veridiano came from humble beginnings, he was exposed early on to the master architects of Manila; and has quickly grown popular for his tailored landscapes. Without the funds to study architecture, the plant-loving Ponce studied civil engineering and, on the side, joined Manila's high-profile garden shows with partner–in–plants, Rodney Cornejo. His exquisite plant arrangements on exhibit caught the eye of garden-lover Linda Lagdameo and led to his first breakthrough landscape project in 1992—the Pearl Farm Resort in Davao. There, on site, he met the architect-icon Bobby Manosa who mentored him to a love for bamboo and organic materials.

As a landscape acolyte in the mid-'90s, Ponce Veridiano apprenticed under master garden artist Yuyung LaO'. There, he imbibed a new array of plants, new forms and stylish ways with home gardens. The gardener from Laguna eventually found his own way to an urbane clientele in Manila and began creating

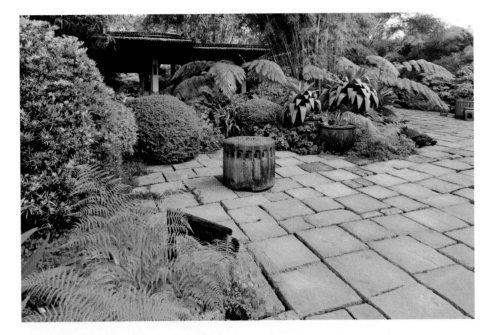

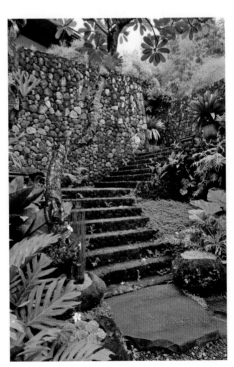

manicured landscapes for their big vacation homes down south. These were house-proud clients like Zobel, Cuenca, Choy and Soriano. Ponce Veridiano is now the favorite modern tropical garden maker for modern architectural projects by the Locsin Architects firm.

Ponce Veridiano
Mandaluyong, Metro Manila
tel no: +63 917 881-0578
email: ponceveridiano@yahoo.com

Michelle Magsaysay
Quiet landscape maker

Michelle Magsaysay studied at the Philippine Institute of Interior Design and worked briefly as an interior designer. While she had no formal training in landscape design, in 1994 she discovered the joy of creating "living spaces" using plants—and "making quiet landscapes" has since taken over her lifework. The two home gardens she has designed that are featured in this book demonstrate her serene touch in landscapes.

Her interest in landscape design was first sparked during a visit to Singapore in 1980. Exposed to a place that focused on the extensive greening of public areas, the sentient 16-year-old was impressed at the lushness of the environment and the state's efforts to create a garden city. However, it was another 14 years before she had her own first taste of landscaping: in 1994, she restyled the garden of her parents' residence.

Magsaysay says, "When I ventured into garden design, I discovered the joy of creating "living spaces" using plants—in contrast to applying non-living items as I had in my interior design projects. I observed how these living spaces continued to *evolve* during my weekly visits to the gardens. The changing elements within these spaces intrigued me. I started exploring garden design; doing gardens for family and friends, and getting referrals to create more gardens. In time, this hobby overtook my interest in designing interiors and has become my present line of work."

As a longtime practitioner of Qigong, a moving form of meditation, Magsaysay now focuses her landscape work on "creating a quiet space or a corner in a garden that will provide people with a place of respite in the midst of the rush in everyday life."

Michelle H Magsaysay
tel no: +63 920 978-0669
email: greeningspaces@gmail.com

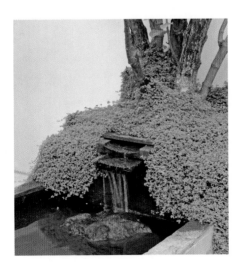

ACKNOWLEDGMENTS

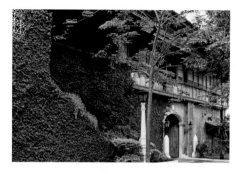

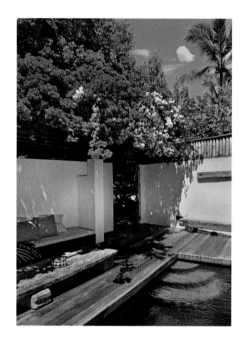

The co-authors and photographer would like to thank a great many people for their help and access during the production of this book of Philippine Tropical Gardens.

Homeowners and Garden Lovers

Metro Manila
Maricris Olbes, Anabel Alejandrino, Emily Campos, Richard Lopez, Roland Andres, Ramon Antonio, Baby S Araneta, Doris Magsaysay Ho, Tessa Prieto Valdes, Roland Ventura, Belen King, Malyn Santos, David and Belinda Lim. Not to forget: Chipsy Yap, Mike Sandoval, Sylvia Oliveros, Maite Araneta, Carmelita Matta, Antonio Carag, Benny Velasco, and Alex Josef.

Antipolo City
Jerusalino Araos, Flor Gozon Tarriela, Carolina Gozon Jimenez, Dr Joven Cuanang, Iggy and Jeannie Tan.

Tagaytay, Cavite
Peter Geertz, Marcia Adams, Ging S de los Reyes, Popo San Pascual, Vicky S Herrera, Tony Boy Escalante, Marilen Concepcion, Anna Maria Sy.

Batangas, Laguna, Quezon
Ado Escudero, Ugu Bigyan, Cecilia Yulo Locsin, John Marino, Bea Zobel Jr, Noel

Saratan, Malyn and Ochie Santos, Lita Tinio Montilla, Sen. Nani Perez, Florentino and Aida Librero.

Cebu and Bacolod
Amparito Lhuillier, Annie Aboitiz, Annabelle Lu Ym, Gretchen Cojuangco.

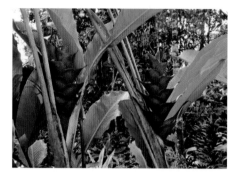

Special Thanks to Consultants...

Pictorial Cyclopedia of Philippine Ornamental Plants, published by Bookmark Inc, Manila, 1995, by Domingo A Madulid, Botany Chair of the National Museum of the Philippines and author of everyone's horticultural bible.
Martin Tinio Jr, gentleman farmer and scholar of Filipiniana;
Dr Benito Vergara, author, scholar, botanist, gardener, UP Los Banos, Laguna
Nonie Dolera, orchid expert of Philippine Orchid Society;
Shirley B Sanders, plant expert of Gardens by Sanders, Inc.

Much Gratitude to Project Hosts

Patis Tesoro, rural style doyenne of Café Salud in San Pablo, Laguna;
Bobby Gopiao, landscape designer with delicious hospitality in Quezon City;
Mrs Edna H Reyes, for constant hospitality for team in Tagaytay, Cavite;
GM Michael di Lonardo, for healthful Farm hospitality in Lipa, Batangas,
Bill Lewis and Ely Bautista for warm hospitality in Alaminos, Laguna,
Cebu Furniture Industries Foundation, for CEBUNEXT hospitality in Cebu,
Marco Polo Plaza, for accommodation in Lahug, Cebu,
Junie Rodriguez, Margie Stevens and Manny

Minana, for great garden leads,
Mercy Gamboa and Mellissa Gervacio, for styling Flor's garden shoot, Antipolo,
Romy Glorioso, for styling maestro Ernest Santiago's garden, Lucban,
Dita Sandico Ong, for loan of modern *abaca* fabrics in a jiffy,
Claudia Bolinao, for loan of transportation in a pinch,
Ricco Ocampo and Tina Maristela, for gracious hospitality in Manila,
Peter Geertz, for communications and access in Tagaytay,
Liwa Araos, for coordination and communications in Antipolo,
Suzanne Ledesma, for coordination and communications in Canlubang,
Teresin Mendezona and Philip Rodriguez for coordinations and communications in Cebu,
Annie Aboitiz and Mary Anne Arculli, for Cebu hospitality,
Charles and Ginnette Dumancas, for Bacolod hospitality,
Mrs Gretchen Cojuangco and Hacienda Balbina staff, for Bacolod hospitality.

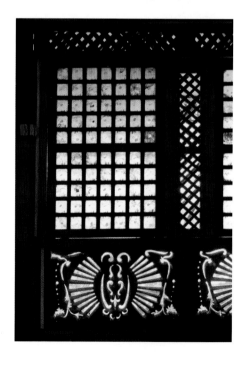

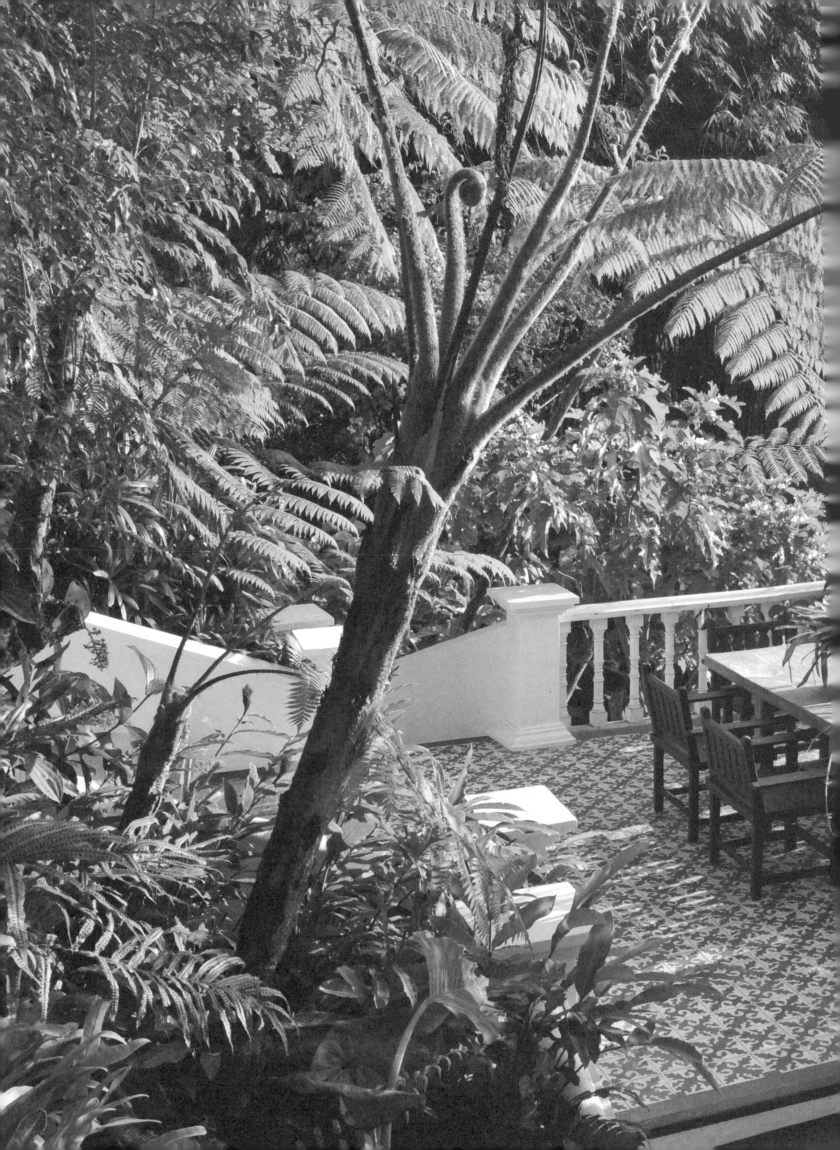